Praise for Appetite for Destruction

'Appetite for Destruction ... has the best of Wall's *Kerrang!* features, each bolstered by new, insightful postscripts. You won't read a funnier rock book in 2010. ****' *Mojo*

'Wall was the lead feature writer for *Kerrang!* magazine in the 1980s, and this hilarious tome is a collection of his finest moments ... Wall had a great knack for getting under the skin of interviewees' *Big Issue*

'An excellent primer to the good and bad of the job ... he never falls into the trap of being too impressed with his own novelty, making this a very good read' *Rock Sound*

'Mick Wall was one of [*Kerrang!*'s] better-known writers and his book contains 31 of his bigger, funnier or generally more significant stories ... what's notable is Wall's approach of reverence where it had been earned and contempt where it was deserved' *Record Collector*

'Wall is firing on all cylinders' *Classic Rock*

Mick Wall is one of Britain's best-known music journalists, broadcasters and authors. Formerly editor-in-chief of *Classic Rock* magazine, his work has also appeared in *Mojo, The Times*, the *Mail on Sunday* and numerous newspapers and magazines around the world. He has also presented his own programmes for Sky TV, Radio 1 and Capital Radio and is a well-known face from countless BBC TV music documentaries. His thirty-year career has also included stints as a high-profile PR, artist manager and record company executive.

By Mick Wall

Diary of a Madman – the Official Biography
of Ozzy Osbourne

Guns N'Roses: the Most Dangerous Band in the World

Pearl Jam

Run to the Hills: the Authorized Biography of Iron Maiden

Paranoid: Black Days with Sabbath & Other Horror Stories

Mr Big: Ozzy, Sharon and My Life as the
Godfather of Rock, by Don Arden

XS All Areas: the Autobiography of Status Quo

John Peel – a Tribute to the Much-Loved DJ and Broadcaster

Bono – In the Name of Love

W.A.R. – the Unauthorised Biography of W. Axl Rose

When Giants Walked the Earth: A Biography of Led Zeppelin

Appetite for Destruction

APPETITE FOR DESTRUCTION

*Legendary Encounters
with Mick Wall*

Mick Wall

An Orion paperback

First published in Great Britain in 2010
by Orion
This paperback edition published in 2010
by Orion Books Ltd,
Orion House, 5 Upper St Martin's Lane,
London WC2H 9EA

An Hachette UK company

1 3 5 7 9 10 8 6 4 2

A CIP catalogue record for this book
is available from the British Library.

ISBN 978-1-4091-2169-5

Typeset by Input Data Services Ltd,
Bridgwater, Somerset

Printed and bound in Great Britain by
CPI Mackays, Chatham ME5 8TD

The Orion Publishing Group's policy is to use papers
that are natural, renewable and recyclable and
made from wood grown in sustainable forests. The logging
and manufacturing processes are expected to conform to
the environmental regulations of the country of origin.

www.orionbooks.co.uk

To Ross Halfin and Peter Makowski,
absolutely without whom . . .

CONTENTS

INTRODUCTION
It Was Heavy, Man . . .

The stories in this collection may come from many different places – Moscow, Berlin, Rio, Los Angeles – but what really characterises them is the time they come from. It seems obvious to say so now, perhaps, but it's worth remembering in this context that back in the 1980s, when I first began writing for *Kerrang!* magazine, the world – certainly in music-business terms – was very different from the one we inhabit now. Without the benefit of the internet and several dozen dedicated music TV channels, and with rock with a capital 'R' still suffering from the stigma punk had bequeathed it as the most singularly unfashionable, indeed offensive – yet, conversely, internationally popular – modern form of music in the world, the only way groups such as Guns N' Roses, Metallica, Mötley Crüe and Iron Maiden could receive any sort of positive exposure from the media was through the eye-searingly background-toned pages of *Kerrang!*. The music industry itself was also reaching a new peak in terms of record (soon to be CD) sales, and record companies had money to burn. Not a week passed back then when I wasn't on the phone organising an all-expenses paid trip to some far-flung corner of the globe (or, as often as I could swing it, LA).

Having spent years travelling around the backwaters of Britain and Europe in various fag-holed Transit vans with a series of punk (or what these days would be called indie) bands, the sudden switch to the limo-driven, Business-Classed realms of heavy rockdom was a welcome one indeed. Never having had a problem with what by then was called heavy metal, mixing my Sex Pistols and Damned records with my Zeppelin and Thin Lizzy, my Stones and my Purple with my PiL and my Fall, I regarded the opportunity to hang out with someone like Ozzy Osbourne or Lemmy as a real treat. Besides, the older rock guys had real stories to tell and that was what attracted me more than anything. Coming from a London–Irish family full of musicians and storytellers, I had grown up sitting around the fire while my father and his various after-dark friends played and drank and smoked and told endless stories of fun, of daring, and of falling flat on their faces. The rock guys were much the same, only for them the drink and the smoke would be augmented more often than not by drugs. Oh, and loose women. What wasn't there to like?

And so it was that I spent the years between 1984 and 1991 travelling the rocking world, making the most of my new-found freedom to overindulge myself and – weirdest of all – get paid for it. No, it didn't always have much to do with music. But this was the '80s and such concerns were considered laughably naive – unless you happened to be writing about earnest palefaces like The Smiths, which, thankfully, I was not. (Always liked that band, by the way; had interviewed Morrissey once in the very early days and was a proud owner of *Meat is Murder* and *The Queen is Dead*, just had no desire whatsoever to, you know, *hang out* with the miserable-looking bastards, the very thought of which still makes me shudder.)

The other thing that should be borne in mind about those days was that air travel was f-u-n; another idea that has all but vanished in these fast-forwarded present days. Me and Ross Halfin – the photographer I worked most often with – would turn up at the airport sometimes with just minutes to go, collapse into whatever private members' club we had access to (and after so many trips, we had access to them all), and avail ourselves of whatever free wine, beer and scotch was on offer, while being 'taken care of' by some good-looking, trouser-suited broad with too much lipstick and the patience of a saint. I remember having a bottle of port for breakfast on one trip to Portugal to interview Iron Maiden, scoffing champagne between connections in New York on our way to Rio (again), and other times when Ross had organised for us to ride the chauffeur-driven buggy they use to transport the sick and elderly (and rich and fat) from club room to plane door, waving our wine-stained boarding passes as we zipped by like old gods dangling their perfumed hankies from the balcony of heaven.

These days, the in-flight staff will treat you at worst like a potential terrorist, a pain in the arse at best. Back then I remember snogging an air stewardess I had met just minutes before in plain view of the entire First-Class section. In the early days, Ross, who was terrified of flying (an odd thought, given that he has spent most of the subsequent thirty years on an aircraft), would knock back a couple of quadruple scotches and a super-strength Valium and be passed out in his seat before we'd even taken off. No one minded, they just objected to the fact that he quite often left his penis dangling from his fly when they came to check he'd fastened his seatbelt. 'Is he . . . alright?' I recall one perplexed but reassuringly non-judgemental stewardess asking. 'He will be,' I assured her.

Things changed in the 1990s, as the last few stories in this collection make clear. After a couple of years out of the game, vainly trying to become an artist manager (what in God's name was I thinking?), I had returned to rock writing, first for the short-lived *Rock World*, then later for *Kerrang!*'s little-brother publication, the now long-gone *RAW* magazine. It was like being released from jail after a longer sentence than the punishment really deserved. I emerged, blinking, into the light: older, hair thinner, belly bigger, appetite ruined. Grunge had happened and like the Big One finally being dropped, the only survivors of the world I'd known were all hopelessly scarred – including me. Considering what I'd been up to as a writer in the years before, starting again with a whole new generation of younger bands was, I realised even then, like checking in for a prolonged spell in rehab. A necessary course of treatment, I sensed, which would be painful in the short term but hopefully cure me of some by then fairly awful habits, even aid my recovery and turn me into the person I hoped to be . . . one day. But you'll see better what I mean when you get there.

In the meantime, for those of you who bought *Kerrang!* in the 1980s – and there are a surprising number of you out there, I discover to my embarrassed surprise as the years tumble by – you'll know that one of the best things about the magazine back then was that we, the writers, always treated you, the readers, as though you were in on the joke, which you always, unfailingly, were. I hope these stories bring back as many fond – if occasionally wince-inducing – memories as they did for me putting them all together into one big pile like this. For as the prophet once forlornly sang: to be a rock and not to roll ... who the fuck wants that?

Mick Wall, Oxfordshire, October 2009

DAVID LEE ROTH, 1988

Never having interviewed 'Diamond' Dave before, I was hoping for something special – or at least something a little outside the normal bullshit. Well, he certainly gave me that.

Ushered into a room backstage after the show, I was treated to Jack Daniel's, cocaine, a huge sack of grass, even a naked dancing girl. All this before we'd even sat down to start the interview. Not that I was complaining. The Average White Band blared from a ghetto-blaster and every now and then Dave would turn to me with that mile-wide smile, familiar from all those Van Halen videos, and howl like a wolf. Beyond words, I just howled right back.

From there, the night just got longer and stranger. The naked dancing girl eventually put her clothes back on and left, as did everyone else in the room, bar me, Dave and photographer Ross Halfin. For the next eight hours we were treated to what amounted to a long stream-of-consciousness rap from the Diamond. Laugh? My face and neck muscles ached for days afterwards. I wished I'd taped it but he wouldn't allow me to. I wish Ross could have got a shot of it but Dave wasn't having any of that either. It was probably just as well. When the demon's eye is upon you, the last thing you need is reminding of it the next day, let alone twenty years later.

The sun was already high in the sky by the time we eventually left the gig – definitely a first for me. Ross, who was off drugs and booze at the time, later complained that it had been one of the most boring nights of his life. Not being off anything myself in those days, I thought it was one of the most exciting. Maybe even a bit too exciting. For when we got back to the hotel and Dave tried to talk me into joining him in his suite for 'a nightcap', I practically ran to the elevators to get away. By then even I had had enough. Only Ozzy Osbourne at his worst had ever made me feel the same way.

If there was ever a real-life Rock School, David Lee Roth would be the headmaster.

Maybe two-thirds of the way through the show, the stage lights dim, drummer Gregg Bissonette strikes up a lookin'-for-trouble cha-cha-chasshhh on the cymbals, and Diamond Dave saunters out from the wings under cover of a lone spotlight. He sashays like Humphrey Bogart up to the mike, lights one, rolls his shoulders and pulls his trilby an inch further down over his face, then looks the audience straight in the eye and holds it. He's about to go into a rap. You can tell. Somewhere far off, a sleazy saxophone begins to wail like a police siren.

'My name is Roth. I'm licensed to carry a microphone,' he begins, the crowd already laughing. 'I was in my office over on Main Street in Worcester, Massachusetts [cue huge roars of approval, Worcester being where the show is taking place] working kind of late one night when I got the call . . .'

He pauses, takes a drag, continues . . .

'She sounded like she needed help, so I told her to come on over. She said OK . . . Sometime later there's a knock on my door. I said, come in. She said OK . . .'

More pauses, more knowing looks.

'She walked in and blew me a kiss so hot I could feel the breeze go right through the buttons on my 501 jeans . . . She was wearing a dress so tight it looked like she'd been poured into it and somebody had forgotten to say when . . . She looked me over and said: "Nice gun." I said, "Nice holster . . ." We got to talking and she told me she was having trouble with the law and wanted to know if I could get her off . . .'

Saxophone sighs deeply as the crowd titter. He continues. 'I said, "I don't know nothin' about the law, sweetheart, but I know I can get . . . you . . . off!" She looked at me and said, "Oh, Diamond Dave! You're just a GIGOLO!" . . .'

BANG! The band womp into the song. The lights are up, the crowd are dancing and wiping the tears from their eyes at the same time. We've got a real show on our hands here! Songs, jokes, props and

lights; the raps and the razzle-dazzle and the blessed rock 'n' roll ...
What hasn't this show got?

Seeing David Lee Roth perform live for the first time since he
last stepped onto the stage with the rest of the Van Halen boys at
Donington four years ago, really brought home to me how mundane
and street-average most rock bands are by comparison.

There's nothing humourless and tense about a David Lee Roth
show; it's just straight-up, high-times excitement from start to finish!
Nothing ever stops moving – the music, the band, the lights, him least
of all. Kid, you gotta be ready when this stuff comes at ya, otherwise
you'll miss something and get left behind!

It begins with a simple announcement, mostly obscured by the surge
of noise from the 10,000-strong Worcester crowd, and by the time the
words DAVID ... LEE ... ROTH!! are boomed from the speakers the
band are suddenly already there and into 'The Bottom Line', Roth in full
Diamond Dave mode, the familiar look of complete and utter astonishment on his face as he throws one leg and then another high into the air,
which makes him look as though he is flying across the stage.

With the crowd already eating it up, the band go almost without
pause into 'Ain't Talkin' 'Bout Love', the old-but-bold Van Halen hit,
pumping out the riff like they were shaking hands with an iron bar:
Steve Vai, sleek and immaculately underdressed, patrolling the bound-
aries of the stage, trying to keep up with his guitar, which seems to go
where it pleases. His opposite number, bassist Matt Bissonette,
hawking it around like Billy the Kid in shades. And on risers deeper
into the stage, keyboard wizard Brett Tuggle, knee pumping, grin in
place, and drummer Gregg Bissonette, arms flailing like a drowning
man, half out of his seat, wild like the wind.

Standing atop half a dozen lighted steps leading to the drum riser,
Roth suddenly cuts the number dead with a single wave of his arm,
leans heavy into the mike, and breathes: 'We ain't just talking 'bout
lurrvve here tonight ... We're talking about going right up to the edge
and gazing DOOWWWNNNN!' The crowd whoop and cheer; girls
scream and throw their panties at the stage; one throws a red rose,
which Roth picks up, sniffs, laughs at, then tosses back into the stalls.
He launches into a rap about his early days living right here in Worcester, which he did for a couple of years as a child. 'That's right, no

shit! I fucking know this town, baby!' The crowd, for most of whom this is news indeed, go completely over the top, trying to climb the air with clawing fingers, eyes white, voices howling like hungry wolves.

The band break into 'Just Like Paradise', Roth starts flying into mad, acrobatic shapes again, the rhythm section kick in and Vai strolls out into the spotlight cradling that baffling but impressive-looking triple-necked guitar thing – just like in the video, ma – and takes it for a spin around the jaw of the stage. Against a backdrop of some vague cityscape outlined in silhouettes, the lighting rig – a row of gigantic diamonds, hovering like a crown above the stage – begins throwing out yellow beams of light into the balconies that trim the stage, and Roth runs the band hard through 'Knucklebones', twirling the mike-stand so fast it starts to flash like a hot strobe ('an old Kung Fu trick,' he tells me later).

A trés butch little strut through the kitsch and beguiling old chestnut 'Easy Street' followed, played for laughs. It got them all singing along, before Gregg Bissonette began pummelling out the raw Red Indian beat that signals the introduction to 'Hot for Teacher'; Vai's spidery guitar lines perfectly matching the original Eddie Van Halen inter-pretation, but adding something around the edges that is all his own; Roth in his element as he wrestles with the footlights and springs like a cat from side to side of the stage.

'Stand Up', the new single, goes down like cold vanilla on a hot day, the Worcester kids and me cranked high enough to hang ourselves, Vai taking off into some Prince-style humping of his guitar, which he lays on its back – still screaming, still itching – across the top of one of the amps in a way only the little girls would understand. Before the guitar solo has grown cold, though, its echo returns to grow into 'Skyscraper', a veritable tour-de-force, Roth descending on a rope from high up in the lighting rigging down the sheer face of the stage in time to reach the mike for the first verse.

After that, it's straight into the hilarious 'Just a Gigolo' routine. 'Crazy from the Heat' is next up and proves to be an unexpected highlight when, halfway through the guitar break, the band suddenly cut out and the lights zero in on the lip of the stage where Diamond Dave is poised behind seven steel drums, whistle in mouth, sticks in hand, ready to blow up a storm of marimba-maramba-let's-go-yamma-

yamma! Eventually, the entire band are at it on the steels, rattling it out like veterans; synchronised, cool; coaxing the house to the tips of its toes.

'Stevie, can you spell Massa-fuckin'-chusetts for me?' asks Dave when the band are back in position behind their instruments. Stevie spells MASSA-FUCKIN'-CHUSETTS for him with his guitar and the crowd goes right with him. The bass starts thumping and the drums start to swagger, and 'Yankee Rose' comes rolling like a wagon-train from the valley of the stage. The number dovetails into an extended guitar break while Roth vanishes from the stage, only to reappear five minutes later at the mixing desk, which is positioned on a five-foot riser in the centre of the arena.

Back on stage, Vai cuts into a camp and over-the-top arrangement of 'The Star Spangled Banner', while Roth begins to climb a rope ladder like Weird Jack right up the giant's beanstalk, pausing every twenty feet or so to swing by one hand and wave, like an outer space ham, to the audience below, which can barely control itself. About 100 feet up he disappears from view once again onto a platform seemingly the size of a matchbox. The band strike like queer lightning into 'Panama' and the platform begins to descend from the sky. As it floats down into view you can see it's actually a boxing ring Roth is riding: ropes, corners, the US flag hanging from one end. The crowd are beyond wild by this time and Dave gives it the full Muhammad Ah-Lee Roth treatment, pausing the number at one point just to receive the adulation of the adoring crowd, arms outstretched just like the real prizefighters do.

And so began the finale. In time for 'California Girls', Roth climbs out of the ring onto a giant surfboard, smoke billowing from its tail, also suspended by wires from above the mixing desk, gliding down to the stage above the heads of the crowd. He's the futuristic lounge-lizard with the *Blade Runner* smile, still singing, still kicking his legs, the Crazy Man who knows something.

The first encore is 'You Really Got Me', which Vai practically reinvents in places, knocking new life into the old standard in a way that would have Ray Davies reaching for the Valium. And then to finish, what else of course but 'Jump'. Preceded by a synthesised excerpt from the theme tune to the movie *2001*, the parping synthesiser intro to

'Jump' is still the one that exerts the most feeling in the crowd here tonight. But Dave knows that, which is why he sensibly saves it for last. Anything after that would be impossible, even now. In that knowledge, Roth and the band squeeze it for every drop it's worth, the way only real pros know how. Breathtaking! She was right, you know. Diamond Dave, you are a gigolo!

We had come face-to-face for the first time the previous evening; when he spun into the room in which I was propping up a beer table, next door to the dressing room, shortly before he went on stage. It was like a hurricane suddenly hit the room. Stomping around in big desert boots, as he talked his body shuddered and jolted, head thrown back in a mile-wide grin, the famous permanently astonished visage mostly concealed beneath a black, floppy beret, dark, impenetrable shades, and the long, yellow mane that falls down his back. He was all angular comic gestures and spitting speed-freak satire, hurling the jazzy one-liners out of the side of his mouth and laughing like a drain before I had time to get a fix on all the punchlines; turning it on for me in his guise as the Guru of Good Times and the reigning King of Ramalama.

'Great, man!' he cried. 'That's fuckin' great! So this shit is gonna be on the cover of the two hundredth edition of *Kerrang!*? Oh, that's COOL! I fuckin' love *Kerrang!*, man. You guys gotta really BAD attitude! HAHAHA! Take no fuckin' prisoners, baby!'

He spun round on his heels and threw out his arms.

'Jesus, I feel high! I'm fuckin' flying here! It musta bin that orange I ate before coming down to the gig. It's that fuckin' sugar, man. It goes to my system like that – zap! Pow! HAHAHA! Somebody fuckin' hold me down, quick, before I explode . . .'

At first I couldn't decide whether this guy was a suitable case for treatment or if he was just putting down a rap – for all I know it was probably both – but I took to him immediately. You'd have to be nine-parts dead not to. When something tickles, you laugh. And when Diamond Dave sings you his song, you listen.

Later, after the show, we got shit-faced together taking turns on his bottle of Jack Daniel's. With the shades off and his gig over, he talks a lot slower, but his conversation is no less animated; standing up and striking poses to explain the point of a certain story, or crouched on the edge of his seat, barking with laughter at another, the conversation rambling all over the place like a drunk looking for the way home.

At one point, we got started in on some travelling stories. When he's not working, Roth likes to take off on his own sometimes: 'Just to see which way the wind blows,' he said. 'Travelling around, you can learn a lot about people and places, and through that you can learn a lot about yourself, too, just by the way you react on the spot to new and different situations. And you can land yourself in some funny shit, too. And that's good for you! You shouldn't be afraid to try and put yourself some place you've never been before.'

He tells me a story.

'I remember driving through the Midwest with a friend one time, we were right out in the middle of nowhere, late at night and looking for a place to stop and have some drinks, maybe. Suddenly we see a truck-stop with a light on, so we decide to pull over and take a look. We walk inside and the place is completely empty except for this one old woman mopping up behind the counter. We ask her for a couple of beers and some sandwiches and she says sure, no problem.

'She brings the stuff out and we get to talking and she's pretty cool, this old gal, so we invite her to sit down and join us for a drink. Well, we put a couple away and I take out a handful of nickels and dimes and tell the old gal to put some sounds on the juke while I went and got us a couple more drinks. I get the drinks, she gets up and puts the money into the juke, then comes back and sits down. Now she doesn't know me from Adam, but the first record that comes on is "Just a Gigolo"! I think, wow, the old gal digs my music!

'I turned to her and said, "You like this song?" She said, "Oh, you mean number fifteen-A? I just love fifteen-A! It's one of my favourite songs on that old jukebox!" I couldn't believe it. Fifteen-A, she called it: the button you had to push on the juke to get the record. Didn't know what it was called, didn't know who it was by, just liked it a lot. So I told her. I said, "That's my song and that's me singing", and she freaked and said, "You mean you're fifteen-A? You!? You're fifteen-A? Oh, my!" I said, "That's me all right, baby – MISTER FIFTEEN-A!" HAHAHA!'

He takes another pull on the bottle.

'At first she got real excited about actually meeting fifteen-A, you know what I mean, but then she turned quiet. I asked her what was the matter and she said: "Oh, I just wish Old Sal was here to meet you. He just loves fifteen-A, too. Old Sal loves that song more than anybody I know." I'm thinking, who the hell's Old Sal? I mean, this lady has got to be pushing seventy, so this Old Sal dude has got to be hitting at least ninety!

'Meantime, she carries on with her story: "Old Sal comes in here most nights of the week and just sits there at that bar, nursing a beer and just playing that old fifteen-A over and over, with a kind of knowing look in his eye." I said, "Oh, yeah? How do ya mean?" She paused, looked straight at me and said, "I think it's because Old Sal's a bit of a gigolo himself." HAHAHA! I tell ya, man, that old girl was worth her weight in gold.'

Somehow we stumbled onto the subject of videos – I think we were talking TV. I was probably trying to sell him on the idea of hosting his own chat-show. Anyway, it transpires that the reason why the colours are so eye-stingingly vivid on the Van Halen 'Hot for Teacher' video is this: 'I was wearing shades the whole time we were editing it and I couldn't see a goddamned thing!' he laughed. 'We'd be shooting segments in which I was wearing these things, then in-between times I would be racing over to the playback console to take a look at what we'd got. Only I never once thought to take off my shades. And I'd be standing up there going, "Hey, man, this looks a little dull. Turn the goddamned colour up!" And it wasn't until much later when I saw the thing on a TV screen that I thought, my God, what is this? How come the colours are so fuckin' high? And then I remembered. Oh shit! Oh yeah . . .'

He grins and continues.

'I'll tell you something else I bet you didn't know about that video,' he says, tapping me on the knee with the bottle of JD. 'You know that bit right at the end, when I'm standing there pretending to be a game-show host? Next time you see that video take a good look at my trouser leg – I'm not telling you which one, you'll have to see for yourself. But if you look real close, you'll see a stain down my leg. That's a piss stain, man! HAHAHA! We were working so hard I didn't even have time to take a piss – literally! So a little got on my leg, so I'm a slob . . . HAHAHA! Take a look next time you see it, though. I guarantee you'll never be able to watch that video again without that piss stain sticking out a mile!'

At another point, I asked Roth if he ever got nervous clambering around on those ropes he uses in his show.

'No, never. Shit, I'm used to floating around at the end of a rope on the side of a mountain, so crawling around in the stage-rigging fifty feet above a stage is not about to faze me. Plus, I've got a guy up there to be on hand if ever I did get in any serious trouble. In fact, he's more nervous than I am. One night I was just about to climb onto the rope and get ready for the part where I lower myself down onto the stage, and I suddenly grabbed him and said, "Oh my God, something's wrong, man . . ." You shoulda seen his face. Immediately he was like, "What is it? What is it? What's up, Dave?" And I was like, "Oh my God, give me your arm!" By this time he's going crazy. "WHAT IS IT, DAVE? WHAT IS IT, MAN? WHAT, WHAT, WHAT?" And I grabbed him by the wrist and said, "It's your watch, man. It's running a little slow, I think . . ." HAHAHA! Now he doesn't listen to a word I say, so we're both totally safe!'

I asked him how he was looking forward to his coming appearance on the bill with Iron Maiden at the Donington Monsters of Rock festival?

'It's gotta be better than the last time I played there with Van Halen,' he said, shaking his head. 'Man, we were not going through happy times. Everything was going wrong between us, we were barely talking. The most fun I had all day was actually being onstage, and even that was a little strained. I remember one particular point, I was starting to get into a number and really fly. I glanced over to the side of the stage and I saw this female photographer with her back to me bending over, searching around in her bag for something. Man, I was already working on my high, trying to get into the set, and then I saw this cute little ass wiggling at me and I just went for it! I ran right over to the side of the stage and got down on my knees and planted a kiss on that sweet little butt.

'And do you know what she did? She spun around like someone had just kicked her in the ass and hit me – whammo! – straight in the jaw! HAHAHA! And that chick packed a wallop, man. It almost knocked me off my feet! I thought, Jesus, this day is doomed . . .'

The night died a lot quicker than the bottle of Jack Daniel's, and it was past dawn before we had crawled out of the dressing room and into

Roth's waiting limo, the coarse yellow sunlight like needles in our eyes. And now here I stand, twenty-four hours on, beer-handed and perspiring a little too heavily in the hospitality room backstage, waiting for Roth to emerge from his post-show dinner of lobster, barbecued ribs, salad, rice and fries, and give me that wave of the hand that tells me it's time to unravel the cellophane from another bottle of old granddad's favourite and turn on the machine.

Suddenly the door flies open and there he is, wise-ass grin in place, eyes a little tired maybe, but still bouncing around on his feet and loose. 'Let me get us a couple of beers and some of this,' he says, indicating the JD on the drinks table. It is, in fact, the only spirit stocked backstage at a David Lee Roth show.

'OK, follow me . . .'

We take off down the corridor and Roth leads us into an empty room and closes the door behind us.

'Awright, I'm open for business,' he smiles. 'Go for it.'

I want to start by asking you a little bit about your current tour. You've always been very athletic, almost acrobatic, onstage, but how did you come up with the idea of a rope-ladder and being hoisted back down into the arena in a boxing ring?

'Well, that, and when I lower myself down a rope onto the stage, or when I ride the surfboard over the audience's heads, they're what I call my tricks. They're not special effects. A special effect is something you buy in a box, that when you take out you need a technician to put together for you. The stuff I do is more pure than just using another set of lasers that anybody with the money can buy. These are tricks that could have been done twenty years ago for roughly the same cost and the same effect.

'I remember when I was a kid going to see a production of *Peter Pan* with my sister, and here was this woman dressed as a man flying from one side of the stage to the other on the end of a wire, and I just thought this was the greatest thing I'd ever seen! There's a certain kind of character displayed in theatrics like that that appeals to me greatly. I don't mean like a cartoon character, I mean in the sense that there's some soul there, there's some heart in stuff like that. And I don't mind having a little bit of that same soul in my show.'

There comes a moment in the show when the boxing ring hovers above the mixing desk in the middle of the arena, and the music cuts out and you stand there soaking up the applause and adulation for minutes at a time. The audience seems to be at its craziest at that moment. What is going through your mind as you stand there with your arms in the air, taking it all in?

'I'm not really thinking too hard at that point. HAHAHA! I'm more just reacting. But I think the people are cheering more from all the combined years of conditioning that seep into your system when you see a boxing ring. And what we have is the real thing. It's a regulation-ring we've got flying around up there. So when you see it, all those years, decades, of watching boxing rings on TV, or seeing pictures in magazines and newspapers or having them described on the radio, when you actually see one it hits you straight away. Question: what happens in the boxing ring? Answer: life, man! You know what I mean? We all deal with the boxing ring on a daily level. Meaning, there is always great hope and potential and there is always potential disaster every time you step into the boxing ring. But like it or not we all have to take that step every day to survive. Just reading those words triggers off something in people they didn't have when they started reading this interview! HAHAHA!

'It's man against man, that's what that symbolises. But both guys can get crushed by time, by the great invisible opponent...' He pauses, self-conscious suddenly. 'Hey man, can you imagine certain people reading this shit? "What's that the dude said about an invisible opponent? Fuck that! I wanna buy a T-shirt!" HAHAHA! But it's in there all the same, buried deep, and that's what makes people go hysterical every time they see me in that thing.'

You're often accused by your critics of camping things up too much as a rock 'n' roll performer, and there's obviously a lot more going on in your head than just wham-bam-thank-you-ma'am mindless metal. Do you ever feel that you have to tie yourself down occasionally, so that you don't go too far above your audience's heads?

'Communication is an art, and music is nothing but communication: how ya feel on a given day and why. That's all music is, and you don't even need words to get the story.'

People seem to either love you or hate you, though. They're either fanatical or they can't stand you. What is it about you that provokes them?

'If they hate me it's because they don't understand me. Either we haven't had a chance to sit and get to know one another, or I'm screwing up on the transmission end. Or maybe they just don't like the changes I've been through with my music over the last ten years. But I never wanted to be a performer that stood for just one thing, one style, one set of moves and that's it. How boring! Nobody reading this right now wants to spend the rest of their lives doing the same thing over and over, so why should I?'

I know from our conversation last night that you're quite a literary person. Do you get many of your ideas for lyrics from the books you read?

'No. Wait a minute . . . I'm such a contrary prick, sometimes. There I go saying no without even paying attention to the question. HAHAHA! I shoulda bin a lawyer. Anyway, yeah, I get inspired by books and magazines. They inspire me to pay attention to things that I wasn't paying attention to before. But I get ideas cooking in my head about all sorts of things – I meet a type of person I never met before, I see something in society I never noticed before . . .

'Anything, man, anything that moves me. I'm always finding new things to get interested in. Sometimes it's a book, sometimes it's other things. You gotta remember, I'm not a natural anything. I got it all out of books, I got it all off a screen, I got it all off the radio, I got it all off other people and put it all together. I hate that term "self-improvement" but that's kinda how it is with me. I'm always looking for something new that's good to add to the stew, you know?'

I'd like to get your opinion, as a renowned live performer, on some of your contemporaries, OK?

'OK, but I'm going to have to say something upfront first. I'm only going to talk about other bands as a music fan, not as someone comparing what anybody else does to me. So if I end up cutting up another band in the press, I want the readers to know that I'm only doing it to complain as a music fan, just the same as they do when they don't like something, OK?'

First off then, Prince. Do you find what he does exciting?

'I think he has a lot of great ideas but most of them are unfinished. I think that . . . ah . . . working with some outside people might flesh out some of his ideas. A lot of his music sounds like jams in the studio that an engineer refined later on in the day, or a remix artist pasted together. And the chief thing about it is it's primarily dance music, very simple chord structures and so on, which to me is a little too much like wallpaper. You use it to change the feel of the room, and not much more. As a live performer I think Prince has got a lot of energy and he's got a lot of heart. But he's hyper-derivative and that I don't find intriguing. I see right dead straight who it is he's copying, and I find that boring, and boredom is the cardinal sin.'

What about Michael Jackson, what do you make of him?

'With Michael there's a more definitive style. Whether you like it or not, it sounds like him. It's definitely his kind of music, it's all his trip. You can't see through the weld marks like you can with someone like Prince. Now that's intriguing to me. Good songwriting, man, and good performance, you know? It's something you've either got or you haven't got. On the other hand, I get the feeling that nobody ever stole this kid's lunch money at school, nobody ever threw a baseball bat at him too hard during recess, and that's an important part of growing up, too. All of that going in the front is what comes out of the back end in your music later on in life. And I'm kinda missing that with Michael's approach. HAHAHA! Some of that man stuff has gotta go into the stew too! Jesus, stop asking me about other people, the readers will think I don't have a good word to say about anybody. HAHAHA!'

All right. What about your own career as a performer – where do you take it from here? You surely don't plan to spend the rest of your life on the road?

'Well, if I want to I could carry this act around for another twenty years, give or take an act of God or Ferrari. I'm certainly in shape for something like that if I want to take things that way. But the next logical step is movies. You know, as one half of the fabulous Picasso Brothers [the other being Roth's manager, Pete Angelus], we made more than three Jack Nicholsons combined, apiece, for the movie we never made [*Crazy from the Heat*]! I mean, hey, we were ready to shoot but CBS went out of the movie business, so suddenly I had to get Darth Vader & Sons as my attorneys and wage doom war on the company.

'But that movie will be made, eventually. I know I talk about a million things at once, but talk don't mean a thing. Come pay day, there's my new record, there's the new tour – that's where my heart is. And up until now there hasn't been enough time to mobilise a hundred and fifty people on a movie set for months and months at a time. What can I tell you? You bet we're gonna get the movie situation together, though. But, typically, I'm already looking forward to recording the soundtrack!'

Is there ever going to be a David Lee Roth that could be a quiet, family man with a wife and kids, et cetera? They say it can happen to the best of us, Dave.

'I surprise people a lot in that I actually spend most of my time by myself. I lived with a girlfriend for a couple of years, but we broke up about a year-and-a-half ago. Before that, I lived by myself for twelve years. And I do again now. And this is . . . how I'm happiest.'

Hence, he said, his passion for climbing mountains and going on jungle expeditions.

'This is all introspective stuff, and I brood. A lot of times people are very surprised if they run into me on the streets. It can be very different from what they expect me to be like in public, or on a stage. I can be the most outgoing, public person in the world or I can be the most private dude you've ever come across. And I like both extremes.'

Do you find, though, that you can adopt the Diamond Dave persona at the drop of a hat when you want to?

'It depends. I mean, I know how to misbehave right on cue! HAHAHA! That's the trooper part of it. But luckily, I've managed to work most of my reality directly into the music, directly into the show, and for the people out there that are familiar with what I've been doing over the years, they know it's never been just one face I've worn, one approach.

'Spirit is the thread that winds all the way through all the chaos, but the faces are different. The face of the person singing "Damn Good" is very different from the person who's singing "Bottom Line", although the spirit is the same.'

The first time I read the lyrics to 'Damn Good' I thought they might have been written about your time in Van Halen. Were they?

'No, definitely not. I guess they could be interpreted that way, and sitting here looking in my rear-view mirror with you, Mick, I see that in the middle of the road, too. HAHAHA! I felt the bump, but I didn't see a thing! HAHAHA!'

Will you have to alter the US show much for Donington and the other European dates you're doing this year?

'Oh, sure, a little. Playing in Europe you're practically playing in a new country every night, confronting a whole new culture at each show, and you have to adjust the set accordingly because each new audience is a little bit different from the one you played to the night before. My job is to guess how different. Like, you speakada language, boy? Well, yes, we do. But the changes won't be drastic, just appropriate. When you're in a drag race like Donington, and you've got six – count 'em! – natural, fuel-burning, top-line, screaming dragster rock metal bands all on the same bill, and they're all eating the stage up, the crowd is totally geared to that kind of action – I mean, it practically tells you on the invitation how to dress! So the fact of the matter is, you're not gonna be the guy who was too cool to put on the style for the Halloween party, you've got to go out there and fuckin' murder somebody, man! It's that kind of event, you know? And I love it, I'm into it. I've got all the hats that I need stashed right there in my suitcase, and I'm ready.'

As you know, this story is for the two hundredth issue of *Kerrang!*. Would you care to say a few words in the way of a birthday greeting?

'Well, *Kerrang!* is the Bible, you know? *Kerrang!* is like Mr Chicken McNugget! Two hundred McNuggets ago it was the only action in town, now suddenly here comes Wendy's and Burger King. What I'm saying is, *Kerrang!* was the first and is still the coolest, right down to the name.

'Now you've got *Bif Pop* magazine, or Metal this, Metal that, you know what I mean? What I like most of all is that *Kerrang!* has always maintained its sense of humour, because it is pretty funny some of the shit that *Kerrang!* somehow always gets to hear about. And there's a sense of honour about it, too. *Kerrang!* has never been afraid to nail somebody. *Kerrang!* is not afraid to complain, because, hell, complaining's more fun, anyway! I know, I do it! HAHAHA! And it's just more human. It's not a fuckin' groupie rag.

'So I'm really proud to be on the cover, man. As long as I don't have to pay for the candles on the cake! HAHAHAHAHA!'

CODA

What I didn't know at the time this story was written was that Roth's career was about to hit the skids. Despite reaching the US Top Ten, the *Skyscraper* album would not go on to become the multi-squillion-selling hit it should have been; most gallingly, its sales were dwarfed by those of the second Van Halen album with his replacement, Sammy Hagar – *OU812*, which hit Number One in the USA that summer. As I later discovered, there was a dark side to Dave, too. My experience of him was that he was a control freak whose obsessions, fed by years of being overindulged by flunkies and yes-men, were now beginning to take control. I recall the glum atmosphere backstage at the shows he did in London later that year, his bassist Matt Bissonette sitting on the stairs with his head in his hands after being bawled out by Dave for messing up some onstage cue. You knew the rot had really set in when his whizzkid guitarist, Steve Vai, politely but firmly walked out on him at the end of that tour. The only times I ever heard from Dave after that were when he was in London and wanted to score some hash. Even then I wouldn't be allowed up to his hotel room to give it to him, let alone share a smoke. I would have to pass it over to 'an assistant', then sit in the bar on my own waiting for him to come down and at least say hello.

Of course, he reformed with Van Halen in recent years, and I'm glad for him. What David Lee Roth is like now, though, I couldn't say, not having spoken to him for nearly twenty years. I still like to think of him, though, in full flow, scraping at the sky and puffing on clouds, the master in his element.

LIVE AID, 1985

These days, whenever it comes up that I was actually backstage at the American version of the 1985 Live Aid concert, even I have to admit it sounds quite impressive. At the time, though, I saw things rather differently. I grudgingly accepted that there did indeed seem to be money being sent to Africa, and that the dreadful 'Do They Know it's Christmas?' single might, after all, be a 'good thing', in that respect. But I hadn't quite got my head around the fact yet that almost everything in the music business is driven by rock star vanity. I still thought it was a bad thing and I cringed every time Geldof came on telly, doing his righteous give-me-your-fuckin'-money thing, or your butter-mountain, or whatever it was. I was convinced that if his group The Boomtown Rats hadn't been a busted flush he would never have come up with Band Aid. Like that mattered.

For some reason, it did matter to me, though, and nothing would have pleased me more than to discover the whole thing was a sham. Hence the rather large chip I appear to be wearing throughout the story . . .

'Not since those star-spangled, guilt-edged nights in 1970–71 when Leonard Bernstein threw his Black Panther party and George Harrison organised the Concert for Bangladesh have so many of the rich and famous stepped out for the poor and famished . . .'

– *Observer*

'By mid-morning the American Telegraph Company reported that the toll-free telephone line it had set up to receive pledges, 1–800–LIVE AID, was overloaded. The 1,126 circuits allocated were simply getting more traffic than they could handle . . .'

– *New York Times*

'Who the fuck are the Hooters?' – Ozzy Osbourne

Ah, yes . . . who indeed? But that's a question you may never get answered. Not here, certainly, not this time. No, we are, after all, professionals with a money-down obligation to address ourselves to only the most important issues, at whatever the cost. So when the boss dished this dirty assignment my way I sat there fingering the soft flesh tyre hanging from my belt, dreaming of pizza and wondering flatly just what a moonage daydream like me could possibly say about this whole meals-on-mega-wheels deal Mr Geldof had christened Live Aid? Gimme a menu and I'll think about it, you know?

Forty or so different singers, bands, actors, comedians and over 90,000 people paying between thirty-five and fifty dollars a ticket just to see it, to finally believe in it, and to go home that night and tell the folks that, yes, they actually witnessed it – Live Aid! History in the making, my little mascara snakes! And why not? Indeed. I remember watching the evening news one night on TV way back in the foul arsehole of last winter, and screwing up my nose when Bob Geldof bounded before the camera with the news that he had assembled his 'friends in the pop business' to record this one song good old Bob had written called 'Do They Know it's Christmas?', proceeds of which would most certainly go, and that means every penny, to the starving Africans in Ethiopia, where the sun always shines and the rain has not fallen in three years. There followed the most atrocious video-clip of several puff-pastry pop bimbos looking dead sincere and as fascinating as a turkey's bollocks, singing this awful, trite little ditty, and blow this for a game of marbles, says I. Waves of cynicism came hurtling from my heart; this is too much, this is just too fucking perfect, they've gone too far this time if they think they can have me choking and weeping on the perfect sincerity of a plan as plainly obnoxious and damned decent as this baby. What's that you see in my eye, Bob? Grass? You bastard . . .

We all know what happened to the record and, it's only fair to point out, we all know what's happened to the money. What Thatcher and her storm-troopers didn't steal in VAT, Geldof and his newly appointed Trust Committee (higher-ups included people like Michael Grade, head of BBC1; Maurice Oberstein, then president of CBS Records; and Lord Gowrie, officially a sponsor) set up to protect the public's money, took care of. The Trust's formation came from a special lesson learnt after the bitter experience of George Harrison's Bangladesh Appeal. The project disintegrated when it got tangled up in the tortuous relationship between Allen Klein, the erstwhile Beatles manager, and the US Inland Revenue. Twice a week, the famine-relief co-ordinator in Ethiopia, Brother Gus O'Keefe, telephones through a shopping list of vital supplies needed to the London offices of Band Aid, in Burton Street WC1, and, according to Geldof, 'It's out there in ten hours!'

That information cancelled my argument somewhat, but I am a grossly cynical bastard at the best of times and I would not give in. Not yet, not so easily this time, friend. But when Big Mama America took up the idea, the £8.5 million already raised by Geldof and 'pop friends' started to look like cold spaghetti. 'We Are the World', featured some genuinely heavy talent indeed – Quincy Jones, Michael Jackson, Stevie Wonder, Diana Ross. That kind of money doesn't haul ass out of leopard-skin couch in Malibu for some dog-shit small-time hustler idea. No, they move when their fine and sophisticated instinct for a deal they cannot refuse wafts by their security-guarded front porch.

As a result, to date – and right now I'm talking about the night before the Wembley and Philadelphia concerts kick off, in approximately five hours – Geldof's little Christmas present to the starving children of Africa has already raised many millions of dollars, a lot of it now stretching into the empty stomachs of Chad, Mozambique, Angola and the Sudan.

So the action is already heavy, and only a certifiable bed-wetter or a cheap stinker out to seriously party-poop this whole nervous deal should raise a hand against it. Only I just can't quite get off on the notion of looking at Live Aid like the good little punter a lot of this material is aimed at. Everybody loves a circus, every man, woman and child wants to join the carnival, and a lot of people like ABC Television network in America know it, and what they know they grow good healthy crops of bucks from. For example, ABC paid an alleged figure of $4 million for the legal rights to broadcast the last three hours of the Philadelphia Live Aid concert. As a result, from 8 p.m. to 11 p.m. Eastern Time, ABC would be the only channel the people of America would watch, and a solid piece of history right there on the videotape too, while the company dished out their thirty-second-long commercial spots to potential sponsors across the world for figures reportedly starting at around $250,000 a throw. Of course, they would also be obliged to run a Telethon, but what the hell, this is good television, so let's roll!

And strange expressions passed across the faces seated in the bar of the Four Seasons Hotel in Philadelphia where all the acts and organisation people are holed-up, when the press report went out that Huey Lewis and the News had decided to withdraw from the concert after what the official document described as 'disturbing news reports about the handling of the food by the Ethiopian government'. A week before the event, local TV news bulletins featured an item that claimed Russian nuclear arms were getting unloading preference over Band Aid food supplies at crucial Ethiopian air-landing sites. It went on to suggest that crates of food were left to rot on abandoned gang-planks, completely and wilfully wasted, man . . .

All I know is, Huey Lewis is a man of conscience, and his band the News are so popular in America and around the world that, unlike one or two names I want to throw around later in this piece, they certainly don't crave the added precedent of massive point-to-point around-the-world-in-a-day publicity. So they thought about it seriously and then they said no. Bear in mind, Huey Lewis had already personally contributed to the USA for Africa single and accompanying video; with the band, together they had contributed a track gratis to the million-selling album that followed, so there was obviously complete agreement with the sentiment expressed, but now they say they will not be convinced sufficiently to perform again until they get hard evidence that the project is being seen through to its ultimate and Godly end.

There's something happening here. I mean, where's Michael Jackson today; at home playing with his pet snakes? Where are you, Stevie Wonder, and what have you seen that we can't see? I mean, I don't believe Stevie Wonder isn't here. Like, why not? It can't be the weather, not today with the sun promising us eighty degrees of slow burn and so many silly motherfuckers like me wandering around with their best smiles on. Whatever the reasons, I hope we never find out. Because if those people I saw at the Live Aid concert in Philadelphia ever get to hear of any scams going down about misappropriated funds by any government, or any one-eyed jacks they can put a dirty name to, then I don't wanna be sitting around on my ass somewhere bashing the keys and telling this foul stinking world, well, you know, I fucking told you. No, that would mean nothing. I hope we would lynch the bastards and slit their throats right down to their rotten putrid gizzards!

Ah . . . but hang on here. How much bile does a person need to suck on before it all just starts to sound like one long bitch of crummy complaints? Let's put the sunglasses on and take a walk around the gig; the weather's nice, after all.

'By mid-afternoon, Phil Collins had finished his duet with Sting in London and was headed across the Atlantic on a Concorde jet to perform in Philadelphia and, more important . . . more than 20 million dollars had already been pledged' – *New York Times*

'David Bowie, Sting, Tina Turner, Mick Jagger . . . there they all were, in glorious, full-colour satellite Dollarvision, being, of all things, nice!' – *Sunday Observer*

I feel like a goddamn fool, but I'm humping around in the queue for the hot dog stand – hoping to lay my molars on some of that fine South Philly cheese-steak ... Mmm-hmmm, with some of those hot cheese fries to go – and I figure, what the hell and why not, so I lean over and with a sudden flash of my bad-teeth smile I am talking to a local Philly Southsider, who says, 'Shit, I know it's for a good cause and all, and I'm glad that's where my money's going, you know, to help people, but like, why I'm here is to see Led fuckin' Zeppelin! You know what I mean?'

You got it. The JFK Stadium – a huge sports arena that in its prime was the home of the big local Philadelphia football team, the Flyers, before the team took their crowd two blocks down the street to the more modern sports complex recently erected – is rarely used these days, except for the biggest events. It is, in fact, the only stadium capable of holding almost 100,000 people out here on the East Coast, and today the old girl look likes she's bought herself a brand new pair of pantyhose, hitched up her drawers and dragged a comb through her hair. The place is alive with colour, rich in good vibes, and swinging on the once-in-a-lifetime security of knowing that what you're doing is right. Straight as a bleeding arrow, mate.

Backstage, the atmosphere is equal to anything going on outside. When Ozzy has finished his three-number set with Sabbath he tells TV interviewer after TV interviewer that no, he wasn't really sure about his feelings before he arrived in Philadelphia, but now, oh now, well that was different – and Ozzy was right. The picture changes when you see the action going on, and fully righteous with it, right there in front of your eyes. Jack Nicholson chats to Ozzy and the two old rogues end up laughing at each other. Rick Springfield you wouldn't know until the TV cameras start to cluster up close, while Bryan Adams walks around in shorts with his girlfriend by his side. Even the loathsome Thompson Twins drop the pop-fart facade for this one special occasion and don't bother the locals too much.

'Good morning, children of the Eighties,' announced Joan Baez, at the very start of the concert. 'This is your Woodstock, and it's long overdue.' We stuck our fingers down our throats for that one, but when the old biddy cranked out a nice and sensible rendition of 'Amazing Grace' I could forgive her those wrinkles around the throat, and anyway, it was only one number, and as a professional I could cope with that.

The Hooters followed and … yes, but who are the goddamn Hooters? Local boyos snuck through the back door of course, should anybody care to enquire. But so what? The Four Tops are a real belly-wobble; quite superb sound, raunchy vocals and saxes hotter than July; no question about it now, Sergeant, we're on our bloody way this time. Why, there are thousands of people over there shaking their booty like Mama ain't never coming home. And then Billy Ocean, followed by Black Sabbath! Yeah, why not? Let's fuckin' go …

It's almost 11 o'clock on this sweltering morning and Crosby, Stills and Big Nose are crying into their guitars. David Crosby is going to jail in Texas before the year is out, say the police and court reports, a five-stretch, say the wise, for getting caught with a room full of guns, cocaine, and … dirty socks, who knows? Stephen Stills looks like Benny Hill on Mandrax for the first time, but they do their bit and what the hell. Judas Priest follow and kill me stone dead. I like this group of Band Aid banditos so much, and when they open their set with 'Living After Midnight', well, here's my fiver, take it to the deserts of Africa with my blessing. When the revolving stage wheels Bryan Adams into view, and the news goes out that we are now – ta-ra! – live and linked, via satellite, to London, the place experiences its first really dangerous explosion of the day. By noon, young Bryan is dipping into the honey with 'The Kids Wanna Rock' and, all right, I give in. Gimme two of those fourteen-dollar T-shirts, I'm all yours …

As the day turns into dusk the stars all come and go. Simple Minds, the Pretenders, Tom Petty, the Beach Boys, Eric Clapton, all introduced so warmly by, uh, Sonny from *Miami Vice*, Chevy Chase, Bette Midler, Jack Nicholson, Jeff 'Whoa! Rock 'n' roll!' Bridges … still no one is burned out, no one is anywhere near ready to quit the good and wholesome action. The tone is growing ever more mellow, not ready to make the jump yet to deep and respectful, but not far to go.

For that final piece of our hearts that says, 'Yup Bob, I gotta hand it to you, I think you did us all a favour there!' we have to wait for Led Zeppelin. Oh yes, you remember, the daddies of them all – Led Zeppelin! That name is worth pure gold in America. The small talk about the Beatles may come and go, but when it was announced that

Zeppelin was to re-form, albeit minus their deceased former drummer John 'Bonzo' Bonham, replaced for this event by Phil Collins and Tony Thompson (Power Station/Bowie/Chic drummer), you could feel the anticipation an ocean away. Was it true? Led Zeppelin, the biggest, the best, and the baddest, just this one last time?

The crunch came as I was standing chatting to Ozzy and Geezer, along the backstage alleyway concourse that led to the stage. All day long the star attractions had wandered amiably around unaffected and wholly uninterested in unveiling their own petty vanities before people who were, after all, suitably regarded as their peers, the least temporary contemporaries, and who would be ass enough to stomp around and play up the whole star-star-superstar boogie, for who would it impress? And then suddenly, large black voices behind our knotty little gathering began yelling: 'Outta the way there! Outta the way! People comin' through here!'

And we shift ass very quickly, being smart, and on turning around to see just who the people are causing this rash disturbance, we spy three no-shit uniformed spades providing a human shield to the angular, distorted crab-like vision of 'Little' Jimmy Page, glassy eyes slitted and raw, his jerky spasmodic gestures a testament to the powers of modern science. Heading up the back with his own court of bully-boy jesters and sprightly laymen, comes Robert Plant, looking every month his true age (fifteen-and-a-half) and bursting with a rouged good health it is hard to ignore.

'Hey, Rob! You big girl's blouse!' cries Ozzy as Plant swishes past, swanning his own unique song for every red cent it's worth (which is at least double any number you or I could come up with, kid). 'Ozzy!' cries Robert. 'Bloody hell! And Geezer too!' And Robert breaks rank, much to the obvious bafflement of his armed guards, and ambles over to greet the two (temporarily) reunited Black Sabbath kingpins. Nice guy, Rob Plant; if he played his cards right I'd really like to interview him.

Minutes later, up on stage, the red, white and blue curtains wind back as Jimmy Page hits the opening chords to 'Rock and Roll' and there isn't a dry brain cell left in the house. Madness! Great huge waves of it erupt into the sky and Band Aid be damned, they really did it this time, and good. 'Whole Lotta Love' follows and the whole thing starts to take on the aspect of some crazy dream. Page looks out of it, Plant looks superb, pencil-thin, knows what he's doing, knows why, too.

At the finale of 'Stairway to Heaven', when Plant closes his eyes and sings, 'And she's buy-uy-ing . . . a stairway . . . to . . . heaven', the crowd all come in on the 'buy-uy-ing' part and cold tingles go up and down the neck of the world. Afterwards, the applause is huge, not just from the crowd of terminal hysterics out front, but from the hard-nosed pay-check-dependent herds of worker ants backstage, me included.

Much later, I am rolling down the highway from Philly, sitting hunched up in the front seat of Ozzy's limo, and on the miniature TV in the back Bob Dylan is sealing the fate of history with his finest old waltz, 'Blowin' in the Wind'. And then Ozzy says: 'Turn that bloody TV off, Sharon. I'm tired.'

Off it goes, the screen dies, and so do my thoughts . . .

'The international accounting firm of Howarth and Howarth, in co-operation with its United States affiliate, Laventhal and Howarth, is to prepare a complete public disclosure of the Live Aid finances'

– *New York Times*

CODA

Although I later had to admit that the Live Aid concerts really had served a higher purpose than that of merely 'resurrecting the careers', as the press still puts it, of acts such as Status Quo and Queen, I still found myself squirming as I sat at home watching the Live 8 show in Hyde Park in 2005. Was it just me, or did the whole thing make the original 1985 version look like a genuinely innocent, heart-warming occasion, designed to give a hand to the poor and the dying? Without being asked to send money, what the 2005 version was about, I don't know. Ending poverty? Raising awareness? Without sending money, what does that mean in practical terms? Does anyone know? Apart from Bob Geldof and Bono, I mean?

I might need another twenty-five years to get my head around that one.

MARILLION, 1985

I have interviewed Fish a great many times in several different locations over the years – from London to Los Angeles, via Aylesbury and Edinburgh. But perhaps the best interview we ever did occurred in Berlin in 1985. It was certainly the most prophetic: Marillion, who he had led from obscurity to the heights of the Hammersmith Odeon, now stood perched on the cusp of their first really big, worldwide success – and, somehow, Fish knew it.

In Berlin to record their third album, *Misplaced Childhood*, from which would come their huge hit single, 'Kayleigh', Fish was already telling anyone who would listen that this was going to be 'the big one'. This was despite the presence of a doubting EMI executive who kept boring everyone stupid with talk of 'demographics' and 'market penetration'. Wanker.

At the same time it was clear that Fish seemed to be undergoing some sort of transition in his personal life. He told me of a girl he had met and become 'obsessed with', who worked as a hostess at one of the glitzy nightclubs he and the band had begun frequenting during their stay in Berlin. (Indeed, not only would she end up the star of the 'Kayleigh' video, but she was soon to become his wife.) He was also still quite heavily involved with cocaine; a rock star's accoutrement he would grow ever more fond of as the band's success began to spiral out of control. Not that I minded, of course. It was the rock stars who *didn't* do drugs that I wished to avoid in those days.

Being the same age, we had a lot in common. I threw in the towel, though, when he suggested going out to a club as the interview finally wound down at five in the morning. He called me a 'lightweight' and, compared to Fish in those days, that's exactly what I was . . .

Five weeks in Suicide City does strange things to a man's head. Berlin is a city of concrete and walls situated smack in the middle of the great East–West divide, its outer limits enclosed by forbidden lands governed by sky-high barbed-wire fences and occupied by soldiers carrying live ammunition guarding God-knows-what from army turrets surrounded by minefields. If you wanna rip it up for a couple of nights in Berlin and shave a couple more years off your life then you can, no problem: the brothels and the clubs and the widespread availability of smack and coke guarantee the action. But if you're planning on spending a month-to-six-weeks in this joint, then bring along your oxygen tent because, boy, you're gonna need it. Not even the hand of fate will help if you want to take a drive out to the countryside maybe, or perhaps just get out and visit friends in neighbouring towns and cities: there simply aren't any. You're trapped until an air-ticket tells you otherwise. Hansa Studios, by the Berlin Wall, is where Marillion have been holed up together these past six weeks recording their all-important third studio album. This is the one they're going to be calling *Misplaced Childhood* and, as you will no doubt have read in issue 93's news story, it's very definitely a concept album, in the tradition, perhaps, of *The Lamb Lies Down on Broadway* or, better still, Pink Floyd's *The Wall*, with maybe just a hint of David Bowie's *Station to Station* masterpiece.

The Wild West of Berlin is groaning under the five o'clock shadow of another rainy Monday when myself and photographer Ray Palmer arrive for our scheduled meeting with Marillion. Us and Marillion, we go back a ways. Shit, we actually like these guys: like talking to them, seeing them, even listening to their music once in a while. *Script for a Jester's Tear, Fugazi, Real to Reel* . . . tell me about it. Marillion? They're special, that's all.

In strictest Marillion tradition, 'business' is scheduled for the following day: meaning it's time once again for all good rock 'n' roll boys to comb the hair of the night, exploring the absolute power of positive drinking. And tonight that means a trip to see Frankie Goes to Hollywood play before 6,000 screaming Berliners. Fish, Ian Mosley and I are sitting in the hotel bar before the show, lining our stomachs on Blue Label Smirnoff and Black Bush whiskey.

'So what do you think of Berlin?' Fish asks me.

'Nothing. I've been here before,' I reply.

'Been here before?' he arches an eyebrow. 'We've been here forever – that's what it fucking feels like. We took a couple of days off for Easter and all went home, and for a few days I was on top of the world again. Then I came back here and depression just hits you the second day – bang! Right in the face.'

'You wouldn't want to live here then?' I ask.

'Fuck, no! How Bowie managed to come here to clean himself up in a place as dreary and insane as this is unbelievable.'

Fish is sporting a beard. I can't make up my mind whether it makes him look like the baddie from some James Bond movie or whether I'm sitting at the court of King Arthur. It suits him, and its dramatic appeal is plain, but what about the face make-up when he gets back on the road?

'Oh no, I'll shave it off tomorrow when we do the pictures,' he smiles. 'I let it grow for a part in this movie called *The Highlander* I was offered, but now the timing has gone all wrong; we'll be touring when they want to start filming, so it doesn't look like it's going to happen.'

Film? Movie? BEARD?! But he's gone, long strides and big hunting boots, towards the elevator doors. The following afternoon at Hansa Studios we're all playing Spot the Walking Amnesia Case – I can't remember who won – and then, with precious little warning, the producer's chair at the mixing console is shoved under my arse and a huddle of hushed grinning Marillion-heads take a deep breath and wait for the tapes to roll. We're gonna hear the single.

Cue: Total Wipe-Out! Stunning, seductive . . . gimme a tequila and let me come back to you on that one. 'Kayleigh' may just be the most perfect song Marillion have yet recorded (remember I haven't heard the rest of the album properly yet), their most perfect song on an LP that boasts just two songs, in the words of Fish from the stage of the Hammersmith Odeon last Xmas: 'Side one and side two.'

The production on 'Kayleigh', by Chris Kimsey, is little short of superb; built around a beautiful cartwheeling rhythm guitar part, child-like in its simple charm and utterly compelling at the climax, while Fish's lyric is all Alice Through the Whiskey Glass imagery, although more understated and refined than we have come to expect and fear from that old 'tongue forged in eloquence'. The voice, too, seems to have finally located the heart and his vocal embraces the whole drama of the song even though the singer remains remote, unreformed, unrepentant.

The other side of the single is not on the album and was written specifically for the 45 here in Berlin: it's called 'Lady Nina' and is named after one of the more infamous Berlin nightclubs the band have read about in their friendly 'Guide to Berlin' tourist information leaflets – and it's a bitch! Somewhere in the back of a taxi-cab, ankle-deep in yesterday's rubbers, stiletto concealed in her purse, driving through the Turkish sector on some unfinished business the law wouldn't understand, sits 'Lady Nina'. What Steve Rothery does with his guitar on this track belongs in the Land of the Unnameable; clawing out the heart of the song and sticking it in his back pocket, while Mosley and the electronic percussion computers erupt and bleed like a volcano between your thighs. The production adds all the champagne touches, the melody pure brandy. When it's over and they've picked me up off the floor, I dry my eyes, take a long swallow of somebody else's cigarette smoke and slump off to a chair in the corner where I sit with my cakehole flapping like a bird in the wind.

Some hours later, Fish is sprawled out on the bed talking on the phone to his ma in Edinburgh. It's the usual Mother Rant: I will, I won't, I did, I don't, shut up ma and I'll see you soon, love ya. On the bedside table sits a large bottle of Black Bush Whiskey, an ashtray, a full glass and two mini-speakers attached to a Walkman. Distant *Fugazi* LP sleeve vibes, ma: Fish as Rock Star, as Poet, Actor, Hedonist and Anti-hero. Just some of the roles that seem to fascinate the man. Like a child, every time he sees a flame burning he wants to grasp it, hold it and know it. I haven't seen him for months and suddenly I realise that I've missed the bugger with the big mouth and broad shoulders. People like Fish, they're in for the life sentence and should be respected because they are so rare. When he gets off the phone, we pour ourselves some decent measures of that fine Black Bush, I pull the cap from a beer, and sitting there cross-legged on his bed, we let it all come down.

Earlier on today you told me you were going to zap me within the first three minutes of this interview and tell me anything I needed to know. What did you mean by that?

'Ah, just get it over and down, get the real heavy stuff over and done with. But it's impossible, you know?'

Why did you come to Berlin to record the album?

'There were a couple of reasons, actually. One of them was that a whole lot of producers we asked to do the LP said no because they thought they couldn't make money off it. They said we had no singles on the album and that the format we were working in was so totally alien to anything else coming out nowadays that they didn't want to touch it.'

I would have thought that might add to the appeal of the project?

'No, no way. A lot of the guys we asked were against a band bringing out a concept album that was like forty-odd minutes long. They were looking at the American market. We carried on searching, though, and then we met Chris [Kimsey]. When he came down to see us the first time we were expecting somebody really straight. The guy's done like five Rolling Stones albums and someone like that you expect to be really big time, but Chris isn't like that at all. He believes in heart and feel and ... emotion, in all aspects of recording, which we as a band had never concentrated on before. That really appealed to us.'

I think because of the more remote aspects of your two previous albums people are always shocked by just how much emotion there is at one of your concerts. It does seem to have been missing, or miscommunicated, on the albums.

'Absolutely. We were aware that we've never been able to put the heart that we have live, and the feel and the angst, whatever you want to call it, down on two-inch tape. Every time we've gone into the studio we've always been overly technical because that's what's expected of bands like us. Chris said that he wanted to go for songs on this album. He doesn't want special effects, he doesn't want over-the-top stuff, he wants to hear a song and he wants to feel a song. Up till now I think I've been trapped by the ego-side of recording an album – like, this is for posterity! And I don't like the temporary aspect of listening to albums. For the album to be truly good you must affect people. There's no point in making people go, "Oh, wow, these guys are really clever", there's no point in that. And I think in the long term it fucked us up because a lot of people who listened to the records were put off going to the gigs.'

The lyrics to the two tracks I heard this afternoon really knocked me out. I've always rated you as a lyricist, but I don't think you've come up with anything quite so eloquent or simple before.

'That's because I've taken a completely new approach. It got to the point after the *Fugazi* album where there were people, like in Canada, coming up to me and telling me that I was walking in the shadow of Dylan Thomas and that I was more than a mere lyricist. Because I don't play an instrument I focus on words all the time. The danger is that you can become so involved with words that it ends up like masturbation; you know, the kick you get is all for yourself and that's not the real kick of being a lyricist.

'It might sound arrogant, but the thing a lyricist should do is try and teach. You must try and explain on a sort of street level so that people can understand immediately what you're talking about. Because the things I go through everybody goes through, and I have the ability to put that into words and I should not try to be condescending or pseudo-intellectual, you know, image-image-image, it's your duty to read into this. Bollocks! On this album I finally realised that by working more on imagery I was avoiding a lot of the problems, a lot of the questions and a lot of the answers that I was trying to put across. *Fugazi* became too wordy from an ego point of view.'

Misplaced Childhood: how personal, or autobiographical, is the story?

'This album is very, very personal. The *Script* . . . album was about the break-ups and the start of the break-ups; the *Fugazi* album was the final break-up, but there was no definitive ending; and this album is the analysis, trying to come out of the problems by saying "yes, that is a limitation; yes, that is a negative aspect of personality". And I realised that if I sat back on this album and wrote it as poetry, or if I started examining it all inside my own head as I was writing it, I would go nowhere and it would be the fucking same as the last two albums. I've always said in interviews that writing lyrics is like an exorcism for me and this album is the major exorcism.'

Why have you been so definite about calling *Misplaced Childhood* a concept album? You know you could be setting yourself up for a major fall?

'I know I've set myself up as A Lyricist completely. Some of it's very manic, very depressive.'

I like your voice better on this album; it sounds less self-conscious, more emotional.

'I think a lot of that's got to do with coming to Berlin. Coming here you've got less contact with the record company, you've got less contact with all the commercial aspects of the music business, so you just go out and do what you fucking want. I've had to come to terms with now – I was becoming too retrospective and my entire romantic life, my personal life, my band life was all based in the past, which is like a complete fuck-up – and I had to pull myself away from that to find my direction again.

'*Misplaced Childhood* isn't so much about an actual childhood, more the simplicities of youth. It's more like someone starting again. You reach a point where your life can get so fucked-up and you try and retrace and you go back and you want to start again, only of course you can't do that. The experiences you have gone through that numb you, that scar you, they are there and you cannot ignore them, the pain is long gone and all they can do is teach you.'

Have you ever suffered from an experience that frightened the shit out of you so much that you refused to go any further?

'Oh yeah, of course. I think it helps to begin with something like that sometimes. We had the idea for the concept of this album just after we'd finished recording the *Script* . . . LP and it was strange that it was never fully realised at the time. I wanted to do an album about, uh, childlike alternatives. The original idea I had for the *Fugazi* sleeve was to have a kid on the cover and the jester going through the window, and when I told Mark Wilkinson [who designs all the Marillion sleeves] he handed me a copy of *Demian*, the Herman Hesse book. And I read it and thought, fucking hell, this is it, this is the album! I didn't have an ending for the album. I knew what I was trying to say but it's like they teach you in school, to have a beginning, a middle and an end. Well, I didn't have the end but I read *Demian* and that gave me the classic ending.'

So how does *Misplaced Childhood* end?

'The guy's looking back on childhood all the time. He looks on his childhood as being the ideal world, the simplicity of then. He can't figure out at which point he stopped being a kid and became an adult and he's wrong because you never stop being a kid while you're still prepared to learn. "Adult" is always supposed to be synonymous with All-Knowing, Wise, Worldly – you're never that! You're always learning, you're always a child.'

Can you still keep your innocence intact?

'Your subconscious innocence, yeah.'

Or faith, in that you won't slash your wrists when you wake up in the morning, there is another day?

'I don't think I had faith when I was a kid. You're still questioning things too much to worry about faith; you're still opening up those dark cupboards and living rooms, which you're told never to open because you'll get smacked on the wrists. You're always doing that and learning and finding out for yourself. Nowadays, there is precious little innocence in childhood.'

You told me earlier that you would hate to be in the situation of being stuck at home, with no option but to 'knob the missus'. That you wanted to 'see life for what it is'. Can you keep that up all the time?

'I dunno. When Mark [Kelly, keyboard player] brings his wife Susie and his kid over to my home I think I really want that, I really, really do want that, and I get very jealous of them.'

Do you feel it would affect the quality of your writing, a settled home life with a wife and kids?

'Yeah, I do. Because of my, um, poetic instincts or whatever you wanna call it, I feel it's part of my job to go out and try and do new things before I come back and talk about them. I've always been attracted to the fringe activities of life, the stuff out on the perimeter.'

What happens if close friends abandon you to your fate because of some of these 'fringe activities'?

'Close friends don't abandon you. My close friends have never known me any other way; I've always been like this. I have to question the morals of the world I was brought up in.'

I know you tend to get bored easily and it seems to be a trait I come across in lots of performers and singers: are the two things linked, are you hung up on excitement?

'I don't like repetition and I don't like playing safe. I don't like it when you go on stage and you're guaranteed a good reaction; when you know that you'll walk off stage feeling like a minor deity or something. I don't like that shit. I like to fight, that's why I want to make sure that I always push myself into other avenues.'

How far do you want to go with these forbidden experiments of personality? If it was in my power to grant you the gift of pure evil, would you take it to find out what it was like?

'No. I still have a mental fuse-wire. Even when I get really, really drunk I never get totally out of order. I don't have blackouts. When I get to that stage where I'm so out of it that Mr Obnoxious raises his ugly pointed head, I either go straight to sleep or throw up. Believe it or not, I do still possess certain morals.'

What laws would you not break?

'Well, religion frightens me a wee bit. Black magic and the occult frighten me. I don't like situations which are totally out of my control. I'm not a great gambler, I'm not even a very good gambler; I like to be sure that the odds are very much on my side. The devil and black magic, you don't play with, and hedonists never play with things. Hedonists who play with things end up as suicides or else completely broken people. The point about hedonism is to experience and learn; the human magpie collecting things, collecting experiences. To me that's how people should work. There's no point hiding away; you cannot get it from TV, you've got to go out and collide and spark with people.'

I remember speaking to you before Xmas about the new album and you told me then that you were convinced it was going to be mega. Are you still convinced that, despite the advice against calling it a concept album, it will be your biggest commercial success?

'I'm confident because it's the first time I've never considered the commercial side. On *Fugazi*, because there was so much pressure that we weren't used to dealing with from inside the business to come up with an album that really sold the band, a record that would give us a degree of established status, I think we had that on our minds when we came to record it. But with this one we've gone in and said fuck it; if you want us, you take us; if not, screw you!

'Berlin has had a lot to do with it, too, because you're removed from it all here, which you're not at home any more. We became pure artists here. Somebody said that Berlin is the focusing point of the world, and it's a crazy place: one minute I hate it, the next I wallow in it. If I lived here I'd go crazy, I'd burn. It would kill me, no doubt about that. This place is more intense than New York. In New York you can walk away; you can never walk away here.'

You told me you still had one more lyric to write for the album. Which one?

'The happy optimistic one!' He bursts out laughing. 'Like, "Sorry man, I haven't got the happy bit together yet, I just can't, you know, relate!" Naw, it's the key lyric but the longer I leave it the more I feel pushed into a corner. It'll happen. But you know what I hate? I hate it when I read somebody saying that they don't want their lyrics to change the world. I don't understand how people can fucking say that: "I don't want to change the world". I'd love to change the world – of course I fucking want to! And anybody who says they don't should be put up against a wall and fucking shot! Nobody can say they're happy with what's going on around them. I would give my life to change the world. Just say the right words. People have forgotten words, nowadays.'

Changing the subject, what's all this about being in a film? What's going on, man, you gonna be the next John Gielgud or what?

'Hahaha! Arise, Sir Fish! Yeah, I've taken on a theatrical agent and she's trying to get me work in films.'

Why films?

'It's another one of those natural steps. I'm a frontman so I'm involved to some degree in the theatrics we have on stage and I want to extend it; I feel pulled into it. Every song is a minor play, they all tell their stories, and eventually you want to extend it. Like as a lyricist. Right now I'm pissed off with writing lyrics, and I'm not being detrimental to the band, but I want to try and do something more. Sometimes I'll get a line which so inspires me that I really want to do something with it other than condense the whole thing down into a song lyric. It's restricting my natural flow.'

Have you ever considered writing a book of prose or poems?

'Yeah, I have. Right now we're talking about publishing deals for books and stuff, and I'm really interested in it. The prospect of recording one of those total ego-job solo albums with the greatest musicians in the land would not be as big a kick as I'd get out of putting the words "THE END" at the bottom of a novel. And it's the same with writing a script or acting in a movie; the kick would be bigger than any solo album.'

Do you feel confident that you could carry the lead in a motion picture?

'No! I am the most unconfident person you have ever met! I have no confidence in myself at all. I am black. Every extrovert is a classic introvert. Always true, and that's what I am. I can talk very easily. I can find safety in words, and in humour. I used to think I was a really funny guy, but it was a safety valve. Actually I'm a vicious bastard with my tongue. It's a very Scottish thing, being fast with your mouth.'

Do you ever wish someone would put a gag in it for you?

'Oh yeah, a lot. Sometimes I hate it, the words and the ability to use them to hurt or whatever. I've had girls in my room who with eight words I have killed stone dead.'

What about when you're with your band?

'It's not my band.'

But do you enjoy freaking people out when you're talking to them? You've done it to me.

'Hahaha! Yeah, I've been freaking people out since I was a kid. This band's terrible for it; we do it to each other all the time. Drummer Ian Mosely is brilliant at it. Ian does it to me; he really fucking freaks me out sometimes. Mind you, I love seeing that shock when you turn 'round and say something and everybody in the room goes "What?! What did he fucking say?!" I love breaking barriers and busting through walls and just fucking people up with their own bullshit. "Lady Nina", for Chrissakes! If you say to someone it's about a guy in Berlin who goes out at night to see this hooker, they turn around and go "You sexist fucking pig!"'

As your career winds on and you begin to take on more and more diverse projects separate from Marillion, how do you react to the responsibility of knowing that the whole Marillion organisation rests on your shoulders too?

'I'm aware of the pressure it puts the people around me under. On April 1st we rang up John [Arneson – band manger] and told him, as an April Fools' thing, that I had all sorts of problems with my health. We said that my throat was bleeding, lots of problems. And John and I are very close, and he's like really nice to me on the phone saying "Don't you worry, you'll get the best treatment, whatever you need we'll have it". And then he says to someone else, "And make sure he does the album, make sure he finishes it". I became aware of it there all right. You wanna hit out!

'Sometimes you just want to walk out on it. Before this album I had moments when I thought, fuck it, I just want to go! It shows on the record. To be starkly honest, I did think about topping myself at one point last year, because I was getting so fucked up with a lot of different things and I just wanted to go away.'

What stopped you?

'A couple of things. One that I don't want to go into, to do with my guardian, my short-fuse, a sort of instinct. And the other because it would have upset a lot of people. I love the guys in the band, they're like my best friends, and I thought about how many people it would fuck-up if I did. Plus, the whole Lennon, Morrison, Hendrix, Joplin thing. I just knew it would be so sordid, and I want to fight it out, I want to say something. Suicide is such a negative statement, and not one I want to make. Like heroin. Heroin is such a negative fucking statement. Like morphine.'

As a singer you inspire followers to whom you must resemble something of a guru. Who's your guru?

'I don't have one – used to have, but not now. I know it sounds very big-headed, but it's myself. Safe in my own words, learning from my own words . . .'

CODA

Fish was another rock star whose career was destined to take a sharp downward turn. If you'd told me at the time of the trip to Berlin that within three years he would have left Marillion for a solo career, or that neither he nor the band would ever again enjoy the kind of career-high they were then on the cusp of with *Misplaced Childhood* – their first and only UK Number One album – I simply would not have been able to see how that was possible. As far as I could tell, they were on their way to becoming the new Pink Floyd, or the new Genesis, at the very least: concept albums and hit singles, a winning combo, surely, especially in America.

As it would transpire, the band never would make it in America. Indeed, it would be some years before they were finally out of the shadow of their former singer and recognised as a creative force in their own right; these days, closer musical cousins to Radiohead than Yes. As for Fish, he has led an increasingly marginal solo career, releasing some truly exceptional albums, but never quite making the smart career moves you need to maintain star status; the sort of star turn you would not be surprised now to see turning up on a 'celebrity' reality show. None of this makes him a bad person or a lesser musical light. He has strayed a long way, though, from the promising path he seemed to be pursuing on that long-ago night in Suicide City.

ROCK IN RIO, 1985

I can't remember how I managed to wangle this one – an all-expenses paid trip to Rio – although I'm fairly sure it had something to do with my old mate Ross Halfin's ability to talk even the most sour-faced editors into anything. I still couldn't quite believe it was happening, even when we got off the plane and got our first peek at the women on the beach – sheer heart attack, and that was just the trannies! It wasn't until I woke up the first morning to find a very pissed-off Ross banging on my hotel room door that the reality of the situation finally began to sink in.

'How come you got a bloody room by the pool and I didn't?' he thundered. I had no idea. Sod's law, I supposed – from Ross's point of view, anyway. Undeterred, he simply moved himself in as my room became the official *Kerrang!* HQ for the next ten days. And what a ten days they turned out to be. Reading this piece again, I'm amazed the magazine allowed us to get away with it. It was still a fortnightly publication back then and so the story – originally run in three parts – took six weeks to eventually reach its somewhat vague conclusion. Yet it went down a storm with the readers – and quite a few of the other writers, some of whom then made it their mission to try and later concoct their own versions, resulting in one very memorable piece on Bon Jovi (before they were famous) from Dave Dickson, that didn't even mention the words 'Bon' or 'Jovi' until the second part had been published. This, needless to say, did not go down so well with the readers or editors.

Rock in Rio, Rio De Janeiro, first published in Kerrang!, *February 1985.*

In this world there are three ways you can fly: First-Class, Club-Class and Cunt-Class. Ross Halfin, who has just been voted one of the world's Top Rock Photographers by the readers of *Creem* magazine (all unfortunate halfwits to a man), has his arse plonked squarely in a First-Class, access-all-alcohol, $2,000 seat. To his right is Rod Stewart and entourage. Rod is looking incredible for a guy who in a matter of hours – at the stopover in Lisbon, on the stroke of midnight, London time – will be celebrating his fortieth birthday. He's sporting an LA tan and LA blond locks swept up in traditional Stewart cock-sparrow style. Every picture tells a story and Rod's eyes, his face, even his nose, are a perfect picture – old rock money built on three ancient Stones guitar riffs and a Dylan love song from Bob's younger days.

Seated on Halfin's left are the boys from AC/DC, who over the years have acquired the unhappy habit of completely ignoring the existence of any living thing outside their own familiar sphere. Very little of any cogent value lies outside their own sightless cosmology of band managers, roadies, bodyguards and immediate family members. Malcolm Young nods a 'hi' to Ross, and Ross offers a copy of the new *Kerrang!* to drummer Simon Wright. Simon sneers into Ross' face and declines. Ah – us and AC/DC, we don't get on any more.

It goes without saying that The Kid has his half-starved arse parked in the pigsty humorously referred to as Economy Class, along with the Rod Stewart Band, several dozen reptiles from Filth Street (the *Daily Mirror*, the *Sun*, the *Daily Express*, the *Observer*; everybody wants a holiday in the sun!), a gaggle of competition winners on a Trip of a Lifetime, and a couple of hundred for-real passengers with only one question they want answered. So tell me, my old doughnut, are you going to the Rock in Rio festival? Yes, we thought so.

All over Xmas and New Year my name has been JAMMY BASTARD to my friends. What my girlfriend was calling me I didn't know how to spell. Yeah, I was southbound on some Varig Airlines skyway, climbing through the heavens to Rio de Janeiro, Brazil. And no one is going to let me forget it. Thirteen hours, including a forty-five-minute stopover in Lisbon, from London to Rio, and all the snow, all the January hassle of a London blanketed in a macabre cloak of black afternoon sky and white treacherous roads would now be history for the next week. Ahead lay, we'd been assured, temperatures in the nineties, the largest, most prestigious rock festival to be staged anywhere on the Earth this year, and, according to the *Daily Star*: '24 HOUR ORGIES' and 'SEX AND SUN AS ROCK MUSICIANS LAY WASTE TO RIO'! Yeah well, we'll see about that, won't we?

As it turns out, Rio de Janeiro is three-and-a-half lanes of traffic populated by Brazilian psychopaths who feel confident enough to drive a taxi without once resorting to clumsy indicators or old-fashioned concepts like keeping at least one hand on the wheel. Shit, these muthas don't even feel a compulsion to focus their eyes on the road ahead, spending most of their road-time chit-chatting out of the far-side window to other equally dangerous and excitable types.

'Keep your fucking hands on the wheel, you stupid homo foreigner!' screams Ross into the ear of our driver, who has just narrowly missed hitting two old women and a dog.

'Si, si, Senor,' grins our friend. 'ESTOSTANOVACALLIMARRI ALBERO COMPLIMENTO!' he cries, winding down the window and gobbing hideously into the kerb.

'Oh gawd, just shut up and get us to the hotel in one piece you horrible, stupid . . .'

Ross Halfin is not a man to be easily impressed, and, so far, what with the three-hour delay going through the antiquated Brazilian immigration, and now the raging onslaught of being subjected to the most dangerous man in Brazil taking the wheel for our round trip to the hotel, Rio is doing nothing constructive for his indigestion.

'A fart for all the people who never gave a fart for me,' he sneers before letting go one of his most evil-smelling emissions. I've travelled with Ross before and have my gas mask duly prepared for this disgusting eventuality. The taxi-driver has not, and consequently nearly passes out over the wheel. This semi-conscious state, however, seems agreeable to his metabolism and his driving markedly improves.

'Welcome to the Rio Palace Hotel, Senor,' hisses the oily desk clerk into Halfin's beetroot boat race.

'Push off, Fernando, just gimme my room keys while I've still got a temper left to keep.' And Ross is off, bell boys laid to waste as the great man slings his giant hook in the direction of the elevators. One of the finest men that ever drew breath, Ross Halfin . . .

The Rio Palace Hotel is situated on the lap of Copacabana Beach in a security-guarded spot as uptown as Rio de Janeiro can offer the casual stinko-riche US tourist out on a middle-aged prowl. It's the best that bread can buy and much of my time is going to be spent by the kidney-shaped pool, dictating memos of regret to a brown Brazilian dwarf and talking rapidly into a pink phone while sinking a suitably large, ice-cold jug of the finest local sangria. That, and watching the browned and bulging torso of Halfin waddling in and out of the sun, calling a spade a spade, day in, day out for the next seven days, is what is going to be happening. That, and wrestling with the languid, sunburn-slow way in which the Brazilians conduct their business. For the first thing you notice is how long it takes to get the simplest thing together here. Now I'm the kind of guy who, it should be admitted, can, on occasion, take bloody donkeys to get the simplest thing together when I'm at home in London, so, you know, I do sympathise, gringo, but God help us, how long can it take a person to hand me one pack of Marlboros? Compared to your average Rio citizen, I move with the catwalk precision of Torvill and Dean on a heavy coke kick.

My first co-ordinated movement, after dropping off my baggage, is to take a walk down poolside, there to find women, mostly American, mostly on the wrong side of thirty, stretched out on plastic floral mattresses, bikini tops discarded. It's all too much for my nerves so I plough gamely into the first six-pack of the afternoon. There is a Whitesnake press conference scheduled for 2.00 p.m., with one for Iron Maiden to follow at 3.00 p.m. But plans are already askew. George Benson, who was scheduled for 1.00 p.m., has turned up an hour late, and the 'Snake boys are left to wander around aimlessly during the interim.

Meanwhile, outside the hotel, hundreds and hundreds of chanting, cheering, hysterical Brazilians push dark, toothy-white faces up against the glass doors and screech menacingly every time a limo pulls up outside. Fame and success and glamour and MONEY and a comfortable ticket on the first flight out of the country are the chief attractions these European rock stars hold for the ticket-buying beat-on-the-street types here in Rio. In a country where you either exist completely on the poverty line, or else are extravagantly rich, ninety per cent of the people walking the Avenida Atlantica alongside Copacabana Beach are making a living from thieving, begging, mugging, prostitution, and all manner of high-turnover petty crime. One of the roadies working for Whitesnake was taking in the sun on the beach one day, his head resting on a travel bag, when two kids simply lifted his bonce gently off the bag and snatched it away (the bag that is), making off down the beach like Carl Lewis with his arse on fire. The guy gave chase, but when he finally caught up with them they turned around and beat the living shit out of him, before proceeding to empty out the entire contents of the bag in front of him, right there on the pearly white sand. The remaining ten per cent of the resident population make their money from carving slices of flesh off the backs of the ninety per cent. That's the way it is, Brazilian style.

Back at the Rio Palace, when the Whitesnake press conference finally begins, the first thing I notice is how well everybody is looking. Singer David Coverdale appears to be in the absolute pink of good health. Within twenty-four hours guitarist John Sykes will have his face plastered across the news pages of all the national Brazilian papers with a banner proclaiming him to be the major sex symbol of the festival. Even bassist Neil Murray is looking decidedly clear of eye, while drummer Cozy Powell gives the appearance of a British mercenary about to burst his taut skin like an over-grilled sausage – brown, brawny, and superfit. The questions are coming slowly and painfully.

'ELTOBRAVO CONNIDENDA QUEL CUMILULU?' asks the man from the paper *O Globo*. The interpreter inclines his head towards the microphone and repeats the question, in English. 'He wants to know what you think about Deep Purple re-forming?' he croaks through a cloud of cigarillo smoke. Coverdale looks bored and flips the guy off with some distant instant remark. Quite right too, for asking such a predictable question, I said to myself, and hurriedly crossed that one off the list of questions I wanted to kick around with David at a later date.

Ten minutes of my time is all the deal is worth so I snake off back to the pool where I fall into conversation with a nice, jolly Texan chap who's in Rio on his honeymoon. His newly wed is down with the shits back at his hotel, so here he is killing time and sinking beers under the Crimplene blue sky. He tells me where I can buy all the Moet Chandon champagne I want for £6 a bottle, so I thank him and take myself back upstairs where the Iron Maiden press conference is about to kick off.

As I saunter through the door, Bruce Dickinson is doing his best to explain the true and lasting nature of band mascot Eddie.

'He's just a phantom really,' he suggests. 'He started life as the band's logo, for records and stuff, and just developed from there.'

'Si, si,' interrupts the interpreter. 'But they want to know who is Eddie?'

After the conference is over, Cozy Powell decides to jog along the beach back to the Copacabana Palace Hotel, where Whitesnake are staying. David Coverdale is already being chauffeured back, while Neil Murray, John Sykes, Maiden bassist Steve Harris and drummer Nicko McBrain, along with a few hardened rock hacks like myself, repair to the poolside bar for further light refreshments. The festival doesn't begin until tomorrow night and there's nothing to do but drink and wait, drink and . . .

On the way back to my room, I bump into Maiden manager Rod Smallwood, who is in his usual jocular form. The word, says Rod confidentially, is that all the security guards operating out at the festival site are really undercover policemen keeping their beady eyes open for any hint of drug-taking amongst the European rock fraternity.

'And that includes the likes of you!' he says, jabbing a finger in my direction. 'The thing is, if they catch you red-handed having anything whatsoever to do with drugs they'll arrest you on the spot and they don't stand bail on those sort of charges here. So be warned! Anyone caught indulging by the local constabulary is liable to be left behind.'

I'm not really listening, though. I'm too stoned . . .

So what's it all about? Why suddenly, straight out of left-field, is there this extraordinarily super-hyped event, Rock in Rio? I mean, when it comes right down to it, so what? There are dozens of rock festivals the world over taking place every year; better organised, more experienced and a hell of a lot closer to home than Rio de Janeiro. With the exception of Queen, who have performed in Brazil precisely once before in their lives, in São Paulo three years ago, nobody else on the bill – which includes Whitesnake, Iron Maiden, Rod Stewart, AC/DC, the Scorpions, Ozzy Osbourne, Nina Hagen and Yes – has ever cared to step onto a Brazilian stage before now. But in London and New York the popular message to the media right now is that there is a vast market for rock music, not just in Brazil, but also in neighbouring countries like Venezuela, even Argentina (where Rod Stewart has already planned a visit). The people of South America, it seems, are just waiting for a little live encouragement before leaping thongs-first into a rock music major overkill. There's bucks to be made from these schmucks and suddenly everybody wants in.

So, yeah, sure. But the most basic research will uncover the fact that over seventy-five per cent of the record buying market in Brazil is much more fascinated with plain old mellow MOR. The biggest names in popular music amongst the hippest factions of Brazilian youth culture are George Benson, Al Jarreau and, mightiest of all, James Taylor.

Nevertheless, we are here and we are, like it or not, getting ready to rock. Certainly, sitting at home in London watching the snow fall outside my bedroom window, Rock in Rio seemed like a grand thing to be happening in the world. Nursing a heavy hangover the morning of the second day, however, with Rock in Rio coming at me from all sides, I'm starting to wonder. *O Globo* is running daily front-page stories and the damn thing doesn't even start until tonight; radio is rampant with the whole deal; and on daytime TV videos of all the bands appearing tonight are being rotated like a spit. First there's Queen, then Iron Maiden; and then it says 'Whitesnake – Love Ain't No Stranger' on the screen but what they're showing is a clip of Ronnie James Dio crowing his head off. Dark clouds crept into the corners of the morning sky . . .

In fact, Rock in Rio is the brainchild of Roberto Medina, who is the president of an advertising agency called Artplan. He is the man responsible for enticing Frank Sinatra down to Brazil a few years back for a gig in front of an estimated audience of 140,000, then roped in all his clients for sponsorship and made a mint out of the whole deal. He is, to all intents and purposes, a sharp-eyed entrepreneur who does a lot of good business out of arranging these 'media events'. He paid for the building of the site – the Barra da Tijuca – situated next door to Rio's Formula One motor-racing track the Autodrome. Erected on what was formerly swampland, it has been furnished with state-of-the-art sound and lights by Gerry Stickle, the expert production technician who does a lot of work with Queen. Medina's initial outlay, therefore, came to a cool $11.5 million! That means that over the ten-day period the festival is scheduled to run for, with tickets selling for between five and seven dollars apiece, Artplan will need maybe 280,000 people there every day to even begin looking at any real profit. Take into consideration the salaries of the hundreds of interpreters working around the clock, the roadies, the security, the bands, the this, the that, and any way you looked at it the money wasn't going to be coming from ticket sales. Indeed, when the festival was over I was told that Artplan had lost over $5 million on that side of the deal, but that the business the several sponsors involved were doing proved so phenomenal it was worth the hit. Top of the list was a beer company called Malt 99, then came Wranglers, McDonalds, the usual crowd.

Now I'm told the plan is to follow up Rock in Rio with annual events. The site has been officially rented from the government for the next four years, and after that the likelihood is that it will be torn down. So the magic of knowing you're going to Rio disperses pretty quickly once you're actually sitting there using their toilets and drinking their beer. Everything feels kind of languid and one-off. Everybody seems to dig the place – a drop of sun, sea and sin is hardly the roughest week on the agenda – but after a while nobody really cares if they ever see it again.

By lunchtime during the sweltering afternoon of the second day, word has it that, with only one major road leading to and from the site, the through traffic promises to be a nightmare and delays of up to three hours are being predicted on a journey that should normally take no more than half-an-hour or so. Whitesnake are scheduled to appear on stage at 9.30 p.m. Even so, Ross and I are advised to leave for the site no later than 4.30 p.m.! Just to be on the safe side. While all the bands – today that means Whitesnake, Iron Maiden and Queen – are being transported by helicopter no later than 6.00 p.m., which will bring them into the site by 6.30 p.m., I hitch a ride with Dwayne Welch, EMI International PR exec and son of Shadows' drummer Bruce Welch. Contrary to information, we reach the gig within forty minutes, arriving at much the same time as the bands. This gives us the next four hours to kill, lucky us. 'Definitely time for a spot of sightseeing,' I say to myself. And by flashing one of the six different passes I already possess before the eyes of the security, suddenly I'm out with the late-afternoon crowd.

So here we are, finally: Rock in Rio, Friday night, and only four hours left to go. I am standing in an area 250,000 square metres in size. The Barra da Tijuca site is trimmed off to the north by large dark hills and a deep, still, blue sky. The actual stage is huge, large enough to hold two bands and all their equipment and props, back to back. At the end of one set the revolving stage simply spins round to bring the next band into view. As a result, the changeovers throughout the festival were always fast and clean, exceptions occurring only when artistic petulance reared its conceited, artistically, uh, sensitive head from time to time.

The sound and lights all belong to Queen. The lightshow is competent and generous, professional in every respect, if slightly less than completely dazzling in scope and imagination. The out-front sound, however, is superb. Apart from the gigantic army of statuesque amplifiers and speakers perched either side of the stage, approximately 100 metres from the front are placed two further towers of power that will throw the sound, as crystal clear as the foul waters of Brazil are polluted with germs and poisons, an even greater distance. However, with the festival capable of containing 300,000 people, the absence of two large video screens to help you navigate the pelvic gyrations of David Coverdale or the head-butting athleticism of Bruce Dickinson (total Neanderthal, baby!) is a strange omission to an otherwise largely impressive set-up. There's a Press Room, replete with typewriters and Telex machines; a shopping centre with more than thirty shops, beer gardens, fast-food restaurants; a telephone centre; a mini-hospital for the severely intoxicated; an information centre for the overly anal; even toilets and – gulp! – showers. I was told that there were also, in fact, two 'video-centres', which were both transmitting the live shows and stringing all the boring press guff simultaneously, but I never managed to locate them personally. I dunno, must have been something I didn't eat.

As I wander backstage again I spot Freddie Mercury standing there at the gates, signing autographs. He's got a superb, quite ridiculous cowboy hat on his head and, my oh my, but isn't he short! I'd always imagined our Freddie to be a lanky matador in shades. In reality he looks more like the villainous cousin of Manolito from *The High Chaparral*, the far side of one too many enchiladas; broad Captain Kirk torso and gaucho Groucho moustache! So he is human ...

In his dressing room, David Coverdale is working out before the show; Cozy Powell, Nicko McBrain, John Sykes and Neil Murray are all wandering amiably around, not quite sure what to do with themselves until show time. Sneaking out onto the stage, however, craftily disguised behind his portable video camera, is Steve Harris. 'I wanted to get the crowd on video just so I could show it to people when we get home,' he tells me. But he's recognised creeping around at the back of the stage within minutes and the crowd start to go crazy. He looks at me, surprised. 'I knew we'd sold a few albums over here, but I had no idea they all knew what we bleeding look like.'

For the final hour before Whitesnake arrive onstage to begin the festival proper – there's already been a handful of local acts geeing-up the audience – I'm holed-up in the beer-locker in Iron Maiden's dressing room. Rod Smallwood is laying down on the couch pondering the life expectancy of the average Marlboro, Adrian Smith is quietly plink-plonking away on his guitar, Bruce Dickinson is squaring up to his mirror reflection, fencing blade gripped in his right hand, repeatedly en guarde, en guarde, en guarde, and tour manager Tony Wiggens is swanning in and out of the door with the urgent calm of a man fully equipped emotionally to deal with at least twelve nervous breakdowns and 550 niggly problems, while still finding time to deal with important stuff like getting the drunken slob from *Kerrang!* a bottle opener. Oh well, tick-tock-fuck-the-clock ...

'LADEEZAN' A-GENTLEMEN ... PLISS WELCUM FROMMA LONDON, INNLAND ... WHITESNAKE!'

Cue instant, immediate, quite unexpected hysteria. Coverdale shakes his tail under the nose of the crowd, John Sykes rattles his long blond locks while ripping out the monster riff to 'Slow 'n' Easy' and

Neil Murray and Cozy Powell lock horns like rowdy stags and suddenly the 150,000-strong audience are full of at least 149,999 smiling upturned faces, relieved as much as anything that the whole shebang is finally off the ground.

The one solitary screwed-up and pissed-off face belongs to Ross Halfin. 'BLOODY JOHN SYKES!' he screams. 'He had me THROWN OFF the stage! They haven't even built the bloody photographers' pit yet so there's no way you can shoot live pictures that mean a shit. Iron Maiden had to fight tooth and nail to get the security to allow me onstage for their set, then I go through the same routine with Whitesnake and thirty seconds before they come on I'm told I have to get off the stage and get off NOW! AND WHY? Because BLOODY JOHN SYKES said he'd REFUSE to play while I was there. BLOODY JOHN SYKES!!'

Ross is not having a fun time at all. Poor old doughnut. Meantime, Whitesnake are battling hard to keep the enthusiasm high for their set. They haven't played live for seven weeks and are still rusty. Through 'Love Ain't No Stranger' and 'Ain't No Love in the Heart of the City', Coverdale's voice cracks at the edges. Cozy Powell's drum solo is cut from the show, and it's clear that a short, sharp shot in the ass is what Whitesnake are out to give Rock in Rio; and, despite the disappointment Coverdale expresses over his croaky larynx after the show, that's exactly what they do. With Mel Galley now out of the picture for good and the keyboards – handled well by ex-Magnum/Alaska man Richard Bailey – tucked inconspicuously behind curtains side-stage, the rambling, bluesy Whitesnake of just a year ago is gone and gone for good. This line-up is stripped and ready for some heavy MTV-type Stateside action. With obvious exceptions like Bobby 'Blue' Bland's aforementioned 'Ain't No Love . . . ', which, no matter how emotively interpreted by Coverdale, will always sound forced and white and very '70s to me, the direction the Whitesnake set is following these days has much more to do with the super-chrome, rear-wheel drive of upfront rockers like 'Slide it In' and 'Slow 'n' Easy', the best numbers of the night. Coverdale ends the set with his usual 'We wish you well, God bless and good night!' And the crowd sighs deeply.

If the response to Whitesnake had been one of unrestrained awe, the reaction Iron Maiden drew from the heart of the vast beast was exultant. 'Aces High' comes roaring out of the speakers with the mega-tonnage of a hub-capped, diamond-starred Sherman tank, the frontline of Dave Murray, Bruce Dickinson, Steve Harris and Adrian Smith hanging over the cliff-face of the outer-stage limits like condemned marionettes suspended by the throats from invisible steel wire. The impact is still on the 'up' when Bruce announces '2 Minutes to Midnight' in semi-fluent Portuguese and the crowd goes even wilder. 'The Trooper' and 'Revelations' follow, and Bruce is climbing the rafters, taunting the crowd to raise their arms and punch chest-deep holes in the star-tinged stratosphere. 'Scream for me, RIO DE JANEIRO!' he screams. 'SCREEEAAMMMM FOR MEEEEEE!!!' Here and there, Union Jacks are sprinkled throughout the crowd, but not to be out-done the Brazilians take up the ferocious chant of 'IRRRON MAYYYDEN! IRRROONN MAAYYYDDEENN!!' With emphasis on those rolled 'rrr's.

'Rime of the Ancient Mariner', replete with taped creaky hull atmospherics, totally freaks everybody out, slaying the audience completely when the band come trooping back for the snarling finale. But the suspension of disbelief isn't truly complete until, halfway through 'Powerslave', the twelve-foot-tall figure of Eddie bounds onstage to cries of utter astonishment from the Brazilians, who know that these English rock groups are, you know, a leetle crazee, but hadn't bargained on the appearance of the surreal rogue phantom, headbanging his savage way across the footlights. Eddie is the ultimate symbol of Iron Maiden's supremacy, and the glazed, phantasmagorical image of Eddie insanely poised, arms flailing behind the huddled figure of Adrian Smith, is something they were still yakking about on the streets of Rio long after the group had left the country to continue their marathon trek across America.

Because they have actually played here before, Queen is without a doubt the best-known international rock act on the bill. So when the stage lights ignite and the taped intro creams from the speakers it's enough to push large sections of the loco public right over the edge. Freddie Mercury senses all this, and with one mighty puff of his broad chest throws his head back and coos like a lovebird nestled on her eggs; prancing and pirouetting, chain-smoking and joking with the crowd, winning their confidence and admiration with every regal flick of the wrist. Guitarist Brian May, bassist John Deacon and drummer Roger Taylor maintain the same super-tight musical backdrop that has been their live trademark throughout their careers, and the set is largely the same as the show the band were touting around the UK last year. The 'Seven Seas of Rhye'/'Now I'm Here' medley is still a feature, as are 'Tie Your Mother Down', 'Somebody to Love' and 'Love of My Life'. It's all the hits and more – 'Killer Queen', 'Radio Ga Ga' (which, just like the video, has the crowd all clapping right on cue: a quite surreal sight), 'Another One Bites the Dust'. The only real moment of serious METAL MAYHEM occurs on 'Hammer to Fall', which sees May and co. playing with the slow-handed, sophisticated aplomb of true early-'70s veterans: mean, moochy and meticulously magnificent. The only pain in the nose is when Freddie and Brian climb up on two stools and make like Frank Sinatra and Dean Martin after a night on the piss for 'Is This the World We Created?', a pure acoustic wimp-out for all the James Taylor junkies in the audience. It's enough to bring a cold tear to my glass eye.

The big fun begins with the encores, though. After the anticipated volcanic eruption of applause, the band bounce back on stage for 'I Want to Break Free' with Freddie sporting the same dark black wig he wears in the video. He looks like a Meard Street tart taking the Monday morning bus home from Soho: faggy, draggy and all shagged out. But the funniest part(s) are the enormous pair of falsies he's wearing! Huge bristols that so excite the lapsed Catholics in the audience that they start to hurl stones and gravel. There's even some that attempt a quick heave-ho over the security-infested stage perimeter, only to be met by devastating blows from the wooden truncheons of the guards. Knuckles are being viciously rapped by long pieces of hardwood, and there's still a ton of gravel flying through the air when the band return for their second encore, 'It's a Hard Life'. This time Freddie's got his blond number-two wig on, but, wily old mistress that he is, he also has a huge Union Jack flag which, when reversed, metamorphoses into the Brazilian national flag. The crowd go suitably ape-shit and a semblance of good order is restored.

Saturday afternoon in Rio de Janeiro is beginning to feel much more agreeable. Me and Boss Halfin, draped over two wooden sun beds by the pool, overhead a marine-blue sky reflecting temperatures nosing into the hundreds, and at our feet the largest glass jug of sangria Ross's Am-Ex card can afford. Tonight, there is a party being held by EMI over at the Copacabana Palace Hotel in honour of several unpronounceable, wholly uninteresting Brazilian acts along with Queen, Whitesnake, the Scorpions, Rod Stewart and Iron Maiden. This afternoon, though, me and Ross are off to play tourists-for-a-day with Maiden's Steve Harris and Dave Murray. Two cars whisk us off to the two main spots any righteous-minded visitor to Rio will go out of their way to see at least once on their journey: Cocavada Mountain and Sugar Loaf. Cocavada is one of the seven wonders of the world: a mountain peak God alone knows how many feet above sea level with an enormous statue of Christ, hands outstretched above the clouds, built on the apex of the deep slopes. Sugar Loaf is another high-altitude rock that rises out of the ocean, bloodlessly penetrating the skyline and approachable only by cable car. Climbing out of the cars, the four of us stand transfixed by the sight of Rio de Janeiro splayed out like a map below us. Even Ross takes a breather from beating on the heads of the grinning locals to contemplate the awe-inspiring scene. Above us stands the super-tall Christian monolith, staring unblinkingly into the arsehole of the sun, while at eye-level all you see are more mountains and hills vying for their place in the currant bun of life.

The Brazilians, whatever else they may or may not be, are by nature an inquisitive bunch, and within minutes of noticing the long-haired young gringos getting their pictures taken so fanatically by Ross, everybody wants to know what is going on. When the security man tells them that the famous English rock group IRRROONN MAAYY-DENN, no less, are in their mountain-top midst, word spreads and causes a commotion. Steve and Dave are still fazed by it all as we drive away an hour later. An hour of being followed everywhere they walk: sixty minutes of smiles and yelps and handshakes and T-shirt buying and ice-cream scoffing. When we arrive at the cable-car station for the jaunt to Sugar Loaf, all that's altered is the location. People surround us wherever we go. Me and Ross have been told by Steve to give up trying to explain we aren't in the group. 'It's easier just to sign the autographs,' he says, laughing at our discomfort. 'Go on – you'll love it!' And so, for the next couple of hours, me and Ross play at being Iron Maiden for the day.

That night at the Barra da Tijuca festival site it's Al Jarreau, James Taylor and George Benson, and therefore not of the slightest interest to the geezers from *Kerrang!* Indeed, we felt it from deep within our bones that it was the EMI party we should be attending. And, sure enough, there everybody is. Jesus! The Filth Street hacks and the rock comix clowns outnumber their prey a solid two-to-one. Queen and Rod Stewart are all there gadding about with their personal bodyguards in tow to 'stop you bastards taking pictures'. Mainly, as far as we can tell, because Rod is sat chit-chatting to a knee-trembling blonde, with pegs that stretch right the way up to her powdered chin, who doesn't go by the name of Kelly. As a result, Justin Focus, intrepid Englishman-abroad lensman for the insipid *Sounds* magazine, is thrown out after the fool tries to turn paparazzi and get a sneaky shot of Rod avec blonde. Meanwhile, Neil Murray wants it to be known that he is not simply here for the beer and that indeed his public image as a, uh, socialite, is wholly unfounded. This while dashing off another V&T and gassing about all sorts of things I have to pretend I haven't heard.

Then Brian May dives into the pool fully clothed – gasp! – as a line of newshound photographers get tomorrow's page-five print-out. I am standing with Michael Jensen, US publicity guru for Rod Stewart, Ozzy Osbourne and Iron Maiden, nose-diving into what Michael likes to call 'some very serious cocktails'. Over there, Robin Le Mesurier (Rod's guitarist) is supping icky-looking green shit with John Sykes from Whitesnake. And over there, Brian May and Neil Murray are discussing, um, technique or something. But, in truth, as these things go, the action is slow, and the wine is turning warm. It's been a long day and anyway, my mind is still stuck up somewhere pinned to the slopes of Cocavada.

Sunday is just another some-day marked by only two events of real significance: 1) Ozzy Osbourne and entourage arrive in town from LA, and 2) Ross Halfin discovers Rio's finest Japanese restaurant. Ozzy has recently been released from the notorious Betty Ford Clinic in California. This is the place you've already read about – a clean-out cabin for alcoholic film stars and family-rich junkie vagabonds from the West Coast. It boasts a one hundred per cent success rate and its clientele in the past has included Robert Mitchum, Elizabeth Taylor, and now – Ozzy Osbourne, the 'wild man of rock' (copyright: the *Sun*). The question is: will Ozzy stay sober? If so, what will he be like onstage? Will the self-proclaimed 'born-again drunk' crack up under the heat and go mad, demanding a barrel of brandy before he hits the boards? And what does this all mean for the rest of us? These, and other equally fascinating questions, are firmly answered the following night when Ozzy makes his first appearance in the bar, looking trim, tanned, extremely healthy and on his best behaviour. Not a single Light Ale dampened his lips all evening, and he won the admiration of even the most hardened cynic (hi, Ross). But the fear returned when later the story went out that Ozzy had broken his vow of abstinence on the flight over, drinking the aircraft dry, finally collapsing in a happy drunken heap into the aisle, where he slept off the remainder of the journey.

Ross discovering a Japanese restaurant around the corner from our hotel was an equally noteworthy occasion. Ross loves Japanese food the way Humphrey Bogart loved Lauren Bacall: with a brutal passion that refuses to accept second best on any level. Halfin is not possessed of a forgiving nature at the best of times, but when it comes to his sushi fish and soy sauce he simply will not tolerate imperfection. A hot, dirty country full of punters ready to swipe your cameras is an acceptable burden on Ross's broad shoulders; he is, after all, getting paid to suffer. A disastrously served sushi with the sake warmed at the wrong temperature is, however, UNACCEPTABLE. On all counts.

'PSSAACHHTT!' he cries. 'EERRGGHHH ... PPSSSAAC-CHHTTT!!' His face is going a horrible shade of purple. 'GOOD GOD ALMIGHTY! THEY CAN'T EVEN GET BLOODY SUSHI RIGHT IN THIS BLOODY HELLHOLE ... PSSAACCHHTT!!!'

Waitresses come running from all directions. But the damage has been done.

'Take it away. It's bloody horrible! You don't even know what soy sauce is, do you? Do you! Oh, go on, clear off and bring me two beers!'

The sushi tremors don't subside until I point out that Moet champers sells for six pounds a bottle in this joint.

'Oh, well. Now that's different,' he sighs.

The rest of the evening is spent watching Ross bill and coo over his cheap champagne into a stunned Brazilian waitress's right ear.

The following afternoon, both the Scorpions and Ozzy have arrived at the Rio Palace Hotel for their press conferences. While the Scorpions file into the conference room, Ozzy is seated by the pool, being interviewed for local Brazilian television. Up on a ninth-floor balcony, Rod Stewart attempts a bit of thunder-stealing by playing his ancient rock and soul tapes as loud as the volume level will allow – which is VERY LOUD! – and the whole poolside area is drowned in wave after wave of Booker T, Chuck Berry and Percy Sledge. Meanwhile, inside the conference room Scorps singer Klaus Meine is explaining to the assembled Brazilian press corps that wherever the band travel throughout the world they always like to learn one of the traditional native songs, and would anybody care to oblige them? Half-a-dozen journalists instantly rise to their feet for an impromptu vocal rendition of some fine old Brazilian folk tune. It's a weird, touching scene, which the Scorpions acknowledge by standing up and replying with a German folk song.

By the time Ozzy takes his spot behind the media-microphone, spirits are still high, but the questions are all coming straight out of left-field. The interpreter informs Ozzy that the press wishes to know if he is going to be biting the heads off any chickens while he's in Rio?

'Tell them I'm off chickens at the moment,' he deadpans. 'I might try a few cats and dogs though.'

The headlines on the front page of *O Globo* the next morning report Ozzy's response verbatim amidst loud, literary gasps of horror.

Tonight is another George Benson, Al Jarreau, MOR-night out at the festival, so in our ceaseless bid to cover the action wherever the hideous trail might lead us, Ross and I do a Judas Priest (as in 'Heading Out to the Highway') over to the Copacabana Palace Hotel, where two lonely bar stools are awaiting our arrival. And in the bar tonight ... It's a bloody rock convention! All of Whitesnake; Ozzy and his wife and manager, Sharon Osbourne; Klaus and Rudy from the Scorpions; world-famous Iron Maiden manager (it sez here) Rod Smallwood, together with various other rock types.

Ozzy wanders by and we shake hands. 'What do you think of it so far?' I ask. 'I think Rio's a fucking shithouse, myself.' He gazes at me balefully. 'I mean, it's a fucking toilet, ain't it? Horrible grub, you can't drink the water, and I can't go outside the hotel because I'll get mobbed. I'll be glad to fucking leave. I tell you what, I feel really sorry for Ronnie Biggs – trapped here! I know people say he did bad things that he never got punished for, but fucking hell, having to spend the rest of your life in this place must be fucking worse! Me, I'd rather have done my time before I'd come running to this bloody place. Honest, I would. And I'll tell you something else,' he says, with a concerned look in his eye. 'I've had the fucking shits since I arrived here.' And he strolls off to a corner table, back to his mineral water and his wife.

Meanwhile, back at the Rio Palace Hotel, a mile or so further up the beach, the action is decidedly more sedate. Rod Stewart and his entourage are joined by Roger Taylor of Queen plus a couple of the Go-Gos. They're planning a midnight dinner, somewhere out on the peak of the Rio social stratosphere, followed by cocktails and empty talk at the nearest available millionaire's shack. And for God's sake don't forget to wear a jacket. That said, AC/DC haven't been seen in days. What does it all mean? Fucked if I know, or care. Let's get back to the bar, pronto.

'I can't be certain,' says Michael Jensen the next morning, 'but I think I've managed to set up an interview for you with Rod. Will it get the cover?' Michael, Rod Stewart's US publicist, is busting his balls trying to do the impossible: organise a Rod Stewart interview for *Kerrang!*

'I don't think you'll get the cover, Michael,' I reply, trying to stifle a smirk. 'Nobody on *Kerrang!* really cares enough about Rod the Mod any more. We're all too young, hahaha!'

'It has to be a cover, or he won't go for it.' There's a nervous edge to Michael's voice. Everybody in Brazil, it seems, wants to rap with Rod, only Rodders ain't interested. But his guitarist Robin Le Mesurier, who I once got drunk with, has put a good word in for me, and now Michael's trying to wrap up the deal.

'All right,' I say. 'Tell him I say he can have the cover. But don't tell him that I told you he won't get the cover,' I suggest, all bushy-tailed.

'Uuuhhhhh . . . no,' says Michael. 'I gotta better idea. Meet me in room 855 at 7.00 p.m., and for God's sake don't be late. Rod will be there. We've organised an informal press conference between him and one or two Brazilian journalists. I'll try and organise something for you then. Just hang out. Make like a fly-on-the-wall for a while and I'll try and introduce you.'

I tell him I'll think about it, and head on down to the pool, wondering what the hell I can ask Rod Stewart after all these years.

That evening I'm scheduled to take a car out to the festival to see AC/DC and the Scorpions strut their stuff before the multitude. Big problem. I didn't see any of AC/DC once, either onstage or off, the whole time I was in Rio. Where were you hiding, boys? And why? Even when I went to the gig it turned out I had been given the wrong pass and so had to stand outside and was eventually forced to seek solace in a bar. It was a damn shame (hic!).

Fortunately, I had the right pass for the Scorpions so the night wasn't entirely wasted. I've seen the Scorpions set a torch to the night in New York and Madrid so far in the last four months and Rio, of course, was no exception. The rock machine that powers the music of the Scorpions onstage thrives on road work, and the band have certainly had their share of that since *Love at First Sting* hit big worldwide. Savvy as ever, Klaus Meine appeared onstage at the start of the set carrying a huge Brazilian flag, which he in turn hurled out into the audience – much to the unbridled displeasure of the tooled-up security guards – before the band launched into a suitably hyper-charged performance of 'Coming Home'. Reaction was rabid but the biggest thrill of the night was reserved for 'Still Lovin' You', a ballad that has already been a hit single in Brazil for the band, and so went down a storm. As I intimated earlier in this never-ending piece, ballads are the big noise in Rio and 'Holiday' was also treated to some very special emotional muscle from the crowd.

Towards the climax of the set, during 'Can't Get Enough', guitarist Rudy Schenker almost topped himself when he did a back-flip at the edge of the slanting stage, guitar still in hand, slipping and cutting a gash over his eye that gushed a fountain of purple blood and later required three stitches to hold his face in one piece. For the encore of 'The Zoo', Matthias Jabs arrived on stage carrying a very low-slung guitar shaped like a map of South America, which, with a bit of imagination, resembled a Gibson Firebird. And then, finishing off the whole event with a real flavour of international bonhomie, the entire band stepped out to the front of the stage to sing the same Brazilian folk song the journalists had taught them, parrot-fashion, back at the press conference the previous afternoon. Oh, there is Wagnerian magic afoot this night.

Earlier, back at the Copacabana Palace Hotel, David Coverdale had just run into the millionth person to ask what he thinks of the re-formed Deep Purple, the publicly touted 'definitive' Mk-II line-up that, uh, doesn't include him. 'I think they look like the bleeding Moody Blues fan club!' he snapped at last, before hurriedly taking his leave. Three feet from certain escape, Dave was collared by weirdo Teutonic chanteuse Nina Hagen, who is also appearing on the Festival bill. They stand together and exchange pleasantries, and when they part Nina breathes into Coverdale's ear: 'You are such a nice man. If I had known what a nice man you are, I would have washed before meeting you.'

Around the same time, in room 855 of the Rio Palace Hotel, Rod Stewart had just walked in to be greeted by half-a-dozen toothy grins from the assembled Brazilian press hierarchy. Only the creme-de-la-creme is granted an audience with Rod the God, and, for once, in my role as Sam Spade fidgety fly-on-the-wall Wall, that includes me. I'm under orders not to participate in this knotty little gathering, with the semi-promise of a few words with his Royal Haircut afterwards, but figure I might just sling a few verbal right hooks his way anyway, if the opportunity presents itself.

Huh! Fat chance! Not with the assembled heavenly chorus of hungry hacks all begging for priceless gems like: 'Eeezze eet troo that yooo were once a gravedigger, Rrooddd?' Or: 'Why deeed yooo leeewe Innland to live inna ELAAAAY?'

I mean, forget it. The moment the inane questions have dried up, Rod is whisked out the door faster than a greyhound out of a trap. I knit my eyebrows and wonder why I wasted my time on this media-Mephisto. Michael Jensen shrugged his shoulders and whispered those famous last words no journo likes to hear: 'Maybe tomorrow . . .'

Much later that night, me and Ross are among a party of guests having dinner with Ozzy Osbourne. The restaurant is Muiro's, reputedly one of the finest meat-eateries in town. While the waiters continuously throw huge skewers of barbecued flesh onto our yawning great plates, Ozzy is reminiscing about his time spent in Black Sabbath.

'It was such a laugh in the early days,' he recalls. 'We treated nothing seriously. Let's face it, we couldn't treat anything seriously outside of playing, we were all too bloody thick! I remember Tony [Iommi] and Bill [Ward] doing this live radio show once, and the interviewer asked Tony who the biggest influence was on his guitar playing and he just sat there and went: "Er . . . um . . . ah . . . er . . . well . . . er . . . let's see . . . er . . . Bert." The DJ was like, "Bert? Bert who?" Stupid sod was talking about Bert Weedon! Then Bill, who's been sat there saying nothing for the last half an hour, suddenly leans over and asks the interviewer if he minds if he just clears his throat. The bloke says "No, of course not", so Bill leans into the microphone and goes: "Bollocks! Fuck! Cunt! Piss! Shit! Bollocks! Fuck! Bastard!" Honestly, it cracked me up.'

He went on to talk about those rock stars who pretend to hate being recognised but secretly love it.

'You see these fuckers hanging out in all-night clubs in New York or somewhere, and they're all walking around wearing bloody sunglasses. They can't see a fucking thing and spend two hours talking to a bloody brick wall, acting cool. Actually, that reminds me of the time I was just leaving this club pissed out of me brains. As I got to the door Roger Taylor from Queen was standing there with his shades on, and he stops me and says hello. I looked at him and said, "Who the hell are you?" And he shoves his bloody sunglasses down his nose, peers over the top of them and says, "It's me, man, Roger." And of course I knew who he was, I was just pissed out of me head. So I looked at him and goes: "Bollocks! Queen just ripped off everything they ever did from Sabbath!" And I walked out the door. Can you imagine his face?' he roars with laughter. 'You should have seen him trying to figure that one out! Queen ripped off Sabbath! What a fucking joke! He hasn't spoken a word to me from that day to this.'

Finally, it's our last night at the festival. There's still another five days to go before things draw to a close, but Ross and I have an important don't-be-late-date in New York and, frankly, we can't wait to leave. We've had enough. The *Daily Mirror* and the *Sun* might reckon this city to be a riot of rude orgies and winter sunshine, but me, I'm here to tell you that's a load of crap. Rio is hot, dirty, dangerous and devoid of civilised recreation. Jesus, of course I'm glad I was there, but not half as glad as I was to leave. Sod what all the other posy press pussies wanna tell you.

So anyway, it's the last night. Two shows: Ozzy Osbourne and Rod Stewart. There have been waves of consternation from the Rod Stewart camp over the prospect of following Ozzy on stage. On the one hand, Rod's guitarist Robin Le Mesurier has already confessed to me that the band are dead chuffed that they and not Ozzy are headlining the show. In the States Rod and Ozzy are approximately neck and neck in purely commercial terms, with Ozzy likely to be the one who will eventually gain the more impressive lead. On the other hand, though, Ozzy Osbourne is one of the greatest rock 'n' roll performers in the world when it comes to delivering the goods to vast open-air festival crowds. Rod ain't no slouch either, but it's going to be far from straightforward converting the excitement Ozzy's metal-plated music generates from the crowd into the more melodic groove-along Rod's confidence thrives on.

'I dunno what he's worried about,' Ozzy shrugs. Stewart's jitters smack of superstar soft-soap, and Ozzy knows it. 'I'm the one that should be nervous. This will be my first time on stage without a drink inside me for sixteen years!'

Classical music fills the night. The lights die and 150,000 people open their throats and howl. Suddenly, flash-bombs ignite, guitarist Jake E. Lee stabs his fist into the beating heart of his flaming guitar and ... Christ! It's Ozzy! Sober and three times as crazy!!

'I Don't Know' opens the deal and the crowd are going mad. Ozzy looks fantastic, pounding the stage with a new-found vigour derived entirely from his own unnatural energy. Your eyes just follow every move he makes. 'Mr Crowley' and 'Bark at the Moon' chunder and boom; the band are choke-tight and the joint is jumpin'. Ozzy's voice never sounded cleaner, and he sings his arse off like a choirboy on speed. 'Revelation Mother Earth', which follows, is just that; a revelation – really. A monster opening and closing its fantastic jaws. The slow build-up, the stake-through-the-heart rhythmic charge of the middle section, then the all-out nuclear strike of the big finale. A real adrenalin fix; the best blood transfusion in town.

Live, 'Suicide Solution' has become the Jake E. Lee show and no mistake. Ozzy throws an arm around Jake's neck halfway through the number and hurls him to the ground. Jake bounces onto his back, still playing, still making magic, points his toes to the sky, arches his spine and begins tipping into a solo that hits the back of your throat like nerve gas. Springing back onto his heels, still playing, still grinning, all his cat-like mobility is shaded in rock 'n' roll malevolence, his guitar a sub-machine gun strafing between the eyes of the crowd. Back up on his padded feet he is flying, fucking flying across the boards, still playing, still edging closer to the limit. 'Iron Man' and 'Crazy Train' close the show in a bloodbath of flash-bombs and animal screams from Ozzy. Forget last year's Donington. Compared to Rio, it never happened – and Ozzy was the best thing all day at Donington.

January is traditionally when the rains fall the hardest in Brazil. Sure enough, towards the end of Ozzy's set the first showers begin to fall and quickly start to grow in strength and sheer bloody-minded persistence. For the opening of Rod Stewart's set we're talking torrential. Built on swampland, the festival site turns swiftly into a bubbling vat of mud-glorious-mud: strictly quick-quag alley. Before he leaves for his hotel, Ozzy blinks into the rain and says: 'People aren't leaving this place, they're just sinking into the mud. It must be a plot hatched by Queen. What they do the day of their second show is, they turn sun-ray lamps on the ground and up pop about a hundred thousand punters waving hello out of the mud!'

Dressed in a canary-yellow shirt and blue strides, Rod comes dancing out of the wings as the band strike up a greasy, trucking version of 'Hot Legs'. The band are tight, guitars swaying in the night, horn section rolling. Rod's in good voice and, despite the thousands leaving the festival because of the appalling weather, those that remain forget the rain and get into it. The last time I saw Rod Stewart was back in the days when he was still singing Jimi Hendrix's 'Angel' and Chuck Berry's 'Sweet Little Rock and Roller' – ah, but that was over ten years ago. How was I to know back then that the next time I saw him perform it would not be with the Faces, and that all my favourite songs – with the obvious exception of 'Maggie May' – would be consigned to the history books.

Funnily enough, it didn't matter. Whatever magic Rod Stewart possesses as a rock 'n' roller will be his for the rest of his life. These days the songs are more Las Vegas – 'You're in My Heart', 'Baby Jane', 'Tonight's the Night', 'Young Turks', 'Passion' – but onstage the athleticism is still all there, the voice still carries that edge and, well, he did throw in a very tasty version of Otis Redding's '(Sittin' On) The Dock of the Bay'. By the end, after half-a-dozen footballs have been shot with Dalglish-like precision into the goal-mouth of the crowd, he's into 'Maggie May' and the time warp is complete. I'm jigging at the side of the stage, plonked right next to the roadie who chucks out the footballs. And I figure, what the hell, it's my last night. So I stoop down and pick up one of Rod's footballs and – this is my chance – this is what I came to Rio to do, I'm convinced of it.

One mighty, drunken kick later and the ball is travelling through the air. Then I turn my back on the stage and pick my way through the dark to the waiting limo . . .

CODA

For all its self-indulgent faults, this Rock in Rio feature would set a precedent: the first of what would be several outlandish trips abroard for Ross and I over the next six years – and a quite unfeasible amount of features that would run to two or three parts. The kind of thing, in fact, that you would never get now, not in these days of box-ticking, marketing-driven features where you write the headline first then construct the piece around it – all before you've even assigned a writer and photographer to the story.

Of course, this sort of rambling discourse had its drawbacks, but the idea was still a good one. Don't assume you know what the story is beforehand; go out there and put yourself among things until the story all but writes itself. And above all, try and entertain the reader; put them next to you wherever you go. In short, writing and pictures that aspired to be as larger-than-life, as colourful and as hugely improbable as the music and artists they attempted to faithfully depict, in all their raging, unselfconscious glory.

KATE BUSH, 1984

This was the first story I was ever commissioned to write for *Kerrang!* I couldn't believe my luck. Crossing swords with Iron Maiden, sliding my nose across a mirror with Motörhead, scoffing chips, perhaps, with Saxon, these are the sorts of things I'd anticipated getting up to in my new gig. Spending an afternoon chinwagging with the delightful Kate Bush – well, not even on the radar, I'd have thought. Indeed, it still seems like an incredibly strange thing to do for what was then an unashamedly balls-out – indeed, the world's only – heavy metal magazine. But Kate had just come top of the Female Vocalist spot in the mag's 1983 Readers' Poll and was extremely thrilled to have done so, according to her record company. And so an interview was arranged.

Strange to relate by today's manicured PR standards, but myself and a photographer were simply given her address and told to pitch up one afternoon. The house was one of her two homes, a South London hideaway where she wrote her songs and perfected the dances she would do in her videos. While she went off to make tea I perused the pile of albums stacked on the floor next to the record player: I recall Bryan Ferry's *These Foolish Things*, some Pink Floyd, some Bowie and various other things you might expect to find in any twenty-five-year-old woman's collection back then.

As we did the interview, we sat crosslegged on the floor. Actually, I sat on a cushion – the only one available in the room – which I did graciously offer to Kate but which she more graciously insisted I park my bony bum on. Not really preparing the interview as I would learn to do in years to come, I simply fired away, asking her stuff like I would any bird I'd just met and rather fancied. I recall asking her if she crimped her hair (I was crimping my own at the time). And somehow we got onto the subject of dope-smoking and she giggled and talked of 'pinning'.

When we were done, the photographer took some snaps. I remember he got her to bend over and scrunch her shoulders together – 'to make her tits look bigger,' he explained to me afterwards. 'Cool,' I said, admiring his professionalism.

It was night, cool and replete, like any other night. I was bedded down in my foxhole, my day-ticket all turned in and chewed over, gliding on a cushion of ozone into the calmer tonic waters of sleep release. In the distance . . . a sound. Darkness surrounded me in opaque chiffon veils, which were lifting casually, layer after layer, from the sweet night ground scented with earth beneath my bare feet.

Oh yes, now I could see; I was standing in a square by a gate. Before me, its menacing grey spires cutting deep incisions into the intestinal sac of the night sky, was an unlit church. I stood, transfixed, before the altar of my own confusion for an uncertain length of time, listening all the while for the sound, mellifluous in its steadily increasing velocity.

Suddenly, the heavy oak doors of the church swung open and a regiment of children carrying ochre candles aloft moved with their own dancing light into twilight view, humming and cooing the ancient songs of their fathers, heretical choruses all.

Breath left me in translucent plasmic gasps. Time stopped. In the centre of these columns of glittering child-light stood a woman. She was quite, quite breathtakingly beautiful. Her face a constellation of feline expression; ancient hieroglyphic image; a saucerful of secrets. The woman, accompanied by her honour guard of tiny laughing folk, moved elegantly up the footpath from the church doors, past where I was standing agape, and forward into the dark velvet forest that trimmed the hills to the north. She was singing. It sounded like: 'Ninny ninny nacky poo, nacky poo, nacky poo . . .'

And it moved me in a way no other singing voice could; it was a delicious, indulgent moment of unspoilt pleasure, a caress that tickled me behind the ears and laid one finger on my groin. My heart was an open wound that would never heal. With the urgent balletic step of one who is possessed, I ran to join the mad procession of twinkling human light, ascending the slopes of impossible desire, praying for the

Autumnal Heavens to spill with naked gifts. And all the while the woman sang, 'Ninny ninny, nacky poo . . .'

Ineffably spellbound, I followed the voice . . . the face . . . the slender moment. And thus it would have remained had not the inexplicably cruel hand of fate touched my shoulder. A second more and I would surely have been lost for eternity, left to walk the oatmeal carpet of stars that connects this world with . . . another. Instead . . .

I woke up! Well, well, only a dream and nothing more. So some might say, but I know better. The realm of dreams is the ultimate reality and one you would be wrong not to take seriously. It cuts time to ribbons, scuffs it up and sends it rolling into the open sewer, and it tells of the future and of the past, and it speaks in tongues of that most inexplicable of all puzzles – the now! I wasn't dreaming of Kate Bush so much as wandering through the white winter world of her songs. Sleigh-bells and waste-laden trains in a merry Easter march, with night and his army approaching . . . slowly.

Kate Bush tells me that: 'I'm very influenced in my writing by old traditional folk songs, handed down by new generations of musicians but with the original atmosphere and emotion still maintained. The sort of music my mother, who's Irish, would have listened to and danced to, and used to play for me when I was very little. It's probably my biggest musical influence; I really like that feeling folk music has – classical music, too – that timeless feeling you experience from the joy of just playing.'

Kate Bush has an astonishing talent for writing songs and an unmistakable singing voice, unique in its intensity and pitch. She explains how her dancing is a more recent acquisition. Although her mother was a prize-winning dancer, Kate began taking classes as late as her seventeenth year, a little over twelve months before her first ever single release, 'Wuthering Heights', reached Number One in the UK charts. She is also the star of a dozen or more lavishly produced videos, the allure of which continues to titillate the jaundiced palate of TV audiences the world over. In their glamorous wake has come a chain of film and TV offers, which, up till now, she has consistently declined. All of this affords the lady a globe-wide reputation as one of the classiest, most outstandingly talented (not forgetting most successful) female pop performers of the last six years. Simply, she's the best! Mind you, and I'll be perfectly straight here, I only discovered the truth gradually. By stages. Three, to be precise.

I'd been writing for *Sounds* for about three months, off and on, when one day a call comes through. The voice says: 'You are reviewing the singles this week.' And me, the tail-wagging, keen-as-a-witch's-breath asshole I was in those days, I said, 'Oh, wow!' I started playing the first of the 250 or so singles that had been released that week at about eight o'clock in the evening, scribbling down notes and silly bits and pieces like that. By four the next morning I had about forty left to go and I was panicking, so wiped out with boredom I was beginning to hallucinate. It was then that I spotted a single in a full colour pic sleeve – a luxury for an unknown artist even today – called 'Wuthering Heights'. A woman, vaguely oriental in appearance, posed erotically on the cover. For a second, I thought this one might even be good, or at least a bit good. I played it.

I still shudder at the memory. I hated it. The sinister attack of the opening vocal lines carved my senses into lead shavings all over the floor. Do you know pain? Well, that's what it was for me, that first time. I pasted the record with vitriol refined into an almighty sneer, pronouncing it dead from the neck up. Three weeks later it was Number One in the charts.

Stage two commenced with the release of 'The Man With the Child in His Eyes', taken from her first album, *The Kick Inside*. That whole album, but more particularly the second single, opened my eyes wide to Kate Bush. It also finally rid me of those prejudices I'd had about her voice. She sang like an angel – the woman with the child in her voice. Then I discovered that Kate Bush wrote her second hit single when she was fourteen and I realised she was some sort of genius.

The last stage began when I was invited by a friend to go and see Kate Bush on her first tour. She was appearing at the London Palladium. Live! Oh, what a night! An evening drawn in exotic inks across the canvas of my mind, an illicit confection of sensations. The lights, the complex choreography made to appear simple and careless, the dancing flesh, evoked an atmosphere that oozed pleasure, that reeked of shameless beautiful entertainment. I, like everyone else there that night, was smitten. Indeed, when I remind Kate Bush of that night

I forget for a moment that she was the bearer of such insouciant warmth and I merely the receiver.

Why had she never toured again?

'I got so incredibly nervous before I'd go on,' she admits. 'All I'd ever really done in the way of live performance before the tour were things like TV shows and videos. I'd never done a big tour . . . and the sort of props and ideas for the show we were carrying around with us seemed a bit ambitious, a bit awesome, at first, but I loved those shows. Once I was onstage I had so much fun. I would like to do more of it . . .'

But? She doesn't say. Meanwhile, her albums just got better and better. Her last, *The Dreaming*, is her best, to quote a cliché. Self-produced, self-written songs, she even picks the ideas for the sleeve graphics, and that's before she sits down to think about what she wants to do with the new video.

Own up, you lather over the videos, right? Something in your head says 'swim' when you hear her on the radio, yes? Then follow me down to Kate's dance studio in South London, where she's sitting cross-legged on the floor, bundled up in wool against the icy January breath of Jack Frost, a tray of tea and biscuits laid between us, your arse and mine parked on the only cushion available, and we'll smoulder away the chill afternoon together . . .

Before you studied dance, did you ever feel you might have a natural aptitude for dancing, performing?

'No. Never. Within the first two weeks of trying – I went to this dance school up in London where, you know, you can just go along part-time – I thought, there's no way I can do this, this is just ridiculous, I'm useless and it's going to take me years and years. I'd really thought that after about a year I'd be a really great dancer. But I got hooked and started going up to London every day. Suddenly, I became a human being – just learning to move.'

Do you employ a choreographer?

'No. The only time I've ever used one really was on the tour, though it can be almost impossible to work at dancing by yourself; you need a teacher. When I'm working on my classes I tend to go up to London because my teacher can't travel. She's too busy.'

In another life, could you have made a career out of dancing?

'I don't know. There was a time, when I'd been dancing for about a year-and-a-half, and I was never really sure if an album was going to manifest itself, that I thought, if you want to be a dancer you should do it now. Because I had people approaching me at the dance class, asking if I wanted to go to Germany and dance in clubs and things, and for a time I really got into the dance thing much more seriously than I thought I would. But I don't think I was good enough. I didn't stand out enough.'

Do you write all the time?

'No. I have to be forced to write for an album.'

You're not very prolific then?

'I used to be. I used to write every day and if it wasn't very good keep a little bit and maybe use it in something else. As soon as "Wuthering Heights" became a hit, though, my whole routine was just blown apart, it was extraordinary how suddenly everything changed. I had such a routine going. It was like, get up, play the piano, go dancing, come back, play the piano, write songs all night, then go to bed. It was like that every day.'

Were you very happy then?

'Yes, I was. I think it was one of the happiest times for me as a person. I'd just left school and I was beginning to find myself as an individual. It was very exciting, but I wanted more than anything in the world to make an album, just to see that piece of plastic. And then it happened, and it was instant, you know, round the world in eighty days sort of thing. It was frightening. I don't know how I did it. I couldn't do it now.'

Do you come from a particularly artistic family?

'Well, my mother's a dancer, she won a lot of prizes cleaning the floor with the opposition, and my father's a musician.'

I know your family are involved in your business, but were they behind you when you signed to EMI at sixteen? Did they freak out? Sex and drugs and rock 'n' roll, et cetera.

'No, not at all. They had seen it coming for a long time. The original idea was to see if we could sell my songs to a publisher, not that I should be a singer or a performer or anything. We had quite modest, curious aims. So it was gradual and they were always supportive.'

Did you ever have singing lessons?

'Yes.'

Did your teacher try to get you to sing in a lower voice? [Stupid joke.]

'No, not at all. I used to go for about half-an-hour a week and the guy would get me to practise my scales and my breathing or something and then ask to hear my new songs. So I'd sing them for him and he helped me more that way. He was really good.'

Do you get self-conscious when you're making a video?

'I get very nervous before I do anything. I feel I have to work at songs for days before I start to produce anything interesting. Before I perform, I'm always worried that we didn't spend enough time getting this or that together.'

You never cover other people's material. Why? Don't you see yourself as The Interpretive Singer? A touch of the 'Rod Stewarts'?

'Actually, I love singing great songs written by other people; it can be fun discovering how beautiful some composers' work is. But I've felt happy recording my own numbers. I regard myself primarily as a songwriter and I don't want to cop out of writing. I get guilty enough as it is when I'm not writing for lengths of time.'

Kate Bush and I carry on talking while the sun goes down behind my back. We talk and she tells me she is currently writing songs for a new album scheduled for the autumn. How appropriate. Do you like the winter?

'I like all the seasons. They each have something to bring,' she replies enigmatically. God, this is getting wistful!

She tells me that she hennas her hair, crimps it occasionally, and that she has make-up artists and hair beauticians available as well as costume designers equipped to run off fantasy threads like the 'Babooshka' number, guaranteed to dry your throat, boys!

She says that she finds it hard to read a book without turning it into a song, and she informs me that Oscar Wilde is probably her favourite author. She is especially fond of his children's stories, which can still make her cry.

All I can say is . . . well, yeah. Me too.

CODA

No need to get into what happened next for Kate Bush here. We did meet one more time, but I was so bladdered I failed to recognise her. It was at the official record company playback for her album *Hounds of Love*, held for some deeply trippy reason at London's Planetarium. I had just gushingly reviewed the album and I'm assuming Kate must have spotted me lumbering about the antechamber where the free drinks were being served, thinking perhaps to offer some small thanks. Having arrived at the party direct from another party and already staggering, all I remember is looking up from staring at my shoes and seeing the most incredibly beautiful woman dressed in what can't have been – but in my memory will always be – the outfit from the 'Babooshka' video. 'Hello,' she said, smiling like a thousand suns. 'Hello,' I said, thinking how much she looked like Kate Bush but too drunk to realise it actually was Kate Bush. After all, what would Kate Bush be doing at a Kate Bush party talking to me? Then I turned back to my much more important drink and ignored her until she went away. Who the hell did she think she was, anyway, impersonating Kate Bush at a Kate Bush party? Oh, I see . . .

DEF LEPPARD, 1987

It was the day after my twenty-ninth birthday and I was sick as a dog – two dogs, in fact. Nevertheless, the record company insisted I get out of bed and make my way to the airport for the flight to Holland. I was still spewing as the plane took off. It was a shame because I'd been looking forward to this one. Way back in the mists, I had almost become the unsigned Def Leppard's PR. Then, just as I'd shaken hands on the deal with their original management team, the band ditched them and signed with a high-powered New York-based management company.

By the mid-1980s, Leppard was the most glamorous – certainly the richest and most successful – British rock band in America. And yet our paths had not crossed since I'd seen them supporting Sammy Hagar at the Hammersmith Odeon back when I thought I was about to become their PR.

Fortunately, the first one I bumped into was singer Joe Elliott, a buff Yorkshireman not about to be put off by the smell of sick or a deathly pale face. He welcomed me to the small, anonymous club the band was appearing in that night, gave me a seat (very welcome) and a beer (even more welcome), and invited me to join them onstage for the encores that night, doing backing vocals on Alice Cooper's 'Elected'. I wished I'd said yes, 'cos that would have made for a better story. But I wasn't feeling that much better yet and was genuinely worried that I might puke all over the stage, so I declined.

Most impressive, in retrospect, were the balls and sheer bloody-mindedness shown by drummer Rick Allen, doing his first major interview since losing his left arm in a horrendous car accident just two-and-a-half years before. I felt like a woozy fake sitting next to him in the dressing room as he rolled cigarettes one-handed and looked straight at me.

I still do.

Interview with Joe Elliott and Rick Allen of Def Leppard, Tilburg, first published in Kerrang!, *9 July 1987.*

I know you've heard it all before, but any day now Def Leppard are going to release their new album. After two-and-a-half years behind closed doors waiting for the mountain to come to Mohammed, the band have finally finished working on what will probably be the most difficult, time-consuming album they are ever likely to record. Four-and-a-half years after the release of their last album, *Pyromania*, one of the most truly innovative hard rock albums produced so far this ill-starred decade, Def Leppard are at last ready to unveil a new masterpiece. It's called *Hysteria*; the first single from the album in the UK is called 'Animal'; they're both released some time around the July / August cusp; and though I can tell that you still don't quite believe me, let me tell you I've heard the damn thing, or most of it anyway. I've even seen them playing half-a-dozen of the new numbers live! In short, I've seen the proof, baby. It's been a long time, been a long time, been a long, lonely, lonely time waiting for them to finally do it, and nobody knows it better than they do, but now, to steal a phrase, Def Leppard are back. And very soon we're all going to have to believe it.

To begin at the deep end, *Hysteria* walks all over *Pyromania* in much the same way that *Pyromania* stomped all over *High 'n' Dry*, their previous album. So it took the best part of three years to make. So what? What have you been doing for the last three years that's so goddamned great? Where's your fucking masterpiece? Me, I'd rather put in the time than settle for some half-assed, frog-marched-through-the-studio-doors piece of rubbish, released regular as taking a crap, every nine months.

A full review of the *Hysteria* album is not possible here. After all, I'm still missing four of the tracks on the tape I've got. However, of the eight cuts I've got my hands on for now, all but one is an up-tempo, two-fisted body swinger, raunchy, swaggering, leatherised. The production by 'Mutt' Lange is quite, quite awesome, as one would expect from one of the most original minds ever to work in the field of hard rock. Breathtaking and intensely dynamic, the production on *Hysteria* is Lange's most elevated work to date, and that is saying something indeed when you tot up all his successes. I shudder to think how he intends following up this one. Meanwhile, the band, far from being blinded by science, play like angels and everybody turns in magnificent performances. 'Animal' and 'Armageddon It' are quintessential Def Leppard: Steve Clark's and Phil Collen's guitars cranking out one deliciously sleazy riff after another, Rick Savage and Rick Allen's rhythm section building like paddies on bonus time, Joe Elliott crooning like a sheep-killing dog. The rest, with the exception of the lone ballad I've heard so far, 'Love Bites', follow suit. In terms of sheer heaviness, the first single in America, 'Women', stakes the biggest claim: huge choruses that erupt out of the mix, underpinned with a guitar riff you could clout people around the head with and – despite its wanton title – a great set of lyrics that avoid slipping into any silly Coverdale-ish aphorisms.

Most impressive, though, are the tracks like 'Rocket', 'Love and Affection' and 'Hysteria', where, in collusion with Lange's almost other-worldly production embellishments, the band really do start to break the mould. The tone is still unashamedly hard-line rock 'n' roll, but the arrangements are so finely wrought, so well-heeled and tastefully delivered, Def Leppard begin to transcend the limited parameters of everyday hard rock, ascending to a more modern musical plain that is going to set the standard for every aspiring superstar rock band for at least the next five years. Quite simply, as of now everybody else is going to have to try to catch up with Def Leppard or they're just going to have to settle for coming second best. When I hear about the new Mötley Crüe album going to Number Two in the American charts, or how Whitesnake's 1987 has already entered the Top Three there, or that the Poison album has just racked up another half-million US sales, I sit back and I say, enjoy it while you can boys, because when this new Def Leppard album finally steps out of its cage in a few short weeks from now, the game will be over. Because somewhere down that long white line that connects the '70s to the '80s, and bands like Led Zeppelin to Bon Jovi, you will find the inspiration behind a recording like *Hysteria*. Raucous, but rivetingly melodic; basic swarthy guitar antics enhanced by the latest state-of-the-art studio technology;

lead vocals that scream while they burn, swathed in lush, multi-tracked vocal harmonies that rush through the room like a burst of fresh air – like broken, dirty fingernails being shaved into a long sharp point – it could take your fucking eye out, some of this stuff. Crammed with monsters and at least eight hit singles! Jesus.

When I finally get into Holland and locate the band – two plane rides, two cabs, too many problems and not enough time – they are soundchecking onstage in a tiny club called the Nooderligt in the small Dutch town of Tilburg. The next Def Leppard world tour officially kicks off in Dublin on 27 August. The *Hysteria* World Tour, all things going according to plan, is expected to run for the hardest part of two years, beginning with the band's first, full-length British tour since the short end of 1983. There's nothing like making up for lost time, is there? Meanwhile, Leppard have slotted in three warm-up dates here in Holland: two nights at the Nooderligt, followed by a late-afternoon appearance before an expected crowd of over 150,000 at the free Park Rock open-air festival in a few days' time. Under-standably, the band are keen to break in their new set before throwing themselves into the spotlight again in Britain and, in particular, America. In America, *Pyromania* may have sold six-and-a-half million copies, but in Holland, at last count, the album had sold slightly less than six-and-a-half hundred copies. Nevertheless, Def Leppard's lack of any real fame in Holland has positively worked to their advantage during the three years they have spent here, off and on, painstakingly piecing together the new album at Wisseloord Studios just outside Amsterdam. No distractions, no intrusions, not too many wayward influences, it's been a great benefit in the long term. Now their domestic lack of prestige in Holland has again worked temporarily in their favour. Tilburg is about as close to Nowheresville as one mega-platinum-selling rock band is likely to get. Walk outside the club and ten minutes in any direction will leave you stranded in countryside: the perfect venue for a low-profile band work-out. The soundcheck is a long one, but the band look like they're enjoying themselves, stretching like cats through a few bars of 'Rock of Ages' or 'Tear it Down'. The out-front sound is just that bit too loud. Good. My ears could do with being pinned back by a bit of Def Leppard. It's been a long time, like the man said. And it must be a relief for them to be back onstage, The Album Actually Fucking Finished, and all that.

'Strangely enough, it doesn't really feel that astonishing to be back playing live,' says Joe Elliott in the tiny dressing room backstage after the soundcheck is over. 'It's been nearly a year since we last played live (at the Monsters of Rock Festival in Germany, last August). But the minute we all got up onstage here this afternoon it felt like it was yesterday since we last did this. Having said that though, the minute we do get out on the road every day and start touring properly, it'll probably hit me how much I've actually missed regularly playing live.'

The relaxed atmosphere amongst the rest of the band seems to echo Elliott's sentiments. The stage and the dressing room may be a deal smaller than the band have become used to over the last five or six years of their career, but the occasion looms just as large. This is a gig; Def Leppard are a band that made their reputation early on, eating gigs like this for breakfast. None of this is really strange, no matter how long it's been since any of them last stepped into a dressing room.

'There's no way this place will be full for us tonight, and it probably only holds about a thousand, maximum,' Joe reflects. 'But that won't worry us. I can remember playing gigs to about eleven people in the early days! I'm just looking forward to getting onstage and playing some of the new numbers.'

When Def Leppard hit the stage at a little after 10 p.m., there's maybe a couple of hundred people there to see them do it. But Def Leppard have always been an exciting and colourful band to watch on stage; handsome and lean and moving around like tigers on Vaseline, the four-man frontline all hang from the lip of the stage and compete for the spotlight. Despite receiving no more than polite applause, the band still make a dazzling entry, Joe Elliott screaming into the mike, 'WELCOME TO OUR SHOOOOOWWWWWW!!' The band flying straight into the manic intro to 'Stagefright'.

At the back, face concentrated, hunkered down behind his beautiful new Simmons electronic drum kit, is the man of the moment, Rick Allen, blowing up the kind of storm most drummers with two arms could only dream about. Since the widely reported car accident in which Rick lost his left arm two-and-a-half years ago, the question nobody liked to ask but everybody was waiting for the answer to was:

would Rick really be able to cut it on his own with the band onstage? He did it and did it well at last year's Castle Donington festival; but could he be relied on to keep it up night after night through another gruelling world tour? The answer is, quite simply, yes. Everything Rick used to do with his left hand he now does with his left foot (always an underused appendage for your basic rock drummer; apart from opening and closing the hi-hat, a drummer in a rock band doesn't use his left foot for much more than booting the odd roadie up the arse, it seems). Rick's specially designed Simmons kit is basically two sets of drums combined: one is played by electronic foot pedals, the other using sticks on electronic drum pads. Over the months since his accident, Rick has developed a brilliant left-foot technique that allows him the scope to play complex drum patterns with remarkable ease. The first kit (the 'Top' kit) is five small Simmons electronic drum pads. The 'Bottom' kit is four specially constructed foot pedals and a Simmons bass-drum pad. None of these drums produce sound, only electronic impulses, or 'triggers', which are sent to a 'Brain' – actually a Simmons SDS7, loaded with a silicon chip containing sampled sounds using a combination of SDS7 Library Samples and samples taken from Rick's own recorded drums. It's this which produces the sounds.

But don't get this thing wrong – these are not goddamned tapes he's using. He only calls on five different sounds, the same five on both kits: bass drum, snare drum, and three tom-toms. Rick still has to beat the hell out of his kit and be able to create the drum patterns himself. That's no robot he's got propped behind the curtain there. It's just another set of drums that you have to learn how to play. It won't make a bad drummer sound good. It won't do a thing until someone shows it how. 'Animal', 'Armageddon It', 'Pour Some Sugar on Me', 'Women', 'Love and Affection' and 'Hysteria' all get premiered before the lackadaisical Noorderligt crowd. The ones at the back in the Slayer T-shirts are waiting to be impressed, but down the front is where they are mostly, nodding their heads thoughtfully, smatterings of spilt applause greeting the end of each number. Even more familiar Leppard material like 'Rock Rock' and 'Too Late for Love' draws only politely appreciative applause.

'It's fair enough, really,' said guitarist Phil Collen after the show. 'Our music simply isn't that well known enough in Holland for us to expect anything else. I mean, you've got to start somewhere, haven't you?'

But when Joe Elliott calls Rick Allen down from behind his kit and says through the mike, 'I'd like to introduce you to my mate, Rick', the crowd finally throw their heads back and cheer. It was the biggest noise they made all night, applauding the talents of this gifted young percussionist whose courage and quiet determination has brought him right back from the brink of tragedy to where he belongs, propping up the beat behind the guitars in Def Leppard.

The afternoon before the band's second show at the Noorderligt, Joe Elliott and I sit catching the breeze on the grass outside my motel room. The sky looks like it's trying hard to rain, grey and perplexed. The night before, we had been sipping brandies with guitarist Steve Clark and listening to some of Joe's priceless Alice Cooper live tapes on the singer's ghetto-blaster. Now we're both nursing our nerves and slurping from glasses of Coke. With only time to kill I start to unwind with a few questions.

The last time Joe Elliott was interviewed by anyone from *Kerrang!* (way back in issue 90), Rick Allen was still at home recovering from the immediate effects of his gruesome accident, and the band were in the Wisseloord Studios with their engineer Nigel Green producing their new album. I ask Joe to fill in some of the gaps for me between then and when Mutt Lange reappeared on the scene some months later.

'Rick's accident happened on New Year's Eve 1984, and we were actually back in the studios in Holland on the second of January '85. I don't know if you can imagine how we all felt, trying to put a brave face on things and carry on working on the album. We were in there going around in circles trying to get things done, but all the time at the backs of our minds we were all thinking about Rick, wondering how he was getting on. For the next four months we carried on like that, but we didn't really do a lot. It hasn't happened to me yet, but it must be like if someone close to you dies, then two weeks after it's happened you're back to work, but you're not really there. You go through the motions and you say all the right things, but your thoughts are permanently somewhere else. It's only natural really.

'The day Rick came back to Holland was the day this band came back to life. We'd never even discussed whether or not Rick would stay in the band. That was always going to be Rick's decision. And his first words to us were that he thought he would, eventually, still be able to do it. He just pitched up in the studio and said, "Don't worry, I'm gonna build this drum kit." He was brilliant, so positive. It really inspired us to snap out of it and not let ourselves down.'

It would take time, of course, for Rick's special kit to be designed, tested and manufactured, and naturally the drummer had to moderate his technique to fit his new circumstances, but as long as Rick was determined to give it a go, the band backed him all the way.

'Nothing ever gets done in a single day,' Joe says thoughtfully. 'I don't expect the Ford Motor Company stuck out the first model they ever came up with. But it was obvious from Rick's brilliant attitude that it was only a matter of time before he was sitting behind a kit with us again. Then he came into the studio one day and played the whole of [Led Zeppelin's] "When the Levee Breaks" perfectly right the way through! We knew then we'd turned a big corner. We could start to breathe again.'

Though there can be no doubt that Rick's unfortunate accident was a major cause of the delay in completing *Hysteria*, by no means was he the only reason the album took so long to make. From the beginning, the project had been dogged by bad luck and worse timing. First they couldn't get Mutt to produce it for them. Although Lange had agreed to spend six weeks with them working on pre-production prior to their departure for Wisseloord in the summer of 1984, after having worked back-to-back on the *Pyromania* album and then the Cars' own mega-successful *Heartbeat City* album, what the ailing producer felt he could not do was run straight back into the studio and begin working on another new album. Mutt needed a break. Badly.

'Mutt knew how big a step this next album was for us,' says Joe, 'and he just couldn't cope with it. At the time, Mutt hadn't been outside a recording studio in something like seventeen years, and he felt he was going to crack up if he didn't take a break. Feeling like that, he knew it wouldn't be fair on him or us to pretend he had the energy and enthusiasm for another Def Leppard album at that time. And that's when we got Jim Steinman in and said goodbye to another two months in wasted studio time.'

Erstwhile songwriting partner of Meat Loaf, co-producer of one fairly average Billy Squier album, and the man who gave it all away to Bonnie Tyler, Jim Steinman's problems with Def Leppard have been well documented in the past. Suffice to say, Steinman did not work out. When the axe fell, the band decided to go it alone with the help of Mutt's regular engineer, Nigel Green. That didn't work out either, though for less spurious reasons.

'Nigel is a brilliant engineer; he can get absolutely any sound you want, which is why he works so well when Mutt is producing, because Mutt likes to experiment with sounds and you have to really know what you're doing to keep up with him. So Nigel was great in that respect. But what he didn't have going for him that Mutt does is that he's not a musician or a singer. Mutt is a brilliant singer and a great musician, there's absolutely nothing he can't play. So there are always ideas and suggestions from Mutt that, unless you're a musician, you'd simply never have in a million years. Mutt can do anything any other producer can do, but he's also a great all-round musician, and as such, a great source of inspiration in this band. We've never hidden that fact.

'Anyway, after scrapping the original sessions with Steinman, and then watching Rick go through his ordeal, we didn't know what else to do except keep plugging away with Nigel. Like I said earlier, because of what Rick was going through, I think we'd lost it by then anyway. Then Rick came back and we started to re-evaluate what we'd been doing. That's when we owned up and realised we weren't actually getting anywhere. What we'd been doing with Nigel and on our own certainly sounded as good as anything on *Pyromania*, but it didn't actually sound any better. And it was very important for the survival of this band that whatever we released next had to be better than anything we'd ever done before. And that's when we decided to scrap those sessions too, and start all over again – again!'

Joe says that, by the middle of 1985, he and the rest of the band were starting to feel that they were fated to enjoy a period of mega-bad luck.

'We were very aware that we'd enjoyed four or five years of nothing but good luck. Even when our albums were stiffing in England, or the singles were going nowhere, or the reviews were crap, we always seemed to ride it all out, we never let it touch us. We never lost the vibe that each new thing we did was better than the last, that we were truly going somewhere. And then of course it all happened for us with only our third album and we became the big band we always thought we were going to be. Overnight almost, everything went from better to totally brilliant and we could do no wrong. So when one thing after another kept going wrong during the first nine months of recording this album it was almost like we had it coming, you know? In fact,' Joe smiles, his mood lightening, 'we were talking about this amongst ourselves the other day, and I'm convinced that all our bad luck started the day Phil and Rick turned vegetarian! Ever since then I swear nothing's gone right!' he laughs.

'To be honest, although all these scrapes affected us very badly when they were happening, and certainly lowered the band's morale for months at a time, looking back I tend to be more philosophical about all those traumas now that we're about to go out on the road again. The thing is we probably had just as many problems in the past, but we were never in the public eye so much before so we didn't have time to sit around and reflect too long about what was going on. Also, it's very hard to get depressed about some problems when you're in a new city every night. But very easy when you're stuck inside the same four walls for three years. It was a bit like sitting in our own shit, sometimes.'

By the summer of 1985, however, things took a dramatic turn for the better when Mutt Lange, now fully rested after his long lay-off, returned to the Def Leppard fold and took charge while the band began from scratch again in the studio. A renowned perfectionist, once Mutt got his teeth into a project, especially one as ambitious as the new Def Leppard album, he didn't let go until he was 100 per cent satisfied that the job had been done properly. As a result, it was to be another two years before Mutt considered it that way.

The album must have cost a fortune to make, I remark.

'*Hysteria* is possibly going to come in as the most expensive rock album ever made,' Joe admits. 'It will probably have to sell something like two million copies just to break even on the costs. But you know, you have to see these things in perspective. Yes, the album cost a fortune to make, but it is the best thing we've ever done. It would be different if we took all that time and spent all that money and still came out with a piece of shit, but it's not. It's got a magic, the new album, that you shouldn't put a price on. And as long as it still only costs a few quid for the fans to buy, then who's lost out? The money was ours to spend and I think we've done it very wisely.

'What else are you supposed to do with money if not spend some of it? It's true we've made a lot of money, a hell of a lot of money. And we've all bought fast cars and big houses and all those things – who wouldn't if they were suddenly rich? That's what it's all for, some of it. But we've also put a lot of it back into the music industry, too. We bought a PA, which has been used by everybody from Dio to Duran Duran, and we put a large part of it back into making the best possible album we were capable of, and I think it was worth every penny.'

Nevertheless, in the past, Def Leppard have suffered a staggering amount of criticism for being, it seems to me, rich and famous, of all things. And not just at the practised hands of the UK press, but even from the mouths of fans – you know, the flash bastards syndrome. Are Def Leppard flash bastards, Joe?

He leans back in his seat and laughs.

'Look, let's get this one straight for the record. It's not as though we won the pools, all that money didn't just fall from the sky. It happened because a lot of people liked our records enough to buy them. Anyway, it's not as though we're that rich. Compared to a lot of bands that I could name, but won't, we haven't even begun fulfilling our earning potential. I can think of plenty of other rock musicians who have all got the big mansion and the big cars and the servants and the perpetual hangers-on and treat everybody that works for them like complete cunts – they always end up getting the "good blokes" profiles in the music press.

'I think because in the beginning when we were first being interviewed by the press we were so young and naive we'd end up sounding a bit too cold and certain in some of the interviews that appeared around that time. Like, if someone asked what we thought of the new AC/DC album and we turned round and said something like, "Oh, it's OK. Good not great", which actually happened when *Back in Black* was Number One in the American charts, we'd end up getting crucified for "slagging AC/DC off"! The letters would start arriving: "Who the hell do Def Leppard think they are?"' He purses his lips in disapproval. 'Things like that and the whole debate over whether we'd Paid Our Dues, man! Three albums! Boom-boom-

boom! Six million sales! People couldn't handle it. Well, we've paid some dues since then. The last three years have seen to that. I mean, tell me about it!'

The world, of course, has not stood still while Def Leppard have been off the road. Strange to relate, when *Pyromania* was released in March 1983 no such things as Bon Jovi or Rätt albums existed; Mel Galley was still in Whitesnake and the *Slide It In* album hadn't even had its first mix rejected yet. David Lee Roth was still at home trying to write lyrics to a new thing Eddie Van Halen had put together called 'Jump'; even Mötley Crüe were still playing the clubs in LA. What's it been like staying quiet in the studio while history was being made by all the other bands, Joe?

'I'd never even heard of Bon Jovi the last time we released an album.' He shakes his head, not quite taking it in. 'The first Bon Jovi record I ever really listened to was "You Give Love a Bad Name". We were in Britain last summer and I turned on the radio and there it was – I thought, fucking hell! Rock music on Radio 1 shock! This is good news! And lo and behold, they've become like the band we should have become. And it's a fair comparison, I think. Bon Jovi on their last album are sort of like we were on *Pyromania*. They're twenty-four years old, it's their third album, a new producer and so forth. I say good luck to them. I love it that I can hear a Bon Jovi record on the radio. Obviously, it just made me want to get out there and do things, too, but I still bought their album! Whenever their singles come on the radio or the TV I still turn the volume up full blast. I'm a fan, I like them! I think it's fair to say as well, and they'd probably admit it, too, that they've stolen things from us. But so what? We stole from Thin Lizzy and UFO, and now somebody will come along and steal from Bon Jovi. That's just the way it works.'

There's no doubting that the success in America of *Pyromania* (and the huge US hit single it spawned, 'Photograph') opened a lot of doors for most of the newer bands that have emerged in the wake of Leppard's phenomenal success there. Just when hard rock and heavy metal were getting the bum's rush again from the bourgeois American media, *Pyromania* came along and sold so many records it was two years before it finally dropped out of the charts. Only Michael Jackson's *Thriller* (the biggest-selling album of all time, don't forget) kept *Pyromania* from the

Number One spot in America – a position no British rock band since Led Zeppelin had been in. Suddenly, hard rock was hip again. But does Joe Elliott feel that, as some have suggested, the more recent successes of bands like Bon Jovi and Mötley Crüe have stolen any of Def Leppard's thunder?

'No, I don't go for all that stuff about Rätt, or whoever else, stealing our audience. It's bullshit. Look at the US charts at the moment – Bon Jovi have just sold nine million albums, Mötley Crüe are at Number Two, Whitesnake are in the Top Five, Ozzy's just been in the Top Ten. So have Poison. Kids don't just buy one band's albums and not others. The same kids who bought the Bon Jovi album have probably gone out and bought the Poison album and the Whitesnake album, too. In that respect, nobody has stolen anything from anyone. There's plenty of room for everyone – as long as they've got something to offer.

'It's true, though,' he agrees when prompted, 'that a lot of bands either rode in on the back of *Pyromania*, or took it as a blueprint for what they wanted to do themselves. I think we set a standard there. It's staggering just how many bands it did influence. And I don't mean just big American bands. I remember meeting Kim McAuliffe from Girlschool in London after their *Play Dirty* album came out, and she came up to me and said, "I'd just like to say I'm sorry". I said, "What for?" She said, "I feel I should apologise because we've just totally ripped your *Pyromania* album off!" I just stood there bemused. I'd never even heard the Girlschool album she was on about. But I went out and bought a copy of *Play Dirty* – it's that album that Noddy Holder and Jimmy Lea from Slade produced for them – and played it, and I couldn't believe it! I swear, there's one track on there, if you took the lead vocals off you could sing "Rock of Ages" over it! The drum sound, the guitars, it was all straight off *Pyromania*. I had to laugh. I mean, you have to take it as a kind of back-handed compliment, really. But at least Kim wasn't afraid to admit the influence, which was nice.'

Joe Elliott downs another cold glass of Coke. It soothes his throat, he says, after burning it on the brandy with me and Steve Clark the night before. I proffer the theory that the band's long lay-off may, eventually, prove to be a real advantage in certain respects. For example, the last Def Leppard album may have sold over six million copies in America but, truth to tell, it didn't really sell doodly-squat anywhere else. However, the fact of their enormous success in America, where, by the end of 1983, Leppard had achieved almost legendary status on a par with any of the old 1970s giants, coupled with the unprecedented amount of time they've taken in order to mastermind a worthy follow-up, has, in itself, reinforced the image of the band with a new and deeper credibility. You may not have bought their last album, but you sure as hell know who they are by now. You may never consider yourself a Def Leppard fan, but I bet you'd like to know exactly what these fuckers have been up to all this time. If you're sixteen years old right now, you were eleven-and-a-half, still wearing short trousers to school and a probable *Beano* fan when *Pyromania* first came out. Surely you will want to find out what all the fuss is about?

'Yeah, I've thought about that, too,' says Joe. 'The plus side in Britain, for example, is that a twenty-one-year-old kid who remembers us from '83 and wasn't a fan probably won't be a fan now, either. If he remembers us slagging off his favourite band, he's still gonna hate us. But if his eighteen-year-old brother, who was twelve or thirteen when we were out on the road playing *Pyromania*, hears the new album and likes it, he's not gonna give a shit about any of the old prejudices that have dogged us in the past. He'll be too busy discovering Def Leppard on his own terms to listen to stupid old arguments that go back to his infancy. Kids aren't interested in history; they're into what's happening now.'

The conversation drifts back and forth a while. We touch on the band's decision to appear on the bill at last year's Castle Donington festival. Joe says Leppard played Donington and the two Monsters of Rock festivals in Germany for no special reason other than 'we were absolutely bored playing to four studio walls'.

The most fun the band had though, he says, was on the five warm-up dates they played in Ireland the week before the festivals began. 'Honestly, it was brilliant,' he chuckles. 'We did one gig in Limerick in this tiny place, and we'd only sold about a hundred and eighty-five tickets come the night of the gig. So we went around to all the local pubs giving the tickets away to anybody who fancied coming along. In the end, we had about three hundred and fifty people in there, although I'm sure half of them had never heard of us.'

It was also while they were out flexing their muscles on those five low-profile dates in Ireland, in 1986, that Rick Allen, appearing live with the band for the first time since the car accident that robbed him of his left arm, first tackled the unenviable task of playing an entire Def Leppard set without the aid of an auxiliary drummer onstage. Former drummer with Judie Tzuke, and now a permanent fixture with Status Quo, Jeff Rich accompanied Rick on the first few dates, then, for a variety of obscure reasons, couldn't make one gig. It took a lot of nerve but Rick said he'd like to have a crack at it on his own.

'We tried Rick on his own at this tiny club in Ireland, only a small crowd, and it worked really well. There were a couple of cock-ups, but basically he did brilliantly. From that point Jeff Rich was history and we were back to being a five-man group.'

That must have come as a great relief, Rick proving he could handle the gig on his own?

'Yeah, it did. But it wasn't entirely unexpected. Rick had been coming along so fast with his new technique that we thought he'd probably be ready to have a serious crack at going it alone at some point. It just happened a year or so sooner than we expected.'

Looking toward the immediate future, Joe tells me that the band's next world tour will almost certainly be their longest and most ambitious yet. Right now, Def Leppard are scheduled to start the ball rolling on 27 August, in Dublin, then creep across the water for their first decent stretch of UK dates since 1983. At the end of September they return to America, where they unveil their most stunning stage show yet. I don't have too many details to hand at present, but I can tell you that it involves a circular stage placed in the centre of each arena they alight on.

'It'll be a completely bare stage except for the band,' Joe tells me. 'Even the amps will be mounted underneath the stage. And we're going to have giant catwalks so we can literally walk out into the auditorium and say hello to people!'

They'll carry on like that for maybe nine months, then plan to return in mid-1988 for an extended European tour. They will then return to America for another six months. All this should carry Def Leppard safely through to New Year, 1989, when there is a strong possibility they will tour Japan. What is this thing you have about touring, Joe? I mean, we're talking about the best part of the next two years out on the road! You're not doing this out of guilt for being away so long, are you?

'No, don't be daft,' he smiles. 'We're doing it because if there's one thing that's detestable, it's when bands make it big in America and immediately settle for doing twenty-date tours of the place in the biggest, most ridiculous places. You know, pack 'em in quick, grab the money and bugger off home. We want to play everywhere we played last time, only this time we want to play two nights where we last did one, three nights where we last did two, and on and on. We want to come back looking, sounding and playing like we're four times the band we were in 1983! And we haven't done anything wrong taking our time about it, either. It was the best thing we ever did, taking three years off from the road.

'And the word is spreading, too,' he assures me, running a hand through his long yellow locks. 'Even in England people are starting to get a buzz about us going out on the road again. This time we're doing two nights at the Hammersmith Odeon, which I know ain't much for a lot of probably less successful British rock bands to do, but for us it's a first! We've only ever been able to sell the place out for one night at a time before now.'

Soundcheck time approaches, and besides, I haven't spoken to the man of the moment yet, Rick Allen. I throw a last one Joe's way, which he handles with characteristic aplomb. I ask him how he would like Def Leppard to be remembered when their time is over and people like me start saying things about them like 'Remember when . . . ?' Just like they do these days about Led Zeppelin.

'I'd like us to be remembered as a legendary band,' he shrugs, eyes crinkling. 'I mean, that's not how I perceive the band right now. To me, a genuinely legendary band would have to be Led Zeppelin, and I couldn't possibly think of Def Leppard in the same way. But I'd take it as the highest compliment we ever had if in years to come that's the way the new generation of rock fans looked back on us. But the only way we'll achieve that is if we never give in and release a dog of an album, and then if we do split up stay that way. Iron Maiden's manager, Rod Smallwood, made a very shrewd observation once when he said to me that the day Deep Purple ceased to be a legend was the day they re-formed. And he was right! I promise you, there will never be any of that with Def Leppard. We'll just go away quietly and not tell anyone we've split up!' One last throaty chuckle and he's gone, soundcheck-bound.

A couple of hours before Def Leppard take to the stage for their second, and last, night at the tiny Nooderligt club in Tilburg, me and Rick Allen and a couple of brown bottles of beer hunker down in a corner of the upstairs production office and – out of the goodness of our hearts – throw down these words onto the tape. I begin by asking Rick how soon it was after his accident he made up his mind to try and carry on as the drummer in the band.

'About two weeks,' he says. 'What happened was, I'd lost my left arm, and I'd busted up my right pretty badly as well. So to begin with my right arm was more or less strapped to my side. To help me sit up straight in bed and move around a bit and make myself comfortable, the nurses placed a hard block of foam in the bottom of the bed so that I could push against it with my feet. Well, it was just in the perfect position for me to tap away on it with my feet. Out of sheer boredom I used to lie there tapping my feet against this thing, and I started thinking, hang on a minute, I can use this. This has possibilities . . . So I got this friend of mine down and he looked at what I was doing and he agreed that the idea of some kind of foot pedal that would at least enable me to get a snare sound with my left foot could probably be worked out and designed. Within a matter of days this guy returned to the hospital with what turned out to be the prototype for the pedals I'm using onstage now.

'The other thing I got into doing, don't laugh, was sitting in my wheelchair and banging on the footplates, getting a rhythm going. And to be honest, what I'm doing now onstage isn't much different.'

Rick Allen may have lost an arm, but he hasn't lost his sense of humour.

'Because the rest of the band were so much behind me as regards, like, you're still in the band, Rick, all that occupied my time while I was in hospital was working out what I was gonna do when I got out. It was great to be able to think positively about the situation, it really helped a lot in the beginning. Because of that, because I had this tremendous urge to get out and actually start again, I was out of there inside a month!'

With an iron will, and displaying remarkable courage, Rick Allen was back in the studios in Holland with the rest of the band within six weeks of his accident. It wasn't easy, he says, making a sudden reappearance. Not at first, anyway.

'I don't think any of us quite knew what to say. It was strange for all of us, to begin with. I think the rest of the band were waiting to see if I was going to crack up or something. Nobody was sure yet how I was going to handle it. But they gave me their support, totally, from the word go. I mean, if they'd have said, "Sorry Rick, we can't really carry on this way", I'd have stepped down gracefully, you know, fine, no problem. But that was never the case at all; they all left it up to me to decide – and that was the spur I needed to try and work things out as a drummer again.'

The technical details for Rick's new specially designed electronic kit were worked out over a period of a few short months. Meanwhile, in the studio, Rick relied mainly on a Fairlight computer to achieve the drum sounds you can hear on *Hysteria*. Outside of the studio, he worked overtime on refining a startling new technique that would enable him to return to the stage the next time Leppard played as a legitimate live drummer. Showing the same heart that dragged him from a hospital bed back into a recording studio inside the space of six weeks, within a year of his return to the band Rick decided he was ready to put his balls on the line and try out some of his big ideas on a stage.

I ask Rick how he felt in the dressing room before he went on for that first gig alone?

'I never, ever drank before I went onstage, but that first night in Ireland using the new electronic kit, even with Jeff Rich beside me on the stage, I was so jittery I downed the best part of a half a bottle of brandy before we went on. And then the minute I got onstage I was straight! I mean, I was just so frightened! And I made a few silly mistakes, a few obvious errors; my timing was a bit off and I kept thinking of things before I was supposed to play them, and then rushing things. Because Jeff Rich was there, though, I didn't have to panic too much. And then over the space of those first few gigs, I started getting it together again. Suddenly I felt a lot calmer and I was doing all right.

'There's an old Irish joke that goes, "When you see a guy with a short leg you can be sure the other one's always longer!"' He laughs. 'It's only a daft joke but there's a grain of truth in there. Losing an arm might have been the worst thing that could ever happen to me. But it happened, and that's that. In the meantime, I feel like the rest of me has grown much, much stronger as a result. Maybe it's just nature's way of compensating for the loss of one part of me, I don't know, but within the space of those first few gigs in Ireland everything started coming together so quickly I think I surprised everybody, myself included. Peter [Mensch, Leppard's manager] had been saying all along that I should try playing live on my own, but I really needed those gigs with Jeff to take some of the pressure off while I got used to the idea of being onstage again, and the new way of playing.

'Then, the second from last gig, Jeff had flown out for a couple of days' work with Status Quo in Germany, and he was supposed to take a flight back to where we were in Ireland on the afternoon of this particular gig. Something happened – he missed the flight, or the plane was delayed – but soundcheck time came and Jeff still wasn't back. We carried on without him, but when it was time for us to go onstage and he still wasn't back, and nobody knew whether to go on or not without him, with just me by myself. In the end, we decided to do it anyway and hope that Jeff would show up soon. We went on as a five-piece, which I must admit felt great, and then we just ploughed into the set and I got on with the drums on my own for about the first six numbers! It was good, too. Nothing too fancy, but I was definitely holding my own. And then Jeff finally arrived and jumped up onstage and the two of us finished the set together.'

Impressed by his solo performance, the following night, their last in Ireland before readying themselves for their appearance at Donington a few days later, the rest of the band encouraged Rick to have a go at the whole set alone. He'd got this far on sheer guts and determination; maybe his new-found technique would carry him the rest of the way.

'I did the gig on my own and Jeff stood out by the mixing desk listening for any obvious mistakes, trying to spot if I wasn't holding my end up on each number, ready to step in and help me if it looked like I couldn't handle it. Well, I got through the entire gig, and afterwards Jeff came backstage and shook my hand and said, "Well, it looks like I'm out of a job then!" It was a nice moment.'

Leppard's appearance on last year's Donington bill was an understandably special occasion: Leppard's first in England in three years; Rick's second on his own.

'When we went on we knew there would still be some people out there who probably thought we had a second drummer hidden somewhere underneath the stage,' he jokes. 'I was really nervous. I think we all were. But we started off OK, the set started building and I just got into the gig. And the longer we played, the more I could sense that people had stopped staring at me and were just getting into it, too. And then Joe started talking to the crowd in between numbers, and then he said something like, "I'd like to introduce you to my mate, Rick Allen!" And the place went mad! I've never seen so many hands go up in the air! I just sat there behind the drums and burst into tears.'

He pauses, looking into the middle distance.

'What we need to do right now is get out on the road, go everywhere we can, and prove to the world that Def Leppard are still a great live band,' he says eventually. 'Since Donington, we've finished the new album and I've had another twelve months to improve on my ability and my technique, and now we're as ready as we're ever going to be. We've been away a long time, but we've got nothing to hide behind. And now we're coming back to prove it.'

Heroic last words from a heroic young man indeed. Later that night, during the show, I crouched down in the darkness behind Rick's drum riser and watched the boy work. I looked on bleary-eyed as he romped through a blistering 'Rock of Ages', his right arm doing what it always did while his bare feet rained down hard and with precision on the pedals. Can he still rock? Is Argentinian tennis star Gabriela Sabatini a horn-ball? Do fish fuck in water? See for yourself in September, then you tell me.

That Def Leppard had to work their asses off to get this small Dutch gathering going is one thing. They got their encores. A wonderfully anthemic 'Photograph', a wired and weird roll through Alice Cooper's 'Elected', which at least kept the grinning fool from *Kerrang!* happy, and a thoroughly bad-minded romp through the most popular number of the night, 'Wasted', all were included as I recall. But ultimately,

Leppard weren't out to seriously wow a new and wall-eyed audience. They went out to oil their gears. And at the end of the second night it seemed safe to say they had their machine ticking over nicely.

The road beckons. This cat's finally outta the bag. You, me, the band, we're all sick of waiting. Well, we don't have to any more . . .

CODA

This story turned out to be remarkably prescient, in terms of predicting just how enormously successful and significant the *Hysteria* album became once it was released.

It was on the trip to Holland that I also first met Def Leppard's flamboyant blond guitarist, Steve Clark; someone who was no stranger to the hangover, either. It was, needless to say, the start of a rather unbeautiful friendship. I ended up travelling with the band through quite a few different legs of the subsequent fourteen-month world tour. It was an eye-opening experience for me, witnessing Steve cut a glamorous dash onstage with the band each night, then sitting with him in the small hours as he bemoaned his lot as the 'second-class citizen' of the band, as I remember being shocked to hear him describe himself. The fact is, his drink problems were so severe it was beyond a joke long before I appeared on the scene: the band had come almost to the end of their tether in terms of waiting for Steve to pull himself together.

It was not to be and he died barely a year after the tour ended, unable to regain consciousness after yet another night on the hard stuff. A huge tragedy in personal terms, it was – perhaps not coincidentally – the beginning of a 'wilderness' period for Leppard, as they struggled to come to terms with the new era in rock ushered in by the early-'90s grunge scene. As we now know, they were one of the few '80s bands to successfully come out the other side. The last time I saw them play live, headlining the main stage at the Download festival in the summer of 2009, they were as good as ever, if not quite as young or as pie-eyed hungry as they were when we met in Holland twenty-two years before. But then who is?

MÖTLEY CRÜE, 1985

I had always looked on Mötley Crüe as something of a joke – and a very bad joke at that. They may have looked the part – if the time the part happened to be in was 1984 and the place Los Angeles – but musically they had never recorded anything that ever remotely turned me on. (That changed later when they released the *Dr Feelgood* album, but even that felt somewhat ersatz and over-sugared.) This, surely, was rock for people who had never seen Adam Ant or heard of the New York Dolls. Or kissed a girl. The only sane response seemed to be laughter. When, however, they called off some UK dates in January 1988 because – according to official sources – they feared snow on the Wembley Arena roof would drag the ceiling down on top of them, the hilarity turned to disgust. They didn't really expect their fans to believe that, did they?

Apparently they did. Meanwhile, word was already creeping out: the real reason the Wembley shows had been pulled, I was told off the record, was that the band's recent tours of America and Japan had degenerated into such a nightmare of drug overdoses, guns, fights and walkouts, that the band's road crew had nearly mutinied at one point, threatening to quit if the band didn't get their act together. Hence the cancellation of the rest of the tour, including those Wembley dates, while the entire band entered drug rehabilitation. Not that they were prepared to actually talk about it yet. In retrospect, then, it's amazing that they even allowed their guitarist Mick Mars to be put on a phone with a nosey Limey journalist. But then this was still the '80s, and so they did.

Interview with Mick Mars of Mötley Crüe, first published in **Kerrang!** *6 February 1988.*

The story so far: just a week before it was due to begin, Mötley Crüe announced the sudden cancellation of what was to have been their first British and European tour for two years. Officially, as reported in issue 171, the cancellation was made because of the band's 'exhaustive and non-stop schedule in 1987'. That's what the official press handout said, anyway. Unofficially, however, the stories continue to pour in: from the sublime to the ridiculous, we must have heard (and printed a good few) of them all. From the alleged drugs overdose Nikki Sixx nearly died from before Christmas, to being told that the real reason the band had cancelled was because they thought the weight of their lighting-rig would put too much strain on the various arena ceilings in Britain and Europe, which would be at breaking point anyway due to all the snow we have in this part of the world around this time of year.

Jee-zus! And those are just the more plausible stories we've been listening to. Ultimately, though, what this all boils down to is that no one in Britain actually believes a word the band are saying any more. The British Mötley Crüe fans smell a rat. That you shouldn't believe every goddamned thing you read or hear about a band, that goes without saying. But something is obviously wrong here. Tired and exhausted Mötley Crüe may well be, but snow on the roof? Naw . . . if Mötley Crüe couldn't get it up for a couple of weeks in Britain, it wasn't just because they were knackered, it was because something had gone wrong with the machine.

When the shit hit the fan here in Britain about the 'real' reasons behind the last-minute cancellation of the Crüe tour, we got in contact with the band's UK record company and asked them to try and get someone from the band to do a quick phone interview, because in Britain right now, the Crüe's reputation is shot. It's in tiny pieces on the ground. We needed to talk to one of them now. The record company said they would try.

Originally, I was going to speak to singer Vince Neil. Then Vince cancelled, we made it for another day, then Vince cancelled again. 'He must have got the days mixed up,' said a spokeswoman for the band in Los Angeles. A pig flew by my window. I growled at her and told her that Mötley Crüe already looked like goddamned fools in *Kerrang!* without any more help from anybody. The only thing left for them to do in order to really kill off the band's reputation in this country, I said, would be to fuck me around right now and blow the only chance they've got to tell their side of the story. She sounded suitably concerned and promised she'd get back to me. It was 8.30 p.m. on a Monday night. *Kerrang!* should have been passed for press by now and the deadline couldn't stand being broken one more time. It was now or never, as Elvis used to sing.

10.00 p.m. The phone rings. I answer it. It's guitarist Mick Mars.

'You wanna talk about cancelling the tour, right?' he asks.

You bet.

'Go ahead . . .'

I begin where the rumours begin here in London: that the Crüe tour of America last year started getting out of hand when Guns N' Roses joined on as the opening act.

'We were doing so many dates, the whole thing was just really exhausting,' he says. 'I don't recall things getting too out of hand, though. No more than usual on one of our tours.'

What about the Nikki Sixx drugs OD story? It's said that it occurred right after that tour ended.

'I heard about that, too, and I just started laughing! It's total shit – just another one of those dumb stories that get put out about us. Honestly, man, stories like that about us go out all the time. Did you hear the latest one about how I'm supposed to be getting married? I mean, COME ON! No way.'

So Nikki Sixx definitely did not suffer a drugs overdose?

'No! None of that happened! Nikki didn't die either – I heard that one, too! It's just dumb shit.'

OK. Moving on to your Japanese tour, which immediately preceded the scheduled British shows, it's here that the stories really start to pick up. It's whispered that it was while the band were weaving their way around the land of the rising yen that the personalities really started to get out of control, a factor said to have contributed greatly to their eventual decision to blow out the UK and European dates. What's the truth here?

'The truth here is nothing like what you might have heard. The simple truth is, we were totally and utterly wasted! Done in; seriously fucking tired! We realised after the Japanese tour that to come to Europe would have been a big mistake. If you ever see one of our shows then you'll know we only ever give a hundred per cent. We wouldn't have been able to do that if we'd come to England straight after the tour of Japan. We were terminally exhausted. You wouldn't have liked us if you'd seen us, it would have been a big disappointment.'

There was a story that had you pulling guns on people backstage in Japan.

'No, no, no. We bought some toy guns while we were out there to keep ourselves amused; we were firing them at each other all the time. But they weren't real guns; they look pretty real, I guess, but they're toys – bought 'em in a store!'

What about the scenes we had described of various band members beating up a party of women they had picked up while you were out there?

'What? That's the first time I've heard that one. Shit, no! We got a little drunk on the bullet train; that was about as far out as we got. The rest is total shit!'

What's the truth behind that plaster cast that Vince now carries on his hand and arm?

'I'm not absolutely sure how he did it, but he cut himself on some broken glass.'

We heard that he did it in a fit of temper backstage one night – that he jammed his fist into a glass jar of mustard and smashed it against the dressing-room wall.

'No, no, no! He cut his hand, all right, but not in a fit of temper or because he had his hand in a jar of mustard. Where do these stories come from?'

Actually, some of the most ludicrous stories seem to come from the band's official sources, I tell him. For example, the absurd we-can't-play-because-of-all-the-snow-on-the-roof story that appeared in the very last issue of *Kerrang!*.

'You got that from an official source!' he cries, barely able to control himself. I read him the whole thing out, word for word, over the phone.

'That is the most COMPLETE and UTTER BULLSHIT I'VE EVER HEARD! I can't believe that came from someone who works for us! You're kidding me! I'm not even going to bother denying it. I mean, nobody believes that, do they?'

One thing I'm not sure whether to believe or not is the latest story hot off the underground wire: that all of Mötley Crüe – Mick Mars included – are about to undergo detoxification at an expensive Californian clinic before returning to the rehearsal studio to begin work on the next Crüe album. I ask Mick for his opinion.

'Well, we're certainly cutting down on all the heavy drinking right now. Next time we go out on tour we don't wanna burn ourselves out so fast. On the recent tour I have to admit that we were in danger towards the end of getting a little bit too out of control, but nothing like as bad as some of those stories say it was. The only way you could properly understand what we have been through as a band this last year is if you'd been there with us. I know it sounds kind of lame, but you'd have to have experienced what we've been through yourself to truly understand how deeply exhausted we are right now. We did the smartest thing by cancelling the tour.'

By way of an official apology, Mick Mars says that the very next Mötley Crüe world tour will kick off with dates in Britain and Europe.

'Believe me, nobody is more disappointed and upset about what's happened than us. But it's like I say – if we had turned up, you would have been more disappointed than if you had to wait a few months until you could really see us at our best. Next time we go out on the road, we start in Britain. That's the deal.'

With recording on the next Mötley Crüe album not scheduled to begin in earnest until July, the likelihood of a tour in the UK by the band occurring much before next Christmas is slim indeed. I wonder how many genuine Crüe fans out there will be convinced enough of the band's integrity to wait that long? Because something is still wrong here, somewhere. The credibility gap remains. Mick Mars didn't laugh off a single one of the questions I asked him. He sounded like he was giving evidence. He sounded tired. Only I still don't know why. Not really.

Maybe he doesn't either . . .

CODA

As we now know from the band's thrillingly explicit 2001 autobiography, *The Dirt*, Mars' admission that their recent touring activities had gotten 'a little bit too out of control' was the understatement of the year, and that my own, in retrospect, mildly put assertions that there was surely more to their sudden cancellation of their UK dates than mere 'tiredness' (or indeed snow on the roof of Wembley Arena), were actually spot-on. In fact, the reality was even worse than anyone outside the band's immediate circle suspected back then. Nikki Sixx had overdosed so badly, at one point, that his heart had stopped beating for several minutes, while Vince Neil had nearly severed the tendons in his wrist after putting his fist through a backstage mirror (apparently because the jar of mayonnaise in his dressing room was smaller than the one in Tommy Lee's – or some such).

Poor old Mick Mars, though. I almost felt sorry for him as he floundered around uneasily on the phone to me, doing his best to keep a lid on things as I probed him for 'the truth'. Not for the first time, Mars was left with egg on his face. Maybe that's why it's always been so white . . .

DEEP PURPLE, 1985

Apart from his extraordinary guitar playing, probably the two big things Ritchie Blackmore was known for back then were: a) his antipathy towards most music journalists, in particular British music journalists, and b) his spectacular wind-ups, of anyone and everyone, including his own band. No one was safe. So when he chose to turn the occasion of what was supposed to be a five-minute phone interview for a news story to announce the newly re-formed Deep Purple's British comeback show at Knebworth, into an excuse to have me fly halfway around the world to meet him face-to-face, I suspected he was indulging both passions: putting me to a great deal of trouble in order to wind up a member of the British press.

When, as you will see, he then gave me the runaround, claiming to have waited for me in a bar he had not actually told me he would be in, I was convinced I was on a typical Blackmore goose-chase. Even if I did manage to pin him down for an interview, I had been warned to expect the worst. 'He hates cunts like you,' a roadie friend told me confidently. What did he mean, like 'me'? 'You know, smart-arses.'

I didn't feel so very smart, though, sitting on the plane from London over to New York. Given just twenty-four hours' notice, I'd barely had time to buy a new cassette-tape and change my kegs, let alone come up with questions clever enough to pique the interest of the Man in Black.

Fortunately, Blackmore turned out to be nothing like I had expected. The air of mystery was all a sham, as he told me himself. There wasn't anything he was afraid to talk about; it was just that most of the questions he tended to get asked were so boring. Most journalists were like sheep: easily startled.

I tried not to bleat too much and even though I didn't quite manage it, he seemed to appreciate the effort . . .

Interview with Ritchie Blackmore of Deep Purple, first published in Kerrang! *June 1985.*

New York City: the Warwick Hotel over on West 54th Street. It's 2.30 in the morning and in Room 1110 the telephone is ringing. A sleepless hand reaches out and grabs the receiver, lifting it tight to a sleeping head. 'Yeah?' the word crawls out of my gob like a snake from a sandpit. On the other end of the wire is Bruce Payne, manager of Deep Purple. 'What happened?' he barks down the line. 'Ritchie waited in the bar for you for two hours! And you didn't show! What happened?'

'Whaddayamean Ritchie waited in the bar for two hours? I get straight off the plane and make it over to the hotel in double-quick fashion. I don't even know for certain if there's going to be a room reserved for me, I don't know when, where or how I'm supposed to be getting together with Ritchie, so what do I do? It's Friday in New York, do I go out on the razz and hit the clubs? Do I crawl on my hands and knees into the bar and launch myself ass-first into a bottle, any bottle? Do I fuck! I sit in my hotel room and wait. I need instructions, I need orders and I am a good boy and so I wait and nothing do I hear, no more do I know until this very phone call. Shit, so what do I do now? Can I talk to Ritchie tomorrow? Is he pissed off? Has the whole deal been shot down in flames and am I about to be the proud receiver of a *Kerrang!*-sized boot up my ass?'

Two long seconds of silence . . .

'No, you wait and sit tight until I ring you back in the morning,' says Bruce, sensing that my nerves are raw and my head's on backwards. The phone dies slowly in my hands.

The following p.m. the phone starts up again and this time I'm ready.

'Do you play soccer?'

'Uh, well, yeah,' I say.

'OK, good. This is what you do. Ritchie says he came to you last night so now it's your turn to go to him. The thing is, Ritchie is playing football this afternoon so he suggests you have a game too and then get the interview together. What do you say? You'll have to take a train out to Long Island and we'll worry about getting you to the airport afterwards.'

Bruce's voice is all smiles. The deal struck, I spend the next forty-five minutes limbering up round the fixtures and fittings in my room, psyching myself up into classic Bryan Robson animal-magic pose. If it's football they want, I am going to make damn sure I can shoot the ball with both feet. But an hour into the training programme the phone is doing its ring-thing again.

It's Bruce. 'There's been a change of plan,' he announces and, oh no, I can feel my mood of doom and gloom in June returning. But the voice inside my head tells me to stay cool and I listen patiently. 'We're gonna send a car over to pick you up and take you to a restaurant in Long Island at six where you'll have dinner with Ritchie and you can do the interview then, while you're having your meal. What do you say?'

I say I'm disconnecting this damn phone from the wall before you change your mind again. Some time later I'm leaning into a fine Bloody Mary at a table reserved for Mr Blackmore and his guests. Out the window I can see Ritchie Blackmore and his friends walking up the drive towards the eatery and my stomach turns over like a Ferris wheel in a force-nine gale. I don't get nervous as a rule – too long in the tooth and knob for that sort of kiddie kick – but hell, this is Ritchie Blackmore! The Man in Black! The One That Never Talks! And what am I but a short-arsed scribbler from Soho? And so I remove my nose from the red juice and stand to attention when the man walks in the room and finally we meet.

I needn't have worried. Contrary to all the preconceived ideas every-body and their milkman threw at me when they knew I was making the trip to meet Ritchie Blackmore, in person he's warm, friendly and very good company indeed. The first thing he does is break all the rules by smiling, and so as we both sit down and I grin back at him it's time to cut the bullshit and do what I came to do – talk.

Do you see the forthcoming Knebworth Fayre show as an important gig for the band?

'Oh, yeah, very important. The pressure is always on in England. Although I don't know too much about the gig itself. Knebworth?

Nah – I'm off to see U2 myself that day!' A wry smile creases the corners of the mouth. (It had just been announced that U2 would be playing Milton Keynes Bowl the same day as Purple headlined Knebworth.)

Why just the one UK date, though? It seems strange after doing a string of gigs elsewhere in the world, like Australia, et cetera?

'We took a kind of vote. Some of the band wanted to do more gigs and some wanted to do one big one. But it's so difficult when you've got a big production to break even when you play England, which is why not too many bands go there. I wanted to do a few gigs – one in Scotland, one in Birmingham, two in London, something like that, but I was overruled by . . . someone, I can't remember who. Someone I met in a pub somewhere I expect,' he deadpans. 'I don't like to be judged on one gig because it's inevitably a disappointment, everything goes wrong. I could say the halls in Britain aren't big enough but I don't really know the answers. I can just see people saying now, "Oh the halls aren't big enough to hold Ritchie's head!" I know if it was down to Ian Gillan the band would do every club and hall in Britain, but I don't know, politics come into play and all kinds of things and it's ended up that the band is doing a European tour with three days off before Knebworth and three days off after so we probably could have done something more. I think it's got to the point where I can't even remember the real reasons why we're not doing a British tour. We're gonna kick off the European tour by playing a small club date in Sweden, actually. Just invite members of the fan club, and do it secretly so the promoter doesn't start charging people a fortune to see it.'

When was the last time you played in a club?

'Oh, Christ . . . a club? Well, I play in a club here in Long Island a lot, a place called Sparks just down the road; it's a heavy metal club. If there's ever a really simple three-chord blues I'll jump up with the band and play a bit. I get into a lot of fights over the football table though,' he chuckles.

Switching back to Knebworth a sec, with U2 holding their festival the same day as yours, do you see the Milton Keynes bash as a threat to Purple's attendance figures, to your prestige?

'I thought it was very strange that they would go out the same day. Originally they were going to hold their gig a couple of weeks later and then suddenly they changed their minds and chose the same day as us. It's not a threat, but it is a challenge, they've certainly got a big audience. We'll be very aware that U2 are playing down the road. I wasn't pissed off when I found out that they were playing, but I was more than a bit suspicious. People in the so-called hierarchy have looked into it for me and they say that it's definitely not a move to deliberately upset us, but at first I thought it was.

'I'm always suspicious of anybody though; there's always undercurrents and undertones of suspicion that I seek out and look for in people. I always look for the bad in people – and I'm sure they see it in me. Mmm, the U2 thing I thought was very strange. Of all the weekends there are in summer to play, you know? I'm sure there's a promoter hidden away somewhere who's responsible, someone who's been crossed in the past with an ancient axe to grind.'

Would you take a poor attendance at Knebworth as a direct snub from the British fans?

'No, not a direct snub, because being English I know how we think and it would just be the luck of the draw. It would be just another concert to go to and it would mean people just weren't interested in us at that particular time. As we have no big commercial hit out we will attract the real heavy staunch followers. We'd like to get through to the people that buy hits as well but if you're not on *Top of the Pops* then, well – I'm still kind of nervous about the event, not sure how it'll turn out. We'll see.'

It's been a good twelve months since the announcement that Deep Purple had re-formed. At the time there must have been a great many personal expectations within the band for the coming album and world tour; have you fulfilled a lot of those expectations, Ritchie?

'Funnily enough, yes. I didn't have too many expectations, I thought "Sod it, let's do it!". I was sick of all the rumours and I said "Let's get on with it", and Roger [Glover] said "I'm with you!". I couldn't believe the business we did and the amount of records we sold. We had to double up everywhere we went – Australia, Germany, America – and I was worried about filling out one show in each city. In fact, we ended up doing two sold-out nights everywhere.

'It's nice to know that so many people wanted to come along to the shows. Deep down inside I'm a very cynical person and I always think no one's going to show up, no one's interested. That's why I shy away from interviews because I can be very negative and I don't want to represent the band in a negative way, the unit that I'm with at the time. I was surprised how well everything worked. I thought it would happen in America, though; having lived here so long myself I knew there was a real buzz, you know: when are they going to get back together? The Americans do tend to stick by their bands, their Black Sabbaths. It takes a hell of a lot longer to make it over here than in England, but once you have made it they don't forget you, which is good from a musician's point of view. You can relax and just play forever.'

When you came to choose the material for the show, how did you reach a decision on what to play and what to throw away?

'What we did is, I sat down and thought, well, what's going to show me off as a brilliant guitar player, and then I told the rest of them what we would be playing!'

It's nice to see Blackmore sparring humorously with his own The Man and His Dark Moods image, and we both sit there laughing at each other again. All the same I press the point.

'I'm so used to manipulating a band, as with Rainbow, that I tend to be very domineering with my thoughts. So I said: "I think this is a good repertoire", and Roger looked at it and thought it was good, but wanted to add another number, I think it was "Mary Long".'

Oh, do you play 'Mary Long' in the show then?

'No. We don't do it, see what I mean? And Jon [Lord] was happy to go along with the set because I think Jon was just very nervous about the whole thing anyway and not particularly into the repertoire, more just how it was all going to sound after so many years. Luckily, everybody feels happy about all the numbers that we play on stage, which is good because sometimes, most times, there's always one or two numbers you don't like playing. For instance, we don't do "Woman from Tokyo", even though it was a big hit here in America and, uh, Camberley, Surrey!'

Do you play any numbers from the *Who Do We Think We Are* album (the very last LP the Mark II line-up recorded before Gillan split for an early 'retirement')? It never struck me as the happiest-sounding album.

'No, it wasn't a happy album, very strained. I can't even remember what was on it, but I don't think we play anything from it, no.'

Would you like to break into the singles market again? You had a lot of hits in the Seventies.

'Yeah, but it's always worked very strangely for us. "Woman from Tokyo" was a big hit here, but I don't think it was even released in England. Whereas "Black Night" was a big hit in Britain and did nothing here. "Smoke on the Water", meanwhile, was only a hit on its third release here in America; I mean, it got to like Number Two but it took three goes to do it. That just goes to show that you have to keep going with something you have faith in even if it means re-releasing things.'

Before the very first reunion gig in Australia, did you or any of the band lose any sleep?

'I don't know. I don't make it my habit to sleep with the rest of the band if I can help it. I think it has been known for some of them to sleep together, though. I have heard rumours about the management and the bass player sleeping together.'

Only if it's been a good gig though, right? He snorts derisively.

'Yeah, right . . . No, actually, for that first gig I just got drunk; whisky comes in very handy, I find. I usually have a level I drink down to before a gig. It's kind of below the label by about an inch.'

Is this Scotch or Bourbon?

'Oh, Scotch; I'm still British, you know! Whenever I think of Bourbon I think of all those silly American boogie bands from the South, what are they called? Molly Hatchet, that's the one. I can see them in the back of their tour bus swigging their bloody Bourbon.'

When I drink whisky it turns me into a raving lunatic with a very bad temper, which is OK if you happen to be John Wayne, but can get you into trouble if you're not, you know?

'Well, when I drink whisky it doesn't turn me into John Wayne. I turn into Oliver Reed! And then I usually punch someone and run, let everybody else get on with it.'

After you've played a particularly exciting gig, how do you relax?

'I try and drink as much water as possible because I'm usually so drunk at that point. I drink all through a gig, and afterwards it feels like my body is saying "no more"! I end up feeling so guilty that I've drunk so much that I walk around guzzling water and pretending I'm perfectly healthy. The reason I drink onstage, though, is because I think I'm actually quite a shy person and to be on a stage you have to project and that only really comes out when I'm drunk. That's why I do it.'

Doesn't that waste you, though, on a long tour?

'Yeah, it does. The travelling doesn't get to me, or the playing, it's the drinking. It's a stimulant which can keep you up most of the night so you might end up taking a sleeping tablet or something, but it's a problem everybody has I think. When we have a day off I never go to the bar, just try and keep the system clean for twenty-four hours.'

Are you into taking vitamins or stuff like that?

'Yeah, I am. It gets ridiculous, though. I started off taking multi-vitamins, then I thought, I need more C, then I thought, well, I'm a nervous wreck so I started taking extra B. Then the real games began because I started thinking my muscles were tense or tired so I started taking more E. Then I found I was lacking potassium from some doctor who told me I needed it, so I took that every other day. I used to have a lot of back problems. I got injured in one of the games of football I played, which developed into a muscle-spasm, which set off all my other muscles, and in the end I couldn't play [guitar]. I was tingling all along my arm. This was just before the last European tour with Rainbow and I didn't think I was going to make it. Every time I put the guitar strap on I pinched a nerve and I couldn't move my fingers properly without pain. I had a masseur on the road with me all the time to massage the muscles and it was always touch and go whether I was going to make the date. During the day my hand kept seizing up.'

Didn't that freak you out?

'Yeah, I started getting really worried. It turned out I had an arthritic joint in the back of the neck. They X-rayed it and told me I had degenerative arthritis. I was immediately panicking, I thought that was it, I was dying, it was all over. But the doctor told me to relax and said that I didn't have any more arthritis than any other normal thirty-nine-year-old man. Degenerative arthritis doesn't mean it's getting steadily worse and worse, it's just that as you get older you naturally get more bouts of it. It's not rheumatoid arthritis, which is the real crippler. So I went to a physiotherapist and started doing all the exercises and now I wear a copper bracelet every time I play. That and the potassium are the minerals you should always have. My mother always wears a copper bracelet, she had rheumatism, and there's always an element of truth in ancient folklore, so I thought I'd wear one too. Over the last two years – touch wood! – everything's been OK.'

Have you recorded any of the dates on the tour?

'I think we have but I'm never usually aware of it when it happens. They record so many dates that it's no big news when I get told before a gig that we're doing it.'

Is there a specific reason for recording live dates, though? Will there be a live album at some point?

'Oh, I think it's a natural habit to record gigs, just bring in a mobile and record some of the dates occasionally.'

What about a live video? Everybody's doing it these days.

'Some of the Australian dates were videoed, I think, which we used as our second video. When it comes to making videos, though, we're a lazy lot; nobody will dress up as an actor or anything ridiculous like that. We don't want to make videos. Sod that! Then the record company say you've got to make a video and we say we won't, and you get this big battle going on about it. The video they used for "Perfect Strangers" was a part of a documentary some people were making. I haven't even seen it yet. If I see myself I get totally self-conscious and turn it off. I haven't seen any of them. I heard there was a part in the "Perfect Strangers" video where you can see me smiling and I tried to get that cut out, but I was overruled!

'We just can't be bothered with videos. I'm a musician, you know? I make a record and then I'm on the road; this video business makes me crazy! There's enough to do to sell a record as it is – to think up the songs, to record them and produce them and then get the record out, and play, and then to be asked to make these stupid videos gets me crazy. I hate them! I hate MTV! I don't know if you've seen it at all but it's awful! You get people like Michael Jackson going completely overboard, spending a million making a video and monopolising the whole thing, which he did.'

I heard that the Tom Petty video for 'Don't Come Around Here No More' cost in the region of half a million dollars to make. From a businessman's point of view in the record industry, is that a worthwhile investment, that amount of bread for one video?

'I think it is. Usually, the record company puts up the money for those sorts of things and usually they pay for themselves. I mean, in terms of record sales. Tom Petty is Top Twenty in the charts here at the moment so I would say it's paid off, yeah. I can't stand it myself. I like to see a good actor and I like to see a good musician. I don't like to see a musician semi act, and I don't like to see an actor trying to play. It's always so weak. And they're always so self-conscious, these people who try and act in videos – I know I am. I play the guitar, I don't want to be an actor or I would have gone to acting school.'

Throughout the years that Deep Purple were no longer an active group there have been huge amounts of compilations and live albums and God knows what else. Now that you're back together, have you witnessed any dark figures trying to get in on the posterity kick again?

'Oh, yeah, definitely. The two guys who used to manage the group in the beginning and are not managing us now are very upset with the state of affairs as far as us being with another management and there's legal battles going on every day. In fact, they are responsible for most of the dreadful stuff that's coming out, like some of those awful Japanese things featuring Coverdale and Hughes – just collections of the same old nonsense that we did years ago. There's nothing new at all. It's very annoying; it can bring you down a lot. I was looking at the world charts in Billboard and in Italy we had something which I'd never heard of in the Top Ten, and also in Germany there was something else. All these LPs that I'd never heard of! I mean, what the hell is this? And they've done this so many times; how can they keep churning out and regurgitating the same old bloody nonsense? But they do. Unfortunately, the kids get taken for a ride; they see a new package and think there's something new on it. It's very hard to guard against it, though we are fighting huge legal battles to stop it. But, you see, it's also the old record company.'

Tell me, if someone left the band now, or there was a recurrence of the Ian Gillan departure of '73, would Purple carry on as it did back then?

'I don't think so, no. I think everybody's amazed at each other's talents at the moment. We're still in that mood. I'll watch the band when I'm offstage and Jon is taking a solo or something. I think they're all amazing, I really do. The way Ian Gillan sings – he's got such a big voice. Every other singer in rock bands these days always seems to have this thin voice which is pushed to the maximum through the PA. With Ian, he ends up shaking the place every night with the sheer power of his voice. Sometimes he loses it, he'll come off stage and he won't be able to talk. But the next night he's back and he is singing! It's great to see that. Ian comes up to me after some of the gigs and says, "You're my hero!"

'Little weird things like that go on all the time, so the band is really into each other on stage. I suppose there still could come a time when politics might again get between us, but when we're on stage we really click because we all respect each other very much. And I love the way Ian introduces songs on stage. Like with "Perfect Strangers". When we were in Japan he used to say "This next song is about a football team back in England who used to live down the road from me in Hounslow." And everybody's going "What? What's he saying? Did he mention cocaine?!" And then he'd go there was this football team and they were from a place called Perfect Street, and this is called the "Perfect Street Rangers"! Everybody was totally lost and I'd be cracking up at the side of the stage, you know? I love that type of dry humour but the Japanese didn't know whether to laugh or send away for pictures of the Perfect Street Rangers!'

Do you plan to carry on with Deep Purple to the total exclusion of doing anything else solo?

'I don't know; every now and again I'll think about that. But I feel that, although Rainbow did some good stuff, it didn't ever have the identity that Purple has. Sometimes with Purple I'll hear the end product and maybe think it should have been more like this or that, but it's always very popular with the masses. With Rainbow I had everything more or less how I wanted to hear it, but it didn't appeal as much to the masses so there's obviously something I'm not tapping into, the pulse of the masses. I don't feel that I was wrong – I had to do something on my own – but the popularity of Rainbow compared to Purple shows me that I'm not right all the time. With Rainbow I had it all my way, totally one hundred per cent, but now Ian Gillan, who is definitely not a normal person, will come up with melodies and lyrics to things I've written which I would never have thought of.

That's part of the chemistry and magic of Purple. Nobody has a voice like Ian Gillan's, and you can't say that about the Journeys, Foreigners, Survivors or Rainbows.'

There's talk in London at present that Ian Gillan is going to do a solo album; how do you feel about that?

'It's bothering me a lot. To be quite honest, I don't think he should. He's obligated to do one because of Richard Branson and Virgin Records. I think it's a very unwise move to make but he's stuck in a corner, he has to fulfil the contractual things he signed before we got together, and I get uptight about the whole thing. We're having about three or four months off and I want it to be time off; nobody should be doing anything. I don't want anybody in the group doing a solo LP because you must take time to relax; then you can come up with good ideas for the next Purple album. If you're in the studio every five minutes, that's not going to help the LP that's coming next. I've always believed in that; it's always been my philosophy to keep out of the studio as much as I can so that when I do go in, something really good will come of it.'

What would happen if Ian didn't do a solo album? Would they sue him for a lot of money?

'Yeah, I think so. From what I know of the situation, it's all very touchy. But I better not say too much or your flight back to London might be jeopardised; you're flying Virgin Atlantic, right?'

Switching the subject, the last two years have seen a lot of re-formations, what with Yes, yourselves, now ELP, and Ozzy and Sabbath doing the Live Aid gig in America; why is it happening now, do you think?

'Yeah, and now Mountain's back together. Good band, you know they're supporting us on our European dates? But you're right, it's amazing how these groups have all come back. I can't think of any solid reason why that should be and there's more than you think: Grand Funk Railroad, Three Dog Night, people that I've read about getting back together. Yes were the first, but we didn't get back together because Yes did. I mean, it took us ten years to do it, but it does seem as if the scene's gone berserk. I think it's good because if people want to go and see those bands, why not?'

Do you think perhaps that some of those musicians might have thought that the market for their music wasn't there anymore? I mean, people like Chris Squire and Keith Emerson are vastly talented musicians but, unlike every member of Purple, they never seemed to do anything once Yes and ELP had expired.

'I don't know, could be . . . it's strange. I don't think Keith Emerson did anything for ages. I know Greg Lake joined Asia for just a short time and I really liked them. Don't know what's happened to them now, though.'

And I hear that Steve Hackett and Steve Howe have formed a band together and signed to Geffen Records.

'Mmm . . . I like David Geffen. I think he expects a lot from his bands, seems to take a personal interest, and he's got a lot of discipline. He tends to crack the whip, which I think is good. I know of a few bands who he's made remix their LPs before he'll put them out for the public to buy. This guy says "No, it's not good enough to put my name to, re-mix it, re-do the whole thing!"'

That happened with the Whitesnake album, *Slide It In*, did you know?

'Yeah, I heard that. This is gonna sound weird, but I really liked the last Whitesnake LP, *Slide It In*. I liked the video to their single, very good song, should have been a hit, but it wasn't. I can't think of the title, though, I wouldn't know it, someone told me what it was. But it's very refreshing. People are always saying "What do you think of David Coverdale?" and I try and remove myself from that and it doesn't influence me. I just see the band Whitesnake as being a good band with a good singer. What I might do to him if he turns up backstage at any concerts is a whole different thing, that's personal! But I'm not that stupid that I would let it corrupt my way of thinking if I hear something. If I hear something I can say "That is good: don't like the guy, but I thought the album was very good." As usual, it wasn't a hit – not here anyway. Didn't do much, and that to me was typical. Makes me even more cynical than ever. Meanwhile, Madonna is Number One which makes you realise just how bad things are. I get these moods where I put the whole business down. I love music and I love playing guitar, being on stage, but the industry gets me crazy.'

Do you think it's got worse in the business since you started out as a musician?

'Yeah, I think so. In '68 when we first started, there was a lot more discretion – people were into whether the band were any good or not. They weren't into the novel approach. Now if the guy dresses up as a girl, or the girl dresses up as a guy, that seems to do a lot for their careers. I don't know, I could go on and on. It disgusts me, most of it. People have said I'm jealous, but I'm not jealous. I've got my audience and I do very well in this business but it does bother me to see good musicians put out of work by these fucking freaks. Your Boy Georges and people like that! They love it over here, they love that novelty gimmick approach; they jump on it. It's ridiculous. I think we're all doomed, basically.'

He's serious but the bitterness is sweetened by another unexpected smile, and a soft shrug of the shoulder.

'And I think England will probably go first,' he chuckles.

Mentioning England, could you ever see yourself living there again?

'It's my favourite country, along with Germany. Yet I find myself not moving from here in Long Island, I still stay here. I've noticed when I go back to London that the unemployment thing has got so bad that if you have a little bit of money and you can afford to buy a round of drinks people start to go "Hey, capitalistic pig here! He's alright, got a lot of money this one! He's got no problems!" And then they start in on you, sidling up to you in a bar and saying "It's alright for you, but some of us have to work for a living". That's their favourite saying: "It's alright for some". There's that kind of chip on the shoulder. But that's true of me as well: I have a chip on my shoulder, but I don't know quite what about. I'll find something. And the English are lazy. I'm lazy! Basically, we all just want to go to the pub and be mellow, hey ... Play darts, who gives a shit? But then again the English, the British, have so much creativity. For some reason we seem to come out with the most amazing things: the medicine side, the music side. The biggest strides that are made in music come from England.

'They have big people over here, but they don't seem to last, they don't seem to make a mark on history. I always put America down when I'm here and when I'm back in England I walk around saying "Typical! Typical! The bastards!" Soon as I get to Heathrow Airport they start: "Oh, you've been abroad, have you? How come you've been abroad and I haven't?" This is the customs man! "What have you got to declare?" Nothing. "Are you sure?" It's like a Basil Fawlty thing the way they look at you and talk to you. "You better come with us, sir." Uh, yes, I'd better come with you. Very English. There are ways of getting through British customs officials, though – wear a top hat and carry a javelin. Then they look at you and go this man is trying to cause attention, he's obviously creating a diversion for this old woman here!' Meanwhile, you walk through with a spear going "Hello! Hello!" Your spear, of course, is full of anything you want it to be. And they go "Naw, too obvious".' He barks with laughter.

Are there any new British rock bands that have sprung up since the '70s who have impressed you? I'm thinking specifically of Iron Maiden, Def Leppard, that generation, you know?

'Maiden have got a great football team. We still owe them a game. They beat us five–four the last time we played, but I'll get them! Steve Harris is a good footballer, got a goal on the volley straight from a corner. That impressed me.'

Steve Harris told me that he thought you were a good footballer but that you could be a bit lazy; wait till you got the ball then use it.

'Yeah, that's right. That's very true, especially in that game. It's my biggest fault; I can't always be bothered with running back. I don't work the field. If I've got the ball I'm alright, but I'm not gonna run up and down. That's very true.

'Def Leppard have a very fresh sound, I can see why people over here like them. They're very fresh, almost like a Beatles thing. It's still a little bit rough, but it's got glamour in it and they look right. America went berserk for Def Leppard the year before last. It was nice to see Van Halen knocked off their perch. They're a little bit smug; they think they've got it all sewn up. Ian Paice is a big fan of Leppard's you know?'

What about Mötley Crüe and Rätt?

'It's all been done fifteen years ago. They don't have that spark of creativity. It's all copying, bits of Van Halen, bits of this, bits of that, I can see everything in them.'

What about The Firm?

'I've seen a few videos, but I haven't seen them play. I think it's good that they're doing something. Paul Rodgers is a good singer.'

Did you ever rate Page as a guitarist?

'I've said it before. He's a strange guitar player. He's not the type of guy you can say is brilliant – no musical theory – but he has a way of writing good riffs, things like "Kashmir" and some of the other Zeppelin stuff. His riffs were great. He's not a player I would attack. He puts down a very coloured construction to a song; he's a very colourful player of the guitar. It's pleasing to hear because I don't feel I have to be on my toes all the time and fence with somebody. He's not the latest gunslinger in town, you know? You can get so fast that it gets silly, but Jimmy's not like that. There are a lot of guys doing that now, though, going berserk on the fret-board and I feel like telling them to settle down, say something, what is all this? It's like quoting Shakespeare at one hundred miles per hour. It's like having sex for five minutes listening to some of these guys.'

You're right. I bet they're not even good in bed.

'Well, I wouldn't know about that, thank you. I think this is where we came in . . .'

CODA

I'm aware that quite a few of these postscripts involve me admitting I could not have imagined what happened next. However, you really would have to have been Nostradamus to have foreseen the unexpected turn Blackmore's career path would take over the next decade. That he would eventually fall out with the other members of Deep Purple to the degree that he would walk out – not once, but twice – before finally turning his back on them for good in 1993, was always a possibility. It was what he did after that that had many of his fans – and not a few critics – scratching their heads. After a false start trying to reinvigorate his solo rock vehicle, Rainbow, he teamed up with his new wife, New York vocalist Candice Night, to form Blackmore's Night, a musical outfit in the Renaissance-style, replete with mandolin, domra, hurdy gurdy, violin, flute and other attendant instrumentation. They even took to dressing up onstage in the garb of wandering minstrels, encouraging audience members to do the same, and specialising in performing in haunted castles and Renaissance fairs.

Needless to say, this turned him into a figure of fun to some people, including this one. Now, of course, I see I was wrong. After all, isn't Blackmore doing precisely what I have recently spent time trying to persuade Jimmy Page he should also be doing – i.e. forgetting about the lumbering dinosaur of a group that made him famous and getting back to the simple pleasure of making music for its own sake?

With folk-rock now enjoying a huge resurgence of mainstream interest in Britain, Blackmore – once again, it seems – is having the last laugh.

IRON MAIDEN, 1988

Although I was hardly a typical fan of their music – it's a long time since I've been a spotty adolescent – I always looked forward to my encounters with Iron Maiden. With the exception of their would-be 'renaissance man' singer, Bruce Dickinson, who always, to me, fancied himself a cut above the rest – until his solo career went belly-up, at which point he was more than happy to be 'welcomed' back into the fold – the men in Maiden were a defiantly down-to-earth, unfussy bunch, as epitomised by their staunchly working-class leader Steve ''Arry' Harris.

Square of jaw and tattooed of arm, I also liked it that Steve refused to bend over for a hit single, even when the temptation to do so must have been tremendous. In a parallel universe, Iron Maiden would have been as globally humongous as their former disciples Metallica. But Steve Harris would rather gnaw off his own knob than work with a commercially sugared producer like Bob Rock. You could argue that it's that kind of bloody-mindedness that has held back Maiden over the years: certainly, they have never been as big in America as they might have been because of it. That said, there has always been so much pride in what Maiden did that Steve would never allow the band to simply cruise among the also-rans of the second tier of rock, the way so many bands that now plough the 'classic rock' furrow are happy to.

Iron Maiden interview, Cologne, first published in Kerrang!,
16 April 1988.

Flight time from Heathrow: 1.30 p.m. Arrive Frankfurt: 4.30 p.m. Drive
to Castle Schnellenberg, arrive: 7.00 p.m. Begin interviews: 7.30 p.m.
Finish: open-ended. It looked like a long day ahead, and another long
night. Working, that is. The one subject I failed in at school. The
important thing, therefore, at this stage, I decided, was not to get too
drunk. I would sink just the one or two on the plane and call it a day
until I'd punched the clock on the interviews. Three, maybe, but that
was max. There, I'd talked myself into it. At last, I figured, I must be
turning pro.

I fill a bag and take a train to the airport. I make it on time, good
old me the pro, and when I get there my old mate, Rangi, is there to
meet me. Rangi has worked for Steve Harris and Iron Maiden longer
than most; part-security, part-crew, and full-time china-plate to 'Arry
and the boys, he has a nice line in gritty Kiwi patter, and fists the size
of my face.

'Hello, my old mate! How are ya?' I say in greeting.

'I'm all right,' says Rangi, his eyes scouring the horizon of the over-
crowded departure lounge. 'But your other old mate isn't here yet and
the flight leaves in half an hour.'

The other old mate Rangi refers to is Maiden drummer Nicko
McBrain. Nicko isn't late yet, but another ten minutes and he will be.
The minutes run away ... five ... ten ... fifteen to go before the big
metal bird flies.

I hear him coming long before I see him.

'MICKEY!' he hollers.

'Nicko!' I cry.

'RANGI!!' he bellows.

'Nicko!' Rangi cries.

'MICKEEE!! RANGEEEEE!!! Am I late? We've still got time for
a wet, surely?'

Suddenly the Mad McBrain is in our midst. With ten minutes to go we manage to make it through customs and passport control and head like men possessed for the bar. DOWN they go, in ones and twos. Then OFF we run like bastards for the plane.

'Always the last to arrive and always the last to leave, my dear,' says Nicko in passing to the stewardess with the stopwatch in her hand as we step aboard the plane. I grab the seat next to Nicko and another stewardess leans over and sticks two drinks in our hands. 'Now that's what I call service,' I tell him.

'MICKEE!' he roars, a big Rasputin smile spreading across his face.

'Nicko!'

'CHEERS!'

And down they go. Just as the plane is starting to go up, up, UP.

We're still doing a forward dance along the ground-to-air diagonal when the next two drinks arrive. At this point the pro in me begins sending out mental reminders about the three-drink-max limit I had set myself. The pro in me sounds very stern, and for a moment I sit there looking at my drink and listening to him go at it. But not for long.

'MICKEE!!'

'Nicko!'

Down they go again, and with them goes the pro in me, on his knees and begging. Nicko calls for the jug. They've just turned the No Smoking sign off. We're still not horizontal, but the pilot takes care of that problem in his way, and me and Nicko take care of it in ours. By the time we've reached our fifth drink, the pro in me is still babbling on. But he's starting to sound like a damn fool, and besides, he sounds like he's been drinking . . .

'MICKEE!!' the voice goes again, only this time it's mine. We kill the fifth drink.

We arrive in Frankfurt at the same time as Steve Harris and Dave Murray. All of the band have flown in from their various hideouts around the world: Steve from his villa in the Algarve, Dave from a holiday in Tenerife and Nicko from Houston, Texas, via London, where he's been out conducting a travelling drum clinic all over America for the past three weeks. Adrian Smith arrived from Nassau earlier in the day and is already waiting for us at the Castle. Bruce Dickinson, who miraculously has not just returned from a fencing tournament, is already in Germany and has driven direct to the Castle alone. The air is rife with the sound of voices barking out the greetings.

'DAVEE!'

'Nicko!'

'STEEVE!'

'Nicko!'

'Rangi!'

'MICKEE!'

'Steve!'

'Davey!'

'Nicko!'

We're all still shouting at each other as we climb aboard the minibus for the two-hour drive from the airport to the Castle. There's a blizzard raging outside. The sky is black but the ground is white-white-white as far as the eye can see. The beers go around the back of the van and the journey is considerably shortened.

'Have you heard the new album yet?' Steve asks me somewhere along the road. I grin and nod my head.

'I've had a tape for the last couple of days and I haven't stopped playing it,' I tell him.

'Well?' he grins.

'Well, that's it, isn't it, you've done it,' I say. 'The ultimate Iron Maiden album! How on earth are you going to follow it up?'

He looks at me and smiles. 'I'm glad you feel like that about it. Everyone that's heard it so far has said something like that. We've never quite managed to pull anything off like this before. For me, it's like the enormous leap we suddenly made from our first two albums to releasing *Number of the Beast* – very much a step forward, a step up,' Steve says, then pauses. 'How we're ever going to be able to follow it up, though . . .' He puffs out his cheeks and blows. 'Fucked if I know!' he laughs. 'We'll just have to wait and see, won't we.'

We sit there quietly for a moment thinking it over. In the distance, perched upon a clump of dark, snow-capped hills – where else? – lies the good Castle Schnellenberg, home for all of us for the next few days. With its medieval towers and creaky, winding staircase, its cavernous wings and concealed corridors, it is the ideal spot in which to unveil the new Iron Maiden album, *Seventh Son of a Seventh Son*, in all its atmospheric splendour.

The official playback for the album – the first of some half-dozen such events to be staged around the world over the next few weeks to herald its release on 11 April – is scheduled for tomorrow night, but already the cream of Europe's media establishment is lining up for a piece of the action. Press lizards, TV barons, radio hams, photographers by the swarm, over the next few days they will all converge on the Castle like hungry bees around a honey pot. Every waking moment the band have will be spent entertaining a production line of interviewers, mikes and cameras thrust forward like swinging lights in their faces, lapping up an endless stream of quotes, jokes, anecdotes, stiff one-liners, all the general upbeat gibberish those things eventually lapse into. And it all starts tonight.

Bang on 7.00 p.m. we pull into the grounds of Castle Schnellenberg and park between two snow ploughs. Inside the Castle all is warm and cosy and nineteenth century. I keep expecting an Igor or a Gregor or something to show up with a face like stone and a candle that never goes out in one hand and bid us: 'Welcome. The master has been expecting you …' But Shaun Hutson couldn't make it, so it never happens. Although their first TV interviews are due to start at 7.30 p.m., the band have only just arrived and nobody has eaten anything yet, so a hasty dinner is arranged and the schedules are unceremoniously pushed back a couple of hours.

Seated around a large round table in a private room to one side of the Castle's main dining hall, everybody – minus Adrian, who's still in his room sleeping off the effects of the long flight from Nassau – tucks into big plates of rich, heavy German sustenance. To my right is yet another old mate of mine, Bruce Dickinson. We last met on New Year's Eve and Bruce was talking incessantly about the new album even then, unable to stop himself raving about it being something like 'a heavy metal *Dark Side of the Moon*', but with a big hit single thrown in there for good measure somewhere along the line. 'Or at least as close as we're ever likely to come to it!' he thundered with laughter, his eyes staring past my shoulder.

We met again a few days prior to the trip to Germany. He was still talking about the album.

'If *Number of the Beast* brought heavy metal properly into the 1980s, which I actually believe it did, then with *Seventh Son of a Seventh Son* I think we've shown the way for heavy metal in the 1990s. It sounds like such a boastful thing to say, I know, but that's how it hits me when I listen to it. I hear new stuff on there I haven't heard before every time I play it. I'm completely hooked on the whole bloody thing! Perhaps I need help, what do you think?'

Bruce repeats the question to me over dinner at the Castle. I've had time to think about it since we last met, and of course I've had a tape of the album to help me make up my mind. And what I think is this: this is it, kiddos! The One! 100 per cent Diamond Maiden! Treasure from the deep nobody expected to find. A 'concept' album in the most direct sense – meaning, it has a beginning, a middle and an end, just like all the best stories – *Seventh Son* . . . is also, surprisingly, the most plausible feat of magic the band have ever worked inside a recording studio. Eight highly stylised original numbers, all bright and polished enough to stand out on their own, worlds within worlds unto themselves, separate and unique, yet bound quite stealthily together by the continually overlapping layers of the strange and beguiling story that gradually unravels.

Which is? Well, put simply, the Seventh Son of a Seventh Son of the title to our story is born into the world endowed, as befitting his occult status, with certain extraterrestrial powers – the power to heal the sick and to foretell the future being prominent amongst his gifts (although the one thing he cannot foresee is his own horrific demise).

'It's the grandest and most fascinating tale of all,' says Bruce at one point. 'The classic story of Good versus Evil, only with no guarantees whatsoever that it's the good guys who eventually come through. Nothing and nobody comes out of his story unscathed! Which is everyone's story, really, isn't it? None of us gets through our lives smelling of roses everywhere we go; everything is a constant battle to try and stay sane, to cut through all the bullshit that gets shoved our way. To find some sort of meaning, some pattern. At the same time, there's more to it than that. It's a quite mythical tale, the saga of the Seventh Son of the Seventh Son, and in trying to tell it we really allowed our imaginations to run free.'

'We've always been at our best, I think, when we've told a story of some kind through the lyrics to our songs,' Steve points out. '"Rime of the Ancient Mariner", "Stranger in a Strange Land", "Number of the Beast" – all of our best stuff has always told a clear story, really. It's one of the things we're really good at, and it's working in a way that is very inspiring for us. Deciding to extend this particular story into an album came naturally. It didn't make the actual writing any easier, though, knowing what the basic outline was; in fact, I probably took longer over the writing I've done on this album than any I've done before. But the stuff we all started coming up with, once we'd agreed that we were definitely going for a fully-fledged "concept" album, really startled me. It was so much better than anything we'd done in ages, and we all started to get really excited about what we might be able to do with it all once we got inside the studio with Martin Birch, our producer.'

Side One opens with the same melancholy chords that later close Side Two: strummed carelessly on an acoustic guitar by Adrian Smith as Bruce Dickinson wails balefully over the intro: 'Seven deadly sins / Seven ways to win / Seven holy paths to hell / And your trip begins . . .'

And then the electric guitars arrive like a siren followed by an explosion, the whole shebang going off like a powder keg, the noise of synthesisers pounding like a strobe in the background, the drums finally raining down in strong, lightning fast blows. The track is 'Moonchild' and it is Maiden at their bones-into-dust best: heightened, exotic rhythms coiled like a snake over everything, the guitars and the drums spinning the world just a little too fast, the voice savage and brutal. I'm not going to sprint through a track-by-track read-out here; that job has already been admirably taken care of elsewhere in this issue by my very old mate, Chris Welch. However, special mention must be made for tracks like the Steve Harris compositions 'Infinite Dreams' and the title track itself: two of the most awesome moments on a collection bristling with grandeur.

A comment on the first single from the album, 'Can I Play with Madness?', is perhaps appropriate, too. Yes, it is by far the most commercial thing Maiden have recorded since . . . oh, since 'Run to the Hills', at least. And I'm glad to see it happen. The band have always been finicky about singles. Brushing playfully with commercialism has never been what you would call a hot pursuit of theirs. And now this. Straight out of left field comes an Iron Maiden song with the legs to carry it into the Top Three! Who would've believed it?!

Interestingly, five out of the eight numbers written for *Seventh Son* ... are collaborative efforts. This has reversed the trend for group members to work alone that began around the time of 1983's *Piece of Mind* album, and reached its apotheosis with the band's last album, in 1986, *Somewhere in Time*, which featured three tracks written by Adrian alone, four by Steve alone, and just one, 'Deja-Vu', co-written by Steve and Dave. On *Seventh Son* ... two of the tracks are credited to Smith/Dickinson/Harris ('Can I Play with Madness?' and 'The Evil That Men Do'); one to Smith/Dickinson ('Moonchild'); one to Murray/Harris ('The Prophesy'); one to Harris/Dickinson ('Only the Good Die Young'); leaving just three credited to Steve Harris alone ('Infinite Dreams', 'Seventh Son ...' and 'The Clairvoyant').

Somehow, the spreading of responsibility for the writing has given the album an injection of vigour, of spirit and excitement usually reserved for the band's more inspired live performances.

'We didn't consciously decide we must all start writing together more,' says Steve Harris, as the dinner things are being trawled away and the first of several TV crews leave the dining room to return upstairs and set up their lights and cameras in time for the first interviews to begin in fifteen minutes. 'It just worked out like that this time. We probably spent more time checking up on each other to see what everybody else was up to, just to make sure the story fitted properly and went somewhere. As a result, it was only natural that we should end up writing together more this time than we have done perhaps on the last couple of studio albums. But these things happen of their own accord; it's no good trying to force something to work. At the end of the day it doesn't really matter who writes the songs, as long as they're good. That's what it's all about. Keeping the ideas flowing; not writing together because we think we should, but doing it when we get real pleasure out of wanting to create a new number together.'

The other mild innovation this time around has been the introduction of synthesisers and keyboards to the quintessential sheet-metal Maiden sound; as evinced best on the new album on tracks like 'Moonchild' and the title track itself. My memory clouds over, but didn't someone from Maiden once say that 'there would never be any keyboards on an Iron Maiden album'? Bruce raises an eyebrow. 'Yes, it was probably me, drunk out of my mind in some foreign bar somewhere,' he chortles. 'Which just goes to prove you should never ever say never to anything! But I was probably a foolish young man back whenever it was that was said. I never knew we'd be able to do this with them.'

The lyrics are uncompromisingly forceful on the new album. Maiden are famous, of course, for not mincing their words, and in the past they have suffered the same slings and arrows from right-wing fundamentalist groups in the USA, such as the Moral Majority and the PMRC, that have continued to dog the careers of acts like Ozzy Osbourne, Metallica, the Beastie Boys – you know the names. Particularly hard to shake was the furore that surrounded the band's 1982 Beast on the Road tour of America. With scattered lines littered throughout the new material such as, 'Don't you dare to save your son / Kill him now and save the young ones / Be the mother of a birth-strangled babe / Be the Devil's own / Lucifer's my name … ', for example, from 'Moonchild', are the band concerned at all at the predictable reaction such material, pulled out of context as I just did, might receive from the right-wing bimbos waiting for them in America with their rolling pins in their hands and their disgusting petitions and vulgar, two-bit pamphlets on full church-day parade?

'You mean from people like Mr Jimmy "Forgive Me For I Have Sinned" Swaggart?' sneers Bruce. 'The man who wrote a book called *Music as Pornography* with a picture of Steve on the cover and has just been discovered crawling around a motel room with a prostitute and then goes on national television to cry about it? You want to know if we're worried about what people like that will have to say about the lyrics on our new album? Listen, the day those people stop having a go at us is the day I'll start getting worried. It rots the brain to even think about the twisted minds of people like that for too long. So we don't. We never give it a thought.'

'You can't allow yourself to descend to their level,' says Steve. 'It's no good getting upset about these fanatics like Swaggart and the PMRC; that's the reaction they want to get out of you. I say let 'em pull any line they like out of any of the songs from any of our albums and twist it around until it suits them, I don't care. I'm not going to let it interfere with writing exactly what I want to. Besides, whatever we write, they'll always find something to pick up on and go mad about. So I just try to completely ignore anything they might have to say about us. It's always the same old clichéd Devil-worshipping thing, too! You'd think they'd have thought of something new by now.'

Indeed, the mention of 'Devil-worshipping', however, inevitably leads to the subject of those bands that still trade on their image under such facile banners.

'Mentioning no names, but this whole thrash and death metal thing really leaves me cold,' says Steve. 'Apart from Metallica, who have done some good stuff, most of the other bands completely pass me by. They've got nothing going for them that I look for in a band. For a start, most of them couldn't write a decent melody line – as in write a real song – if their lives depended on it! I often wonder if it's got something to do with the fact that most of these bands don't seem to have very good singers, not in the traditional heavy metal sense of really good singers, anyway. You know, like they can only sing in one really gruff style. I had a similar problem in the early days of Maiden with Paul Di'Anno singing in the band. His singing voice simply wasn't versatile enough, and because of that I could only write songs in the one style he was able to sing them in. With a singer like Bruce in the band, of course, the whole thing changes because there's probably nothing that Bruce couldn't sing if he put his mind to it, which enables me to write songs in any key, any style, any time, any rhythm that I want to because I know Bruce will always be able to handle it.'

Nevertheless, bands like Metallica, Anthrax and Slayer, for example, have all been making impressive inroads into the international scene these past two years. How aware were Maiden when they went into the studio to record *Seventh Son* ... that there were now newer, younger bands out there snapping at their heels?

'Not in the least bit,' says Steve. 'We never consider what any other band, no matter who, are doing when we go to work on a new Maiden album. I'm not interested in what everyone else is doing. I'm too into what we're doing ourselves to think any further than that. You say there are all these bands out there waiting to steal our thunder, but I don't feel like that at all. Good luck to whoever comes along next, that's what I say. There are plenty of good new bands around who I do like, and I follow them all, but that's as far as it goes. I don't feel like there's anybody about to overtake us.'

I leave the boys to their TV interviews and decide to hit the long wooden hills to Bedfordshire. Tomorrow is another beer, as they say.

The following afternoon at Castle Schnellenberg finds the band trooping from room to room, from interviewer to interviewer, while outside half-a-dozen different TV crews zigzag through the snow in search of the ideal location shot, haggling with the roving press photographers for exclusive rights to the choicest spots they can weigh up through their viewfinders. Along one wall in the basement bierkeller of the Castle sit a line of journos listening to Walkmans, all with the new Maiden album blasting out of them. Nobody gets to talk to the band until they've heard the album at least once. Every twenty minutes or so another journo will get a tap on the shoulder and be led nervously away to one of the distant wings of the Castle where one or more of the band will carry out their duties as gentlemen hosts.

By evening another one hundred or so media faces have arrived in coaches. The playback, at 8.00 p.m., is a huge success, the room erupting into applause at the death of Side Two, the rest of the evening lost in a ferocious feast of back-slapping and yaw-hawing as the wine goes down and the room starts to get loose, everyone relieved as much as anything that the whole new Maiden deal is finally, officially, off the ground and running.

3.00 a.m. and the last guests have long since called it a night and fled the Castle. The last to leave are Steve, myself, Maiden's indestructible manager, Rod Smallwood, and the band's London PR, Roland Hyams. Steve invites us to desecrate the mini-bar in his room, and so, not to be impolite, we agree. Once up there and glasses filled, the talk turns to Steve and the band's forthcoming headline appearance at this year's Castle Donington festival.

'One thing we're going to make absolutely sure of,' says Steve, 'is that on the day every band that plays sounds good – and loud! The big criticism of Donington for the last couple of years, it seems, has been that no one except the band headlining ever sounds any good. Well, all that's going to change when we play there. It's going to be our only British date this year and we want to make it the best Donington ever!'

The band's next world tour, already christened the Seventh Tour of a Seventh Tour, is due to kick off in Calgary, Canada, in May, and run continuously for the next seven months through twenty-four different countries, playing to more than two million people along the way. What is it about playing live that makes Steve Harris and Iron Maiden want to do it for up to seven months solid without a break?

'Playing live is ultimately what it's all about for a band like us,' he says. 'The albums are the most important things we do with our music. But once it's written and recorded the real test comes with taking it out live to the Maiden fans and finding out what they've got to say about it all. The strength of the band, the way we've evolved musically, has all come through spending so much time on the road together. We've always been a live band first and foremost. So touring is like the bedrock of everything this band stands for. Without it, our music wouldn't be the way it is. We'll never do another tour as long as the one we did when we released *Powerslave*, though. That went on for eleven-and-a-half months! We were probably lucky to come out of that in one piece. It would have finished off some bands I know.

'And at the end of every tour I'm always glad to be able to go home to my wife and family and forget all about Iron Maiden for a while. But the only reason I can be so relaxed about it then is because I know I'll be back out on the road at such a time as me and the band are ready to go out again. It would be terrible if I didn't know when next I was playing. That's what would really make me go off my head.'

Steve's mini-bar went dry about the same time the sun was just starting to creep through his window. Shakily, a bit full of beer and wine and so on – a lot full of it, in fact – I get to my feet and point myself in the direction of the door.

'I have to leave now,' I tell everybody.

'You're drunk!' cries Rod. 'Look at you, you're a bloody disgrace! Go on, bugger off to bed!'

I think it was the seventh sup of the seventh drink that finally did me in. That, or the seven I had after, I don't recall.

*

Footnote: Nicko McBrain would like to take this opportunity to apologise to the staff and management of the Castle Schnellenberg for breaking the toilet seat in his room. And no, I don't know how he managed to break the toilet seat in his room. But then, according to Nicko, neither does he. But that's another story . . .

CODA

Although none of us knew it then, the above story found the classic Maiden line-up of Harris, Dickinson, Smith, Murray and McBrain at their dizzy peak. By contrast, the 1990s saw the band struggling to cope with the new post-thrash era of metal. No longer the new dicks on the block, when grunge arrived to make the 1980s seem positively obsolete, and Bruce left to surf that wave as best he could, for a while it looked like they might not survive. That they eventually did says something about Dickinson's pragmatism – he returned an older, wiser, more interesting head in 1999 – and a great deal about Steve Harris's own brand of stoicism.

As a result, Maiden today occupy their own unique position in music. They are what they are and fuck what anyone else has to say about it, including me. And I like that – a lot. If there was a little bit more of that piss-off attitude in rock generally, the music business would be less of a back-slapping boys' club and more of a place for real men (and women) to feel at ease.

PUSHEAD, 1990

Visiting Pushead at his home in San Francisco was a bit like going behind the screen to meet the Wizard of Oz. To the public, he was the weird and somewhat sinister-seeming figure whose skull-infested images had enlivened artwork for no-shit bands like Metallica and the Misfits. In person, he was Brian Schroeder: skinny, somewhat anal, skate and comics buff who objected to me smoking, only drank orange juice, and looked severely disapproving when I suggested – half-jokingly – that some of his more outré images had been inspired, perhaps, by his own adventures with psychedelic drugs, or at the very least some of that strong home-grown weed Frisco had long been famous for. Absolutely not, said Brian. He also confessed to seeing himself as a sort of 'underground renaissance man', having started out as a singer in his own obscurantist metal band, Septic Death, and as a writer for tiny-circulation-but-deeply-cool rags such as *Skateboarder* – or whatever the hell they were called. (I have still never seen – let alone read – one.) He was a character, though, and storytellers need characters like fleas need dogs and dogs need lampposts. Whatever he was up to or however he'd got there, you couldn't help but be impressed. And besides, Metallica had given him their endorsement and that was better than a royal seal of approval back in 1990.

Pushead lives in a spartan one-bedroom apartment in San Francisco, along with his pretty Japanese-American girlfriend and his vast collection of skulls. Cow skulls, monkey skulls, alligator skulls . . . human skulls.

'Everything I have in the apartment I use as a reference – it's always best to use the real thing. Human skulls always inspire me the most – especially for my Metallica stuff,' he says nonchalantly, walking me through to a sunlit bay-windowed lounge. 'I'm actually pretty low on human skulls at the moment. Since they stopped importing them from India and Pakistan – where they used to dig 'em right out of the grave – it's been really expensive to buy good human skulls,' he adds wistfully, running a long bony hand through unkempt shoulder-length hair.

Pushead is a man who knows all about skulls; human or otherwise. He's drawn, inked, painted, sprayed, printed, faxed and fabricated enough of them in his time. Indeed, he has made a career out of it: most famously with Metallica, of course, although latterly his clients have included more commercially mainstream acts such as Aerosmith and Mötley Crüe. Now in his early thirties, Pushead – Brian – lived with his family in southern California until he was four. He began drawing as a tot, 'just copying stuff out of comic books. Both me and my brother did. We used to enter little competitions and things. Then I started to do my own stuff. That's when I found out how messed up I was, 'cos I couldn't do the muscles right or whatever.'

School wasn't much help. 'The art teacher hated me. I was the class anarchist. I just didn't wanna be taught by him.' Pushead objected to being asked to draw 'butterflies and flowers. I still got good grades for my still-life, I just hated having to draw that stuff. I always wanted to draw strange creatures and things.'

For a while he contributed drawings to the High School newspaper. 'I had this funky little cartoon style that I did; it was really popular for a while but I got bored with it.' Instead, the young scribbler turned to a new craze that was then sweeping the West Coast of America for the first time: skateboarding. It wasn't as exciting then, though. 'Plain old plank of wood, heavy iron wheels. Then, in 1968 my family moved to Idaho and the kids up there were like, "Hey, what's that you're standing on?",' he remembers with a laugh. 'I stopped for a while after that – the boards were broken and there was nowhere local to get them fixed. Then, around 1974, skateboarding suddenly came back. Some kids at school brought one in and I just got right on. I've been skating ever since.'

What, even now you're approaching the age most other men would be happy just to skate into the couch and veg out in front of the TV while the wife and kids ran riot all around them, I teased.

'Sure,' he shrugged, not seeing the funny side. 'I haven't been for a while 'cos I've been so busy. But yeah, I still skate.'

Drawing and skateboarding aside, the true passion of Pushead's brattish youth, he says, was music. 'Listening to the radio is one of the first things I can remember. Stuff like the Beatles – my brothers always really liked the Beatles. I never liked the Beatles.' He says Iron Butterfly were his big favourites back then, as were Cream, Creedence Clearwater, early Doors . . . 'And not forgetting Hendrix. Though Hendrix wasn't all that popular where we lived in Idaho.'

When Pushead quit high school in the mid-1970s, he began working at a local record store. 'Just to get closer to the music, really.' That was where he bought the first Montrose album – 'Blew me away!' – discovered he didn't like glam – 'Hated it' – and bought the first albums by Rush, AC/DC and Judas Priest: 'AC/DC were considered a punk band back then. Me and my friends all bought *High Voltage*. But after Bon Scott died, we hated them. I still don't like it.'

Like a lot of young dudes of his generation, in the late-1970s Pushead started mixing his taste for underground metal with some of the more extrovert punk sounds that were then starting to emerge. The Sex Pistols were 'really cool, but I preferred The Damned. They were more fun.'

Interestingly, however, the NWOBHM scene – so long the pet subject of Metallica's Lars Ulrich, among others – which followed in punk's wake, failed to strike any sparks at all. 'That was a big lull for me; I didn't like any of that stuff. Except Iron Maiden – with Paul

Di'Anno. I've never liked Iron Maiden with Bruce Dickinson. The early stuff, though, was great.'

Instead, says Pushead, he spent the early- to mid-1980s listening to heavy-duty anarcho-punk metallists such as Black Flag, the Germs and Discharge: 'About two or three times a year I would drive down to LA to a store called Vinyl Fetish and pick up obscurities by Circle Jerks, Discord . . . and I'd read all the fanzines that were starting to come out then – getting scened-up.'

Eventually, he started writing record reviews for *Skateboarder* magazine (later to become *Action Now*). He also found a way to indulge his passion for drawing by designing some posters and handbills for a couple of local Idaho bands. That was when the Pushead nom-de-plume – a nickname since the playground at high school – first became embedded in stone. Or should I say skulls . . .

'At first I didn't sign my name at all, I just wanted it to be "artwork", you know? I wanted it to be looked at for what it was, not who did it. But the more I did, the more I found it hard to keep track of them, so I had to give things a name suddenly.'

But why something as frankly obnoxious as 'Pushead'?

'Well, it went along with the punk thing at that time, but it was more about how people treated me. From when I was a little kid and did monster drawings, or when I skateboarded, a lot of my friends' parents considered me a bad influence. I don't know why,' he shrugs again, 'but I was never treated as though what I liked doing was in any way normal. I was regarded as this sort of subversive influence on other kids. It was weird, I didn't understand it.'

One of the first posters Pushead ever made was for an Exploited gig. Although the gig was later cancelled, the band liked it so much that they used it as the sleeve for their next album. Good news for the budding illustrator, you would have thought. Except for one thing: the band neglected to pay him for it.

'Yeah, they liked it so much they stole it,' he recalls sardonically. 'And the thing is, they're still using it to this day on their record labels and stuff. It even says on one of their album sleeves – "No Thanks To Shithead". Wattie's a dick,' he mutters, dismissing the Exploited leader from his mind.

But you know what they say: once bitten, twice smitten, and

Pushead's output grew increasingly prodigious: drawing and designing posters, flyers and eventually his first record sleeves for bands all over America. 'Small bands, small independent labels – half the time I'd get ripped off and earn nothing. Other times I was doing it for a box of the albums with my picture on them.'

In 1981, Pushead did the inevitable and formed his own band. 'It was called Septic Death, but we weren't supposed to play gigs or make records or anything. We just liked getting together to jam,' he says self-effacingly. Eventually, of course, Septic Death did play: at a local pizza parlour, where they lasted exactly six numbers before being 'dragged off for being so awful'.

Nevertheless, Septic Death thrashed around for another three years before splitting, when Pushead did – for LA. 'I got a job working at Rough Trade's warehouse, loading records, and I just began to check out the local scene.' Then, in 1985, at a Venom concert in LA, he made the connection that brought the name Pushead, if not fame exactly, then certainly recognition on a grand scale, when he was introduced to Metallica singer James Hetfield at the gig. 'He'd seen something I'd done for the Misfits, and he asked if I could get him a T-shirt of it. I said, sure, no problem. Then he wore it on the back of the *Master of Puppets* album, and that's when the whole Misfits cult thing took off.'

James had also asked Pushead to come up with a drawing Metallica could use somewhere on the inside of the *Master . . .* sleeve. 'He wanted a drawing of the four of them like zombies.' But a wrong phone number kept them out of touch until after the album was released and they bumped into each other in San Francisco, where both Pushead and Metallica had relocated to. James was still interested in Pushead doing something for the band, and suggested Pushead do something for the next Metallica T-shirt.

'It was the "Damage, Inc" T-shirt. James wanted something like an animal-type thing – like a wild beast. I still have the original drawings of this beast-type skull. But I didn't like it, it didn't work for me. So I went to a human skull and made the head a little bigger. James wanted fangs, so I drew them in, and he wanted the mallets, so I did that. Then they all came over and I showed it to them and they loved it. In fact, everybody I showed it to loved it. They said, you've got something there with the skull, stick with it, it's different. So I did.'

Next came the 'Crash Course in Brain Surgery' T-shirt; an awesome example of classic Pushead skull splat. His twisted, gruesome, sometimes wickedly funny illustrations have adorned every legitimate piece of Metallica merchandise ever since. Had there ever been anything he'd done for Metallica, though, that they didn't like?

'Yeah, the "Thing That Should Not Be" T-shirt. I think they thought it was a bit too H. P. Lovecraft – all teeth and tongues and hot colours. Lots of symbolic sort of gore,' he chuckles throatily. 'It was a little over the top, I guess,' he shrugs, unrepentant.

And although he was responsible for the eye-stabbing designs on the 'Harvester of Sorrow', 'Eye of the Beholder' and 'One' singles, he has never done a Metallica album cover.

'I'd love to, obviously,' he says, eyes already glinting at the thought. 'But they haven't asked me yet, so we'll have to see. The way I do it is, I look at the lyrics James has written, then discuss what ideas they conjure up in my mind with him and he either says, yeah, cool, or just plain, no. It works real well. Luckily, he nearly always says yes.'

Artistically, Pushead says he draws inspiration these days from contemporary comic book artists such as Kevin O'Neil, famous for his *Torquemada* series in *2000AD* (Pushead has an original piece of 'Be Pure. Be Vigilant. Behave!' O'Neil artwork); legendary 1960s poster king, Rick Griffin; Kent Williams. 'And right now an English artist called Simon Beasley, who's amazing and does the covers for *Doom Patrol*. I got my art dealer looking for him but he can't find him. Plus another guy called Alex Nino, who lives here in San Francisco. I really like his stuff, it's so bizarre and intense I can't take my eyes off it.'

He's a great collector of other artists' work. 'It took me years to get this stuff together, though I knew I wanted most of it already.' He says his favourite comics currently are titles such as *Elektra*, *Wolverine*, *Metazoic*, *Hellraiser*, unknown to the outside world, yet gold dust to comic connoisseurs.

How long does it take him to complete a finished piece of work – a T-shirt, for example?

'It varies. If I go crazy I can do a piece in a day – if I really have to. 'Cos when I start something I don't stop till it's finished, not unless I have to.'

Flicking through some of the more outlandish examples of

Pushead's portfolio – eyeballing such illicit delights as the 'Hand of Fear' (Pushead's logo), 'Birds Eye' or 'Seek & Reach' – it begs the question: are these images the product of a twisted mind?

'No, I'm not twisted,' he says quietly but firmly. 'I think some of the drawings are quite beautiful, actually . . .'

Does he, I can't help wondering, indulge in any recreational drugs for, uh, visual inspiration when he's drawing?

Shakes his head vigorously.

'No, I've never taken drugs and drawn. I'm straight, I've been straight since I was in high school,' he says, a little indignant at the suggestion. 'I don't even drink coffee.'

As *Kerrang!*'s own in-house metal designer, Krusher Joule – a man not usually known for dropping compliments anybody's way other than his own – said over my shoulder while I was writing this article, 'I hate to admit it but Pushead is without a doubt the leading heavy metal artist in the world today.'

These days, as I indicated earlier, it's not just Metallica who have regularly begun to use Pushead's unique skull-shaped talents, either. The Mötley Crüe skulls-in-straight-jacket T-shirt was the second most popular item of merchandise on their *Dr Feelgood* tour this year.

'But the great thing is I'm still doing exactly what I want to,' he points out. 'I won't just do anything. I've been offered all sorts of stuff. But Mötley Crüe was a fun thing to do. And so was Aerosmith. And the cool thing about it is I don't get to paint myself into a corner by just doing Metallica all the time. Which is something, say, I think has happened to Derek Riggs, Iron Maiden's [official] artist. Where it's like, Derek Riggs *is* Iron Maiden and you never see him do anything else, I don't have that with Metallica.'

CODA

As far as I know, Pushead is still living and working in his SF garret, turning out artwork for bands you may or may not ever have heard of. He finally got to design a Metallica album sleeve in 2005, when they let him loose on *St. Anger* – ironically, or perhaps not considering Brian's punk origins, their most un-Metallica-like album ever. He even started his own boutique record labels, putting out records for original Bay Area punk and metallists such as Poison Idea and Final Conflict. And, of course, there is the inevitable website where you can buy numbered limited-edition Pushead posters and whatnots, but then, hey, who doesn't have one of those these days, right?

BON JOVI, 1990

Despite having known and interviewed him for many years, including long before he became nauseatingly world-famous, I still don't really know what I make of Jon Bon Jovi. Happy to play the big giggly kid just thrilled to be there in the days before he made it, once his career took off like a rocket he became so long-faced and serious you wondered what it was he was actually in this for – apart from the money, which was spectacular, of course.

For a pretty boy, to me he always seemed so old for his age; so consumed by his own crippling self-absorption that he couldn't even bear to poke fun at himself. Ironically, of course, this has only made him an even bigger figure of fun to certain sections of the rock media than he might have been had he simply owned up to his status as a pop pin-up and forgotten all about his not-so-secret dreams of being the new Bruce Springsteen. But from my vantage point he just doesn't seem to have been able to help himself, looking on with disdain at those who treat him like a pop star, while bristling at the very suggestion that he might have anything to do with hairy-assed heavy metal. No, to borrow a phrase, whatever you think Jon is, that's what he thinks he's not.

Maybe that's the tragedy of being such a good-looking and successful rock star: other guys simply don't take you as seriously as they do the singers who look more like Lemmy. Whatever it is, it's hard for the rest of us to really care. When someone as blessed as Jon comes along – dripping chicks, money, fame, even a certain amount of talent – it's almost impossible to feel sympathy for any so-called 'problems' they might genuinely be having. And yet to meet Jon, especially around the time the following interview took place, four years after the chart-molesting *Slippery When Wet* album first set him on the road to megadom, was to meet a man who clearly felt he was walking around with the weight of the world bearing down on his tanned and gym-toned shoulders. You actually felt sorry for him. Then you went home to your one-bedroom apartment and he went home to his million-dollar mansion . . .

Jon Bon Jovi interview, New York, first published in Kerrang!, *28 July 1990.*

It's July and hotter than hell's kitchen in New York City. The heat clings to everything like a second skin: the buildings, the sidewalks, the people. Eyes rolling like hard-boiled eggs in saucepan faces blurred by sweat and car fumes. Jon Bon Jovi and I are perched on the veranda of his manager's second floor suite of offices on Central Park South in Manhattan, elbows resting on the railings, gazing out at the piss-coloured taxi cabs, the hawk-faced pretzel pedlars, the blank-eyed bums and the power-dressed office shirkers pretending to ignore them.

As we look out, Jon tells me this is the very spot he and the rest of Bon Jovi first met with Doc McGhee, their powerful and influential manager, to plot the seeds of a success story that now spans more than twenty-five million albums and has generated maybe ten times as many millions of dollars.

'Back then we didn't have the price of a cup of coffee between us,' he says, running a restless hand through his long, rust-coloured hair. 'That was seven years ago. You ask me has the success changed me since then, I say, sure, man. It changes everybody. Deep down I still have all the energy and enthusiasm I ever had as a kid. But on the outside I'm a lot more cynical these days. A lot more.'

Indeed, Jon does look remarkably cool and unbothered for someone whose new single is rapidly climbing the US charts in a Top Ten-bound trajectory, and looks almost certain to do the same here in Britain. The track is 'Blaze of Glory' – the Bon Jovi-penned theme tune to the upcoming *Young Guns II* movie, in which Jon makes his debut appearance on celluloid as one of the good-looking young guns who gets it (and good) early on in the story. An album – full title: *Blaze of Glory: Music From and Inspired by the Movie Young Guns II, Written and Performed by Jon Bon Jovi* – follows in the UK on 6 August and features such famous sidekicks as Jeff Beck (the lead on 'Blaze of Glory'), Elton John (singing harmonies and banging the ivories on 'Dyin' Ain't Much of a

Livin'') and Little Richard (doing much the same on 'You Really Got Me').

In fact, the star of our story looks positively down-in-the-mouth today. Not depressed, exactly. Just somewhere else, deep within his own thoughts. He says he's happy enough to do the interview and goes as far as to congratulate *Kerrang!* on reaching the ripe old age of 300. 'Three hundred, huh?' he chews his lip. 'Well, you don't look it!' he jokes. But it's clear his mind is on other things, other dates, other times, other places.

The first time Bon Jovi received any attention in *Kerrang!* was in 1984 when a positively glowing review of the first Bon Jovi album was ungainly matched by an absolute trashing of one of their early shows in the live reviews section.

'I remember it very well,' says Jon with a crooked jester's smile. 'Bon Jerk-off I think the guy called us. It's funny 'cos I can't really remember what the album review said. I just remember it was great. It's funny how you always remember the bad things people say about you and very seldom any of the good.'

The Happy Birthdays over, we get down to business. There's a lot I want to ask him. There's a lot he has to say right now: about his future with or without the rest of Bon Jovi. Specifically, about guitarist and long-time 'best bud' Richie Sambora, with whom he has reportedly fallen out. And about – oh, a lotta stuff you'll just have to wait for. Meantime, back to that ledge in New York City . . .

Let's start with the new single, 'Blaze of Glory'. This is your first solo record, right?

'No! I've gotta keep saying that. I don't want anyone thinking this is a solo thing. I have to restate it time and time again. This is a soundtrack. It's for a movie, and that's all it's supposed to be. I mean, I had to write it to fit a certain parameter. So I don't want anyone thinking this is a solo anything. It's not. The parameters I had to write under were so limiting, you know, I could only write songs for particular scenes that some other guy came up with.'

How did it all come about?

'Well, how it started was they wanted to use "Wanted Dead or Alive" [from the 1986 *Slippery When Wet* album] in the movie. I was told that they wrote the first *Young Guns* movie with "Wanted . . ." in

mind, that it was a big influence on the movie and I was really flattered.
I like the first *Young Guns* movie a lot. And I always said that if I'd ever
acted in a movie, it would have been in *Young Guns.'*

Were you approached to be in the first movie?

'No, no, not at all. But anyway, it turns out they decide they wanna
feature "Wanted . . . " on the soundtrack to the follow-up. Lyrically,
though, it wouldn't have really worked. You know, "On a steel horse
I ride . . . ", it just doesn't fit the movie. So I said, if you want, I'll write
you something in that vein to fit this part of the movie. I knew where
it was going, they told me what it was about, and I went there with a
song in my hand, which was "Blaze of Glory". I wrote it just by what
they told me over the phone. So I took it to 'em. They liked it. And
then I came home and wrote three more. So now we've got four songs,
all based on what they'd told me about the movie. So they said, "Great,
let's do an album!"'

But isn't it true that you were looking for some form of solo expression outside of the band, anyway?

'I honest to God had no intention whatsoever of doing a solo
venture, because to me Bon Jovi records are my solo albums. There's
not any songs really that I adamantly didn't want on any of the Bon
Jovi records. If I didn't want something, it wasn't there. I mean, my
interpretation of what was going to happen to us as we had these
discussions in January, was that we were gonna go home and Richie
was going to go do his solo record. It was gonna be Richie Sambora
and Friends. It was gonna be all his friends playing cover songs, playing
some of his songs, playing some things that me and him do together.
Meantime, Dave [Bryan] was gonna do a New Age record and I was
gonna mix the Bon Jovi live album. And that was what the year was
gonna be. That was the plan anyway.

'But come February, when the tour was ending, the one thing in my
mind was, if something comes up that you don't do every day of your
life, do it this time. For the first time when you say you're going to do
something, go out and fucking do it! If you finally want to go somewhere where there isn't an arena, then go there, you know? Like,
I always say I wanna go to Utah and ride motorcycles and I never
fuckin' do. So when Emilio [Estevez, one of the stars of *Young Guns II*
and a long-time pal of the singer] was so adamant about me coming

out there, I said, "Fuck it, I'm gonna get on an aeroplane, without the band, without my road manager, without my wife, all by myself and go and do this!" That was a big step for me, to go and do something by myself. It's a big deal for me to come to New York City, an hour-and-a-half from my house, without picking up my dad on the way and saying, "Hey, you wanna take a ride?" I'm not used to doing anything by myself. I just don't do it.'

So are you pleased with the results?

'I'm very excited by the album. By playing with those guys. Even if I didn't play with those guys. I was real excited to just get up, 'cos I wanted to get up, write ten songs for an album, go produce it and have people be happy with it. When I did it, I was excited. When the single came out here I was waiting with bated breath to see what would happen. Just like I always am before I release a record. But now that it's out, it's beyond me. So now there's a sigh of relief and what happens, happens.'

You've got a lot of big names on this album with you – Elton John, Jeff Beck, etc. How was it they ended up on the record, and why them exactly?

'Why them? It was the idea that ... Well, I've always loved Beck's playing and I loved his sound. So the idea was, who would you get to play on "Blaze of Glory"? It wasn't a matter of four songs or ten songs, it was one song. My first choice of guitar player was Jeff Beck. I mean, if you're shooting for something you may as well aim for the sky, you know?'

You had already met before, hadn't you?

'Yeah, he's been to some shows. He'd been to Wembley, he'd been to Hammersmith, he's been to see us before, yeah. I thought he was a nice enough guy, so what the hell, give him a call and see what he says. He said yes so quickly and hung up the phone, that I would have sworn he wasn't coming. He was like, "I'd love to do it, man. Have your manager call my manager. It sounds like a great idea. And, er, I gotta go!" I was like, yeah, sure, man. We've all heard the rumours about what he's like, you know. Well, the fucker not only flew out to LA to do it, but he was in the studio in the morning before I was and wouldn't leave until I physically said, "I'm not gonna do this anymore, go home!" I mean, he worked his ass off! He dispelled all the rumours about him, he was a consummate professional.'

What's Beck like as a person, though?

'Jeff is a little boy. He loves to play. He wants to go to the movies. We went to see *Total Recall* together [the new Arnold Schwarzenegger flick]. He loves to drive around in this car. He wants to go out to dinner and goof off. I mean, he loves to go play around, but when it came time to work, he was right there on the money every time.'

Were you nervous working with someone like that?

'No, you see because though I like Jeff Beck, I didn't buy his records when I was a kid. He was a great-sounding guitar player, but for me it was always Rod Stewart. I was a singer, I played guitar to write songs. I never grew up wanting to be Jeff, I wanted to grow up and be Rod Stewart.'

What about Elton John? What was working with him like?

'Ah ... again, there's a guy that's a songwriter, consummate song-writer and performer, and Elton is a great guy as well. Fortunately I got a feeling meeting Elton – I think the first time was when he came to see us – I got a feeling meeting Elton that he was one of the guys. He was a real sweetheart who just loves playing piano. Then I played with him at Madison Square Garden and I felt that I had a friend in Elton. When he was in Los Angeles at that time I thought that he would be perfect. It wasn't name value so much as the fact that he was perfect for the part. Roy Bitten was booked, but Bruce [Springsteen] wouldn't let him do it.'

Why, because it was you?

'I don't think so. I think because he's co-producing his album.'

It wasn't a bit of New Jersey boy rivalry?

'If Bruce Springsteen is afraid of me then I'm flattered. But I doubt that that is the case. I think that it's just purely that Roy's co-producing the Springsteen album and he couldn't do it. But with Elton being there, he said he'd love to do it. So I had him come over and one song in particular that I wrote on piano really lent itself to Elton: "Dyin' Ain't Much of a Livin'". To me it sounds like an Elton John song. To me it was like he's the only guy who can play this song. Then in the control room he started to sing the harmony. All along I was dying to get him to sing the harmony and he started doing it, so there was my in. I went, "Hey, why don't you sing it?". So we did it live and the vocal was right there.'

Are you an Elton John fan?

'Like, the biggest! When he was on the cover of *Time* magazine in '74 or '75, I remember in grammar school as a class project I made a red, white and blue guitar and wrote "Elton" on it. I had the *Caribou* album and *Goodbye Yellow Brick Road*. That whole era, he was the biggest to me, I listened to him religiously. So to have him play on it was real exciting. Then in an old art deco '50s-ish diner right next to the studio – this was prior to Jeff flying in – we said, "Who else can we get?", just joking around. Like, what legends are there left in this business? And we thought, Keith Richards! Let's get Keith Richards!

'The one thing about Keith was, everyone in the room played guitar, everyone, me, Aldo [Nova], and everyone, fought to play on the record. Finally I said to Danny Kortchmar [Jon's co-producer], "Who's record is this, man? It's mine, I'm playing the parts." It's like everyone wanted to play on this record. Another time, I said, "Let's get Little Richard to play this song" and everyone dropped their cheeseburgers! Like, "You know Little Richard?" I said, "Yeah, I do, he played with us on the last tour." So I called him up and he came down and it was fucking great 'cos it was the one thing I could do. Jeff Beck knows the Stones, the Beatles, he's played with everybody. But even he asked me to introduce him to Little Richard, so I did. I asked him to introduce me to Rod Stewart and he did that.

'So I call Richard and he came down and Jeff was so excited and nervous. When Richard walked into the control room – and I know this 'cos I've done it myself, you feel foolish afterward – but Jeff couldn't help himself and when Richard walked into the control room his fingers started playing "Lucille". Richard put his hand out to me and Jeff jumps out of his seat and gives him his hand and says, "It's so nice to meet you, you're the reason I got into this business", and asks him for his autograph. You have to slap yourself once in a while and say my life is so lucky that I get to be in the company of people like this. To watch those things happen is just a thrill.'

It's always been one of the biggest buzzes for you, hasn't it, people such as Jimmy Page getting up onstage with you?

'I've been so lucky with that, it's been so much fun.'

What happened to the Keith Richards idea?

'Well, with five guitar players already we decided to just steal his licks instead!' He laughs.

Have you ever met him, though?

'Real briefly, at an album launch party for him in Los Angeles.'

The $64,000 question, though, is whether there is going to be another Bon Jovi album?

'I hope so.'

But you don't know so?

'I don't know so and I can publicly say it, to you, because the truth is *Kerrang!* started this whole fucking fiasco. We were in Mexico, at the end of the last tour, with nothing but wonderful things happening. We were finishing the tour doing stadiums, which is just how we wanted it to end, and we were feeling real good. Then *Kerrang!* says Tico [Torres] is leaving the band ['America Calling' column, issue 274]. Suddenly we got drummer tapes and pictures and everything coming in. It was like, "Hey, Tico, are you quitting the band?" He was like, "First I've heard of it, man!" That was amazing, but that's when it started. But we pushed it away, I threw the magazine out the window. I was upset 'cos I knew it wasn't true. I think the quotes were like the drummer's quitting and the band is breaking up. I thought, what the fuck's this?

'So then the English papers, I think it was the *Sun*, or one of those gossip rags, got hold of it. The headline ran "All Ovi For Bon Jovi". It said that Sambora was out and there were money problems, that he wasn't happy with his cut and he was leaving for Cher and all this shit. I'm reading it out of the fax thinking what is all this shit? Then phone calls start coming in, people calling me saying they want the gig. I tell you, four months later I'm not entertained by it any more. It's got to this point because the five of us haven't been in the same room together since before the last show and it's added fuel to the fire. So now all of us are believing there are problems. I can't tell you what the problems are about, but we think we've got problems.'

Jonathan King asked me when we were in Moscow last year whether you and Richie were having problems. He said in the early days you were never apart. Now it's like one walks in the room and the other walks out. Have you grown apart?

'In the state of things at this time, yeah. Right now, in July 1990, yeah. Things are not happy in the Bon Jovi camp, that's for sure, they're not happy at all. I don't want the band to break up, 'cos the five of us . . . It's like, you can only play your first time at Donington once. Your first headline show in London [at the Dominion, in 1985]. Those gigs were what made us. We were spitting in the eye of the fire and we didn't give a fuck about anyone. It was us and we were gonna make it. Regardless of money and stadiums, or who I played with, if that was the band tomorrow and Elton was my new keyboard player, it would never be the same. All of that would be lost and I don't want that to happen. I definitely don't want that to happen. I want to keep it together 'cos these are the guys who seven years ago were here when we sat on this ledge for the first time, when we didn't have enough money for a pretzel across the street and no one knew whether Bon Jovi was jeans or what the fuck it was. We had to fight for everything we got and we had to fight even on the *New Jersey* album to prove that we were gonna be around. It's a rewarding feeling to know that the band as a unit did this. I could play with better musicians, or different musicians, and they could play with a better songwriter and singer, but it wouldn't be the same – ever.'

Do you think that everyone has to get their solo albums out of their system first?

'I don't know, you'd have to ask them. Richie was always, "Oh, I'm gonna do it", to the point where things weren't happening for him and he joined this thing. Everyone gives Rich a lot of attention – and well-deserved it is, he's a fine musician and a fine singer – but I don't think it's fair to harp on about him all the time because it was us and the band. For the first two albums, he never wrote any of the singles. Dave Bryan co-wrote the singles. It was Dave and I who did it. Richie came in on the third album when he had begun to understand the way I like to write. It wasn't until the third album so it's not fair for everyone to pick on him because it's . . . the press I mean, it's not fair.'

It's like the Jagger/Richards thing, though, isn't it? You and Rich always were the stars of the show.

'It's so stereotypical of what's supposed to be, though: John Lennon and Paul McCartney, it's the same thing.'

With respect, though, if the drummer leaves the band, it's not the same story. But when the lead guitarist leaves, that's news.

'Yeah, you're right. I don't know how much I like that or dislike that but it's true. I missed him very much when Little Steven left Bruce, it just wasn't the same anymore. I don't want this band to break up. But there aren't any plans to make a record at the moment.'

Where does that leave your career at this point?

'Promoting the *Young Guns* record first and foremost. Promoting the *Young Guns* record as a soundtrack for a movie, and then I'm going to go and produce other things and get them out. I just produced Hall & Oates' next single. I wrote that with a couple of other guys.'

Sooner or later, though, you're going to want to get back on the road, right?

'I went to see Alec [Jon Such] and he said to me, "The Al that was out there in South America and Mexico isn't the guy that you know now." I didn't think he was being any weirder than usual. But he says, "I was so burned out I couldn't take it any more, but you wanted to keep going so we had to keep going." I didn't know what to say. I felt great this tour so I kept pushing and pushing, I didn't give a shit. I'd have stayed out there forever. I love touring but I can turn it off; when I'm done touring I'm done. I don't have any desire to go down the Stone Pony [a club in the Asbury Park area of New Jersey] on a Sunday night and play a song. I don't have any desire to do that at all.

'I'm really excited by the avenue that's opened up, though, doing this soundtrack. And I'm blown away that Daryl Hall and John Oates have asked me to work with them. I was even happier afterwards when they would tell people, "He's a real producer". I guess coming from them, that's a compliment. But Aldo [another long-time buddy] on the other hand, I've got fifteen tunes with Aldo and we're gonna go into the studio in October. So that's my next project, to get Aldo out on the road. We'll see what happens. Skid Row are gonna want to do their own album next time, too. I don't think I'll be writing anything with them this year. So there's a lot, you know. But in the meantime I'll be watching, I'll be checking out what's happening.'

Briefly, the acting thing in the movie when you get shot, is it like a Sam Peckinpah slow-mo bloodbath or a John Wayne trickle down the cheek?

'It's in the middle of the two. I'm in it for thirty seconds. Don't mistake this for an acting career! I was freezing my ass off in Santa Fe, New Mexico, in February, dressed the way you would dress your three-year-old kid, you know, snowsuit, gloves, feet-warmers, just freezing my ass. I was thinking, why am I out here with these idiots, you know? I was miserable, while the stars of the movie are running around in T-shirts and jeans, riding horses, moving around, running, shooting and I'm going, "Fuck this, I'm a spoiled brat, I wanna go home!"

'They said, "Be in the movie then" and I said, "Great, give me something to do, I hate this!" And they did. So, for thirty seconds I escape from this jail with the writer of the movie, who was the fan who started all this off. I escape from this jail with him. We grab the deputy in the jail. The sheriff sees me and loads up his gun and I take one hit to the chest and there's blood everywhere. It's in slow motion and in close-up. And that's it. It took me longer to explain it than it did for it to happen.'

Do you think there will be any teenage girls having heart attacks seeing Jon Bon Jovi being splattered like that?

'Do you know what they're really gonna have heart attacks over? The seven bucks it costs them to get into the movie – 'cos I'm in it for thirty seconds max! Nobody blink!'

Considering you're hardly in the movie, the publicists in Hollywood are certainly making a meal out of the fact that it has Jon Bon Jovi in it.

'Tell me about it. I mean, I don't want 'em taking advantage of our fans, making believe like this is my first big film part or anything. Like the album. I'm pissed off because first they were gonna use at least four of the songs in the movie. Then it was three. Now I'm afraid that the last cut was only two. So here's gonna be my friends and fans and family going to see a movie that I'm in for thirty seconds and I have two songs in. But they're marketing it like it was my first major film role or something.'

How, in your own mind, is the soundtrack record different from a Bon Jovi record?

'Musically, it's real different. If I were to do a Bon Jovi record for this film, I would look foolish and they would look foolish for hiring me. It had to be different. It had to be a little off the wall. With that in mind, that's why I did it.'

What is it about the cowboy image that appeals to you, though? Is it the same as the rock and roller type of thing?

'I think it's that kind of lifestyle. The truth of the matter is, like the way we wrote "Wanted Dead or Alive", I feel that you ride into town, you don't know where the fuck you are. You're with your "gang", stealing money, getting what you can off any girl that'll give it to you, drinking as much of the free alcohol as you can and being gone before the law catches you – before someone wakes you from this wonderful dream and says, "You're an asshole, you're going to jail." Because it's not the real world I'm living in, it's a dream sequence, a big fucking wet dream.'

Rätt's new album features you doing backing vocals on a track called 'Heads I Win, Tails You Lose'. It's a great track. How did you end up doing that?

'Well, they asked me and I said, "Yeah!" I was doing my record in LA at the same time as they were [and] I think that the years that have passed have helped both of us as bands to be allies. When we opened for them in '85 it was hell. Me and [singer] Stephen Pearcy definitely didn't get along. Now, I truly like Stephen a lot and I think both of our bands are very good friends. The thing is we both grew up, I think, and have seen the highs and the lows and realise that there is room enough for everyone. Both of us came down off of our high horses and realised that it's a friendly sport, you know? I like the new Rätt record, they've got some good shit in there.'

Do you think that you're a nicer person than you were five years ago, before the fame and the money?

'Maybe, I hope so. I think I'm a little more cynical and sceptical. I hope I am nicer, but you'd have to tell me that. Other people would have to tell me whether I am or not.'

All I remember is a very energetic and excited kid.

'I still think I have a lot of energy and I am excited. That's probably another reason why the band is going their own ways. We are supposed to, like human beings do, take some time off. I gotta settle down. The way I figure it is, if I was to sit with Freud or one of those guys, he'd tell me it was because I hate my wife or my mother or something. Because all I like to do is go and work. I dig making records.'

Do you think that your individual fame has forced you to make a conscious decision not to turn into an asshole and to try and stay a 'human being'?

'No. People will say about you what they want. I mean there's a DJ here in New York named Howard Stern who went on a rampage for about a year saying what scumbags me and my organisation are.'

Why?

'Because I couldn't go to his radio station the week "Bad Medicine" came out. He literally went on a tirade for a year and it really upset me. I was a true friend of his. Then there's the good stories about how I helped a little girl across the street one day. Everyone's got their stories, you gotta deal with them. I just hope there's more good than bad.'

Mike Tramp of White Lion told me that when he was having problems with his voice, he got you on the line straightaway trying to help him. That's unusual in this business, isn't it? Something for nothing?

'Sure. I guess it is. But I just don't get it. To me, when I was in a young band all I wanted was for the Scorpions – or whoever we were playing with – to say, "I dug this band". No one ever said that. As a headliner now, I look down on my opening bands as a part of my organisation. With Cinderella, every night we would bring them out on stage with us at the end, every night. What's great is that now Cinderella are doing that with their support bands, Winger and the Bullet Boys. Every night they do a jam. I had something to do with that. Tommy [Keifer] is a great guy, he has no ego.'

Are you disappointed with the Skid Row situation, where Sebastian Bach – who bad-mouthed you from the stage while supporting Bon Jovi – doesn't appear to appreciate what you've done?

'I guess he doesn't. But I can punch the bastard in the face and be very happy I did it.'

Does that kind of thing make you less inclined, though, to be so charitable to your support bands?

'No, definitely not, that would never happen. One thing that I heard someone say, I think it was Billy Squier, was, "If you're ever afraid of your support band then you don't deserve to headline." So I would give my support band anything to help them. It only makes the show better for the people who come to see us. I don't give a shit about the ego involved. All I expect is, like, if this is my house then treat it nicely, don't spit in the house, you know? That's all I would ask of anyone. If you don't like us then fine, go about your business but don't ever slag it because that's why you're here.

'Fortunately for us, we don't need a support band – it's like whoever we want to put on our bill. When you're the one selling all the tickets then who gives a shit? Then you're doing it because they are your friends. The Skids are wonderful guys, though. I just spent a week's vacation with [guitarists] Snake and Rachel. I still love them very much – and Sebastian's probably a good kid, too. I don't spend enough time with him to find out. It's tough for him to grow out of my shadow. I mean every fuckin' interview they were saying "Jon did this for you, Jon did that." I'm sure he got sick of it, like "Fuck Jon!". I understand that.'

So after two of the most successful rock albums of the 1980s – *Slippery When Wet* and *New Jersey* – what comes next? What are you actually going to do?

'I don't think I can write "Livin' on a Prayer" again. I just think that it is old. We did it. I think that our public is more intelligent than to expect that. I think that our organisation is more intelligent than that. It wouldn't be fair to us or our audience to do the same thing. I think that the songs on *New Jersey*, like "Wild is the Wind", which were never released as singles, are bridging the gap to where we're going.'

Which is where?

'Just to do something different. I see big bands on MTV now with their new albums and it just looks and sounds the same. That's great and all, but fuck, I can't do it again. It's just not right.'

I was reading someone who said that arena rock has become 'the professional wrestling of the '80s': just going through the moves, the formula, knowing what gets the crowd crazy, and that's it.

'I agree with that. I figured that out. I don't think that that's the way we're going, that's for sure. From what I hear of what Richie's doing and judging by this soundtrack that I just spat out, that's not where we're going.'

Would you risk your commercial impact to diversify artistically?

'Yeah, yeah. But defending Bon Jovi albums, I never in a million years thought: "This is a commercial album therefore it's gonna sell a lot of records." I didn't set out to do that on *New Jersey*. With *Slippery* . . . , who knew? We had no fuckin' idea. And definitely not with *New Jersey*, no way. With this soundtrack it's the same deal. I set out to write ten songs. I hope you like them, end of story.'

Is there one person of whom you could say 'That's the nicest superstar I ever met'?

'When I was a gofer at the Powerstation studio, Mick Jagger was very nice to me. The second time he came in he remembered me enough to say, "You keeping up those demos? You keep on it." I never forgot that. Maybe that's a part of the reason I'm here today. I mean, that was a buzz 'cos I was just a shit-head little gofer with a tape. It was very nice of him, you know. You don't forget. The Scorpions were also very good to us on our first tour. .38 Special were real good to us on the *Slippery* . . . tour. They were legitimately nice guys. Southside Johnny has always been a great guy. Ten years ago Johnny let me open for him and he's still a great guy.'

I hear that you met Prince. I'm intrigued by the idea of you and Prince working together.

'I'm intrigued, too! Prince and I met at Tramp [club in London] one night. We chatted over a bottle of wine – seeing Prince drunk is great.'

I didn't know he drank.

'He did that night! He was a real sweetheart, he was great, he was funny. He was real candid. He came to see us in Minnesota and invited us back to his place after and we all went, it was a lotta fun.'

What's his Paisley Park place like?

'Oh, it's ridiculous, amazing – a ten-million-dollar recording studio. I'd like that. I think that he is a genius lyrically, and somewhat musically. "Sign of the Times" is a real good indication of that. I would like to do that. I would like to write a "Sign of the Times". I'm intrigued by guys like him. It's something different. I'd like to be responsible for going "left".'

Have you discussed this with him?

'Yeah.'

Why does he want to work with you?

'Good point, I don't know. I couldn't honestly give you an answer, so it's not fair to guess. He told us he liked our music. He came to our show, right?'

Did he get up onstage and jam?

'Nah, he chickened out! Well, it's a whole different vibe than his kinda thing. We had rehearsed a version of "All Along the Watchtower" at the soundcheck, but he backed out. We were ready to do it, but between the encores he said he didn't want to do it. But later that night he had an all-night jam session at his studio with us and Living Colour.

'But the idea behind working with Prince is to do something different. We have a couple of tracks – we never save songs usually, I throw them away – from the last album where you'd never guess it was us. One song is called "Let's Make it Baby" and it's just about fucking. Just a nasty Prince-style fucking song! The other one is called "Diamond Ring", that's about what a wedding ring can do to you. It's like that song "Fever" by Peggy Lee or something like that. It's just slinky and quiet and spooky. It doesn't have a fully fledged chorus and it's real different for us. With that in mind, that's where we need to go. That's where we want to go. Somewhere just a little left of where we've been before. It might fail miserably, but at this point there's no timetable and there's no parameters which we have to keep in. So we can make an album and if it sucks then we can throw that album in the garbage and write another one. For the first time we have my studio, which is finished now. It's a full twenty-four-track studio. So nobody has to hear it if . . . it won't get stolen and sold as bootleg demos.'

I was talking to somebody about how bands around today will stand in history. Who do you think will still figure in twenty years?

'Prince will still be important. And Madonna, I think Madonna has been incredibly important to the 1980s, musically. She was a little disco queen who lost the baby fat and became an icon, an '80s version of Marilyn Monroe.'

What about Bruce Springsteen?

'I wanna hear Bruce's new stuff as much as anyone else 'cos I wanna hear which way he goes. Nobody, except the people who've played on the record, who say it's real good, have heard it yet. I don't know what Bruce means to everyone else. For someone from New Jersey that's not a fair question. He was the hometown boy, so to us he was Jesus when I was in high school . . . [But] I really don't know about Bruce.'

Any rock artists? How about Aerosmith?

'I don't know if they count or not: they've been around for seventeen years as it is. But they have influenced so many bands who came up when I did. Not us particularly but Rätt and Mötley and all those kind of bands.'

Guns N' Roses?

'Good question. They've still yet to be proven. I don't know whether Axl is a genius or a psycho. I've heard that this song "Civil War" is amazing and I think that lyrically if he is going after that then he has real potential of being there [in twenty years].'

How about Metallica?

'I don't know any of their music except for that song "One", which I saw on MTV. They were better than I previously thought they'd be. But I've still never heard a Metallica album and I never saw them when I played with them. It's not that I'm not interested, I respect those guys a lot. But they have given Bon Jovi a lot of stick. I actually sent them a telegram when their bass player, Cliff Burton, got killed because I knew that the bond that they have is similar to what we have and I really felt bad for them. Apparently they never received it. When we played Donington they thought we cleared the backstage area but of course the band never knew anything about it and Metallica carried a chip. Metallica have been important to heavy metal, but I don't know enough about them.'

Mötley Crüe?

'I don't think that the Mötleys are at all influential. I don't think that they ever had enough to say lyrically, musically or personally. Again, because of the mud they've thrown over here, it made better press for them to slag us than to slag Doc McGhee [one-time co-manager of both Bon Jovi and the Crüe] 'cos no one knows who Doc McGhee is. But I swear that I did not set off those lasers and pyro in Russia. If that was so important to them then maybe they didn't deserve to headline. All power to them, they just made their most popular album yet [*Dr Feelgood*], but I don't think they'll stand the test of time.'

Where do you think Bon Jovi will be in twenty years' time?

'I want us to be together because it's afforded me all these things. It's really been my love and I feel a loyalty to those four guys that I only feel toward my immediate family. I hope that I can keep it together, but I'll only keep it together if it's fun. I can't do it for money and I can't do it to keep the record company happy. I can't do it unless it's going to be a good time. Unless I still want to have a beer with those guys every night like we always have, then . . .'

He pauses, looks over the railing, thoughts elsewhere, then continues . . .

'We always grew up hearing "Boy, Van Halen were so dumb to split." But none of us in the general public know what the real problem was. Same with Journey, same with Aerosmith. I'm giving you these examples so you can tell your readers that I'm as confused as anyone. I want it to stay together because it's been so good but I don't want it if it is no longer good. [Former Journey singer] Steve Perry said to me, "You're right where I was when I walked away from it and I miss Journey." You go like, "Wow, I don't know if I should walk away from it."

'I know that I'll still make records and I'll still be able to tour but who cares about the money? That's not why I'm doing it. It's only if it's going to be fun that I'll continue with those four guys. Time will tell . . .'

CODA

I didn't have much to do, personally, with Jon Bon Jovi after that final interview, although our paths would continue to cross professionally, not least when I became editor-in-chief of *Classic Rock* magazine in the late 1990s. In the earliest days of the magazine, his record company wouldn't even send us copies of his albums to review. Jon was still dreaming of being on the cover of *Dazed and Confused* and didn't get it that his fans were actually buying a magazine for – pause to clear throat – older rock fans. It all changed when suddenly younger rock mags like *Kerrang!* stopped putting him on the cover and the *Mojos* of this world wouldn't feature him at all. That left . . . well, me and *Classic Rock*.

He didn't appear to have lightened up in the intervening years, either, smiling for the cameras, scowling behind the scenes, making demands via his various PRs and endless management flunkies. Still, however, his star continued to rise, and, yes, his music also improved – to the point where he has lately come perilously close to fulfilling his Springsteen fantasies. And let's face it, not even the Boss has ever appeared in an episode of *Ally McBeal*.

I had to laugh, though, when he and the band were seated in the front row of the UK version of the Rock and Roll Hall of Fame show in 2006, and the MC made some quip about needing a mosh pit for the 'Bon Jovi boys'. The cameras zoomed in on Jon and the 'boys', expecting to find them yucking it up. Instead, it came across a bunch of long faces and stony expressions. Bon Jovi left the mosh pit behind – if indeed they were ever really part of that culture – a long time ago, amigo. If only the rest of the wide world would just recognise it, eh, Jon?

MOSCOW PEACE, 1989

Unlike Live Aid in 1985, which, despite my inbuilt cynicism, I can't help but look back on as some sort of achievement, the Moscow Music Peace Festival – held four years later and barely remarked on outside of rock circles – is hard not to regard as something of a sham. A puny, self-serving spectacle by comparison to the Live Aid event it was meant to echo, the whole thing was so obviously a get-out-of-jail card for Doc McGhee (who, at that time, managed all the major acts on the bill, bar Ozzy Osbourne), rather than an honest-to-goodness attempt to raise money for the various drug charities it purported to support, that it was almost impossible to report on the whole thing with a straight face. So I didn't: I took the piss, and this time rightly so.

As for Moscow, I hear they have a McDonald's there now but that the queues for the few food and clothing stores are just as long as ever. God help them. I have been to India and Brazil but I've never seen poverty like the kind I witnessed in Russia; the kind that starves you mentally as well as physically. Coming home after a week in that grey place, Ealing Broadway on a Saturday afternoon looked like Santa's grotto, it sparkled and shone so much.

Moscow Music Peace Festival, first published in Kerrang!, *2 September 1989.*

It all began when a man named Ward approached me in the bar of the Soho Brasserie in London and began babbling excitedly about Russia, punching the air with his fist on certain key phrases like 'Media event!', 'History in the making!' and, most ominous of all, 'Once-in-a-lifetime experience!' That did it. The shutters came down. I have accepted enough offers of a 'Once-in-a-lifetime experience' to know to steer well clear of anyone blind or stupid enough to offer me another one now. Nevertheless, something about his manner endeared Ward to me. He was thirty-ish, dressed in a crumpled suit and worried tie, and he looked like he hadn't slept in several days. He spoke in rapid bursts, like quick-fire speech bubbles, and he had the wild red eyes of the True Believer.

He began to throw a few names around – Bon Jovi, Ozzy Osbourne, Mötley Crüe, the Scorpions. Then he stirred in a few ripe images – Moscow gripped by such a fearful heat everyone that can flees the city; Red Square at night beneath the shadow of the Kremlin; the vast and imposing Lenin Stadium getting ready to Make a Difference . . .

I had to admit, it sounded like my kind of scene. Jon Bon Jovi in the back of a Russian-made Zil limousine waxing lyrical about Nelson Mandela; Bob Geldof and the impossibility of obtaining a cold beer in Moscow; Ozzy in Red Square in the pissing rain, philosophical as ever: 'If I was living here full-time, I'd probably be dead of alcoholism, or sniffing car tyres – anything to get out of it. I can understand why there's such an alcohol problem here. There's nothing else to do!'; the Scorpions hamming it up onstage at the Lenin Stadium with a turbo-charged version of 'Back in the USSR'. I could see it all splayed out before me like a giant map.

Ward kept the drinks coming and eventually a deal was struck: I was contracted to present a thirty-minute documentary film for Sky Television, who were broadcasting highlights of the second of the two scheduled concerts, attempting to explain the purpose of the event and exploring some of the reasons for holding it in the first place.

This was to be Total Coverage From Every Angle, a veritable blitz-krieg of prolonged media gibberish centred on this deal called the Moscow Music Peace Festival. Ten days later I was drinking vodka in Moscow. Well, it's like Ozzy says: there simply is nothing else to do.

I don't know what images the name 'Moscow' conjures up in your mind, but I suppose the archetype must be of a large, grey, unhappy citadel full of cold stares and food queues. The reality of the situation, however, is much worse than that. The first thing you learn when you settle down to spend your first night in Moscow is that There Is No Food. At least, nothing actually edible. There are restaurants, of course, but mostly they are closed. Usually for 'cleaning'. Which seems to take place approximately six nights out of seven. When you do find a restaurant open, it's a take-it-or-leave-it deal: you can have the worst chicken kiev you ever tasted in your life or you can go drive a tractor.

Learning to survive on the road means learning to eat anything. Fussy eaters are the first to throw in the towel. As a result, over the years I have – at various trying moments – found myself: eating smoked reindeer and bear steaks in Helsinki; drinking from the foul tap water of Rio de Janeiro; quaffing large fistfuls of chilli-dogs and fries at fast-food counters all over Los Angeles; and gorging myself on raw fish and cold rice in Tokyo. All because it was either eat that or eat my own dick. But never in all my travels have I come across anything so frankly vomit-inducing as the chicken kiev in Moscow. 'Why do you think there are no dogs on the streets of Moscow?' whispered Dimitri, our official KGB-approved 'guide' and 'interpreter', conspiratorially as I pushed away my plate again one night.

So, all right, you can't eat. Rule number two: There Is No Such Thing As Russian Money. Well, actually, there is – it's called the rouble, but no self-respecting Russian accepts any home-grown currency. Officially, a rouble is supposed to be the equivalent of one pound sterling. But on the black market, they'll give you up to ten roubles for one pound. Even then, they're not worth having. The only thing you can buy with roubles are wooden dolls and big furry hats. The only real consumer variables available are on sale in the Tourist-Only stores, which take all major credit cards including American Express. Records or tapes are purchased on the black market.

In fact, the main currency in Moscow is US dollars. Or better still, packs of Marlboros. At the hotel bar (no beer, no wine, just Teacher's whisky, Vladivostok vodka and a seemingly limitless supply of Bounty bars), I paid for all my drinks in dollars. If I didn't have the exact amount I'd throw in a pack of Marlboros. For change, I'd receive an assortment of dollar bills, ten-franc pieces and the occasional silver Deutsche Mark. For small change I'd get handed a packet of orange-flavoured Tic-Tacs. I'm not kidding.

We were staying at a 'five-star' £125-a-night bread-and-water joint right in the heart of Moscow, one block from Red Square. Prostitutes lined the entrance to the hotel and dark-suited security guards checked the ID of anyone wishing to enter. Fat black cockroaches obviously high on life clung lazily to the walls and ceiling of the lobby. The night I arrived in my £125-a-night room up on the sixteenth floor, I was advised by one of the advance crew to check my bed for bedbugs before settling down for the night. In my bathroom the water running from the taps was the colour of yesterday's piss; in the soap dish there was only a rotting apple-core. The only towel provided was hanky-thin and crisp as an old rag. Two cigarette stubs floated lifelessly in the toilet pan. I was truly baffled. What the fuck happened back there when they had the Great Revolution? Didn't anybody come out on top at the end of it? And if anybody did, where do those guys go to eat? I didn't bother to check for bedbugs. I just pulled back the sheet and got in. I settled my head back on the pillow and turned out the bedside light.

By now you've read the reviews, and/or seen the telecast or heard it on the radio, and the question on everybody's lips is: so what the hell was all that actually about? Officially, the Moscow Music Peace Festival was about raising money for the Make a Difference Foundation – an anti-drugs and alcohol abuse agency set up late 1988 by Bon Jovi's manager Doc McGhee, as the lion's share of the community service programme McGhee was sentenced to by an American court after he pleaded guilty to funding a multi-million-dollar operation to smuggle eighteen tonnes of marijuana into the USA some years before.

After the 'production costs', all proceeds from the two concerts held in the Lenin Stadium are earmarked by the Make a Difference doyens for various drug and alcohol 'rehabilitation centres' and 'substance-abuse awareness' programmes, specifically in the Soviet Union, where until the onset of Gorby's perestroika it was not officially admitted that a drug or alcohol problem even existed. So far, so worthy. But, as Jon Bon Jovi was the first to admit, there's also the extra icing on the cake of doing something no other rock band has yet done. History and mystery and millions of dollars' worth of free publicity all rolled into one death-defying leap of the imagination.

'You know, at this stage of the game, it's like you ask yourself, what can we do that Zeppelin or the Stones or the Beatles didn't already do?' Jon told me from the back of his Zil. 'And being here is it. Not only do we get to come over in a good cause, we also get to put on the kind of rock show never before seen in the Soviet Union.'

And the whole world gets to watch. MTV had an American crew on board the airliner – the *Magic Bus* – that transported all the bands from the West that would be taking part. If that baby had gone down it would have taken the casts of Bon Jovi, the Scorpions, Mötley Crüe, Ozzy and his band, Cinderella and Skid Row with it. But it didn't, and waiting to greet its arrival at Cheremetyov Airport are TV crews from ITN, the BBC, Sky, CNN, some sombre-faced chaps from the official Soviet TV network, plus a couple of hundred print hacks flown in from various far-flung editorial outposts around the world, all edging for position. It was just the beginning of a media merry-go-round that would test the patience of a saint, never mind a road-hardened rock 'n' roller.

The press conference, like all press conferences everywhere, is a bore. Soft soap and bullshit. De-dum de-dum. Most of the questions from the Western press corps are directed at Jon Bon Jovi. Most of the questions from the Russians are for Ozzy. This comes as no surprise to anybody, except perhaps Ozzy. Doc McGhee paid for a survey to be conducted long before any of the bands arrived in Moscow to determine just how aware his potential Russian audience was of the acts he wanted to bring with him. Ozzy's name came top of the list.

'I was very surprised when they told me that,' said Ozzy. 'Surprised and flattered. Though looking 'round, I can see how my music or Sabbath's music makes sense here. It's bleak all round, isn't it?'

Right. Yet twenty-four hours earlier Ozzy had threatened to pull out of the event after McGhee suddenly changed his (Ozzy's) placing on the bill from third to fourth, upgrading Mötley Crüe – like Bon Jovi, the Scorpions, Skid Row and Gorky Park, all an integral part of McGhee Entertainments – to the slot above Ozzy. McGhee took the threat seriously enough to return Ozzy to his original placing on the bill, just below the Scorpions and Bon Jovi, and Ozzy kept his promise and boarded the *Magic Bus*. The farce repeated itself on the night before the first show when McGhee made another attempt to have Ozzy accept the fourth spot on the bill below Mötley Crüe. Again, Ozzy threatened to pull out, and again McGhee relented. What Mötley Crüe thought of all this is not generally known, although there were a lot of heated discussions taking place behind closed doors over at the Ukraine Hotel, where all the bands were staying, during the hours leading up to that first show at the Lenin Stadium.

For all their sweet talk to the media about this being a show where it's not important who headlines or who appears where on the bill, privately all of the acts gathered here in Moscow were fiercely competitive on this point. For example, there is no way in the world Bon Jovi are ever going to appear anywhere as anything but headliners ever again. The Scorpions, the only band from the West on the bill to have played before anywhere in the Soviet Union (ten sold-out nights in Leningrad in March '88), rightly lay the strongest claim to the second spot on the bill. As for Ozzy, he's always been happiest second or third on the bill.

'Like at Donington in '84,' he explained. 'The pressure's all on the headliners. You can just go out and enjoy yourself. I've done some of my best shows ever when I've been second or third on the bill at one of these big outdoor festivals.'

Mötley Crüe, who got their first taste of what it was like to play before a big arena crowd opening for Ozzy on his 1983/84 American tour, would these days never dream of appearing so low on a bill of this size – Make a Difference or not – anywhere else in the world. This is Moscow. You do what you're told.

Cinderella, Skid Row, Gorky Park and the other locally based and government-sponsored (read: no royalties) Soviet acts are all essentially along for the ride. But as long as they get their cut of the prime-time action that comes with it, they're happy.

Which is, at heart, what this trip is really all about: free publicity on a global level. And lots of it. And why not? Ask Sting, he'll tell you. The charity thing is pure gold. Bob Geldof's been dining out on it for years.

'I don't know,' Jon Bon Jovi shook his head when I talked to him about it. 'People are always ready to question the motives behind why a bunch of rock stars would want to get together and do something like this. And, sure, inevitably you get a clash of egos occasionally. It's not exactly the easiest thing to organise in the world; we sure found that out! But at the end of the day, I look at it like this. I wouldn't have known about Nelson Mandela's situation like I do now had I not been drawn to it because of the artists on Amnesty. Or I don't think that I would've ever known about Ethiopia the way I do now if it wasn't for Bob Geldof. So there is a wonderful icing on the cake. You get to see all these big performers that I enjoy, too, but there's ultimately a cause behind it. And that's what raises your awareness.'

Indeed . . . and yet a spectre still looms. That of Aerosmith, who not only pulled out of the event at the eleventh hour but also insisted their contribution to the official *Make a Difference* album (a version of The Doors' 'Love Me Two Times') be lifted from the final pressing, after expressing private concern over where exactly all the proceeds were actually going. Officially, the word is that Aerosmith are still busy putting last-minute touches to the release of their new album and the start of their own world tour, in Europe in October. Off the record, everybody remains earnest and tight-lipped on the subject. Something's gone down, but nobody's saying what. Besides, there's too much to do. The forty-eight hours leading up to the first show are spent in a blur of interviews and 'photo-opportunities'.

Everybody gets to go to Red Square. Ozzy is interviewed there for the Derek Jameson show on Sky, and Jon Bon Jovi, Richie Sambora and David Bryan arrive to view the scene, armed with a posse of about fifty photographers and at least six TV crews. Ozzy is telling Sky, 'It's not that I make millions out of playing Russia, I just want to play music to them, that's all. Maybe I'll give someone a smile on their face for a day in Russia.'

Meanwhile, back at the Lenin Stadium, I run into Vince Neil and Nikki Sixx and ask them the obvious question: so what the hell are Mötley Crüe, the ultimate all-American sex, drugs and rock 'n' roll band, doing in Russia, of all places, appearing at an anti-drugs concert? Sixx bares his teeth and smiles:

'It might be an anti-drugs concert for some people, but it's not for us. It's anti-abuse we're talking about. That's our belief. We're not here to preach. If you tell a young kid not to do drugs, he's gonna do it anyway. I know I did,' he goes on. 'We just say, if you cross the line between use and abuse, then that's really tragic. I've crossed that line, many times. And I know from experience that it's bad, and I try to tell kids not to cross the line. The rest is up to them.'

Klaus Meine from the Scorpions had a simpler message:

'There's everywhere a drug problem, all over the world. So I think it's good that the bands stand together on one stage and give a message to the kids in the world: forget about the drugs. The best drug is music.'

The last time I saw Jon Bon Jovi was in Red Square on the evening before my departure (we had to be back in London to edit the film in time for Sunday's live broadcast of the concert, so I never got to hang around and see either of the shows). He was still looking for a cold beer. 'Have you discovered any of the nightlife here yet?' he asked me hopefully. I shook my head. I had spent the last three nights prowling the streets of Moscow, TV crew in tow, in search of something even faintly resembling the sort of nightlife we take for granted in the West. Only, like everything else in Russia, the only bars we discovered that catered for music, live or otherwise, were always closed or being 'cleaned'. We never found a single club open the whole time we were there. It made the high street in Sheffield on a cold Tuesday night in December seem like the most glamorous place on Earth.

I left Jon Bon Jovi still trying to Make a Difference on the steps of St. Basil's Cathedral in Red Square. It was drizzling rain and the sky was the colour of chilled vodka. The changing of the guard at the gates of the Kremlin was about to take place and a great crowd of tourists and out-of-towners gathered along one side of the Square to watch.

Me, I stick another dime in the jukebox (baby) and watch the discs go round . . .

CODA

The Make a Difference Foundation – the short-lived organisation that was supposedly behind the event – has, to my knowledge, never been heard of since. As for the money raised by the show, I don't even want to speculate where that all went. Of course, it would be nice to think that a goodly portion of it went where it was supposed to, but I don't recall too much in the way of follow-up as far as keeping the media informed of those developments. I just remember all the bands bitching and fighting about where they were going to be on the bill.

It almost goes without saying that barely anyone these days even recalls there *was* a Moscow Music Peace Festival. Any laughable subsequent claims – and there were a small few, usually made by fans looking to justify the whole sorry affair – that it was one of those events that helped bring about democracy in the former Soviet Union ('Oh, look, comrade, it's Ozzy Osbourne; quick, let's pull down the Berlin Wall!') – were thankfully ignored, and certainly by those of us that were stood there in the pissing rain, trying to make sense of it.

OZZY OSBOURNE, 1989

Inevitably, most interviews I did for *Kerrang!* were of the tell-me-about-the-new-album variety. So when I got a call from Sharon Osbourne asking me to come and speak to her husband about his latest mis-adventure – being banged-up on an attempted murder charge – I felt a strange mixture of excitement and apprehension. It wasn't every day I got asked to do something like that. But then, that was probably at least half the reason I got into rock writing as opposed to straight news reporting: I didn't see myself as the guy who could write with any insight on a topic as serious as, uh, murder. Naw, getting pissed and stoned and getting my rocks off to some noisy arse-wiggling rock band was about my level. That and pulling chicks – and even that was not always within my reach, as a writer or a fighter.

On the other hand, it wasn't every day a major rock star tried killing someone, and I was just sober enough at the time of the call to understand that this might actually make one hell of a story. Well, I was right about that . . .

Interview with Ozzy Osbourne, Buckinghamshire, first published in Kerrang!, *21 October 1989.*

Just like everybody else, the first I heard of the arrest of Ozzy Osbourne, at his Beel House mansion in Buckinghamshire, was when I read about it in the newspaper. 'DEATH THREAT' OZZY SENT TO BOOZE CLINIC! screamed the headline in the *Sun*. BAN ON SEEING WIFE! HELL OF DRYING OUT! According to the reports, the police had arrived at the house in the early hours of Sunday morning, 3 September, and subsequently arrested Ozzy for allegedly threatening to kill his wife and manager, Sharon, or 'intending her to fear that the threat would be carried out' as the official police report put it.

The phone got to me before I got to it – America's *National Enquirer*, the *Sunday Snort*, the *Daily Angst* – and all with the same questions: what happened? Did he finally go mad? Or better still, has he always been mad? And what about all the, you know, rumours? That Sharon had been having an affair and it was the discovery of this fact that prompted the fight between them. That Sharon's father and a former manager of both Ozzy and Black Sabbath, Don Arden, was about to step in and retake control of his estranged son-in-law's career? And that this move would precipitate the re-formation of the original Sabbath line-up, including Ozzy?

I realised straight away that these were the sorts of questions only my answer-phone could answer, so I switched the thing on and sat back to think it over. As chance would have it, I had seen both Ozzy and Sharon the day before the incident, at the studios of Capital Radio in London, where Ozzy had been taping an interview. He looked a mess. Eyeballs popping out of his skull, his face a mask of sweat; his mind drifting in and out of the conversation. Sharon smiled indulgently and hid whatever was going on inside her as she always does when Ozzy's having one of his 'bad days'. They were on their way to Hamley's toy shop in Regent Street, to pick up a present for their eldest daughter, Aimee, whose sixth birthday it was the next day.

I asked Ozzy how he was enjoying being home again after his long recent world tour.

He shook his head and frowned: 'It's alright – I'm bored already, though; I don't know what to do with myself. Why don't you come up to the house for a drink sometime?'

I said, sure, why not? And that was the last time we talked before the whole shithouse went up in flames. Then a couple of nights after the newspapers broke the story, with Ozzy safely installed in Huntercombe Manor in Buckinghamshire – a private rehabilitation centre for recovering alcoholics and 'substance abusers' – Sharon called me at home. Other than checking that she was OK, I found myself asking the same dumb questions as everybody else: what happened? Did he just go mad, or what?

'Yes.'

Sharon spent her formative years working for her father, Don Arden, whose reputation in the music business for being a hard-boiled example of the Old School, with a bite to back his formidable bark is as well known as it is well founded. Later she split acrimoniously to manage and marry Ozzy, one of Don's hottest properties. Following that experience, Sharon is a lady used to dealing with tough situations. 'She can be a hard bastard, my old lady,' Ozzy once told me. 'Anybody who fucks with her – watch out!' On the phone that night, however, Sharon sounded frail, upset, weary and concerned.

'Alcohol is destroying his life,' she sighed. 'To be an alcoholic means you have a disease. If Ozzy had cancer, people would feel sorry for him. But because he's an alcoholic, people don't understand. He just needs to get help.'

Even though Sharon has since dropped her charges, the legal ramifications have yet to be untangled fully and the police may yet bring a charge to court. It would be unwise therefore to attempt a full blow-by-blow account here of what happened that night. Nevertheless, it's easy to put the pieces together: Ozzy was celebrating his daughter's birthday by getting smashed on his current favourite tipple, Russian vodka. He has a meandering drunken argument with Sharon that begins over dinner and continues throughout the rest of the evening, culminating in Ozzy attacking his wife with such ferocity she felt compelled to call for the police.

'It wasn't Ozzy and that's what terrified me,' said Sharon. 'Ozzy would never, ever, ever have done that to me, or anyone, because he's just not capable of it. But when Ozzy is loaded, Ozzy disappears and someone else takes over.'

Following his arrest, Ozzy spent the next thirty-six hours in a cell at nearby Amersham police station, while he waited to appear before Beaconsfield Magistrates Court on the Monday morning. Waiting for him inside the courtroom that day were over fifty reporters and photographers from the world's tabloid press. After a brief hearing, Ozzy was placed on bail under three conditions: that he should immediately check himself into an alcoholic rehabilitation programme at a live-in centre of his choice; that he should not make any attempt to contact Sharon; and that he should not return to Beel House. Instead, Ozzy was driven from the courthouse back to Amersham police station, where he was met by his long-time friend and employee, Tony Dennis, who drove him directly to Huntercombe Manor, a £250-per-day rehab joint already familiar to the errant singer. (He had stayed there twice before for brief periods earlier this year and last.)

For the time being, he's staying put there. If a trial date is set, it could be as much as three to six months away. Even if he doesn't have to attend trial, it will be at least three months, by his own doctor's reckoning, before Ozzy will be anywhere near ready to go home.

'Whatever's wrong with Ozzy, it's not something that's going to take six weeks in a rest home to cure,' says Sharon. 'It's going to take a lot longer than that to get Ozzy well again. But no matter how long it takes, the children and I will be there waiting for him. I am not divorcing him. I just want him to get well.'

Although I have been friends with both Ozzy and Sharon for some years now, that Ozzy might want to meet and talk with me at this precise moment had never occurred to me. I had imagined him far too busy with doctors and lawyers, his senses irretrievably dulled by medication, to even think about doing an interview. So when Tony Dennis called a week after my conversation with Sharon and said Ozzy wanted to talk, I was surprised, to say the least. 'He's got a lot he wants to get off his chest,' said Tony. 'But he doesn't trust talking to anyone else from the press.'

Significantly or not, I don't know – it hardly seems to matter under the circumstances and yet in another way it's almost too rueful – but Tony and I decide to meet on the steps of the Hammersmith Odeon, scene of so many triumphant and not-so moments from Ozzy's twenty-year career. From there, Tony drives me the rest of the way to Huntercombe Manor, a large building in the style of a traditional English country house. It lies up a long, winding path shaded by trees, somewhere off the M40. We arrived at about 7.30 p.m. on an already dark Sunday evening, two weeks to the day since Ozzy's arrest. Sundays are one of the two days of the week that the 'guests' at Huntercombe are allowed visitors.

The main reception area is part hotel lobby, part dentist's waiting room. People mill around casually and at first it's hard to distinguish the 'patients' from the 'visitors'. Eventually, a pattern emerges: the patients are the ones smiling and looking relaxed; the visitors are the ones shuffling uneasily in their best shoes, chain-smoking and snatching furtive glances at their watches. I wait in the TV room while Tony goes off to locate Ozzy. He arrives, typically, in a nervous panic, not a little self-conscious perhaps, immediately fumbling for a cigarette, groping for a light.

'Allo, Mick. Sorry I kept you waiting . . . I was in a meeting with my therapist . . . Have you got a light?'

He keeps up the chatter all the way down the corridor and up the stairs to his bedroom on the first floor. Inside, his room is something like the size and quality of a suite at some well-to-do provincial hotel: one large bedroom with bathroom and shower en suite and a smaller adjoining room, a large bed, the usual bedroom furniture and a couple of chairs. No TV, though. And no smoking allowed in the room.

'It's a bit like a hotel room,' I remark casually.

'Yeah, except you can't go downstairs to the bar,' says Ozzy, straight-faced, whipping out an ashtray from where he's got it stashed under the bed and lighting up his cigarette.

We settle down in opposite chairs at the table by the window and I pull out the tape-recorder and set it down between us amidst a pile of chocolate bars, packs of Marlboros and cans of Diet Coke that already crowd the table. Despite everything, Ozzy looks better than I've seen him in some time. Certainly more focused than the stoned and bamboozled figure I ran into the day before his arrest. And far more alert and together than the lost and distant character that sleep-walked his way through the Moscow Music Peace Festival back in July. Dressed in black T-shirt and black slacks, he looks trim and in very good (physical) shape. Mentally, though, it's harder to tell straight off. It's clear Ozzy's very uptight about the things people have read into, and in some cases read about, his present dilemma, and for that reason says he wants to 'set the record straight once and for all, and then everybody can fuck off and leave me and my family alone to get on with the rest of our lives'.

The words raced out of his mouth and at one point I feared the torrent of emotion would turn into a flood and that he was on the point of bursting into tears. But just when I thought he might be stepping over the edge and winding himself up unduly, he would suddenly bring the conversation right back down to Earth again with a small joke, or, more often, a fitful shrug of the shoulders. Which is exactly where Ozzy says he wants to be these days: back down to Earth. What follows is a ninety-five per cent verbatim transcript of the conversation we had that night, in Ozzy's room, illicitly smoking cigarettes next to the open window and sipping decaffeinated coffee. Under the circumstances, you'd hardly call it an 'interview'. More a conversation between sober boozing buddies that tends to jump around a lot. Anyway, for better or for worse, Ozzy was on a roll. Mostly I just sat back and watched.

Let's start at the beginning, Ozzy. How, in your own words, have you ended up in this mess?

'Well, what happened was I tried touring sober, and I did very well for about four-and-a-half months, and then I started messing around again with it [drinking], you know? And I came back from Russia, went to Los Angeles, and I had this Russian vodka. So I tried a bit of that. And it was all right for a week or so, on the vodka. Then I became like a closet case, you know? I started drinking in the closet and not telling anybody I was drinking. Till in the end ... apparently Sharon and I were having a few words, she was getting on at me for ... I think she suspected ... I mean, my paranoia stepped in, you know? And I just went into an alcoholic blackout.'

How long have you suffered from these 'alcohol blackouts'?

'I became a blackout drinker about a year ago – as far as I know.

I may have been one for many years before that and never really realised it. Anyway, I went into a blackout and don't remember anything of the incident. I vaguely remember going to a Chinese restaurant with Sharon. Just bits and pieces, you know? I'd drunk a bottle of vodka that day. And then when I woke up in the jail and all my face was scratched where Sharon had tried to defend herself, I didn't really know what had happened. I could remember being nicked, but I thought maybe I'd fallen over when they were dragging me out of the house. I just couldn't remember. It was like a mad dream. At the time, in the police car, I thought I was dreaming. I thought, this is not real, you know? Police in my house, taking me out of my house? But I went to jail. They kept me in Amersham jail for two days. They were all right, in the jail. The jail conditions were disgusting, though. I mean, I know they're not supposed to be built like Butlin's, but they were terrible, you know?'

In what way?

'Real disgusting places, shit on the walls ... not fit for a rat, you know?'

Were you sharing a cell?

'No, I was on my own. They were all right to me, though, the people in there. They gave me cigarettes and chatted to me once in a while. What really bothered me was the press. They've built the whole thing way out of proportion. I'm not divorcing Sharon. We've met several times since the incident. I'm not rejoining Black Sabbath. I'm not going back to Don Arden. I just wish everybody would back off and leave me and my family alone, you know? Leave us alone!'

The ugly rumours have certainly been spreading since your arrest.

'There's a lot of rumours about Sharon and I breaking up and that she's been having an affair, and all that. As far as I know it's all rumours, it's not true. All I can say at this point is I'd like to thank all the fans who have sent me lots of letters. I am gonna record a new album again with my band. I'm not gonna be touring so much any more. I mean, I'm not gonna tour for eighteen months at a go any more. I'm gonna cut it down. My band are very loyal to me, though; they've all been down to see me. Zakk [Wylde – guitarist] and Randy [Castillo – drummer] flew across from the States especially to see me. So I've still got the thing there, it's just that I went off the rails for a while, you know? The pressure of the tour got to me and I just blew up. That's what happens to me. I've got no other way of getting rid of the frustration, it just happens, you know? Other people go to the pub and have a few drinks and mellow out. I can't do that. I'm a chronic alcoholic and I'm in a chronic phase, and so on the Wednesday before the weekend the incident happened I'd already checked into this place. But my alcoholic mind was telling me, "Don't go Ozzy, just pull out at the last minute and go up north to some drinking friends of yours and get smashed for a week." And this was all planned in my sick head, you know?'

Did you go up north?

'No, no – I got nicked on the Saturday night, didn't I? I'm just so glad I'm here now, though. I miss my kids and my home, but I have a lot of hope now, you know? I have a real lot of hope, because I don't wanna go any further down the scale than that. That was pretty bad, what I did.'

Do you remember attacking Sharon?

'I can only take what's been told to me, but I assume she's right because . . . I mean, it really shook my wife up. Really, what I suppose it's true to say happened, was we had a domestic argument that went a bit over the edge because I was pissed. Which happens every night of the week to some people, but when it happens to me everybody gets to hear about it. Everybody rows. I suppose I was pissed and I took it a little too far and threatened to kill her. But it's snowballed yet again, same as all the other incidents. It's just gone way out of proportion. I just wish everybody would back off. I'm very much still in love with my wife, you know? I don't wish anyone any harm. But just leave us alone.'

I heard that both Don Arden and his son, David, tried to get in contact with you when you checked into this place.

'They tried to call me in the jail. I got telegrams and all that. I mean, I appreciate the thought, but I think they need to take care of their own business and leave me alone. Me and my family are doing OK as we are. I don't need their help. I'm a big boy now. I'm not the vegetable that they used to call me any more.'

Do you think something like this had to happen before you came to your senses and decided to really do something about your drink-related problems?

'Maybe so. It's not fear that makes one want to quit drinking, though. Alcoholic people, the same as drug-dependent people, don't understand why they're doing it. I don't understand why I get drunk. I don't understand any of it. But you've got to be on your guard twenty-four hours a day, or suddenly you're lying on the floor the next morning with an empty booze bottle by you and you think, what happened? How did I get here? My intention on Saturday morning wasn't ... I mean, I didn't get up and think, "Oh, it's a good day to go up the pub, get smashed as a rat, come back, drink another bottle of vodka and strangle the wife!" That was not my intention. I just wanted to have a few drinks and mellow out. But I just go crazy with booze now. Today, when my children left me, that was enough for me to want to stop. They were all crying, looking out the back of the Range Rover, and my heart broke. And being in a place like this, it's kind of lonely, you know? You don't know if they're gonna put electrodes to your balls or what.'

What's it actually like here?

'It's all right. It's like a therapy thing, you talk in a group to other alcoholics. I really can't give too much more about the place away because it's supposed to be anonymous, you know? But there's a lot of different people here from all walks of life and we sit in a group and we discuss our problems and we recognise similarities. Anybody that's an alcoholic, you always think you're the only one that does these crazy things. But you find out later that everybody who's an alcoholic does exactly the same things. There's a pattern to it, and so you talk it out instead of bottling it up. I'd say something like, whenever I have the third drink I go a bit funny in the head. And the guy in charge will ask if anyone else relates to that and someone will say they can. So it makes you feel a little bit more at ease with yourself. I'm not gonna try any of these aversion therapy things though, where you take this pill and have eight bottles of vodka and throw up. I used to do that without having a pill! I mean, Sharon and I have had a pretty rough year this year, with the work schedule. Sharon's been working her arse off with the Quireboys, Lita Ford and me. She never stops working, which kind of gets on my tits sometimes. Because when I come off tour I wanna be with my wife and family, and she's still a manager for other bands.'

Does that make you resentful?

'I get pretty resentful over it, then I get bored. But I've got to work it out somehow or other. I still love her very, very much. But it was hell for me on that last tour: fourteen months! Trying to get sober on the road is ... Everybody I've met that's got sober said to me, "Ozzy, you're heading for major destruction, you're heading for a major calamity", because you haven't got a chance on the road. I was whacking cortisone in me twice a month, and all that shit just to keep going. And it's all mind-altering. It's all a drug. It's a steroid. I was fucking crazy when I came off that last tour! Absolutely insane! I'm still not sane now. I'm still on medication in this place.'

What sort of medication are you on?

'Anti-depressants mostly, because the side-effects of cortisone make you very depressed and you think the world's coming down on your shoulders all the time. And I'm on various anti-fit pills, because I became a fit-drinker, I became a spasm-drinker.'

What's a 'fit-drinker'?

'It's like, when I was withdrawing one time I went into like a spasm, because I didn't have a medical detox. This was about six months ago. It's not such a major thing. It doesn't mean I'm gonna have a heart attack. I'm pretty well healthy, I train every morning on my bike and I run around the field a bit. It's not as bad as it sounds, but if you've got a record of having these seizures they keep you on this medication. I'm on all kinds of different stuff. But I'm glad I'm here, as I said before. It's the best place for me, and it's the only place I've got a chance. Even if I wanted to drink, I can't, you know? And I want to stay here for as long as it takes. I'm not gonna leave here until I feel that I can cope with the real world. I've got to get well this time because it could have been a darn sight worse; I could have ended up killing my wife, which I would never have forgiven myself for till the day I died.'

You have spent time in places like this before and it doesn't appear to have had much lasting effect. What makes you think that this time will be any different?

'Because I'm not gonna start work until I'm well enough. I'm not even thinking about work, Mick.'

*

So how long are you actually in here for?

'Indefinitely. The usual thing is four to six weeks. But I'm not even thinking about that. I'm thinking about three to six months, or maybe even longer. There's no time limit. I'm not gonna go out into the real world until I'm well again. My wife's still in shock. My kids ... We're all still in shock over this episode, because it wasn't me in my full ... I didn't mean to ... You've known me, Mick, for a long time. In my wildest dreams I wouldn't have wanted to do that. I just wanna try and stop these fucking sickos accusing my wife of having affairs, of me having affairs. Everybody's fucking trying to get on our case to destroy the marriage. It's always the same, people want to clean their own doorstep before they start trying to clean mine. There's plenty of shit on everybody else's doorstep to clean. Leave us alone and we'll be all right.'

So are you going to have to stand trial eventually?

'If it goes to court, it goes to court, you know? I mean, the difference between me and everybody else is all my dirty laundry comes out in the open. When we have a row it's in full view of the whole fucking world! That's enough pressure on its own. My wife is in red ribbons, I'm not very well. And the pressure we're under is phenomenal.'

What would be the best way things could turn out for you right now, Ozzy?

'That Sharon and I are still together. That we're all back to normal, and I can learn a bit more tolerance. And that we have happy days for the rest of our lives, you know? I can't speak for Sharon because I've learnt in this place not to speak for anybody else any more. I presume, at the end of the day, she wants to settle down, though.'

But you'd like to keep working, wouldn't you?

'Yeah, but keep working in a more civilised manner. I mean, what do I wanna do a fucking gig in all these far off places for? Russia was OK, it was a very interesting place. I wouldn't mind going there again one day. But I don't want to be on the road forever. I've bought a house in Buckinghamshire and in the two-and-a-half years since I bought it, I must have been there about three months! At the most! I mean, what's the point in me buying all this property and buying all this stuff if I'm never there to appreciate it?'

This, it seems to me, is the saddest part of all. You're one of the world's biggest rock stars; your albums have consistently sold in their millions over the years, with or without Black Sabbath. Now you come home from one of your – admittedly longest – but certainly most successful world tours ever, to be with your wife and three beautiful children. And on paper, you should be the happiest man in the world.

'Instead, you end up in a rehab joint on an attempted murder charge. Happiness doesn't come from high finance, though. It helps a great deal. I mean, people say, I'd rather be wealthy and unhappy than poor and unhappy. And I'm not going to give it to some far-off fucking charities, you can forget that! But it's like, what's the point in working if you don't appreciate what you're working for? I'm never there to take part in anything, so I build up a lot of resentment. Not personally against Sharon, but I build up a lot of resentment within me. Like, why didn't I do that? And why didn't I think of that? Because I'm always working. And then coming home is an anti-climax, you know? I think, when I get home I'm gonna take Jack [Ozzy and Sharon's three-year-old son. They also have two daughters: Kelly, aged four; and Aimee, whose sixth birthday it was the day Ozzy was arrested] out on my bike, I'm gonna buy the girls a little paddling pool. I wanna do all those little things that fathers are supposed to do. And when I think about how it's gonna be, I think it's gonna be sunny, it's gonna be this, it's gonna be that. And when you finally get home, it's never how you pictured it. It's either raining, or they've run out of paddling pools, or the bike's broken that you were gonna take Jack out on . . .

'Also, after living such an active life for a year or so, you come home and people just live ordinary lives, and it's hard for you to wind down. I mean, I understand how people go into meditation and all that, you know? I suppose it's a good way of winding down. You get bored so easily, too. I've got a concentration span of about thirty seconds. I've just been seeing my therapist in that room before you came and he said, you've got to learn some relaxation. I said, I've never relaxed since the day I was born, I can't sit still for a moment.'

Have you actually tried meditation or any other relaxation techniques?

'Well, part of the therapy is a kind of a meditation exercise. When I say "meditation" people out there will probably think I'm talking about the guru and all that. But it's nothing like sitting there going,

"OOMMMM!" We just shout "PINTS!"' He laughs. '"PINTS!" and "BROWN AALLLEEEE!!!" No, it's all right. I feel safe here, you know? It's when I'm out there . . . I walk out the house, in the yard, in my studio, out of my studio, in my yard, back in the house. I'm like a bloody preying mantis! Yet when I'm on the road for long periods of time, it's worse. I've been on the road for over twenty years, you know? And I really don't enjoy being out on the road for huge long periods of time. It would be worth it if I could go home every two weeks or something. But it don't work like that.

'And I get resentful when I'm away for too long a time. My kid starts to walk, my kid goes to school, my kid takes part in the school sports, and I'm never there for any of it. And I just get pissed off with it. I think, why am I out here on the road all the time? I mean, I get on the phone and they go: "Aimee came second in a race at school today". And I go, "Oh wow, great. What the fuck you telling me for?" You could tell me Aimee just became the first child cosmonaut in the world! I wouldn't know anything about it. And every time I leave my kids, a little part of me dies, you know? I mean, they came today, and they were all crying in the back of the Range Rover when they had to leave me. And I looked at the back of that Range Rover and I thought, that's a good enough reason for anybody to quit fucking boozing.

'At this point, Mick, my number one priority is to get sober and stay sober. I never again want to be in a bar. I've said this a million times before, I know, and always ended up in a bar. But I have hope that I can kick this booze thing and get straight once and for all. It's like a love affair I have with booze. It's like, you know it's killing you but you can't stop. It's like any addiction. You know it's killing you but you just can't put the stuff down. No alcoholic person out there goes, "Oh shit, yeah, I got pissed for a week, I don't wanna talk about it". I mean, Sharon used to drink a lot of booze many years ago. But she got up one morning, we were in Monmouth, and she said, "Fucking hell, Ozzy, I feel like shit, I'm never gonna drink again". And she's never drunk since, as far as I know.'

Do you seriously believe you will be able to quit drinking for good?

'I hope so. I've got to go to constant therapy classes for the rest of my life, I suppose. I've got to go to meetings. I've got to start reading lots of books. I've got to meet up with other recovering alcoholics.'

Do you have any close men friends?

'No, not that close!' he guffaws. Then becomes serious again. 'I'm involved in a fellowship, where we all sit around chatting about how it was, what it's like now and, you know, how you got here. Two alcoholics can do more for each other than any psychiatrist or therapy. Two alcoholics talking it over can do a lot for each other. And I've met people a lot worse off than me that got well on this programme. Ultimately, I've got two choices: either get it right this time, or screw up again. And if I don't get it right I'll either die or go insane. I mean, I don't even *like* drinking. The feeling of being drunk is oblivion for me. I don't drink for the taste, I hate the taste! I drink it for oblivion from this planet, you know, get me off!'

They say that a lot of alcoholics are actually allergic to alcohol, and that's what makes it so addictive. The body becomes addicted to the poison and the rest is all a major allergic reaction.

'I heard that before, yeah. Maybe I am, I don't know. All I know is, I am an alcoholic and my name is Ozzy. And I've got to take certain steps to try and arrest the disease. Because I'm either gonna kill myself, kill someone else, which I very nearly did, or I'm gonna go insane, I'm gonna be locked away in an insane asylum. It's got to that point now where I don't get happy-pissed, I go bulldozing around. I don't even know what I'm doing or where I'm at. Sharon says she's terrified when she sees me drink now. It upsets the whole family, close friends and everybody that works for me. You should do an article on some of the people who have been around me the last twelve months. I've been like Dr Jekyll and Mr Hyde, you know? And I'm really like that when I get drunk – from Dr Jekyll to Mr Hyde, every time. But I can't keep saying, "I'm cured, mate!" You know, "cured" in inverted commas. Because I never will be cured from it. I accept that now. I've just got to take certain steps. I've got to be on medication for a while because I became a manic depressive from the cortisone shots. I mean, major depressions. But if I can just reaffirm, I'm in treatment. But there's no guard outside the door. I'm not in shackles. I'm not getting electrodes 'round my bollocks.'

It's nice to see you've been able to keep some of your sense of humour about this.

'All in all, that's about the only thing I have got, which cheers not only me up but all the rest of the people here. We have a scream here. Somehow it's easy to laugh at your troubles. Yet I can have double-platinum records and all the rest of the shit and I'm still unhappy about it. I'll always find a fucking fault in anything. That's the artistic temperament, I suppose.'

What was the main reason you asked me here this evening? What is it you want to tell the world the most?

'I just wanted to set the record straight. I picked up the newspaper and I read "Ozzy gets divorced", and it's not that at all! I mean, not as far as I'm aware of. Sharon was 'round this afternoon. I asked her then, "Are you going to divorce me?". She said, "Absolutely not". And I want to say that I'm not gonna let people from the outside fuck my marriage up. Nobody thought we would last as long as we have, but we have. And I hope to God that we last as long as the rest of our lives.'

It's hard to imagine you and Sharon apart. If the worst came to the worst, though, and you did split up, would you go back on the bottle, do you think?

'The very worst thing that could happen to me would be if me and Sharon were to split up. But if it did happen, I wouldn't drink, no. Because I can't drink. Because that would fuck everything up even more. And that's what I've gotta say to myself – no matter what, I don't pick up that first drink. There's no such thing for me any more as just-have-a-half-Ozzy. One's too many and ten is not enough for me. Once I'm off I'll drink the fucking planet dry! And when you hear of people like Phil Lynott dying, or Bonham and all that, you think: that will never happen to me. But it fucking will! It's catching up with me rapidly. I don't wanna be the next fucking victim, you know?'

Aside from the alcoholism, do you think you suffer from any other problems? Paranoia, insecurity?

'Oh yeah, I've always been a paranoid person. Always. Ultra-paranoid. I'm very nervous and shy, too. When I'm performing, that's a different person again. The performing Ozzy is nothing like the person you see now. At least, I fucking hope not. I mean, I don't suppose Laurel and Hardy walked around in the silly hats when they were offstage, and neither do I. But some people look at me and they expect me to walk around with a fucking bag full of bats! Hi there, wanna bat? It's not real, you know? It's called entertainment.'

What about the rest of the people in this place – were they at all wary of you when you first arrived?

'No, I keep everybody smiling down here. We have a bit of a laugh sometimes. It's all right here, it really is all right here. I mean, it's tough in the respect that sometimes I think, what the fuck am I doing in another dry-out zone? But you know, if you're in a facility like this one and you don't put your heart and soul into it, then you ain't gonna get anything out of it, you know? I mean, I can sit here looking out of my window in my two-hundred-and-fifty-pounds-a-day fucking room and think, I'm here, what now? But you've gotta get down to some work. You've got to give it your time. When I saw my kids go away today in that car crying, I thought, "What a fucking arsehole you are Ozzy. What a total dickhead! You're saying goodbye to your kids again and you should be at home with them."

'I beat myself up about it, you know? I get really down, because it wasn't my intention to fuck everything up again. But whatever happens, I am definitely not splitting up with Sharon. And even if it came to that, I would never go with Don Arden again. And I am definitely, definitely not rejoining Black Sabbath. And that's from the bottom of my heart. You can kiss that one straight off. I will never rejoin Black Sabbath. No fucking way! Not in this life or the next.'

Has Sabbath guitarist Tony Iommi tried to get in touch with you?

'Yeah, he's phoned me. I wouldn't pick up his call, though. I haven't spoken to the fucking dickhead since Live Aid and even then he didn't say goodbye. So what's he suddenly become my old pal for? I mean, I'm not that much of a dickhead that I can't see that. I'm stoned, I'm not fucking brain-dead! Not yet, anyway, old bean. Not yet . . .'

CODA

Weirdly, when I reminded Ozzy of this story not long ago he swore blind he couldn't even remember me coming to see him – which says something for the state of mind he was in at the time, poor bastard. Not that it took him long to snap out of it. Just over a year after this story first ran I spent the evening with Ozzy at the apartment he was then renting in LA, drinking brandy, smoking a bong and snorting our brains out together. Not even an attempted murder, it seems, would be enough to stop Ozzy in his tracks for long. Only increasing old age and the even more unexpected success of the realest 'reality show' ever to hit TV would do that.

These days Ozzy is fit and well, and doing better than ever. As such, he is an example to all of us who lived through the good old, bad old days with him. And he's still my favourite rock star.

POISON, 1988

After it was published, this story quite quickly became known as the one where I was 'locked in a cupboard'. What was even stranger to me back then was just how long the piece was talked about afterwards – literally, for years. Flattering though that is for any writer, the reasons it became so well known to *Kerrang!* readers had little to do with how well (or not) the story was actually written. In retrospect, it was simply because that, for once, rather than broadly praise the subject of one of its features, *Kerrang!* had allowed one of its writers to put the boot in. While this was a fairly regular occurrence in the reviews section, it was rare enough within the features pages – let alone in one of its cover stories, which this was – that it immediately became one of the most talked-about stories I ever wrote for the magazine.

With very tired eyes, Ross Halfin looks at me and asks the 64,000 dollar question: 'Do you have the slightest idea what's going on here?' It's 8.15 p.m. Ross and I are standing alone, chair-less and cheerless, unable to escape, in a large empty room backstage at the Nassau Coliseum in New York. In the distance, we can hear Poison onstage, rattling their jewellery for all it's worth, fifteen minutes into a tight, strictly-no-encores, forty-minute-long opening spot for David Lee Roth. Ross should be in the photographers' pit, shooting the show; I should be out there, scribbling half-arsed little notes and reviewing the damn thing. It is, after all, what Ross and I do best, which is why Poison's record company, Capitol Records, spent all that money flying us out here in the first place. At least, in our mutual madness, that's what we'd assumed.

Well, not according to the band, baby. What me and Ross should be doing is standing in this goddamned room, pulling our plonkers and counting the bricks in the walls. Escape is impossible. Two hours we've already been trapped in this room, and it will be two more before we finally get the hell out of here, and the weirdness is compounded by the fact that neither of us understands why any of this should be happening. And yet here we are and here it is. Three doors out of the room; two of them guarded by men who are not interested in our stories, only interested in our passes, of which we have none because nobody will give us any; the third door, leading to Poison's dressing room, slammed and locked shut to us.

'Mickey,' Ross groans. 'What's going on? I don't understand it. If they don't want us around, why don't they just tell us to fuck off? Why have they stuck us in a fucking room and left us here to stew? I'm dreaming, aren't I? Go on, tell me I'm dreaming.'

Five p.m. precisely, as requested, we had turned up at the gates of the Nassau Coliseum. Backstage passes were to be collected; a pre-show photo-session was to have taken place; there was business to be taken care of; some rock and rolling to be done; a show to see; who knows, maybe even destiny to write. Kidz, as far as Halfin and I were concerned, for the next twenty-four hours we were going to make *Kerrang!* Poison's oyster! And then the shit started.

'Sorry boys, no Halfin or Wall down here on my list,' drawled the sweet old uniform on the backstage gate, just like something out of a B-movie. 'I'll try calling the production office for you, though.'

He calls, he tries. Nothing. He has to repeat our names four or five times before whoever he's talking to on the other end of the line is able to tell him for sure that there are no passes back there for any Halfin or Wall. 'Sorry boys.'

OK. A mistake, a mix-up; we've seen this movie, too. The band haven't arrived themselves yet, we are told, so we decide to sit it out and wait. An hour-and-a-half later we're still waiting outside. It's cold, we can't come in, but it's an hour's drive back to where we're staying and there's no car to take us there, and anyway, what the fuck, this can't go on for much longer. The band will get here, there'll be apologies and smiles, we'll get what we can done, cover the show, bang bang, yeah yeah. Where the fuck are our passes?

At last, someone arrives to take us through. A roadie; young, hair, solemn.

'I've come to take you guys in.'

We ask him if he has any passes for us.

'I don't know anything about any passes. I was just told to take you guys through.'

We get taken to Poison's dressing room, where another roadie tells us we cannot stay.

'You'll have to wait in the corridor outside.'

Only then yet another roadie tells us we cannot wait there either because we don't have any passes.

'You'll have to wait in here.'

'Here' turns out to be the room Halfin and I will not leave again for another three-and-a-half hours. Adjacent to the band's dressing room, The Room You Cannot Leave is a derelict space cluttered with empty, abandoned bookshelves and a couple of bare tables. Two roadies shift the bookshelves in order to make some space for us to stand in. Then they leave us to it. We stand there looking at each other, Ross and I, sharing this horrible sinking feeling.

At 7.15 p.m., Poison arrive. Not with a bang, but with a whisper. Standing in the room next to theirs, going out of our minds with boredom, we hear them at it. It's obvious they don't know we're in here. Rikki Rockett, Poison's drummer, suddenly sidles into our bit with an 'I wonder what's in here?' look on his face. What's in here are two very uncomfortable Limeys left with no pass, no class, and no arse, in a windowless room fortunate enough to at least boast a toilet, saving us the indignation of having to piss on the floor like chained dogs.

'Hi guys, how're ya doing?' Rikki smiles uncertainly. Ross and I can't help staring at him as though he was a person from another world. 'OK – see ya later,' he says, disappearing into the dressing room. A minute later Poison's bass player, Bobby Dall, appears in the doorway connecting our two very different rooms, clutching a sandwich, again with no more curiosity than a mouse. 'I wonder what's in this old room?'

By now the vibe Ross and I are filling this room with is very bad and Dall seems to pick up on it straight away. He just looks at us for about three seconds, throws us a barely perceptible nod, and turns on his heel back into the dressing room. Two minutes later the band's personal security man walks in, says nothing, just yanks the door connecting us to the dressing room closed with a thud and locks it, checks the lock is good, then leaves, job done.

With fifteen minutes to go until Poison take to the stage, Ross and I have been waiting around, inside and out, for nearly three hours. We're starting to lose it, giggling inanely at each other like inmates in a nut house, singing Poison songs under our breath like 'Talk Bullshit to Me', 'I Won't Forget This' and 'Nothing Like a Good Time', and we're sweating and starting to stink, the weirdness of it all starting to seep through our clothes.

Scotty Ross, Poison's tour manager, walks in. 'Hey guys, the band got held up getting here and now everything's in a panic,' he begins. We ask Scotty for our passes. The rest can wait. 'The passes I have won't get you anywhere,' he tells us. 'It's not worth having them. But don't worry, I'll take you both out to watch the show from the mixing desk.'

'The mixing desk?' interrupts Ross, appalled. 'That's no good for me.'

'Well, you can stay here and set up your stuff for some shots after the show?' Scotty suggests, remarkably calmly considering the impact his words are having on Ross, whose eyes are almost popping out of his head. Scotty leaves. Everybody except us that comes into this room manages to leave within thirty seconds! What's wrong with us?

By the time Scotty Ross returned to take me out of that filthy goddamned room and actually to see some of the Poison show, it was 8.22 p.m. exactly. I know, because I made a point of looking at my watch when he walked in the room – just for the record, as they say. 'Hey guys, I'm sorry!' he begins again. 'I didn't forget about you, I was just busy getting all the photographers organised in the pit.'

This is the last straw, the final insult, the banal cherry on the whole rancid, ridiculous cake. I'm frightened Ross is going to explode. 'Anyway Mick, I'll take you out to see the show now.'

At best, there is less than fifteen minutes left of the Poison set, and frankly my dears, I no longer give a fuck. 'Frankly Scotty,' I begin, 'I didn't come here to see the last fifteen minutes of the show, I'm supposed to see the whole thing. And I have to say that with no pass I have no confidence whatsoever that once my fifteen minutes are up I will be able to get back here.'

I'm still trying to be polite. I don't know if Scotty understands me fully or not but I'm trying to tell him this whole stupid thing is a shambles and a disgrace and wondering what he proposes to do about it.

'OK,' he says, completely unruffled. 'You'll be ready to go with your shots when I get them in here after the show?' he asks Ross, but Ross isn't listening anymore. 'OK – fine. Good, good,' mumbles Scotty. He leaves and I help Ross set up his gear. We work in silence, the distant drone of Poison still echoing far off down a corridor we will never see. We hum along, thin sticky grins marking our faces like scars. I think we're beginning to like it in here. Another couple of hours of this and we'll be completely habituated and then we'll never want to leave this room again.

*

And it had all started so nicely as well. Only the day before our Nightmare at Nassau, I had met with singer Bret Michaels and drummer Rikki Rockett in a room at their hotel in New York, and for half an hour – while we chatted for the benefit of my tape-recorder – we seemed to have something going. We joked and talked about the new Poison album, *Open Up and Say . . . Ahh!*, and when I asked them if it was true that the success of their debut, *Look What the Cat Dragged In* (three million sales in the USA alone last year), had turned them all into temperamental, ego-tripping thugs – as had been told to me more than once during the weeks prior to our meeting – they sat there and tried to convince me with their laughter that nothing could be further from the truth.

'Listen, the only thing about us that's changed is that now we get a little more freedom to enjoy ourselves,' says Michaels, the baby-blues twinkling. 'Before we were successful I was out to prove to everyone what I was like – this is the way Bret is: I drink too much, I smoke too much, I party too much, I fuck too much. Now I've learned how to enjoy it more than trying to prove it. After the show tonight, if I feel like going to my room alone and writing a song, I'll do it. Before, I thought I had to get drunk and fucked before I did anything else. Now I can sit back and let people decide whether they like me for what I really am, or whether they like me because of some kind of facade I'm trying to create.'

Michaels smiles so sweetly as he says this, so sincerely, I almost believe him. He wants me to write that Poison have, contrary to all rumour, actually matured as a result of their staggering and unpredicted success last year; that the brat-pack LA trash image that still clings to them like last night's mascara is unwarranted and unfair; that all these boys wanna do is have FUN! I've heard all this stuff before, of course, from countless other bands in Poison's present second-album-make-or-break position. But then I've been around a lot longer than Poison have, so I decide to cut them a little slack and wait to see with my own eyes what this shit-stick called success has or has not done for them.

The following night, an hour after Poison have left the stage, still stuck in my favourite room, a line of girls walk in dressed in nothing except after-show backstage passes. Outside in the auditorium, as pass-less and clueless as Halfin and I, are sixteen Heads of Department from the British and European offices of Capitol Records, all flown in Business Class specifically to see the show then go back afterwards and tell Poison how hard they are all going to work at making the band as big throughout the rest of the world as they are presently in America. None of them, though, can get back to meet the band. I'm told the next morning that the Capitol execs gave it an hour of waiting around being hustled by deaf, dumb an' blind kid security guards before giving up the ghost and skulking back to their hotels. Lucky buggers! At least they didn't end up getting the full Cell Block Number Nine treatment.

Is this what Bret Michaels means, then, when he talks about life being 'just a popularity contest'? Now that they've sold three million albums you can hate them all you like because they simply don't give two shits about anybody else anymore? Hey, it's only a question.

Back to the previous afternoon with Bret and Rikki: I ask them if it's a pain in the arse being recognised in the street?

'If people come up to you in the street and they like your band, it's never a pain in the ass to stop and say hi to somebody who recognises you,' Bret tells me. 'The only time it's a pain is when they stop you and they hate your guts! You know what I mean?' he smiles.

'It's weird though when we walk into a club here in New York, or in LA,' says Rikki. 'Sometimes it's like walking into an old Rod Serling movie where the whole room starts moving in slow motion. You can feel all the eyes swivel 'round like beams of light that just land on you!' he laughs.

'I remember on my birthday being taken to this club in LA called the Cathouse,' says Bret. 'And the place was full of people that all seemed to know me and want to party with me, and for the first couple of hours I was loving every minute of it!' he exclaims, wide-eyed. 'Then I said to myself, wait a second here, I've just got to get my bearings. I remember sitting at the bar, in the end, like an old man, just drinking by myself, looking straight down at the bar, face grey, you know what I mean? Fame's great, man, but sometimes you just need to be left alone for a while and given some space to remember who you are.'

I know just what Bret means. Actually, me and Ross could re-commend this very nice room we know. Lots of space – nobody to bother you or come near you for hours . . .

Poison's second album, *Open Up and Say ... Ahh!*, has just been released. I never read the music press so I don't know what everybody else is saying about it, but here in *Kerrang!* Poison's album has already met with loud yawns and disappointed grunts of derision. Geoff Barton it was who put the glitterised moon-boot in. A long-time fan of Poison since the days before those three million American units had been shifted, and a world-renowned and completely remorseless devotee of glam, Geoff's main complaint was that the new Poison album lacked all the sordid bite and puppy energy of their debut. 'You never quite know where Poison are flouting their stilettos: on their heels or in their hands' is how the gist of it ran, I believe. For Geoff, first time out Poison carried their stilettos in their hip pockets; second time around, though, they moved like they had 'em jammed up their arseholes.

For myself, listening to the new Poison album is much like listening to the last Poison album – dumb, tacky, glitzed-up to the eyeballs, as sparkling as fake diamonds and twice as cheap. But with one crucial difference: no 'Cry Tough', no 'I Want Action', no 'I Won't Forget You' and no 'Talk Dirty to Me'. No obvious hit singles whatsoever this time, in fact. The first single released from the new album, 'Nothing But a Good Time', is the most obvious candidate for Hit City USA (which is presumably why they released it first), but though it comprises the predictable Poison mix of second-hand guitar riffs and sugar-plum, pop-metal choruses, it's about as memorable as old whassisname.

'Love on the Rocks', 'Look But You Can't Touch', 'Every Rose Has its Thorn': all, I would guess, are destined to become singles at some stage this year, though how many become hits – and make no mistake, that's what Poison thrive on – I will leave Capitol Records to gamble their money on. Recorded in a week-and-a-half in 1986, and paid for in peanuts and dreams, *Look What the Cat Dragged In* is the Poison album with all the wit, the laissez-faire charm and conceit. *Open Up and Say ... Ahh!*, recorded over a three-month period around the end of '87, beginning of '88, with a dollar-rich budget and famed LA producer, Tom Werman, backing them, fails to capture the stinging adolescent verve of its predecessor. Tracks like 'Tearin' Down the Walls', 'Your Mama Don't Dance' or 'Bad to Be Good' (all of which sound just like their titles suggest) have all the cosmetic appeal of earlier Poison ravers like 'Talk Dirty to Me' or 'No. 1 Bad Boy', all the cheap flash and frills, but none of the real straight-to-the-viscera hooks. Most of all, they lack visible charm and identity. Poison never did sound very deep, but here they're as shallow and forgettable as a lip-glossed pout.

The pressure was on for Poison to deliver the goods second time around. No question. Maybe that's what spoiled the album. I had asked them: how much of the pressure they were under to come up with a credible (not to mention commercial) follow-up to their first mega-hit album came out in their work in the studio?

'Sure, we felt the pressure, a lot of pressure,' said Bret Michaels. 'I still feel like that. You know, first time around, it was like when you've got nothing, you've got nothing to lose. This time round we have everything to lose. But we work good as a band under pressure. We know that people are waiting to see if Poison's going to fail or if we're going to succeed this year. We're that kind of band – it might all go up in smoke at any moment! We hope not, but we don't really know. And that kind of gives everything we do that edge and it's what keeps us excited. You know, the thing with us, we're the kind of band that was voted the best and worst band in every magazine going last year!' He suddenly bursts out laughing. 'Best new band and worst new band, you know what I mean? At least they have an opinion on us, good or bad, right or wrong, they all want to see what happens next.'

What happens though if there are no hit singles this time?

'I don't think we're a band that lives or dies by hit singles,' says Michaels. 'If we lost the crowd that only come to our shows to hear the singles, this band wouldn't die. I think we have a much larger core audience there that know Poison are first and foremost a rock band, not a bunch of pop stars. At the same time, "pop" means popular, and if you're popular you must be doing something people like, and that's all right with me too.'

'Also,' Rikki interjects, 'we didn't become successful last year because radio played us. It happened because the fans were calling up all the radio stations and asking them to play our records. The people that first got into us did it by coming to see us play, and that's where we really score.'

'A lot of people have told us that they never gave us a second thought until they saw us play live,' says Bret. 'Poison is a band that was built for and grew up on a stage. And if you wanna know what makes this whole thing tick for us, then you make sure you're there tomorrow night and see for yourself!'

'Yeah,' drawls Rikki. 'We'll have a couple of beers and have a good time.'

Uh-huh . . .

At 9.30 p.m., four-and-a-half hours after we first arrived at the gig and three since we were taken to The Room of a Thousand Yawns, Poison at last troop in to have their pictures taken by Ross. They shuffle in – Bret, Rikki, bassist Bobby Dall and guitarist C.C. DeVille – nonplussed and nonchalant, faces like wax. I stare at them and wonder who they all are. Ross gets five minutes of group shots in the shower, and a couple of minutes with each of them individually, except for when it comes to Bobby Dall's turn he refuses, snapping at Ross: 'We don't do individuals!'

'Well, this should look great for a cover story, shouldn't it!' cries Ross, utterly exasperated. 'One group shot in the shower, no live shots and no individuals. Is that what you want?'

Without missing a beat, Dall says OK to individuals. 'But I guess you know how much I'm enjoying doing this,' he says out of the side of his lipsticked mouth. Two minutes and half a roll of film into it in the shower with Ross, Dall says, 'I think you have enough pictures now,' and strides off, not a backward glance.

'That's what I like, working with real professionals,' spits Ross.

In another corner of the room Bret Michaels suddenly approaches and asks me into the dressing room to speak with me. I follow him into Poison's dressing room and he asks if I'd like a drink or anything. It's the first time in five hours of arriving at this hell-hole that anybody has bothered to ask whether either Ross and I were at all hungry or thirsty, dead or alive, fags or putzes, gimps or fans, men or dogs.

'No, thanks,' I tell him.

We sit down and Bret asks why I didn't see the show. I tell him. He acts like he's just been told the world really is round and starts shoving the blame back and forth – the fuck-ups getting there late, the lack of passes, the this, the that . . . I didn't have time for it then and I don't have time for it now. I leave Poison's dressing room and return to the room of my dreams to help Ross load up his gear. All of Poison are also in the room chatting to their guests. We manage to ignore them and they manage to ignore us without too much embarrassment. When Ross and I are finally shown the way out the door, only Bret Michaels notices us leaving.

'Hey, you guys, I'm really sorry about all this, you know what I mean?'

Actually, I'm not sure that I do. It's been a real pleasure talking dirty with you, boys. Fix me up a nice empty room for a few hours and we'll do it again real soon . . .

CODA

What was less well known about the 'locked in a cupboard' story was the fact that I ran into Poison again just a couple of weeks after its publication. I was in LA, hanging out with Slash from Guns N' Roses, when we got wind of the fact that there was a Poison party on in town that night. Slash had once, very briefly, been in the band, but now professed to hate them. Partly, he explained, because they had 'turned into a bunch of posers'. But mainly, he said, because 'that asshole' C.C. DeVille had recently taken to wearing a top hat onstage – the top hat, by then, being a Slash trademark, of course.

Given our mutual antipathy towards the band, I saw no reason why we would want to go to their party. Slash had other ideas, however, and a couple of hours later, much the worse for wear, I found myself face-to-face with Bret Michaels.

'I don't know whether to be nice to you or not,' Brett pouted.

'I don't know whether to be nice to you or not,' I parroted.

'I think we already know how you feel, dude,' Brett countered.

It was a fair point. I burst out laughing.

'Let's have a drink and forget about it,' I said.

And to his credit, that's exactly what we did. As a result, I would go on to pen more features on Poison, including the last thing I ever did for the magazine, which made the cover in October 1991. Poison, after all, was one of the better – certainly one of the most entertaining – of the great '80s hair-metal bands. But of course nobody ever remembers the stories I wrote where I said that . . .

JIMMY PAGE, 1990

An air stewardess once told me that the nicest people on the plane were always the ones in First Class. 'They've made it and have nothing to prove,' she explained. The people in Economy were usually nice, too, while the ones in Business Class – caught quite literally in the middle between First and Economy – were almost always the worst. 'The ones who haven't quite made it but still demand all your attention,' as she put it, 'the know-alls and wannabes.'

I have found the same can often be said for rock stars. Put simply, the bigger the star, the easier they are to deal with. This is certainly true of Jimmy Page. An artist with nothing left to prove – except perhaps to himself – he has always been remarkably free of 'attitude' whenever I have spoken with him. A gentleman in every sense, I have always struggled to put the guy I know next to the dark-eyed evil-doer we have all read about in other books.

And yet, as he would be the first to admit, that doesn't mean he has always been a saint. As you can see from this interview, he freely acknowledges that much of the life he lived in Led Zeppelin was, in his words, 'quite hedonistic', and that he and the group actually fed off that dark energy, using it to inform their creativity and their personal appeal. Perhaps surprisingly, however, to those who only know Zeppelin from the books, Jimmy remains utterly unrepentant, describing his years in Zeppelin as some of the 'happiest of my life'.

That said, Jimmy has always been somewhat shy of divulging his true feelings about Zeppelin, over and above acknowledging how 'proud' he is of their musical achievements. Of all the many interviews I would do with him over the years, this was the first time that he really opened up about it. The first time I realised, in fact, how much he still missed those days and what he would give to actually put the group back together. If only Robert Plant felt the same way too ...

Interview with Jimmy Page, first published in Kerrang!, *October 1990.*

A word to the wise guy. This month has seen the release of the first legitimate Led Zeppelin 'product' for over a decade. First was the triple-album *Remasters*. Now this week comes the real McCoy: *Remasters Boxed*: a fifty-four-track, six-album/four-cassette and/or four-CD collection of some of the finest moments from arguably the most legendary rock band of all time. The tracks for both were officially selected by the three remaining band members – Jimmy Page, Robert Plant and John Paul Jones – then compiled and remastered from the original studio tapes by Page.

The story of Led Zeppelin has, of course, been well documented over the years; the tales of road madness and red snappers, cocaine and mind games, always with the suggestion of something darker lurking in the background, are as well known and often-repeated as a favourite dirty joke. But never has the case for Led Zeppelin been put so forthrightly, so imaginatively, or so poignantly as it is throughout the duration of this collection. A good time then to talk to the man responsible not just for the remastering, but who wrote, played on, produced and directed – both musically and artistically – every important move Zeppelin ever made. A good time then to talk to Jimmy Page.

We meet up at the house in Hampshire Jimmy lives in these days, along with his pretty blonde wife, Patricia, and their two-and-a-half-year-old son, James Patrick. Now in his mid-forties, on the day we met Jimmy was looking fit, well, tanned even – about as un-Zeppelin as you can get, in fact. And, in case you're wondering, our preferred choice of beverage throughout the interview was tea.

To start with, whose idea was it to put this box-set together?

'I don't know who had the original idea. It came from Atlantic Records and it was just put to us. I, for one, was very keen to do it because, primarily, the CDs that have come out of the Zeppelin material in the past didn't sound as good to me as they should. I had nothing to do with them. When we made the records I'd always gone through everything, producing, mixing, right down to checking the test pressings. I always saw it right through to the end. The way they remastered those original CDs, though, there wasn't much to it and there were a few things which annoyed me – like the cough that was cut out at the end of "In My Time of Dying". It wasn't until I started working on it in the studio I realised how into it I really was, on every level.'

How did you pick the tracks? Did you actually get together in a room with John Paul Jones and Robert Plant and discuss it?

'No. We just all made a list of the ones we wanted. Given the time and the situation, I think, Jones just sent through a list. I don't think Robert even did that. It came to the point where I sent a proposed running order out to the chaps and they seemed happy with it. That was it. There was also a couple of extra numbers included that weren't on any of the original Zeppelin albums. One of them, "Hey, Hey, What Can I Do" was the B-side of the "Immigrant Song" single. And there are a couple of tracks salvaged from the vaults of the good old BBC: [Robert Johnson's] "Travelling Riverside Blues", from a *Top Gear* session, I think it was. A John Peel thing, anyway. And another one from those sessions, "White Summer/Black Mountainside".'

How long ago would that be?

'Oh, that's right from the early days! Late Sixties, early Seventies. And there are the two Bonham tracks – "Moby Dick" and "Bonzo's Montreux" – I didn't want to leave one or the other off, so I had a crack at joining the two up with a Fairlight. It starts with the "Moby Dick" riff, then it cuts into the solo part of "Bonzo's Montreux", and then the riff comes back in again. It works great, actually. I think John would have been quite happy with it.'

Looking through the running order it occurred to me that there are very few rock bands anybody would want to wade through fifty-four tracks for, and yet every one's a winner here.

'Yes, it's sort of surprising to me, too. I was going through the albums taking things off this one and that one and leaving a lot behind. At the end of the day, with fifty-four numbers there, I hadn't realised we'd written that many good songs. And there was still a lot left.'

Before you started this project, did you often dig out the old Zep albums and have a blast while you were on your own at home?

'Oh, yeah. Every day! I like a little blast every now and then,' he says, crinkling his eyes.

Once you'd chosen the tracks, how long did it take to remaster them?

'It must have been about five days. I'd have to check, because I was punchy after the first three. I got off the plane in New York and went straight to the studio to begin working. During that process, though, I certainly lived my life over again. It was quite incredible, really. I'd be listening to a track and start thinking about where it was done and under what circumstances, and funny little anecdotes about it. Sometimes a really joyous feeling, sometimes a little sad. Nevertheless, it was evident what a brilliant textbook Zeppelin was. Especially in the different areas we approached. We went boldly where few men have been before, let's put it that way.'

And where few have been since, in your opinion?

'Yeah, maybe. 'Cos we had a licence to do it. It was all album-oriented material. It wasn't about having to come up with something to fit the singles market.'

It seems like you've deliberately rearranged the original running order of the tracks to add a further element of surprise. For instance, it comes as a real jolt to the system not to hear 'Livin' Lovin' Maid' come belting out of the speakers straight after 'Heartbreaker'.

'Yeah. I think the good thing about that is it sheds new light on those tracks. It's the same picture in a different frame. Like "The Song Remains the Same" from *Houses of the Holy* now goes into "Ten Years Gone" from *Physical Graffiti* instead of "Rain Song". But it works great!'

You mentioned that working on the box-set brought back a lot of memories. Can you give me a for instance?

'The sessions we recorded at Headley Grange immediately spring to mind. We had three or four different spells there. They were really good times for us, very productive because we were living in and we came up with a lot of material we definitely wouldn't have done otherwise. I remember one night I came downstairs and Jonesy's mandolin was lying there. He always had loads of different instruments lying around. I'd never played a mandolin before but I picked it up and started messing around with it, and I came up with all of "The Battle of Evermore" [from the untitled fourth Zep album]. That would never have happened if we'd just been in a normal studio situation.'

Do you miss that kind of creative camaraderie; four guys in a band just hanging out together and making music?

'Ah, well . . . in the writing sense I do, yes. In those days there was a purpose behind it. I knew exactly who I was writing for. If I was writing something I was hearing Robert singing it, and you knew you were going forward all the time.'

What ingredients defined the Led Zeppelin sound for you?

'Well, I think that the first album had so many firsts on it, as far as the content goes. Even though we were heavily involved in a sort of progressive blues thing, one of the most important parts was the acoustic input. Things like "Babe I'm Gonna Leave You", which had the flamenco-type bits in it. The drama of it, I don't think had been touched by anybody before. With the acoustic input you had this sort of embryo, which was good.'

It was always very exotic-sounding music, I thought.

'It was very passionate, that's for sure.'

Other guitarists have commented in the past on how strange and unpredictable many of your guitar chords are on certain Zeppelin songs. 'Rain Song', for instance, is said to be a particularly tricky one to learn. The guitar doesn't appear to follow any 'normal' rock progression.

'That comes from the tuning. I was constantly fooling around with tunings on the acoustic. Sometimes they'd progress onto the electric. Like "Dancing Days", things like that. But a lot of the acoustic numbers had different tunings. "White Summer" [originally Jimmy's acoustic showcase with the Yardbirds], that was a standard folk tuning. "Friends" is a different kind of tuning again.'

Did that interest in experimenting with tuning come from your well-known fondness for Oriental music?

'Mmm . . . It's like, "Black Mountainside/White Summer", I call that my CIA – Celtic, Indian and Arabic. It's got all those influences in it. I was always interested in ethnic music. Still am.'

When you first put Led Zeppelin together, did you have a clear idea of what you wanted the band to do, how you wanted it to be?

'Yeah, definitely. I'd come from the Yardbirds, which was a guitar-oriented band, and there were lots of areas which they used to call free-form but was just straight improvisation. By the time Zeppelin was getting together I'd already come up with such a mountain of riffs and ideas, because every night we went on there were new things developing.'

How do you feel when people say Zeppelin was modelled on the group formed by your brief sparring partner in the Yardbirds, Jeff Beck?

'Well, it wasn't. It wasn't modelled on Jeff's band at all. For a start, Jeff had a keyboard player in his band, he was attempting an entirely different thing. The only unfortunate similarity was that we both did a version of [Willy Dixon's] "You Shook Me". I didn't know Jeff had recorded it too until our album was already done. You know, we had very similar roots but we were trying for a completely different thing, in my opinion.'

What about the overtly mystical slant of much of Zeppelin's lyrics: was that a sign of the times, or are you just like that, anyway?

'I was like that at school. I was always interested in alternative religions. These days it's alternative medicines, isn't it?' he kids. 'But, yes, I was always interested in mysticism, Eastern tradition, Western tradition. I used to read a lot about it so consequently it became an influence.'

As Zeppelin began to grow bigger and bigger, did you feel you were tapping into something greater, some form of energy more profound than 'good-time rock 'n' roll'?

'Yeah, but I'm reluctant to get into it because it just sounds pretentious. But, yeah, obviously, you can tell that from the live things. It was almost a trance state sometimes, but it just sounds, you know . . .' He looks away.

'That was what was so exciting about it, though, certainly. Once we'd recorded the numbers and then started playing them live we were pushing them more and more, making the numbers work for us. Like on the live soundtrack to [the movie] *The Song Remains the Same*, you hear all this energy roaring through it. That energy and intensity that there's no escape from.'

When you were at the height of your power in Zeppelin, were you ever afraid, as you stood on stage, that things were in real danger of getting out of hand, beyond your control?

'No. The only thing that became apparent was that there were more and more people wanting to see us. It just kept increasing right till the very end. If it ever did start to get like that some nights, if it was getting too rowdy, we used to stop the concert and get them to cool down. If you didn't do that and allowed it to fester, it could get . . . Well, someone could get hurt. We wanted people to go home happy rather than with a few bruises – or worse.'

Did you remain matey with the three other members of Zeppelin right through to when John Bonham died and the band broke up?

'Yeah, I think so.'

What about towards the end when it's said you used to walk offstage and immediately disappear into your own world, away from the others?

'Well, I'm a very private person, and still am, so maybe people played that up into something else.'

Do you feel you're still living down the image that continues to linger from those days – the bad man with the guitar in one hand and the bag of tricks in the other?

'Well, there's no smoke without fire. I guess I'm a pretty complex person.'

You once told me you had what you called an acoustic side and an electric side to your personality. Can you expound on that a little for me?

'It's true. But there's light and shade to everyone, I would presume. I mean, I'm obviously a different person offstage to what I am on.'

You were always very flamboyant – what about the famous suit with all the symbols woven into it? Was that your own creation?

'Yeah. I came across this person who wanted to make me some stage clothes and I said, "Try this!". It was incredible. It had dragons going up the side and the astrological symbols and stuff. It's a work of art, that suit.'

Did the astrological symbols have a specific meaning?

'Yeah, like my sun rising sign . . .'

Are you very into astrology?

'I'm interested in astrology, yeah,' he smiles self-deprecatingly.

You're a Capricorn. What characterises a Capricorn?

'Stubbornness, but reliability, I'm sure.'

Onstage you had the fantastic costumes, yet offstage you seemed to guard your privacy jealously.

'I tried to get . . . Because of the whole spectacle and energy of the shows, you couldn't live your life like that. You had to reach some balance in-between. You know, coming back from a tour, instead of setting up a two-hundred-watt stack, I'd pick up an acoustic.'

Can you describe for me a little of what it was like to be on the road with Led Zeppelin in those days?

'Well, you know . . .' He pauses, lights a cigarette. 'Most of it was so cocooned. We used to leave the stage, jump into the cars and get whisked off to the aeroplane, which would fly us to the next gig. Our feet never really touched the ground.'

The aeroplane in question – the notorious *Starship* – couldn't have held much more than a couple dozen passengers and yet the amount of people who have since claimed to have ridden on it with you would be enough to fill a Jumbo.

'Yeah, right. But we never actually let too many people on the plane.'

And for those of you who did actually ride on the plane, what was the truth? Were the after-show parties really as wild as some of the scenes that have since been described in endless books and articles?

'Oh, yeah, there was always a lot of theatre. There always is on rock 'n' roll tours, though I think we might have pioneered a lot of it. In fact, I know we did!' he chortles.

When you see bands like The Who and the Rolling Stones, much older bands than Zeppelin, getting back together and doing great things, doesn't it make you want to do it, too: re-form Led Zeppelin? I mean, could you see it?

'I'm sure there's a lot of people who would like to see it. Me being one of them. The telling thing about the Stones was that even with Mick and Keith's differences, at the end of the day they owned up to the fact that the band was bigger than both of them. Whereas with us, we've all collaborated through the years. I played on Robert's album. He played on mine. Jonesy and I collaborated on the *Death Wish II* soundtrack album. So I don't think it's impossible that we could do something in the future.'

Does it worry you though, that the moment might be gone and that Zeppelin couldn't be revived?

'I've never doubted for a minute that if Robert and I sat down and started writing that we could come up with some really good stuff.

We've already got ten years of music to prove what we can do.'

It's been a decade since Zeppelin broke up, which is almost as long as the group was together. And yet in a way the band is bigger now than it ever was.

'Absolutely, no doubt about it.'

How does your lifestyle compare now with your years in Zeppelin?

'Well, I was never unhappy in those days, let me tell you, and I'm certainly not unhappy now. The only difference is I'm not doing so much touring as I used to. Which is something I intend to rectify when I finish working on my next solo album.'

You've certainly clocked up the old guest appearances this year: Bon Jovi at Hammersmith; Robert at Knebworth; Aerosmith at Donington and the Marquee. 'Yeah, I'll be giving jamming a bad name soon.'

When you joined Aerosmith at the Marquee, that was the first time I ever saw Joe Perry smile on stage.

'That was great. They're such a good band to play with as well, let me tell you. They really know what it's all about, all right.'

I never saw so many musicians in the audience.

'Yeah, we'll have to have some more of it, eh Mick? Hopefully, when I get my new band together next year.'

You've got a young son now: Patrick. Will he be musical, do you think?

'Yeah, sure. He's coming from a musical family, so if he wants to, sure. I'd like to see him enjoying the guitar like I do. At the moment, though, his hands are too small to get round a guitar, even a small custom-built one. But as soon as I think they're big enough . . .'

Let's go back and talk about your earliest experiences as a musician. How did you come to form Led Zep? Did it happen suddenly, or was it just part of a natural development?

'Well, I'd been in a band when I left school. One thing led to another and I ended up going to art college. But nevertheless I was still playing guitar. By then I was playing in the interval band at the Marquee, supporting Cyril Davies. I was sort of plucked out of that to do a session. Someone just came up and said, "Would you like to play on a record?"'

It's rumoured that you played on just about everything in those days, from 'Walk Tall' by Val Doonican to 'You Really Got Me' by the Kinks. What actually was the first session you ever played on?

'The very first session I did was "Diamonds" by Jet Harris and Tony Meehan [Number One in the UK in 1963]. Do you remember that? That was the first thing I did. The A-side was all right, but the other side meant me reading music and I hadn't got a clue about all that, so I wasn't seen again for a while. Then when I was in the interval band at the Marquee I got to play on this other record and it crept into the bottom of the charts. After that the phone started ringing more frequently; my art studies sort of stopped and I carried on with the studio work. At that time the Beatles and the Stones were just beginning to happen and the studio producers needed a young guitarist who knew what was going on. Then that started to progress into other things and I'd be doing folk sessions and jazz sessions and film music.'

It must have been great training for what came later.

'Yeah, it was really, really good for that, because I had to get to know all these different techniques. It was good discipline, too. The studio discipline was essential for later days.'

Was it during this period – the early- to mid-1960s – that you developed your interest in ethnic music?

'I was always interested in ethnic music. I had a sitar in those days that I'd had imported from Bombay. I didn't even know how to tune it. Fortunately, listening to Ravi Shankar, I learned how to do it.'

This was before George Harrison and the Beatles got their hands on one?

'It was certainly before they were using them, as far as I know.'

Although you soon became known for your prowess and versatility as a session guitarist, it wasn't until you joined the Yardbirds in 1966 that the wider public became acquainted with the name Jimmy Page. How did the Yardbirds thing originally come about?

'I replaced Paul Samuel Smith, the bass player, to begin with, and then I took over on guitar as well with Jeff [Beck], which was something that we'd always wanted to do anyway. Then Jeff sort of had a flare-up on tour and left the band.'

His own freak-out or a freak-out at you?

'No, no, his own thing. The whole Yardbirds thing became fragmented after that. What the manager did was to take the two acts as an overall package to producer Mickie Most, who was starting his own label, RAK – Jeff Beck, his solo thing, and us, the Yardbirds. But the material we were doing was all wrong. I wanted to try a different approach and they seemed to want to do it on their own.'

And so you set out to form your own band?

'Yes. Keith Relf, the founder member, was really disillusioned towards the end. I can understand why. But I had all these ideas that I wanted to explore with a band, especially the acoustic stuff. So I knew from the kick-off what I wanted the backbone of the outfit to be.'

What about the improvisational aspects of Led Zeppelin: was that another area you deliberately set out to explore from the start?

'Oh yes, right from the very first live performances there were these stretched-out improvisations.'

Which is, perhaps, what gave Zeppelin their edge live – not being able to predict what was going to happen next?

'Yes, absolutely. There was always that energy, which just seemed to grow and grow. It could be almost trance-like some nights.'

In some of the audience shots from *The Song Remains the Same* movie there are some incredibly beautiful, sophisticated young women and some very intense-looking young men in the audience. Led Zeppelin didn't just attract screaming teenagers and long-hairs . . .

'I hadn't thought about that, but you're right. It was like the Rolling Stones' crowd, there was a real cross-section of people into us. It went right through the age groups. That was what made it so great.'

You once told me you had a large collection of vintage live Zeppelin recordings spanning the group's career. Weren't you tempted to use any of that on this new box-set?

'I think that the live stuff would be better in a collection of its own. In fact, before [the posthumously released final Zeppelin album] *Coda* I'd decided to make a chronological album with the live tapes, 'cos we had tapes going right back to the Albert Hall in 1970, right through to Knebworth [Zeppelin's last British gig in August 1979].'

Why didn't you do it in the end?

'It wasn't done because there wasn't enough interest between the band members. Whether any of that stuff will surface in the future or not . . .' He shrugs.

Of course, Zeppelin's reputation was solidly founded on the fact that it was a determinedly album-orientated band. Hit singles were never a consideration. Do you think if the band was around now you'd be pressured into releasing singles?

'It's just a totally different ball game now, because in those days there was the music "business", there wasn't the record "industry" – the corporate industry where every band is viewed purely as an invest-ment and there's the whole package that goes with that. We certainly wouldn't have been able to explore the areas that we did and feel no pressure. Because we weren't putting out singles we didn't have to worry, thinking about what was going to be the follow-up single when we were recording the next album. All we concentrated on was trying to make a statement of where we all were. That's why all the albums are so different, I think.'

Success came very quickly for Zeppelin. According to *Rolling Stone* magazine, during its first year of release *Led Zeppelin II* sold over five million copies in America alone. Were you taken aback at how quickly the band took off?

'I wasn't even aware of it, really, to be honest with you. That's the truth. We knew the albums were doing better each time. *Zep III* prob-ably didn't do as well as *Zep II*, but we knew that there was a bigger audience out there each time.'

To the point where you stopped having anybody else on the bill opening for you.

'That happened purely because the set we had when we first went out playing just increased as our catalogue grew. We had real difficulty dropping any of the older numbers 'cos we enjoyed doing them so much! So the set just started to get longer and longer until it got to about three hours' long, sometimes three-and-a-half, and there just wasn't time to have anyone else on the bill!'

In September, it was the tenth anniversary of the death of John Bonham. Are you aware of that date when it comes around each year?

'The time of the year, yeah, sure.'

One of the great rock 'n' roll tragedies.

'Musically, that's for sure . . .'

For you personally, too?

'Yeah, definitely. It was a real blow at the time.'

Did John's death sour your memories of the band?

'No. I was basically numb for a while afterwards. As I'm sure one is; it's quite natural.'

What do you remember as John's most important contributions to the band?

'Just his whole input. People always underrated John's input into the songs. Everybody always knew he was a phenomenal drummer; what they missed was how much he had to do with the writing of the songs. A lot of those songs simply wouldn't have been written or come out how they did, if it had been anyone other than John playing in the band.'

He also had a pretty fearsome reputation.

'He was a great leveller to have in the band. At group meetings, if people were waffling on he'd just say, "Ya what?" When anyone used to get a little too far out, John would always be there to pull them right back down to earth.'

Obviously this box-set is very much your own work: of the three surviving members of the band, you were the one who sat down and did all the hard work.

'As well as all the hard work in the early days! It's true. I was thinking in the studio when I was remastering the tracks, "My God, the amount of time I've put into this over the years!" It really was . . . It was my life, you know?'

If it means so much to you, isn't it somehow wrong to just let the story end there – with Bonzo's accidental death in 1980? Don't you almost have a duty to get Led Zeppelin back together at some stage?

'We've all kept in touch, we've collaborated here and there on each other's albums, so I don't think it's completely beyond the realms of possibility that we could all do something in the future. It would be the logical conclusion.'

If Zeppelin were to get back together, would you do like the Stones did and record a new album first?

'I don't know about an album, as such. As I say, I'm sure we'll collaborate in some shape or form in the future. But it's premature to say when or how, really. At this point in time, this year Robert's out on tour, and when I've not been working on the box-set I've been writing my next solo album, which I hope to begin recording quite soon.'

You're intent on pursuing a solo career then, for the time being?

'You bet your life I am! I've only had one solo album out so far, and I'm determined to have a second. Which will be better than the first, of course.'

Robert has talked vaguely of the possibility of there being a new Zeppelin film being put together, made up of footage from the band's private collection. Is that true?

'The truth is that we were searching through old footage to see what there was. We started to look through the outtakes from *The Song Remains the Same*, which wasn't really the best place to look. We have got some unused footage lying around, but sadly not as much as other bands probably would have. We haven't got as much footage as we have live tapes. In that respect, it's probably a good thing that *The Song Remains the Same* came out, otherwise there wouldn't be any documentary evidence at all of what was happening. That's the truth of it.'

Do you see much of Jason Bonham these days?

'I haven't seen Jason since his wedding.'

Have you seen his drum kit with the Zeppelin album sleeve designs painted on it?

'Yeah. I think it's got a bit over-the-top, all that. He's forgetting who he is. He shouldn't keep leaning on us. I think he's been totally ill-advised by his manager. The whole thing's questionable, to say the least.'

But almost everybody wants to be Led Zeppelin these days, don't they? Did you hear the track 'Judgement Day' from the last Whitesnake album, by any chance?

'No. Why?'

It's 'Kashmir' all over again. When I asked David Coverdale about it he just said, 'It has nothing whatsoever to do with woolly jumpers.'

'I think that's silly. The fact is, "Kashmir", that track especially, is totally original. We may have built stuff around old blues numbers but the riffs were always totally new. Something like "Nobody's Fault But Mine", for instance, doesn't bear the slightest resemblance to the original. That's one thing about Zeppelin – the riffs and what we could do to them were always totally new ground. Always.'

You looked like you were having a gas on stage with Robert at

Knebworth this year. Does the 'spirit of Led Zeppelin' still move you when the two of you get on a stage together?

'We were having a really good time that day at Knebworth. We'd had a rehearsal before we did it and that was great fun.'

Is it a relief to be able to launch into something like, say, 'Rock and Roll'?

'Oh, yeah. It's really good playing all the old numbers. Especially "Wearing and Tearing", 'cos we never actually played that live with Zep, apart from recording it. It's a really tricky number because it's got some silly sequencing, and verses and choruses with odd bits in the middle. It really was on a wing and prayer that we went on with that at Knebworth. We were back to living dangerously again.'

It's plain you miss touring regularly.

'Oh Lord, yes. But as I say, I intend to rectify that as soon as I can, and the way to rectify that is to get my solo album finished, and I'm well on the way to doing that.'

And until then?

'I don't know. Another cup of tea, I think. Shall I put the kettle on?'

CODA

As discussed, at length, in my 2008 Zeppelin biography, *When Giants Walked the Earth*, I find it immensely sad that in the twenty years that have passed since Jimmy and I did this interview, his views on Led Zeppelin have changed not at all – and nor have Robert Plant's. It all boils down to this: Jimmy would re-form Zeppelin in an instant, has, in fact, been working towards making that happen, one way or another, almost since the day they broke up. Robert, meanwhile, would rather cut off his own arm. Indeed, he has spent just as long doing everything in his power to demonstrate he doesn't need Zeppelin. Now, with the enormous success and critical acclaim – the latter of even more importance to Plant than the commercial rewards were, having already scaled that mountain in Zeppelin – that his collaboration with Alison Krauss has brought him, there is even less chance of him ever agreeing to join Jimmy in a re-launched Zeppelin.

That Jimmy Page still refuses to accept this, in the sense of at least moving on, musically, and attempting something different – not least at a time when his stock as an artist of immense importance is higher even than ever it was while Zeppelin was actually alive – is shocking to me. Not for what it says about his curtailed horizons as a musician – although that in itself is enough for deep regret, when you consider how innovative he once was – but for what it says about him as a man now approaching his seventies. I, for one, am less interested in what a 'new' Zeppelin might have to say, musically, than what someone as deeply fascinating and talented as Jimmy Page might have to say, through his music, about what it's like to be such a man.

RED HOT CHILI PEPPERS, 1990

Still largely unknown outside of hip circles, it was a good time to meet the Red Hot Chili Peppers. Barely famous, let alone rich yet, singer Anthony Kiedis arrived at my LA hotel room unaccompanied by PR or management flunky. He looked a little lost, actually, gazing out at the swimming pool as he tucked into the egg-whites-only omelette I had bought him. Bumming cigarettes off me, after the interview he drove us to the photo-session at Ross Halfin's studio in an old jalopy that juddered and spluttered as he pushed the speedometer past 70 mph.

Recently off all drugs and alcohol, he was doing his best to stay 'clean and serene', which had the knock-on effect of keeping me sober that day, too. I couldn't compete with his muscles, though. Even though I was something of a gym-rat myself at the time, Kiedis looked like he'd been training for the weightlifting event at the Olympics. 'I was the buffest junky you ever saw,' he joked when I mentioned it. And like a lot of ex-druggies and drinkers, his only real pleasure now was sex. He told me he'd recently hooked up with an eighteen-year-old model he'd met in Japan and that she 'demanded sex at least five times a day'.

I didn't know if he was joking or not, but sensed there was always at least one grain of truth in anything he might say. I was also surprised to discover he was a Charles Bukowski fan. In those days I still thought I was the only one who'd ever heard of him. When I showed him a new copy of Bukowski hero Céline's *Journey to the End of Night* that I'd just bought, though, he admitted he was impressed. 'Wow,' he said, looking at the cover photo of a man clearly on the edge of despair, 'he even looks kinda like Bukowski.'

I decided to give him the book. I'd be able to have a drink after he'd gone; he would only have the book to read. (And the model to fuck, but he made that sound like a chore.) He gave me a CD of a group called the Digital Underground. I decided he was the nicest, most down-to-earth and – just possibly – most honest American rock star I'd met in a long time. Possibly ever.

Interview with Anthony Kiedis of the Red Hot Chili Peppers, Los Angeles, first published in Kerrang!, *2 June 1990.*

I'm sorry, ladies, but when he appears in the doorway, immediately I'm struck by how small he is. Onstage with the Red Hot Chili Peppers, Anthony Kiedis looks like one of those classical Greek statues; large, muscle-bound, big willy dangling. In person, however, the singer with the original 'hardcore, bone-crunching, psychedelic, sex-funk band from heaven' looks much more manageable. Five feet eight maybe, long, straight, tea-coloured hair, younger-looking than his twenty-seven years; dressed in shorts (natch), T-shirt and sneakers. Still with the big muscular arms, though. As for the willy? Well, he never showed it to me, which is a shame. Maybe if he had, I might have sued him and made some money out of it. He explains how a similar situation came about.

'It was backstage after a show and I was changing and there was a girl there. We were all joking and laughing together and when she left, no one was under the impression that she was perturbed by my nudity in the dressing room.'

Within twenty-four hours, however, the girl – a student at the George Mason University, in Virginia – had sworn out a complaint and Kiedis was tried and convicted on misdemeanour charges of 'sexual battery' and 'indecent exposure'. He was fined $1,000 on each count. He paid the fine for indecent exposure, but is appealing against the sexual battery charge. She claimed Kiedis had dangled his dick in her face. Had he?

'No,' he says sharply. 'I'm not that type of person. I'm a very fun-loving, friendly person. The fact that I was found guilty of misdemeanours and given a nominal fine pretty much indicated to my attorney and to hers that it was a pile of shit.'

Unlike the singing voice, which has rapped, yapped and crowed its way through four albums with the Red Hot Chili Peppers, the speaking voice is even-tempered, almost monotonous, or would be if what he had to say wasn't so interesting. We meet on another typically red-hot day in Los Angeles. Actually, I'm lying. It was pissing with rain, chucking it down. I just liked the line.

'I love the rain,' Kiedis tells me, glancing out the window of my hotel room. 'It's very important to Los Angeles; the air pollution is so deadly here that without the rain we would die. So, you know, we're very lucky to have rain today.'

We digress to discuss the environment. Kiedis says it needs all the help it can get. I don't argue. We sit there looking thoughtful. Then the conversation steers itself back onto safer ground: more sex crimes. In March, performing during MTV's Spring-break party in Daytona Beach, Florida, bassist and – along with Kiedis – co-founder of the Red Hot Chili Peppers, Michael 'Flea' Balzary, and drummer, Chad Smith, were arrested by beach rangers after they had leapt off the stage to much commotion, and Flea allegedly threw a young woman over his shoulder while Smith spanked her. Both face charges for battery, with Flea facing additional charges of 'disorderly conduct' and 'solicitation to commit an unnatural and lascivious act'. Kiedis remains tight-lipped on the subject. It's clear he thinks the whole thing has been blown out of all proportion. Maybe if it had been solely a Red Hot Chili Peppers gig instead of a variety show, the girl would have understood, maybe even demanded it . . .

'Most people who come to our shows understand that there's a humorous element to what we do and not necessarily intended to offend anyone,' Kiedis says, straight-faced. 'The First Amendment of the American Constitution gives you the freedom of speech and the freedom, you know, to do what you will from the stage.'

Tell it to the PMRC, I tell him. Or the Governor of the state of Minnesota, who is trying to introduce an over-twenty-one law for all major-league concerts in the state, whether the venue is selling alcohol or not.

'That's a terrible concept,' says Kiedis, shaking his head. 'I hope they fail miserably. Creativity has always been threatened by certain right-wing factions of society. But they've never succeeded and I don't see why they should now.'

Nevertheless, the last Chilis' album, *Mother's Milk*, came complete with 'Explicit Language' stickers plastered on its sleeve.

'That doesn't bother me at all,' he says. 'Our lyrics are very explicit, whether it's about sex or friendship, or love for life in general. If they wanna inform the buying public that it is explicit, I have no problems with that.'

However, when a certain large chain of American stores wanted to buy 50,000 copies of the album, they balked when they saw the sleeve (the naked upper torso of a young woman cradling the four miniature figures of the band in her slender arms). The band's US record company, Capitol, got around the problem by redesigning the sleeve to make the bodies bigger, in order to obscure more of 'Mother's' breasts. Fifty thousand records later, Kiedis says he is comfortable with the decision and denies any implications of selling out. Yuk! Horrid words.

'The art of the Red Hot Chili Peppers is first and foremost that of our music, and we never change our music as a compromise for anybody's desires or tastes. That we should have to enlarge ourselves on the record is really not that big a deal. It's what's inside that counts,' he points out pragmatically. 'These things are so arbitrary, anyway. Nobody kicked up any fuss over our T-shirts.'

The two most famous being the legendary socks-on-cocks number, and the less well known woman-masturbating shirt: 'It's a drawing of Madonna masturbating, and she's dreaming of the Red Hot Chili Peppers,' Kiedis explains with a straight face. It's not known if Madonna herself has actually seen it. 'I think if she saw it, she'd want one, that's the type of girl she is. I mean, I don't think she's ever denied masturbating. Or denied masturbating to the Red Hot Chili Peppers, for that matter.'

What about the serious side of the Red Hot Chili Peppers, though? All play and no work makes Jack a dull jerk. Does it concern Kiedis that some people might not be able to see past the silly faces in their photos, the smutty T-shirts, the whole zany, kinky, mama-we's-all-crazy jive? That some people might not take the Red Hot Chili Peppers seriously at all?

'But that's like people going to see Jimi Hendrix play and coming away from the concert with nothing more to say than, "Wow, that guy can play with his teeth!",' he says. 'This is show business, and we are here to entertain. We like to entertain people. The visual value of it is there, but there's a lot more to it than that. People who are truly interested or concerned will find that out eventually.'

On the other hand, of course, some people take the Red Hot Chili Peppers almost too seriously. To the point of actually wanting to be them. No, I'm not talking about Faith No More: just their singer, Mike Patton. I ask Kiedis straight for his opinion on the matter: did Mike Patton rip you off hook, line and sinker, or what?

'Yeah,' he says, no hesitation. 'My drummer says he's gonna kidnap him and shave his hair off and saw off one of his feet. Just so he'll be forced to find a style of his own.'

Is this genuine bitterness here, or just another joke?

'It used to really bother me. I thought, what a drag if people get the idea that I'm actually ripping him off! Especially in the UK where Faith No More are much better known than us. In America, it's a different story, people are aware of the profound influence we had on them. But after it stewed in my stomach for a while, I just decided to accept it. He is just a kid. Besides, without his left foot he's going to have to change.'

In America they have just received a Gold record for *Mother's Milk*. It is only now, though, that the Chilis have started to make any serious inroads into the British or European markets. This month they return to the UK for a clutch of dates and TV appearances. How important is it for the band to be a success this side of the ocean they named after a record company?

'Everywhere we go in the world we try our hardest and we play our hardest every night we play. That's basically what we have to offer Britain. The way the industry's set up over there, the only way to get across is go over there and play. It's to expose what you have to offer to the entire world.'

Does he actually like it, though, in Ye Olde Country?

'To be blatantly honest, England is not our favourite place to go,' he admits without guilt. 'It isn't because we're not as well known as we are in America: it's the weather we don't like, and it's very far away, and the food's not very good – they tend to overcook the vegetables.'

He adopts a teasing, bitter English accent: 'You know, steak and kidney pie is not really me favourite. I think that sooner or later, though, it's inevitable that we will conquer England, as well as Scotland, Ireland and the rest of the world.'

This without a hint of an exclamation mark in his voice.

'It's very much like the long-term process of making love to some-body: you start off with the foreplay, you kiss them and you suck their neck and you titillate their sensory areas with your fingertips, with the first couple of records. Maybe you start giving them head with the third record, then you finally slip it in for the fourth. That's essentially what we've done with our career up to this point. *Mother's Milk* was incredibly well received in America. Basically, we're still involved in the foreplay section with the rest of the world, since they didn't really get our first two records.'

Sex – it all comes back to sex with this guy. Almost as soon as we met, Kiedis told me he was on a 'sex diet'. And he had the love-bites – one either side of the jugular – to prove it.

'I've got a new girlfriend. She's eighteen years old and demands rigorous sexual activity several times a day.'

For those of us who need to know, Kiedis' sex diet consists of 'no fattening foods, lots of protein, and a lot of exercise before and after you eat. Basically, you just can't afford to have an ounce of fat because a sexual diet is for performance. But it's also for aesthetics: she's a model and she's quite perfect in her physical structure.'

So is this lurve, Anthony?

'Love is a word taken much too seriously sometimes,' he says enig-matically. 'People are afraid to say they love somebody, but the fact is I do love her. I'm not gonna marry her and I'm not gonna dedicate my whole life to her, because I need to devote time to myself and to my music. But she understands. I just broke up with the girl that I lived with for two years. To get out of the frying pan and to go straight into the fire would be stupid right now. We've decided we're gonna be blatantly honest about all our feelings, at risk of hurting each other. But I do love her and she loves me. She's the biggest sexual genius I've encountered in the last ten years.'

He strikes a post-coital pose and lights a cigarette. Excluding sex, smoking is his one remaining vice.

'My guitar player [John Frusciante] is such an avid smoker, and he really loves the quality it gives my voice, the raspiness. But he's the kind of guy who was heartbroken to find out that John Waters, his favourite film-maker, had quit smoking at the age of forty-four.'

Once upon a time, of course, smoking a cigarette was the least of Kiedis' problems. Heroin abuse, alcoholism, both had threatened to take him over for much of the band's seven-year career. Then his guitarist, friend and co-conspirator in the twilight world of drug addiction, Hillel Slovak, died.

'Like me, Hillel had the disease of drug addiction,' Kiedis says, not flinching. 'He didn't die of an overdose; he died from having a disease. No one wanted to accept that this young man with so much to offer was just gone, you know, wiped out in a second. But in a strange way, we found strength from that. It forced me to make a choice. I could either join Hillel or I could try and finish my life.

'I've been completely off all alcohol and drugs for twenty-one months now. I mean, completely. I don't drink or use anymore. But I don't do it by myself. Hillel tried to do it by himself and he died. I do it with the help of other addicts that have cleaned up. That's the only way I know how to deal with it.'

A new Red Hot Chili Peppers single, 'Taste the Pain', the third to be taken from last year's excellent *Mother's Milk* collection, is released by EMI to tie in with the UK shows. A new video, directed by Alex Winter (the weedy, blonde guy in the movie, *Bill & Ted's Excellent Adventure*), has already been shot, and features, says Kiedis with obvious satisfaction, 'some very twisted images of pain and brutal reality. It's impossible to describe. There's a sense of surrealism to it all as well.'

When he's not devouring his new girlfriend, Kiedis says he likes to spend his spare time reading (Bukowski is a big favourite, as is Capote, Hesse, Bach); listening to music (*Sex Packets* by the Digital Underground is a current favourite, he tells me). But mostly, he insists, he has sex. Well, it's a hobby, I suppose.

While still discussing his sex diet and all the exercise involved, I eye his bulging arm muscles (like Popeye) and enquire how often Kiedis lifts weights?

'No, no weights,' he deadpans. I look surprised. 'Where did you get those big arms from then?' I asked. 'Sex,' he replies. 'No way!' I laugh. What does he do, carry them around over his head before he gets them into bed? At last, he allows himself a small chuckle, amused by my puffing and blowing, my envy and disbelief.

'The only exercise I ever get, unless I force myself to do push-ups, is sex and being on stage. Stage is the cardiovascular scenario, you know, an hour-and-a-half running around every night. That's a perfect exercise. And sex. You'd be surprised. I mean, you're holding yourself above a girl for any length of time, you know, utilising your pelvis, or whatever. Don't you feel pumped up after you've had sex?' he asks me, face a perfect mask of sincerity.

Outside, it's stopped raining . . .

CODA

The Red Hot Chili Peppers are now, rightly, one of the most successful and highly regarded rock artists in the world. Yet this is another one of those instances where I could not have predicted at the time what the eventual outcome for them would be. Indeed, I felt they were already becoming left behind, in terms of recognition, and not just by Faith No More, but by the beginnings of the first wave of what would, over the next ten years, become known as the rock-rap nu-metal crowd.

I do remember thinking, though, that if – as I suspected – their postmodern melting pot of musical styles and fashions represented a glimpse into the future, that the 1990s would be a far more exciting and fulfilling place to flap your wings around in than the '80s had ever been. So it proved. The only snag: I wasn't around to enjoy much of it, spending most of those years doing everything I could to get out of writing about music. As a result, I never actually met Anthony or the Chilis again, merely watched from the sidelines like everyone else – usually on TV – as they took on and beat the rocking world at its own irredeemable games.

WHITESNAKE, 1990

The fact that I interviewed David Coverdale so many times in the 1980s that we became quite matey – swinging by for drinks whenever we were both in town – just shows what a gloriously two-headed beast the music business is. For the very first thing I ever wrote about Whitesnake was such a scathing review he actually referred to it in a radio interview he gave some time later. Asked whether bad reviews ever bothered him, he had laughed. 'Only once,' he said, citing almost word-for-word my own review, before concluding: 'All the guy had to do was add that my wife was ugly and he would have finished me off completely.'

The irony was that the Coverdale/Hughes era of Deep Purple had been my favourite, and still is. After my initial cynicism, I had even warmed to Whitesnake – particularly after they'd added guitarist John Sykes to the line-up in 1984. The album Coverdale co-wrote with Sykes, the multi-platinum *1987*, wasn't just the best Whitesnake album, it was one of the best rock albums of its era. Hence, my determination to write more positively about the band.

Coverdale, for his part, never referred to my original review, although one-time Whitesnake bassist Neil Murray once told me that behind the scenes David had mentioned it several times whenever my name came up.

Welcome to the music biz, baby. Anyway, by 1990, when this piece was written, me and David were Big Pals. Not only that, he now had whiz-kid guitarist Steve Vai in the group, another of my Big Pals back then. We were all LA people, just trying to make a megabuck, and doing pretty good out of it, although none of us ever quite so good as permanently young, permanently handsome Mr Coverdale.

Interview with David Coverdale of Whitesnake, first published in
Kerrang!, March 1990.

Whatever you may think about David Coverdale, you gotta hand it to
him: he's a handsome motherfucker. Sitting in the lobby bar of a plush
hotel in Cincinnati, immaculately attired in a sleek black-and-white
herring-bone coat, cream wool jumper and matching scarf, tight black
jeans (no VPLs, girls) and black suede ankle boots – the only visible
'rock 'n' roll accessories being the elegant silver chains that adorn the
boots, the bleached-blonde not-too-teased hair and a lone silver hoop
through the left ear – he is the image of the debonair English rock star.

Sipping black tea (no sugar), smoking Marlboro 100s and charming
the pants off everyone from the middle-aged businessman who
requests an autograph – 'for my son. He's gonna die' – to the pretty
waitress who serves him his tea, Coverdale exudes a certain kind of
cool that is both studied and warm.

He lays it on, sure, and there's ice within the fire – you can bank on
it – but mostly he is just old-fashioned nice. Polite, attentive, and with
eyes that don't miss a trick, he's the kind of guy your mum would
adore and your dad would admire.

Not for this rock star the savage storm-the-hotel-bar shenanigans of
the more reckless young blades in his profession. Coverdale is a dig-
nified member of the thirty-something rock gentry, early-'70s vintage.
He's been there, done it, done it again (the dirty dog), and then done
it some more when most rock bands in the charts these days were still
sitting around the table in highchairs.

After seventeen years in the business, the reason he's still doing it, he
says, is 'purely for the music, I just do it for the music. I love rock 'n'
roll. For me, it's still the most exciting thing in the world, so why
shouldn't I keep doin' it?'

Why indeed? It's certainly not for the money: some estimates put
the Coverdale personal fortune somewhere in the $50-million-plus
region.

Meantime, the Whitesnake machine rolls on. And very good business it's doing, too. Despite the lack of a first-out-of-the-box hit single with 'Fool for Your Loving' – astonishingly, at least to me, a flop both here and in America – *Slip of the Tongue*, the eighth Whitesnake studio album, went Top Five in Britain and is already certified double-Platinum (over two million sales) in the USA.

Inevitably, though, given the always dubious status of 'follow-up' thrust upon it by the unprecedented ten-million-plus success of the previous Whitesnake album, *Slip of the Tongue* has a way to go.

'Hey. Two million fuckin' albums ain't too shabby, dude, in less than three months, if you'll excuse the vernacular,' he says, smiling unapologetically.

'But the thing is, I don't equate it like that. When we last spoke, I told you I've never done an album before where every one of the guys has been happy with it, with themselves and their performances. This time we are. So, you know, artistically we were successful before we'd even given it to the record company. That's my attitude.

'The situation now is there's gonna be a lot of work and we're prepared to do it. Why? Because we love what we do.'

Indeed, Coverdale and the band are currently a month into their latest world tour, a jaunt that threatens to take up the next eighteen months of their lives, including headlining Monsters of Rock appearances at Donington and in Europe this August, plus the promise of a full British tour possibly before the year is out.

So far, however, word has it that the early dates on the current American tour haven't exactly been selling out. But with the second single from the new album, 'The Deeper the Love', starting to kick into the US Top Thirty, attendances are picking up.

For example, the 17,000-capacity Riverside Coliseum in Cincinnati, where Whitesnake would be appearing later that night, would be about three-quarters full by the time the band walked onstage.

For Coverdale, though, 'the glass is always half-full, not half-empty. You can do your homework and see that the tour is doing better than a lot of others that have been through the North East recently. We've had some great attendances and we've had some shabby ones, but we've still put on the same show. Nobody goes away disappointed.'

It's been over eighteen months since Whitesnake last toured. Since then, of course, they've brought in former David Lee Roth guitar maestro, Steve Vai.

Coverdale, who made his reputation working with some of the tastiest rock guitarists of the last twenty years (Ritchie Blackmore, the late Tommy Bolin, and John Sykes immediately jump to mind), admits that in Vai he has found a jewel for his crown perhaps more precious than any before.

'The first show we did was serious thrash metal. It was wild!' says Coverdale, with relish. 'We all just exploded onstage. We kept colliding into each other. No cohesion whatsoever, just going for it,' he says, shaking his mane.

'Working with Steve is a ball. I think he has to settle yet, though. He's a very intense young man. Very, very intense. I mean, I think I've found somebody who's actually harder on himself than me. A very passionate man.

'And of course he's great onstage. The whole band is. It's a very passionate show. We're doin' more numbers than we did last time out, and they're all ball-breakers. It's the hardest set I've ever done.'

The majority of the current fifteen-song American show is understandably drawn from *Slide It In*, 1987 and the latest album (the only three Whitesnake albums that ever made the US charts), with only the reworked arrangements of 'Here I Go Again' and 'Fool for Your Loving' representing the more distant (and frankly more muddled) Whitesnake past.

'Strangely enough, I've started to get requests for things like "Ain't No Love . . .", which were previously only known in Europe and Japan. But that's because some of the Whitesnake back catalogue has now started to sell in America.

'As for playing stuff like that live over here, I don't see us dusting anything like that off until we get to England for Donington in August,' he says. 'We only bring things like that out on special occasions.'

One of the innovations of the new show is Steve Vai's solo spot, in which he plays snatches from 'For the Love of God' and 'The Audience is Listening', two tracks from his forthcoming solo album, *Passion and Warfare*.

I remark that it's not often Coverdale has allowed so much of the spotlight to fall on a Whitesnake guitarist. Even for just a couple of minutes.

'Oh, it's a beautiful piece, yeah. But it lasts longer than a couple of minutes,' he laughs. 'I mean, it's early days. Steven is so instrumental – kind of a musical director, getting a lot of the songs together for the show while I was being a promotional tool.

'So there was a lot of stuff there, and when it came down to it he'd worked on everything apart from his own feature. So it's still finding its way. It's very interesting though. Very, very interesting. But we'll have it finished soon.'

After only a fleeting glimpse right at the end of the otherwise strangely mediocre video for 'Fool for Your Loving', Tawny Kitaen, star of all the hit videos from the 1987 collection, and these days of course better known as the second Mrs David Coverdale, is back with a vengeance in the vid for the new 'The Deeper the Love' single.

As ever, she features more than any member of the band with the exception of her hubby. But then again, who wants to see Tommy Aldridge in stockings and stilettos or Rudy Sarzo lying up to his tits in a suds-filled bathtub just itchin' to run his tongue down the soap dish?

'We have no shame. No shame at all,' Coverdale shrugs, his brown eyes glinting wickedly. 'Also, because the three 1987 videos were so over-the-top in terms of people's awareness of them, she's become like the Whitesnake woman to a lot of people.

'I know many people don't like it, but there are twice as many – if not more – who do. So it's a dilemma for me. Who do I put in, you know? You've got to admit, she does the job well. Show me someone better, I'll consider a change. But I've never indulged my wife in those circumstances. I mean, anybody that thinks she's in there just because she's my wife doesn't know me. She's in there because she's an ace. As is Vai, as is Vandenberg. You know, if you've got an ace, play the fucker.'

Mention of Adrian Vandenberg leads to talk of how he and Steve Vai are managing to blend, not just as players but in partnership as live performers.

'It started off totally chaotic,' Coverdale admits. 'I mean, they're both so flamboyant in their own separate ways, we had snakes flyin'' every fuckin' which-way across the stage!' he chuckles. 'There's not a lot of co-ordination going down at the moment. It's every man for himself.'

You have to be fit to keep up. So except for 'an occasional glass of wine after the show', Coverdale eschews all drugs and alcohol and works out every day in a gym: a strict personal regime he began on the 1987 world tour.

'It makes sense. I wouldn't be able to do the shows otherwise. It's that simple. And it's not a high price to pay at all. I've been through all the superstitions of needing a couple of cognacs before I go on. That's just a self-perpetuating myth.'

More tea arrives on cue, more cigarettes are lit, and talk winds inexorably towards the big one: Donington 1990.

'I'm delighted that they got the licence after such an unfortunate tragedy [the two teenage fans who died in 1988 during Guns N' Roses set], which, God willing, will never be repeated,' he says. 'But I'd be much more scared about letting my children go to football matches than rock concerts, to be honest.

'My policy has always been if I see any disturbances going on in the audience, I'll stop the band – no performance is that important. I've done it twice already on this tour.'

Any chance of revealing who else you're talking about for the rest of the bill?

'I can tell you it's gonna be a major stack of bands. And of course we've got Aerosmith as very special guests. But the rest have yet to be finalised so I can't really say. But you will be the first to know. Special treatment for you, Michael,' he winks, ever ready to ham it up.

After the unnerving reviews the new *Slip of the Tongue* album received from the British press, not to mention unexpected little gripes like coming top in the *Kerrang!* Readers' Poll 'Worst Album of the Year' section, it would not be hard to understand if Coverdale never wanted to set foot on British soil again.

'I'm pissed off but I'm not bitter,' he says, matter-of-factly. 'I refuse to go away. If I'd listened to the press I'd have completely abandoned playing rock music after I left Deep Purple, and gone disco.

'I think people have a lot of misconceptions about me: the big head syndrome. Certainly with the success of the last album, I get the feeling some people think I'm smug and gloating, which isn't the case at all. I'm in a very, very positive place right now, real positive; privately and professionally. It's so weird because under normal circumstances, in a man-to-man situation, I'd probably smack 'em in the mouth. But nobody from the press has ever been rude to my face, ever.

'But I tolerate it because it's the only way I can get certain points across to people who genuinely care about Whitesnake. You know, the audience which has stayed so incredibly loyal to this band through the years.'

Which, whether it gets reported enough or not, is even more vast and imposing than the crowd who turned up to watch the first time Coverdale and Whitesnake headlined at Donington in 1982. Seventy-two thousand of the buggers are expected this year, with even more on the eventual British tour afterwards. How do you top that?

'I'm not intending to try and top anything I've already done. That's not part of the master plan,' he says. 'My motivation comes from the fact that this is the most wonderful way to express myself. I love rock 'n' roll and have done from the beginning.

'When I was in London recently, I picked up, like, *The Best of Sweet* and *Best of T.Rex*', all these bands that are unsung here in America. And I got the best of the original Fleetwood Mac, and I picked up some old Jeff Beck, all on CD, mind you. Lovely!

'It's great listening to all that stuff again. I'm still such a big fan of music. It all sounds as fresh to me as it ever did. I still get goosebumps. I mean, I care. I really genuinely care about what we do. I care that people have fun, I care that the players have a ball, you know? I've been doing it when it was miserable.'

The following night at the Riverside Coliseum, it's my turn to get goosebumps. It's been a while since I last voluntarily subjected myself to the balls-out orgiastic splendour of an arena-sized American rock 'n' roll show. I'd almost forgotten how LOUD these things can be.

When the lights in the hall die and the spacy dry-ice intro to 'Slip of the Tongue' begins, the screams begin echoing around the giant hall. Then the band hit the stage, a bank of bright white lights behind them, casting them as silhouettes until Coverdale reaches the mike and starts to croon like a sheep-killing dog: 'Sometime after midnight / The heat begins to rise / Girl, you'd shame the Devil / With the look that's in your eyes . . .'

Great. Dressed head-to-toe in black, and scarecrow-thin, he launches himself at the mike stand and into the song, steamin' from the off, his voice as raw and emotional as a wounded lion's, the mike stand whirling in his hands.

Steve Vai, of course, is simply from another dimension. Not only is he, as the boys keep reminding me, probably lick-for-lick the most talented rock 'n' roll guitarist in the world right now, but he is also, as the girls never cease to point out, the sexiest. Where other lesser beings woulda stomped, he glides like a candle across the stage for the intro to 'Slide It In' – his patented Ibanez seven-string special slappin' his thigh.

Adrian Vandenberg – or the 'blond-haired Viking from Hell!', as Coverdale is currently introducing him on stage – provides a nice visual contrast to Vai's agile strut. Adrian's fair, whereas Steve is dark, and fleet-fingered finesse is not necessarily the name of the game where the flying Dutchman is concerned: instead, he gnaws at the guitar break on 'Slow 'n' Easy' like a dog with a bone that needs burying. So to speak. Well, this *is* Whitesnake.

As for Rudy Sarzo and Tommy Aldridge, they're still up to their same old tricks: Tommy soloing with his hands; Rudy with his tongue. Seasoned pros with their chops together and the ability to put on a good show for the back-row fanatics.

'Is This Love' sends the crowd into a swoon, and 'Judgement Day' provides the first really solid high of the night: a strong and compelling performance, the air suddenly charged with promise.

Hilariously incorrigible, Coverdale pauses to toast the crowd.

'Ah, there's a nice selection of titties down the front tonight. Gentleman, isn't it awfully nice to have a penis?' he deadpans, quoting from Monty Python. 'Ah, yes – it's delightful to have a dong,' he muses grandly, as the band strike into a thundering version of 'Kitten's Got Claws'.

'The Deeper the Love' has the aisles swaying and 'Cheap an' Nasty' is just that, while 'Crying in the Rain' is positively awesome. 'Fool for

Your Loving', meanwhile, is greeted like the big hit single it never was and damn near brings the house down.

Steve Vai's solo feature follows and is, as advertised, an absolute gem: featuring the triple-necked red baby first made famous in David Lee Roth's 'Just Like Paradise' video, and a couple of sensitive seven-strings only brought to life by the special touch, or sometimes just a glance, it seemed, of the master. For me, the second most moving moment of the night.

But 'Here I Go Again', which followed, walked away with the first prize. It was Whitesnake's first Number One and has become almost a signature tune for Coverdale and Whitesnake. It's pretty, with a beautifully soulful lead vocal for sure, but it's the 'My Way'-type ingredient of the lyrics – 'I've made up my mind / I ain't wasting no more time' – that does it to ya every time. Coverdale sings it so this time you *know* he means it.

A bottle-totin' version of 'Bad Boys' breaks the trance and the crowd are left chanting for encores they know David is far too polite to refuse them: first 'Gimme All Your Love' – complete with singalong chorus – followed by a blood-curdling version of 'Still of the Night', that would have a dead man rattlin' his picked-clean bones in excitement.

Earlier in the show, David Coverdale had raised his glass of mineral water to his lips and shared this thought with the audience: 'If it's in hard and it's in long and it's in heavy … it's indecent! Boom boom! God bless you!'

Looking handsome as hell, and with the screams of delight from the crowd ringing in his ears, he convinced me it's going to be a very rude Donington.

But then, you probably already knew that, right?

CODA

Little did any of us know that within eighteen months of this article being published, Vai would have left Whitesnake, I would have left music journalism, and Coverdale would have left Tawny Kitaen. In fact, you might say it was goodbye from me and goodbye from him – and him. And even her . . .

Not that the story ended there, of course. Coinciding with the massive revival in classic rock generally, the last few years have been some of the best ever for Coverdale and Whitesnake. They might not sell albums in their millions any more, but they certainly sell tickets. Now a grandad – albeit the handsomest, most fit and tan grandad on the block – the last time I spoke to David, he told me how these days he felt like he had 'bluebirds coming out of every orifice', he was so happy with his life.

And, of course, Steve Vai has had bluebirds coming out of the neck of his guitar for many years now, too, recognised – as he is – as one of the greatest living guitarists in rock. Even the redoubtable Tawny has enjoyed another, brief, but scorching moment in the spotlight, through the unsparing lens of US reality television. But then almost everybody ends up on TV these days, even me, God help us . . .

METALLICA, 1991

As with a lot of rock bands that became stars in the 1980s, I had known Metallica since before they were famous. So while it definitely felt weird watching them make it so big in the '90s, one thing I felt sure of was that their drummer and chief spokesman, Lars Ulrich, would not change much. He would become a lot richer, of course, but I still envisaged him, like Steve Harris of Iron Maiden, keeping his wits about him and being able to tell the fools and the fakers from the old friends who had helped him along the way.

Certainly that was the attitude I still had at the time of this interview. What I hadn't anticipated was that the self-titled album they were then recording – now known as *The Black Album* – would sell so many millions of copies it would turn Metallica into the Bon Jovi of the thrash generation. Change was coming, you felt, but I could not have envisaged the scale of it. Instead, I assumed Metallica would be more than happy to become the Iron Maiden or Motörhead of their generation: wealthy, venerated, famous and immeasurably cool. Instead, they were destined to become not just bigger and more famous than bands such as Maiden, but – alongside Guns N' Roses – the biggest, most famous rock band on the planet.

At the time of this interview, though, Lars was still Lars and the future was something nobody really worried too much about. Or so I thought . . .

I catch up with Lars Ulrich on a grey and chilly afternoon in North Hollywood. He's in the recreation room at One on One studios, where Metallica have been holed up these past six months, recording their new, as yet untitled, album with neo-legendary producer Bob Rock. Neither Kirk Hammett's saw-toothed guitar nor Jason Newsted's belly-rumbling bass are required at the studio today. But James Hetfield is seated in the next room – Studio One – guitar cradled on his lap, patiently laying down the ponderous melody that makes up the cyclical guitar part to a song called 'The Unforgiven'. Lars chomps on a hastily slapped together cheese-and-pickle sandwich and shows off the amenities: pinball machine, video game, pool table, punchbag . . . Punchbag?!?

'For fucking tension!' Lars exclaims, crumbs spluttering from his lips. 'You know that shit; you're in a studio and you're trying to get something down and you can't get it down right and you just need to hurt something. Then you receive the bill for it next week. You can hurt that and not have to pay for it.'

James has been using it a lot lately, apparently.

'But now that Jason has started doing his bass he uses it a lot too!' Lars chortles loudly.

Cut to a side room further down the corridor. MTV is murmuring from a screen in one corner and – nine-line phone positioned on a table by his side – Lars settles his whip-thin body down into an armchair and fixes me with that piercing, squinting stare he reserves for such occasions.

'So what do you want to know?' he spitballs in his graceless Danish-American drawl.

Well, there's a lot of things about the new album that I'm curious about, I tell him. Firstly, the idea of you working with Bob Rock. When I think of the name Bob Rock, I immediately think of very different bands to Metallica; more commercially minded outfits like, say, Mötley Crüe or The Cult.

'I think that's the main thing I've been asked about. Everybody asks me about Bob Rock.'

Let me be more specific, then. People choose Bob Rock to get hit records.

'Yeah, that's a fair comment,' he nods his head solemnly. 'But I look at it a little differently. Last summer, when we started writing this shit, we were just thinking we'd do what we usually do, be safe and predictable and record the album like we always do. But we'd never really liked the mixing on . . . *Justice*, *Master* . . . or . . . *Lightning*. So we were thinking, who can we get in to do the mixing? We felt it was time to make a record with a huge, big, fat low-end and the best-sounding record like that in the last couple of years – not songs, but sound – was the last Mötley Crüe album. We really liked the really big fat sound on *Dr Feelgood* [produced by Bob Rock]. So we told our manager, "Call this guy and see if he wants to mix the record". He came back and said not only did Bob want to mix the record, but he saw us live when we played Vancouver, and really liked us and would like to produce the album. Of course, we said, "We're Metallica, no one produces us! No one fucks with our shit and tells us what to do!" But slowly, over the next few days, we thought maybe we should let our guard down and at least talk to the guy. Like, if the guy's name really is Bob Rock [it is], how bad can he be?'

James and Lars flew to Canada last summer to meet the producer at his home in Vancouver.

'We're sitting there saying, "Well, Bob, we think that we've made some good albums but this is three years later and we want to make a record that is really bouncy, really lively; just has a lot of groove to it." We told him that live we have this great vibe and that's what we wanted to do in the studio. It's really funny 'cos he turned around and said, "When I saw you guys live and then heard your record I thought that you hadn't come close to capturing what you do in a live situation." He basically said the same thing as we had and from then on we thought that maybe we shouldn't be so stubborn and maybe see where the fuck this would bring us.'

The only snag was Rock's notorious reluctance to record anywhere outside of his own Little Mountain studios in Vancouver, home of the hits for Poison, Bon Jovi, Mötley Crüe, The Cult, Aerosmith,

David Lee Roth and so many others it hurts my wallet even to think about it.

'We really didn't want to do it in Vancouver – everyone comes to him. For a while I didn't think it was going to work out. Bob's got a big family and he wasn't that keen on coming to LA. Then when we played him the stuff, I could see his eyes light up. We'd built a little eight-track studio in my house and made some rough demos; just me on drums and James, not really everybody, just really rough. Bob was like, "Wow, this could be the 'Kashmir' of the Nineties!" He's saying all this stuff and me and James are looking at him thinking, he's listening to one guitar and one set of drums and a vocal melody that goes "na-na-na-na-na"? Anyway, as soon as he heard the stuff things started livening up. We brought him here to One on One studio, and in this very room, on that machine over there, I played him the next two or three songs we'd been working on. It was like, boom! From there it was pretty much a done deal.'

And the band's reaction to the results of their, on the surface at least, offbeat new studio relationship? Thus far, it would seem, judging by Lars' pixie face, nothing short of elation.

'The way I look at it is that Bob Rock brought out the best that Mötley Crüe had to offer and made the best Mötley Crüe record. The same with The Cult or Bon Jovi. If you listen to *Slippery When Wet*, he made the best Bon Jovi album, he brought out the best that Bon Jovi had to offer at that time. Looking back on our last four albums, they were great records, I'm not going to say anything bad about them. But we never thought that we'd done one where you think, there it is. That one album is it. You're never gonna be able to make a record like that but as close as you can get to that one album, this is fucking it. The new stuff that we've been writing is like a breath of fresh air. We're just really excited in a way that I don't think we've been excited before. Bob says he thinks it shows we've got a lot of soul, or . . . what's another word for soul?'

Depth? Emotion?

'Yeah, we have a lot of emotions that we don't let out easily, 'cos we're very guarded as people. He says that he could see through that right away. He says that one of his things on this album was to try and let us take down our guard and let out the shit that's in there.'

Do you think that it was also because the time was right for you as people? Perhaps you were waiting for someone to say, 'OK, let's drop this big bad Metallica attitude for a second and find out who you really are.'

'Yeah, but I also think it's a combination of us getting pretty bored with the direction of the last three albums. They were all different from each other, but they were all going in the same direction. You know, long songs, longer songs, even longer songs. Progressive, more progressive, even more progressive. It was time to take a sharp turn. The only way to do that would be to write one long song to fill the whole album or write songs that were shorter than we had done before. And that's what we did. I don't need to tell you again how I feel about being pigeonholed with the whole thrash metal thing. But the new shit's just got a whole new vibe and feel that I never knew Metallica were capable of. Before when we've gone into a recording studio we've always frozen up and tried to be too perfect. It's like, five minutes after I could play drums, Metallica were going, and the shit just roller-coastered. Suddenly we're making demos, then we're touring, making our first record after only being together a year-and-a-half – all of a sudden it was like, well, we have a record out but we really can't play. So I had to take drum lessons and Kirk's doing his Joe Satriani trip.' (Kirk takes regular guitar lessons from the San Francisco-based guitar ace.) 'I think we spent a lot of years trying to prove to ourselves and to everyone out there that we can play our instruments – you know, listen to this big drum fill I'm doing, and Kirk's playing all these wild things that are really difficult. When we were first starting out in 1981, the two big bands in America that year were the Rolling Stones and AC/DC. I clearly remember sitting at James's house going: "The worst drummers in the world are Charlie Watts and Phil Rudd! Listen to them, they don't do any drum fills, they're not doing anything. Listen to that, it's horrible! Give me Ian Paice and Neil Peart." So for the next eight years I'm doing Ian Paice and Neil Peart things, proving to the world that I can play. Now it's like my two favourite drummers at the moment are Charlie Watts and Phil Rudd. At the end of the last tour, "Seek and Destroy" had practically become my favourite song in the set. It had so much bounce and groove I could really just sit there and play it without worrying about when the next quadruple-

backwards-sidewards paradiddle came in. About halfway through the
... *Justice* tour I was sitting there playing these nine-minute songs
thinking, "Why am I sitting here worrying about how perfect these
nine-minute songs have to be when we play stuff like 'Seek and Destroy'
or 'For Whom the Bell Tolls' and they have such a great fucking vibe?"'

So is that why you would occasionally record songs like Budgie's
'Breadfan', or the covers on the 'Garage Days Re-revisited' EP? That
was 'fun', but your own songs were 'serious'? Now it's more integrated,
rolled into one?

'Yeah, that's probably true. Yeah, that's a very good way of putting
it. We were finally able to let that happen. I never really thought of it
like that. I guess there was this thing lingering inside of us that wanted
to do things like that, but when it came time to sitting down and
making the record ...' He shrugs his shoulders fitfully. 'If you look
back on the albums, next to the song titles, the times are always listed.
I used to be really proud of it. In the past we'd do a rough version of a
song and I'd go home and time it and go, "It's only seven-and-a-half
minutes!" I'd think, "Fuck, we've got to put another couple of riffs in
there". Now I'm not bothered either way.'

But wasn't that always Metallica's forte: jamming in as many riffs as
you could snap your neck to?

'I guess the point I'm trying to get across is, I used to be really
concerned with the timing and lengths of a song when we were writing
them. But this time I didn't even want to think about it. There is one
six-minute song – "Friend of Misery". It wasn't written on purpose,
though. It was the last song we wrote and we did the usual to-the-
point verse and chorus and came up with a cool thing in the middle,
which is a bit longer. Most of the tracks are about four minutes,
though.'

With twelve tracks already slated for the finished album, is this
going to be your *Hysteria*? The big seller, loaded with hits? The record
company must be rubbing their hands in glee at the prospect of so
many potential hit singles.

'They are!' he snickers. 'I'm sure we're gonna get a lot of people
saying we're selling out, but I've heard that shit from *Ride the Lightning*
on. People were already going, Boo! Sell out! Even back then.'

Isn't it a self-made cross, though, refusing to do videos: the whole underground 'you-don't-tell-us-what-to-do-'cos-we're-Metallica' kind of thing?

'I really don't look at it like a cross. Everybody should know by now that we get really bored easily with things we do. We move between this really serious album to a stupid cover version EP. You know, serious videos, goofy videos. We're a band of extremes and we keep changing, keep following our instincts in whatever direction our heads takes us.'

OK, but have their heads taken them to a point where we're gonna see four or five singles (plus videos) pulled from this album?

'It's much too early to say. One side of me wants to sit there and defend it – just 'cos they're short songs doesn't mean they're any more accessible. Then the other side says, I don't give a fuck. I know what these sound like.'

So what do they sound like? Lars played me very brief, very rough snippets of three tracks: 'Sad but True', 'The Unforgiven' and 'Don't Tread on Me'. The first thing that hits is that, Bob Rock or not, half the length maybe, this is still Metallica. Fearful as a widow's wail, stark as a new moon; it could be no other.

'They all have these big fat guitar riffs,' says Lars with relish. 'But instead of after the second chorus steering into another fucking universe, they stay in the same one then go back into the chorus. Then we go to another universe on the next song. Whatever people want to think of that, they can. But for me that's how I look at it.'

Which song was it Bob Rock said could be 'the "Kashmir" for the Nineties'?

'Aarrgghhh! I asked for that one, didn't I? It's "Sad but True", but I'd like it to go on record that I don't agree with that, ha! It's just one of those songs that has one of these monstrous guitar riffs that you latch onto right away and the drums kinda cruise in the background and just lay down a solid thing. It's about how different personalities in your mind make you do different things – and how some of those things clash and how they fight to have control over you. From the mind of James Hetfield, you know? Don't ask me . . .'

What about 'The Unforgiven', the track they were currently working on. What was that about?

'It's about how a lot of people go through their life without taking any initiative. A lot of people just follow in the footsteps of others.

Their whole life is planned out for them, and there's certain people doing the planning and certain people doing the following.'

One I didn't get to hear but liked the title of, 'The God That Failed', Lars says, 'is about this thing that's going on in America. This kind of religion thing where they don't believe in medicine. So if their kids get some heavy illness it's like, "Please God, heal this sick child", and three days later the child is dead. It's stirring up a lot of shit over here because the courts are going after these people now and nailing them with murder. But it's not necessarily against or for. It just tells a story.'

Lars says his favourite song is always 'the one we're working on today' but that he has a peculiar affection for the next song they begin working on after they complete 'The Unforgiven' – another strangely titled artefact called 'Enter Sandman'.

'That song has been on the fucking song titles list for the last six years,' he smiles coyly. 'The way it works is James and I sit with a big list of song titles and throw them at each other. We might pick one that will work with a specific guitar part. Others that don't catch straight away, we just leave on there. I'd always looked at "Enter Sandman" and thought, what the fuck does that mean? Me being brought up in Denmark and not knowing about a lot of this shit, I didn't get it. Then James clued me in. Apparently the Sandman is like this children's villain – the Sandman who comes and rubs sand in your eyes if you don't go to sleep at night. So it's a fable and then Metallica turn it into . . .'

Freddy Krueger?

'Nooo . . . James has just given it a nice twist. Hahaha! But it's this classic example of having something lingering around. People might say "Is that 'cos you can't come up with something new?" No, not at all. Six years ago I looked at "Enter Sandman" and thought, "Naw, let's write 'Metal Militia'." Metal all the way, you know?' He squinted his eyes, then chuckled self-consciously. 'Six years ago, yeah . . .'

I said I wanted to move the conversation onto some broader issues and Lars smiled like a cat: 'Mick, after all this time you can ask me whatever you want and I'll try and give you the best answer I can.'

I'd forgotten how good he is at this interviewing lark. OK, well, it's finally been announced that Metallica will be appearing at Donington this year, second on the bill as special guests to AC/DC. Why don't we start with that?

'Yeah, it's cool,' he says. 'Obviously, we're lucky to be in a position not to have to support a lot of bands. But in the last couple of years we've opened at festivals and a few big outdoor things, and it's been great. My personal hard-on was playing with Deep Purple. We did that three or four years ago. James's personal hard-on was opening up for Aerosmith when we did a show together up in Canada last year. Now I've been really getting into the AC/DC stuff again. In fact, the only band left that I really want to play with is AC/DC.

'Plus it fits in so perfectly,' he continues, eyes skyward, squinting into the future. 'Cos the new album's gonna come out hopefully sometime in August. We were gonna start touring in America, because we'd never started in America before and we wanted to turn it around. But you can't tour in America really until at least three months after the album comes out. So after the album came out we were gonna have to sit there for, like, twelve weeks playing with ourselves. Then this came up, which is basically playing stadiums in Europe with AC/DC, and I couldn't ask for a better situation. Playing with AC/DC, which is, like, the only band that I actually want to play with – I mean, really!'

It's no secret, of course, that Lars is an AC/DC fan from way back. How did he view their newer recordings, though?

'Obviously, the golden era of AC/DC was from *Dirty Deeds Done Dirt Cheap* to *For Those About to Rock*,' he said. 'But the new album I've listened to a lot, too. "Thunderstruck" is a great track, and "Are You Ready" is really bouncy, too. I didn't like [former AC/DC drummer] Simon Wright's stuff. I think Chris Slade has brought back a lot of that bounce. I'm really looking forward to playing with them. Are you kidding? It's exciting. When you're a kid you sit there and dream about stuff like that. When I saw the name Deep Purple and then Metallica's logo underneath it on a poster, it was, you know, major jerk-yourself-off time!' he cackled. 'It's the same thing here playing with AC/DC. AC/DC is just cool to me. It could have something to do with the fact that I was one of their biggest fans from, like, '76 to '82. But their new album's great and I look forward to the whole thing tremendously. I think it should be fuckin' something.'

This will be Metallica's third time at Donington. Their first appearance was in 1985 with ZZ Top when they were 'third from the bottom', he reminded me. 'It was Magnum, Rätt, Metallica, Bon Jovi, Marillion, ZZ Top.' Then in 1987: 'It was Bon Jovi, Dio, us, Anthrax, W.A.S.P. and Cinderella.' And now Metallica are second on the bill. They didn't think they could have headlined this time then?

'Donington? No!' he shakes his head. 'Obviously, anybody can headline it, but whether anybody fucking shows up is another situation! I don't know, it's kinda weird,' he goes on. 'If you look at America versus Europe over the last six years: six years ago in America, Metallica was like down here.' He places his hand down by his knees. 'Now in America, Metallica is, like, boom!' His hand rockets through the air like a salute. 'From one hundred thousand records to three million! But in Europe, six years ago we were *here*.' Hand waist-high. 'And now we're *here*.' Chest-high. 'The increase has not been as big. If you compare it, I don't know if we're as big in Europe anymore as we are in America. We headlined Wembley and the NEC, in Britain, but I really don't think we could play Donington yet.'

Nevertheless, it remains an ambition?

'Obviously!' he cries. 'It would be a great ego kind of thing to do it. But it's got to be right. I think Iron Maiden probably did it better than anyone else; they waited until the time was exactly right. Me and every other fucker would like to headline Donington, but you wanna do it when the time is right. This seems like the right thing to do, go around Europe once more. Maybe with album number six – which will hopefully come out sometime this century,' he laughed sarcastically. 'Maybe on that we could headline Donington.'

I steer the conversation onto the juddering rise and rise of Metallica over the last five years. From wise-ass no-names with more riffs-per-song than an octopus has tentacles, to million-selling Grammy award-winners in the space of four dark, sometimes comic, frankly brutal albums. It took something but even Lars had a hard time explaining what. A long, rambling discourse ensues ...

'I've finally come to a conclusion on what it is,' he begins, staring solemnly at his sneakers. 'It's because we look so good. Ha-ha-ha! God, that was hard to say with a straight face,' he splutters. 'I don't know,' he tries again. 'I guess a lot of it has to do with the fact that early on we had a very distant attitude to the business side of things. We firmly stood our own ground on things like what we played, how we looked, how we presented ourselves. Or how we *didn't* present ourselves. Just doing what we were doing. The thing is, there weren't really any decent independent labels going in America when we were starting out. You really had to be the right package to get a record deal in 1982. But we said, "Fuck that!", and just plodded away doing our own stuff and feeling great about it. Then suddenly there is an independent label and we do have a record out and a lot of people start buying it because there was never quite anything like this in America before.

'In America everything would have to go through the record companies, then the record companies would package it in a way they thought was saleable to the public. The record company philosophy in America has always been, well, give the public a choice of A, B or C but the menu stops there, and we'll decide that a band like Metallica will not be on the menu because they are not saleable. So all the people got to listen to hard rock through Styx or REO Speedwagon or whatever. And then this band Metallica came out and they thought, "Wow, where has all this shit come from? How come we haven't heard this before?" Because the record companies never believed that anything like that could actually sell.

'So we start selling a shitload of records and at the same time James' lyrics are different from all the clichéd crap that all the older metal bands spew out, and people started to take notice of that.'

But why are Metallica so fashionable these days? More than an entire universe: Megadeth, Slayer, Anthrax et al – even Guns N' Roses – why are Metallica, above all others, regarded as not only the hardest of the hardest, but the smartest of the smartest, too?

'We've been very lucky with critical acclaim from a lot of fashionable magazines,' he shrugs, 'you know, *Rolling Stone* and the *Village Voice*, the *LA Times* and the *New York Times*. All these writers who would spew about Bruce Springsteen or Prince, usually. Metallica's kinda been lumped into that crowd in America.'

Why Metallica, though? I persist. Why not, say, Slayer?

'I think a lot of it has to do with our approach lyrically, and about wanting to confront issues that were more realistic and had more to do with things that were happening around us. I'm the first to line up for a Slayer record when it comes out, 'cos I think Slayer are the best at what they do. But lyrically, it's a whole different kettle of fish. We've always been very adamant about shying away from the metal clichés. One of them being the whole sexist, Satanist crap. And as a consequence it seems, all the trendsetting journalists have been throwing acclaim at Metallica right, left and centre. Not doing a video and then finally doing "One" and everybody going, "Wow!"'

He looks nonplussed for a moment. I quote him something he once told *Time Out* magazine: 'We get more publicity from not doing a video than doing a video'. Was it really that thought out at the time?

'Naaw! That's just how I look back on it,' he insists, his cherubic features contorting into a wicked smile. 'We just said, "Well, the formula for record company stuff is: here's the band, here's the look, here's the safe radio song and here's the video." We just thought, "Fuck that!" It took us a long time to realise that you can use a video as more than just the obligatory promotion tool.'

He scrubs at his unshaven chin with the back of his hand: 'You know, you can use the medium and make it as much fun and as creative as it is to make a record. So we sat down and made a video that was as creative and fun as when we make a record; not just have some kind of running-down-a-corridor bullshit.'

I wondered if he'd seen the new Skid Row retail video, *Oh Say, Can You Scream*. To say that it 'borrows heavily' from the home-shot techniques pioneered by Metallica's groundbreaking 1987 *Cliff 'Em All* video would be to say an elephant shits mighty big ones: an understatement, and then some.

'Yes, I think it's a lot of fun,' he smiled politely. 'Sebastian [Bach – Skid Row singer] told me where he got the idea from, too!' he chortled. 'I saw him the other day. He goes: "Dude, have you seen our video yet, dude? You don't mind that we got the idea from *Cliff 'Em All*, do ya, dude?" I said, "Naw!", 'cos I don't mind. I guess over the years, looking back on it, it makes me kinda uncomfortable trying to figure out why exactly Metallica is so cool. It's like, part of the reason that Metallica is so cool is that you don't sit there and think it out, you just go with your instincts,' he reflects earnestly. 'An idea happened in one of our heads to make a video from all the bootlegs that were floating around. That's it! You don't second-guess it. You don't go, "Gee, but will it sell?"'

Did he get a sense of pride, though, from knowing that people in the music business also respected the band's work? To the point, in fact, where they had now handed the band a Grammy two years running? His eyes dance.

'Ha-ha-ha! I know that Cliff [Burnstein] and Peter [Mensch] take great pride in managing Metallica, and yeah, it is cool. I'd be lying to you if I didn't say that I'm proud of the shit that we've done and the doors that we've opened.'

The whole business of getting a Grammy – sneered at by those never nominated for anything other than the bargain bins, yet so coveted by those used to breathing the rarefied air of the US Top Ten – did that make him proud? He thought about it for about three seconds – which for Lars means he really thought about it – then nodded his head slowly. 'Yeah, I am.'

Even though they should have got it for their ... *And Justice for All* album in 1989 – the year that Jethro Tull walked off with the Heavy Metal/Hard Rock award (go figure) – instead of for Metallica's version of an old Queen song? ('Stone Cold Crazy' from Elektra's fortieth-anniversary album *Rubaiyat* – a two-disc CD collection of cover versions).

'Well, we got the first one last year for "One",' he points out. 'This is our second Grammy. But I know what you're saying. Let's put it this way, if we release anything for the rest of the Nineties, every year we'll get a Grammy for it just because they fucked up that first year.'

Is that what he really thought?

'Honestly?' His eyes drop and his voice assumes a serious air. 'Yeah, I do. Nobody's gonna want me to say that but that is where it's at. Listen man, we go into the studio in January last year and spend about fifteen minutes – give or take a day, the shortest visit we've ever had in the studio, anyway – and we put down a cover version of a Queen song from 1973, for an Elektra compilation album, and it's track eleven on Side Three, right, and it wins a Grammy over fully fledged albums by, like, Judas Priest and Megadeth?' he sneers. 'Don't you think that it has anything to do with, "Gee, how can we rectify how we fucked up in 1989?" Nobody's gonna like me for saying that, but let's be honest.

But do I like winning a Grammy? Of course I like winning a Grammy!'
he grins. 'I want a Grammy as much as the next guy; even *more* than
the next guy.'

When I ask where he keeps them at home, I swear he almost blushes.

'Erm, the first one, I'll admit it, it actually sits in the living room . . .'

On the mantelpiece?

'Yeah . . .' he snickers.

In a display case of its own with laser beams bouncing off it from
the ceiling?

'Ha-ha-ha! No, I haven't quite gone that far! I kinda have one shelf
with the awards on it that we've won, you know, Bammys [Bay Area
Music Awards] and Grammys. I guess I'm proud of all those things,
yeah . . .'

Suddenly he jerks up straight in his chair. 'I'm just sitting here
thinking nobody has asked me if I'm proud of it before,' he says
ruefully. 'Come to think of it, I'm really fucking proud, I really am!'
He looks me hard in the eye: 'I used to always think it didn't mean
much, you know? But the truth is, I guess it does.'

He sits there thinking it over.

'I guess I'm just proud of the persistent stubborn belief in ourselves
and not ever altering or toning down what we do in any way, shape or
form to get anything,' he decides at length. 'That has paid off and
opened up a lot of doors not just for us but for a lot of other bands,
and shown a lot of people at record companies that there's a lot of
people out there who don't want their music and their bands all nicely
packaged. We were the band to do that in America, in the Eighties.
I'm really proud of that, too.'

With that in mind, I let Lars return to the interiors of One on One
and make my way back to my hotel to play back the tape. Roll on
Don-ing-ton . . .

CODA

The Black Album turned Metallica into the biggest, coolest rock band on the planet – until Nirvana came along with *Nevermind,* released later the same year. This was a fact that Lars plainly resented when I later spoke to him about it. 'If he [Cobain] hates success so much, why doesn't he just bow out?' he'd snarled.

Of course, Kurt would do just that a short time later. The point here, though, is that, as a result of all this, the Lars Ulrich I used to know – as represented by this interview – was not going to be around for much longer. The unbelievable money – as one mutual friend put it, 'The fountain in his courtyard is bigger than my house' – the colossal fame, the self-confessed drug problems, all would soon conspire to turn the Lars I once knew into someone I didn't know at all. Where once he would phone and ask to crash on my couch if he was in town, now he flew into London incognito to buy his antiques and art.

Frankly, who can blame him? If I'd been blown away by that kind of zillion-dollar deal at his age – he was barely thirty when *Black* hit Number One – I'd have probably been worse; a lot worse. Anyway, this piece captures him on the cusp of that massive lifestyle change, back when he still lived among mortals and was forced to take drum lessons by the producer. I didn't realise it then – not fully – but Lars knew exactly what he was doing. He certainly achieved what he set out to do, and how many musicians out there can really say that?

DAVE MUSTAINE, 1990

Dave Mustaine was always one interview I really looked forward to back then as he was always so incredibly cynical and bitter, and honest and tough. This was the guy, after all, who'd been booted out of Metallica for karate-kicking James Hetfield and bullying poor shy-and-retiring Lars Ulrich. I wasn't sure how this one would go, though, as I'd been told Dave was just out of rehab. Mustaine off the gear? Hard to imagine back then. He'd always seemed so impregnable; what would he be like now that the head doctors had actually gotten hold of him? Weak, vulnerable, needy?

No chance. In fact, the Dave Mustaine I encountered that day in 1990 was even more self-assured than I remembered. Losing the booze and the drugs had enabled him to shed whatever last traces there were of self-doubt or – whisper it – insecurity that had still lingered during his Captain Smack days.

He had a new drug, he said – sky-diving. That is, sky-diving and sex, although obviously not in that order. Oh, and music. That was the other thing he was newly enamoured with. Having seen Metallica finally penetrate the US Top Ten with their ... *And Justice for All* album the previous year, he was now in a hurry to show that his band, Megadeth, could do the same. Which, rather sensationally, they would do with their about-to-be-released collection *Rust In Peace*.

Interview with Dave Mustaine of Megadeth, first published in Kerrang!, *September 1990.*

Love him or hate him, Dave Mustaine is a strictly one-off personality.

It's a cliché, of course, just like all the other clichés regularly used to describe him down the years: genius, ghoul, junkie, cool ... none of them are right, none of them are wrong. Mustaine just is.

He started his career as the singer/lead guitarist in Metallica, of course, playing on and writing much of the original 'No Life 'Til Leather' demo tape, which won the band a record deal. But he was fired before recording the first Metallica album, after giving James Hetfield a bloody nose in a fist-fight.

Bowed but unbroken, he formed Megadeth in 1983 with bassist Dave 'Junior' Ellefson, and a trio of gnarled, slit-eyed albums followed: *Killing is My Business ... and Business is Good* (1984), *Peace Sells ... But Who's Buying?* (1985) and *So Far, So Good ... So What!* (1987). All of these earned the band substantial worldwide sales and a vast hardcore following.

However, the exposure Mustaine and his band received appeared to be a double-edged sword. Mustaine the Thrasher became Mustaine the Mouth.

Some said he was an asshole. Actually, a lot of people said he was an asshole – and quite often they were right. Worse, the contrived profanities and the vulgar machismo charm tended to overshadow the music he was also busy making – some of the most innovative heavy metal recordings of the 1980s. And you can hang your skeleton on that one.

But, of course, Mustaine was a junkie then; a self-confessed heroin addict. Had been for more than five years, during which time his 'disease', as he now calls it, cost him a manager, a long-standing girl-friend, several Megadeth line-ups (Dave Junior being the only constant factor in Mustaine's life, professionally and personally, throughout this period) – and perhaps some of his sanity.

The Dave Mustaine I met in Los Angeles recently, however, appears to be a changed man; a reformed character, almost saintly in his devotions to his new-found toe-hold on reality.

Seven months ago Dave Mustaine quit heroin, alcohol, pot, cigarettes and every other drug you might care to name.

'Yup, I finally saw the light. Praise the Lord,' he says sarcastically, as we sit down to talk about it over dinner at a small, otherwise empty Thai restaurant on Hollywood and Vine late one afternoon.

I can't believe how well he looks. We've met two or three times before over the years but somehow he looks taller, much taller. He looks huge, in fact. Not fat, though. Just tall and broad and strong. The kid I remember was half this size.

When I remark on it he smiles and says, 'Yeah, but that's because I was always stooped over in those days, ready to nod off at any moment. Like I was dead or something. I probably was.'

Well, not any more. With the new Megadeth album *Rust in Peace* about to hit the streets and with yet another new line-up in tow behind him and Dave Junior (Marty Friedman, guitar and Nick Menza, drums), and with the worst of his drug addiction apparently behind him, Mustaine could almost be described as Born Again. Except that he'd probably land one in the kisser of anyone who dreamed of putting it so crassly.

He's that type of guy: full of contradictions. Just like all the other bad guys and geniuses you've ever known.

But I'll let him tell you about that.

Let's start with the personal renaissance of you and Dave Junior. About a year ago I thought you were both so far down the hole that you were never going to come up again.

'That's not the extent of it, either. We'd been so fucked by everything that the only way to deal with our feelings was to cloud our thinking. It went a bit far with the heroin, but it wasn't just heroin. It was alcohol, too.

'As a kid, everyone always said that I was going to end up an alcoholic like my father. You see, alcoholism is hereditary, it's in the genes. I just could not drink.

'Well, I choose not to drink now. I don't do a lot of things now, and I'm healthier than I've ever been. I fuck like a beast and that's my main concern. Eat, fuck and sky-dive, that's it.'

You even quit cigarettes, didn't you?

'Yeah. But you see, I've got iron will. If I set my mind to do something, I do it.'

What was it that finally made you stop abusing yourself and see sense?

'I was the best at being loaded, but I wanted to be the best as a musician too. This music is intense, it requires a lot of work. And I'm sick and tired of people saying, "Dave's dead". I hear that still from a lot of people and I think, "Shit, I'm still standing up" ... you know? I must have done a good job.'

The stories that used to circulate around LA about the house you were living in with Dave Junior were pretty scary.

'Give me some examples and I'll tell you if they're true.'

Mainly that you were both just out of your heads on heroin all the time. How much of the material on the new album was written at that time?

'Almost all of it! Although one song – the title track – is over ten years old. I wrote it when I was in Metallica. And then "Hangar 18", which is one of the most melodically strong tracks, I wrote once I decided to straighten myself out. Everything else we'd done inebriated.

'At first I had doubts about getting cleaned up but now I just enjoy being coherent. I get just as high when I jump out of an aeroplane with a parachute on. I get just as high after I've done boning my girlfriend. I get just as high after I've had a great meal and I'm racing around in my car. I'm getting pleasure from the things that are in my life right now rather than the things that were in my system.'

It took you several attempts inside a private clinic to come off heroin, didn't it?

'Yeah, about ten times.'

There were horrendous stories of you making phone calls to people in the middle of the night, trying to persuade them to smuggle heroin in to you.

'Shit, you know it all, don't you? You've got good sources. Yeah, I did do that.'

Why did you start using heroin in the first place?

'I started off using. Then it turned into abuse and then into full-blown addiction. It got like I couldn't see what was going on.

'I was powerless. I got people to bring me stuff 'cos I wasn't ready to quit. Now I want to quit. I've got so much going on in my life right now which is positive.

'When Dave and I first hooked up together, the extent of our getting high was just beer and pot. But we were hanging out with these jazz players, and jazz is synonymous with drugs. And they'd be saying, "Dude, all the greats do heroin! Charlie Parker, Miles Davis, blah blah blah."

'I was kind of fascinated by the thing of being a junkie, too. I felt like I had something on everybody else. I was a bad boy. I didn't realise I was tainting my image. Now I can say that I've been there, I've done that. I was spending five hundred dollars a day for five years on that stuff.'

And is it all over for you now, finally?

'It's over for today. It might start again tonight. I may leave here and go down the street and pick something up. I don't want to, but it's like a disease with me and it's not something I can say I'm cured of. I'll always be a junkie, but right now I'm not a practising junkie.'

Do you worry whether you'll be able to come up with the goods now that you're straight?

'Worrying is just a lack of faith. I have faith in myself, this band and the record company.'

When you listen to the old Megadeth albums, does it remind you of your bad old days?

'Oh yeah. "In My Darkest Hour" – I live the whole thing every time I hear that. "Poison is the Cure" off the new album is about that. It's about having this big hole in myself and the only way I could fill it up, instead of with spirituality, was with drugs.'

Spirituality?

'Sure. Religion is for people who don't want to go to hell. Spirituality is for people who've already been there.'

And how does that affect you?

'It manifests itself through daily practice and being aware of how I should treat myself, and how I should consider other people's feelings. I may not subscribe to their point of view, but their feelings are still valid just like my point of view is valid because those are my feelings. There is no right and there is no wrong.'

Do you think that's why you used to make such outrageous statements – just to shock people gratuitously?

'A lot of that was just stuff that would slip out. I have no right to put down other people's sexual preferences, or other people's points of view. Just 'cos I like the model with two holes instead of one.'

'I've wondered what is so interesting about Dave Mustaine and what makes him so "profound" – 'cos I read this stuff and I think I'm an asshole!

'A lot of the way I used to come across was to do with the fact that I was living in a narcotic haze and I thought everybody and everything should be my way or the highway. Now, you know what? I think, "Fuck it." I just don't care.'

You look extremely fit and well. I remember a skinny kid; angry, funny. Now I see a man.

'I am. I'm also kick-boxing right now. That's another one of my thrills – getting beaten up. In my childhood, I did martial arts, and then I started getting into dope and thought no one could fuck with me. In reality, if anyone had tried it I would have been destroyed.

'Now my reflexes are back. My stamina is way up. And so I figure my ability to satisfy an audience, the intensity of my live performance, is going to escalate. Nothing's gonna keep me from reaching my goals, unless I die.'

Do you believe in 'sex magic'?

'Yeah. I used to get a heroin boner that would last for six hours but I just couldn't come. Not that I'm sure I could keep going! As I say, that's what I'm into now: eating, fucking and sky-diving.'

Maybe that should have been the title of the new album?

'Yeah, right.'

Do you think people sometimes mistake your sense of humour for something more sinister?

'People try to sift through my lines and find some meaning, but they can get too wrapped up in what I'm saying. Every day is an ongoing experience for me.

'I'm constantly learning new things about myself and the people I work with. I'm constantly making amends to people I've fucked over, which is a slow, ongoing process because I've hurt a lot of people.'

OK. Let's do the sensible thing and talk about the new album. Let's begin with the first single from it, 'Holy Wars'. Does that have anything to do with Northern Ireland and the time you spent there on the last tour?

'Bingo.'

What are you trying to say in this song?

'What it says is that people are killing for their religion, and this whole feud has gotten so out of control that I think they've lost the whole meaning and reasons as to why they're fighting. I mean, how the fuck can one religion say anything against another religion? Anybody who's for God is right whether they're Buddhist, Muslim, Jehovah's Witness, or whatever.

'Ireland was a bad experience all round for us. The pissing part for me is that I'm a quarter Irish and I'm not embarrassed about my ancestry or anything, but we won't play Ireland any more.'

Not even Southern Ireland?

'No. They spit all over us. It's not so bad that they spit on us but spitting on the equipment . . .'

Do you think that's because there's a punk element to Megadeth?

'I don't know, but I wish they'd stop doing it! 'Cos we'd like to go back to Ireland, but our past experience is that one idiot ruins it for everybody. True fans of Megadeth, regardless of their nationality, will still come to see us.'

Getting back to the new album: what's the track 'Five Magics' about?

'That's alchemy, thermotology, wizardry, sorcery and magic. The five types of magic. The character of the song possesses the five types of magic.'

Where do you get your information from? Do you read occult books?

'I try to. A lot of it depends on the imagination and remembering what I've been dreaming. Sometimes I have these really weird dreams.

'Take "Dawn Patrol", a song which Dave wrote the music to. I woke up one morning and grabbed my notebook; I had the words just in my mind. All I had to do was copy them down.'

Dave Junior said the record was not as dark as the older stuff.

'Alive maybe? Sober? There's a big difference. A lot of it has to do with being positive. It has nothing to do with whether I choose to drink or do drugs or not.'

You said that most of the songs were written during your drug period. In 'Tortured Souls' there is a line: 'The future looks bright / I think I've seen the light'. Is that a post-recovery song?

'It is, as a matter of fact. I'd just come out of a relationship after six years. I remember that morning; I was tired of her. She was using with me. Our sex had just gotten so fuckin' bad, I nearly had to be stood on my head and have concrete poured inside me to get myself hard any more.'

Is that how you feel now – that there's light at the end of the tunnel?

'Yeah. There used to be a train bearing down on me, in my life. Now it's like I'm starting to get a little closer to safety. Life's starting to actually not smell of diesel any more. I can stomach myself. I can stare at myself and like what I see.'

You and Dave Junior have been through a great deal together. Would you describe him as your best friend?

'He used to be my girlfriend before he had the sex change . . .'

He stuck by you when everyone else fled.

'Yeah, I couldn't get rid of him! It wasn't that he stuck by me, more like we were stuck to each other.'

Would he have followed you down the hole if you hadn't come up again?

'Oh, he was ahead of me. I was bringing up the rear. He was the one making drug runs all the time. But we're both doing good now. I forgive him and he forgives me and we're both dealing with it.'

The new LP is a very busy record with a lot of variety. I think anyone who labels it as just a thrash metal album is missing the point.

'We've been labelled as the state-of-the-art speed metal band, and I'm proud of that. What we've done is get right to the fuckin' nucleus, man. We've split the atom!

'We're not putting blinkers on and being narrow-minded about our audience, though. We don't write songs just to sell tickets. I never have, 'cos money just got me into trouble. Money doesn't matter. It just gets me to where I'm going.'

So tell me about this upcoming 'Clash of the Titans' tour, with Slayer and Anthrax.

'It's like the best of black metal, the best of thrash metal, the best of punk metal and the best of metal, period. Not that I consider us to be any of that shit.'

How do you think you're going to handle being on the road straight for the first time?

'I'm prepared for it. Before, we used to spend a lot of time sleeping and a lot of time staying up. Right now, we'll maintain our health and happiness and convalesce between gigs and cater for our following. We want to offer them something we haven't offered them before.'

Have you ever done a gig straight before?

'The only thing I've done sober so far is rehearse and record this album! It may require a bit of regrouping from me now to go wider with it. I've got the full use of my faculties, though. If I want to put someone in their place I can do it with a lot more finesse now.'

I wonder what kind of high you'll experience when you do a really great gig straight for the first time.

'I don't think we've done our best gig yet. I think that the best gig will be when we're playing for the big guy upstairs.'

No, I mean the best high.

'Oh, the best high. I haven't experienced the best high. Right now the best high is sitting here talking to you and not running to the bathroom every ten minutes. Every party I used to go to, they'd put the toilet in the front room just so I'd be there, you know?'

Metallica, the band you helped start, had their biggest hit with the ... *And Justice for All* album while you had your head down the toilet. Did you ever look at the 'One' video on TV and think, 'That should have been me?'

'I did in the beginning. But, you know, this town was never gonna be big enough for the two of us. That's how it was with me and James (Hetfield). We'd have to set up at opposite ends of the arena to play the same venue.

'I sit there sometimes and think, you fuckers! But I'm at the point now, though, when I realise that my guts spoke a lot louder than my brain did in those days. Basically, James does a brilliant job and I think there's a lot of similarity in what we do.'

So what's the bottom line, Dave? How much of the 'evil Dave Mustaine' image is real and how much is bullshit?

'I was born at the witching hour . . .'

Actually on the stroke of midnight?

'Two minutes after.'

So you believe in all that?

'I believe in the supernatural. My elder sister is a white witch. I dicked around with her stuff when I was a kid. I found a "sex hex" and I used it on this girl I had the hots for. She was this cute little babe, looked like Tinkerbell. She didn't want to have anything to do with me. So I did my little hex and the next night she was in my bed.'

Have you done any more hexes since?

'One time I did one on this guy who picked on me when I was going to school. He was enormous. But without going into it too much, I did a chant, basically asking the Prince of Darkness to devastate this fella and stop him messing with me.

'Later, the guy broke his leg and he can't walk straight now. I stopped messing with witchcraft after that, but it made me feel good at the time. Retribution.

'Me and Dave once had a suicide pact. We decided that if this band ever went down the tubes, we were going to handcuff ourselves together and do it.'

Was that in a dark moment or would you still honour it?

'I'd still do it if he would. If the band was over. 'Cos life or death, it doesn't matter. I'm happy with where I'm at right now, but if I'm dead then I go to sleep as far as my mind goes.

'I'm very happy right now, though. I'd like to live on, but if my time comes . . . then it comes. I have no choice in the matter.

'If anything, I hope people can see that, as fucked up as I was, I pulled out of it and now I'm smooth flying. "Friendly skies, I like to fly United!" – you know what I mean?'

CODA

Reading this story back now, I remember very little of it. My abiding memory, in fact, is of what happened after the interview, when Dave showed me something he called the 'sex hex'.

He said he had known a white witch and that when he was young she had taught him many magic spells, including the sex hex. He listed the things you needed: virgin parchment; hair of a cat (or dog), or maybe a broom; something from the object of your desire (more hair, or maybe just a cigarette butt they had smoked); some other stuff. Then you took the virgin parchment and drew a vagina on it along with her name and a penis (erect) with your name. Then you wrapped all the goodies up in it and burned it, all the time concentrating really hard on the person you were hexing. Then you sat back and waited.

'I guarantee you, within twenty-four hours that person will be banging at your door, begging to be let in,' he smiled.

'And then?' I asked.

'And then, my friend, she will fuck your brains out.'

'Cool,' I said.

I thought about it.

'And you've tried this yourself?'

'Sure.'

'And it works?'

'Fuck, yeah!'

'Wait,' I said. 'Tell me again. I want to write this down.'

I produced a notepad I had taken from the hotel I was staying in and he very patiently wrote it all down for me, drawing the vagina and the erect penis and indicating where you put the names. When he had finished, he handed it to me and I sat there looking at it, wondering.

He must have seen the look in my eyes because he added another proviso: 'Don't forget, this fucking works, OK? So you gotta be real careful who you do it on.' He looked at me, serious suddenly, and added: 'Don't go doing it on Princess Di. You might wind up dead.'

I took his point and mentally crossed her name off my list. Then I carefully folded up the piece of paper and put it in my wallet and we went back to our noodles and green tea.

When I got back to my room that night I pulled out the piece of paper and studied it. *The Sex Hex*, it said at the top of the page. I thought about it: who would I do it on? I couldn't think of anybody. Or rather, I could, but I couldn't be arsed to try and find some virgin parchment and cat hairs and so on. Maybe one day I would feel differently, though. I carefully folded up the piece of paper again and put it back in my wallet, where it stayed for years. Until one day when I looked, it was gone. I don't know what happened to it, but I never did get around to using it. Hopefully Dave wouldn't be disappointed . . .

W. AXL ROSE, 1990

Because they came out at about the same time, people have understandably tended to assume that the reason my name ended up in 'Get in the Ring' from the Guns N' Roses album *Use Your Illusion II* is because Axl Rose objected to my 1991 GN'R biography, *The Most Dangerous Band in the World*. Not so. There were many reasons why Axl got his knickers in such a twist over me, but, essentially, the main one revolved around the following article. As we now know from the Mötley Crüe autobiography, *The Dirt*, published eleven years later, Vince Neil was so pissed off when he read Axl's rant about him in the interview with me, he decided to take Axl up on his offer and agree to duke it out with him. Of course, as we also now know, Axl – whose mouth has always exceeded his trousers by some considerable distance – then decided he'd never said any such thing and went as far as telling friends and associates that I had made up the whole thing. Gee, thanks, pal.

This, in turn, led to a series of verbal skirmishes that eventually led to me leaving *Kerrang!* after the then editorship was told they would be denied all further access to the band until they had eradicated the 'problem' – i.e. me. In fairness to the lily-livered hierarchy at the magazine back then, I had not helped my cause by becoming almost as megalomaniacal as Axl himself by that point, and when I deliberately failed to turn up for the party to celebrate the magazine's tenth anniversary at the end of 1991, it was a snub that effectively signed my own death warrant. My name was unceremoniously dropped from the editorial masthead a week later.

For all those reasons – and several more it would take a separate book to try and explain adequately – this turned into quite a momentous article, for me and Axl both. The moral might be: don't ever bite the hand that feeds you. If only morality had been something people like me and Axl Rose cared about back then . . .

Interview with W. Axl Rose of Guns N' Roses, first published in Kerrang!, *21 April 1990.*

W. Axl Rose is pissed off. Not, thankfully, in the grand manner to which he is sometimes accustomed: no glass-smashing, no room-wrecking. But he has a bee in his bonnet that he wants squashing, and so what if it's nearly midnight, why don't I come over right now and take down some kinda statement?

Well . . . why not? Sleep's for creeps anyway, or so they say in LA. So I hot-rod my tape-machine, scuttle down a coupla quick beers and head over to Axl's West Hollywood apartment.

Axl meets me at the door with eyebrows like thunder clouds.

'I can't believe this shit I just read in *Kerrang!*' he scowls.

'Which shit are you referring to?' I ask.

'This shit,' he growls, holding up a copy of *Kerrang!* dated 4 November 1989, in his hand, yanked open at a page from Jon Hotten's interview with Mötley Crüe.

'The interviewer asks Vince Neil about him throwing a punch at Izzy [Stradlin, GN'R rhythm guitarist] backstage at the MTV awards last year, and Vince replies,' he begins, reading aloud in a voice heavy with sarcasm: '"I just punched that dick and broke his fuckin' nose! Anybody who beats up on a woman deserves to get the shit kicked out of them. Izzy hit my wife, a year before I hit him." Well, that's just a crock of shit! Izzy never touched that chick! If anybody tried to hit on anything, it was her trying to hit on Izzy when Vince wasn't around. Only Izzy didn't buy it. So that's what that's all about.'

He goes on, still furious.

'But this bit, man, where Vince says our manager, Alan Niven, wasn't around, and that afterwards [Vince] walked straight past Izzy and me and we didn't do a thing, that's such a lot of bullshit, I can't believe that asshole said those things in private, let alone to the fuckin' press! The whole story is, Vince Neil took a pot-shot at Izzy as he was walking offstage at the MTV awards, after jammin' with Tom Petty, because Vince's wife has got a bug up her ass about Izzy. Izzy doesn't know what's going on, Izzy doesn't fuckin' care. But anyway, Izzy's just walked offstage. He's momentarily blinded, as always happens when you come offstage, by comin' from the stage lights straight into total darkness. Suddenly Vince pops up out of nowhere and lays one on Izzy. Tom Petty's security people jump on him and ask Alan Niven, our manager who had his arm 'round Izzy's shoulders when Vince bopped him, if he wants to press charges. He asks Izzy and Izzy says, "Naw, it was only like being hit by a girl" and they let him go.'

He smiles mirthlessly.

'Meantime, I don't know nuthin'. I'm walking way up ahead of everybody else, and the next thing I know Vince Neil comes flying past me like his ass is on fire or somethin'. All I saw was a blur of cheekbones! I tell ya, man, it makes my blood boil when I read him saying all that shit about how he kicked Izzy's ass. Turn the fuckin' tape-recorder on. I wanna set the record straight.'

He carries on ranting about wanting to give Vince 'a good ass-whippin'' as I hurriedly set up the tape-recorder; about how he wants to 'see that plastic face of his cave in when I hit him' (referring to the rumour that Vince had recently reportedly had plastic surgery).

Are you serious about this, I ask him? He nods vigorously.

'There's only one way out for that fucker now and that's if he apologises in public, to the press, to *Kerrang!* and its readers, and admits he was lyin' when he said those things in that interview. Personally, I don't think he has the balls. But that's the gauntlet, and I'm throwing it down. Turn on the machine!'

We settle back in the only two available chairs not smothered in magazines, ashtrays, barf-balls (one squeeze and fzzzttttt, it's Johnny Fartpants a-go-go), and other assorted crap. I fix up my machine and we start to roll.

Axl scrunches up on the balcony window, which affords an impressive cinema-scope view of the twinkling footlights of the billowing Hollywood hills below. It reminds me of the sort of backcloth you might see on something like *Late Night with David Letterman* (the American TV talk-show Jonathan Woss wipped off). I wait for the band to cool out and the applause from the studio audience to die down before I hit tonight's star turn with my first question.

You don't seriously believe Vince Neil will take up the gauntlet and arrange to meet you and fight it out, do you?

'I've no idea what he will do. I mean, he could wait until I'm drunk in the Troubadour one night and come in because he got a phone call saying I'm there and hit me with a beer bottle. But it's, like, I don't care. Hit me with a beer bottle, dude. Do whatever you wanna do but I'm gonna take you out – I don't care what he does. Unless he sniper-shoots me – unless he gets me like that without me knowing it – I'm taking him with me and that's about all there is to it.'

What if Vince was to apologise?

'That'd be radical! Personally, I don't think he has the balls. I don't think he has the balls to admit he's been lying out of his ass. That'd be great if he did though, and then I wouldn't have to be a dick from then on.'

I heard that David Bowie apologised to you after the incident at your video-shoot.

(The story goes that Axl got pissed off with the ageing soopastar after he appeared to be getting a little too well acquainted with Axl's girlfriend, Erin, during a visit last year to the set where the Gunners were making a – yet to see the light of day – video for 'It's So Easy'. The upshot, apparently, was that Axl ended up aiming a few punches Bowie's way before having him thrown off the set.)

'Bowie and I had our differences. And then we talked and went out to dinner and then went down the China Club and stuff. And when we left, I was like, I wanna thank you for being the first person that's ever come up to me in person and said how sorry they were about the situation and stuff. It was cool, you know? And then I open up Rolling Stone the next day and there's a story in there saying I've got no respect for the Godfather of Glam even though I wear make-up and all this bullshit. It's laughable.

'I was out doing a soundcheck one day when we were opening for the Rolling Stones [at the LA Coliseum in October 1989] and Mick Jagger and Eric Clapton cornered me. I'm sitting on this amp and all of sudden they're both right there in front of me. And Jagger doesn't really talk a lot, right? He's just real serious about everything, and all of a sudden he's like ...' He adopts an exaggerated Dick Van Dyke-style Cockney, '"So you got in a fight with Bowie, didja?" So I told him the story real quick and him and Clapton are going off about Bowie in their own little world, talking about things from years ago. They were saying things like when Bowie gets drunk he turns into the Devil from Bromley. I mean, I'm not even in this conversation, I'm just sitting there listening to them bitch like crazy about Bowie. It was funny.'

But you and the Thin White Duke are now best of buddies, is that right?

'Well, I don't know about "best buddies". But I like him a lot, yeah. We had a long talk about the business and stuff and I never met anybody so cool and so into it and so whacked out and so sick in my life. I remember lookin' over at [GN'R guitarist] Slash and going, "Man, we're in fuckin' deep trouble" and he goes, "Why?" and I go, "Because I got a lot in common with this guy. I mean, I'm pretty sick but this guy's just fuckin' ill!" And Bowie's sittin' there laughing and talking about, "One side of me is experimental and the other side of me wants to make something that people can get into, and I DON'T KNOW FUCKIN' WHY! WHY AM I LIKE THIS?!" And I'm sittin' there thinking, I've got twenty more years of ... that to look forward to? I'm already like that – twenty more years? What am I gonna do?' He laughs.

Speaking of the gigs you did supporting the Stones last year, you announced at the first show that you were going to 'retire' and that the band was going to split up. Was this a serious-minded statement at the time? Or was it nothing more than a publicity stunt?

'No, no. The thing at the Stones show was definite and it was serious. I mean, I offered to go completely broke and back on the streets, you know, because it would have cost us an estimated $1.5 million to cancel the show. That means Axl's broke, OK? But I didn't do that because I didn't want the band to have to pay for me cancelling the show. I don't want Duff to lose his house because Axl cancelled two shows. I couldn't live with that. But at the same time, I'm not gonna be a part of watching them kill themselves. I mean, we tried every other angle to get our shit back together, and it didn't work. It had to be done live. Everybody else was pissed off with me but after the show Slash's mom came and shook my hand, and so did his brother.'

They say that every successful band needs a dictator in the line-up to kick butt and keep things moving. Do you think that's one of the roles you fulfil in Guns N' Roses – the dictator of the band?

'Depends who you ask and on which day. We got into fights in Chicago, when we went there last year to escape LA and try and get some writing done. Everybody's schedules were weird and we were all showing up at different times. But when I would show up I was like, "OK, let's do this, let's do that, let's do this one of yours Slash. OK, now let's hear that one Duff's got." And that's when everybody would decide I was a dictator. Suddenly I'm a total dictator, a completely selfish dick, you know? But fuck, man, as far as I was concerned we were on a roll. Slash is complaining we're gettin' nothin' done and I'm like, "What do you mean? We just put down six new parts for songs!" We've got all this stuff done in, like, a couple of weeks. So suddenly, like, everything's a bummer and it's all my fault.

'And he was like, "Yeah, but I've been sittin' here a month on my ass waitin' for you to show up." I'd driven cross-country in my truck to Chicago from LA and it had taken me weeks. So suddenly, like, everything's a bummer and it's all my fault. But after working with Jagger it was like, "Don't anybody ever call me a dictator again. You go work for the Stones and you'll find out the hard way what working for a real dictator is like!"'

Apart from that one brief conversation about Bowie, did you get to 'hang' with Jagger or any of the Rolling Stones when you supported them last year?

'Not really. Not Jagger, anyway. That guy walks offstage and goes and does paperwork. He checks everything. That guy is involved in every little aspect of the show, from what the backing singers are getting paid to what a particular part of the PA costs to buy or hire. He is on top of all of it. Him and his lawyer and a couple of guys that he hangs with. But basically, it's all him. And this is where I sympathise. I mean, I don't sit around checking the gate receipts at the end of every show, but sometimes the frontman ... I don't know. You don't plan on that job when you join the band. You don't want that job. You don't wanna be that guy to the guys in your band that you hang with and you look up to. But somebody's got to do it. And the guitar player can't do it because he is not the guy who has to be communicating directly with the audience with eye-contact and body movements. He can go back, hang his hair down in his face and stand by the amps and just get into his guitar part.'

How do you manage to 'communicate directly' with the crowd when you're playing in one of those 70,000-seater stadiums like the one you played in with the Stones?

'You have to learn how, but it can be done. You know, like someone goes, "You're gonna have this huge arena tour next year, dude!" And I go, "I know, but that's the problem. I can work a stadium now." And I can. And if I can work it, then that's what I wanna do. It's just bigger and more fun.'

Tell me about how things are coming together for the new LP.

'It's comin' together just great. 'Cos Slash is on like a motherfucker right now. The songs are comin' together – they're comin' together real heavy. I've written all these ballads and Slash has written all these really heavy crunch rockers. It makes for a real interestin' kinda confusion.'

What about Steven [Alder], your drummer? First he's out of the band, then he's back again. What's the story right now?

'He is back in the band. He was definitely out of the band. He wasn't necessarily fired; we worked with Adam Maples, we worked with Martin Chambers, and Steven did the Guns N' Roses thing and got his shit together. And it worked, and he did it, and he plays the songs better than any of 'em, just bad-assed, and he's GN'R. And so if he doesn't blow it, we're going to try the album with him, and the tour and, you know, we've worked out a contract with him.'

So you told him he had to stop taking drugs or he was out of the band?

'Yeah, exactly. But, you know, it's worked out. It's finally back on and we're hoping it continues. It's only been a few days so far. It's only been since Thursday last week, and he's doin' great. We're all just hoping it continues.'

How different has it been writing these new songs compared to the way you wrote the songs for *Appetite for Destruction*?

'One reason things have been so hard in a way is this: the first album was basically written with Axl comin' up with maybe one line and maybe a melody for that line, or how I'm gonna say it or yell it or whatever. And the band would build a song around it. This time around, Izzy's brought in eight songs, at least, OK? Slash has brought in an album. And Duff's brought in a song. Duff's said it all in one song. It's called "Why Do You Look at Me When You Hate Me?" and it's just bad-assed! But none of this ever happened before. I mean, before the first album I think Izzy had written one song in his entire life, you know? But they're comin' now. And Izzy has this, like, very wry sense of humour, man. He's got this song about . . .' He half-sings the lyrics, '"She lost her mind today / Got splattered out on the highway / I say that's OK." Hahaha! It's called "Dust and Bones", I think, and it's great. The rhythm reminds me of something like "Cherokee People" by Paul Revere and the Raiders, only really weird and rocked out. It's a weird song. But then it is by Izzy, what can I tell you?'

You seem very happy now you're back with the band in a recording studio. You like recording?

'Yeah, I do. I prefer recording to doing a live gig, unless I'm psyched for the gig. Before the gig I always don't wanna do the fuckin' show, and nine times out of ten I hate it. If I'm psyched it's like, let's go! But most of the time I'm mad about somethin', or something's going fuckin' wrong. I don't enjoy most of it at all.'

Is that partly your own fault, though? Some people have accused you of having a very belligerent attitude.

'I don't know exactly. Somethin' always fuckin' happens before a show. Somethin' always happens and I react like a motherfucker to it. I don't like to have this pot-smokin' mentality of just letting things go by. I feel like Lenny Kravitz: like, peace and love, man, for sure, or you're gonna fuckin' die! I'm gonna kick yer ass if you mess with my garden, you know? That's always been my attitude.'

Do you think that attitude has hardened, though, with the onset of this enormous fame and notoriety you now enjoy?

'Meaning what exactly?'

Do you act the way you do because your fame and popularity allows you to, or would you act that way anyway?

'I've always been that way, but now I'm in a position to just be myself more. And the thing is, people do allow me to do it, whether they like it or not. It's weird.'

Do you ever take unfair advantage of that, though?

(Long pause.)

'No. No, usually I'm just an emotionally unbalanced person,' he smiles. 'No, really. I'm usually an emotional wreck before a show because of something else that's going on in my life. I mean, as I say, something weird just always happens to me two seconds before I'm supposed to go onstage, you know? Like I found William Rose . . .' Axl's natural father, estranged from the family since his son's infancy. 'Turns out, he was murdered in '84 and buried somewhere in Illinois, and I found that out like two days before a show and I was fuckin' whacked! I mean, I've been trying to uncover this mystery since I was a little kid. I didn't even know he existed until I was a teenager, you know? 'Cos I was told it was the Devil that made me know what the inside of a house looked like that I'd supposedly never lived in. So I've been trying to track down this William Rose guy. Not like, I love this guy, he's my father. I just wanna know something about my heritage – weird shit like am I going to have an elbow that bugs the shit out of me when I get to forty 'cos of some hereditary trait? Weird shit ordinary families take for granted.'

You say your father was murdered?

'Yeah, he was killed. It was probably like at close-range too, man. Wonderful family . . .'

You've taken a lot of personal criticism for the more brutal aspects of the lyrics to your songs – 'One in a Million' being the most obvious example. Do you think your critics miss a lot of the humour in your songs?

'To appreciate the humour in our work you gotta be able to relate to a lot of different things. And not everybody does. Not everybody can. With "One in a Million" I used a word ['nigger']. It's part of the English language whether it's a good word or not. It's a derogatory word, it's a negative word. It's not meant to sum up the entire black race, but it was directed towards black people in those situations. I was robbed, I was ripped-off, I had my life threatened. And it's, like, I described it in one word. And not only that, but I wanted to see the effect of a racial joke. I wanted to see what effect that would have on the world. Slash was into it – I mean, the song says: "Don't wanna buy none of your gold chains today". Now a black person on the Oprah Winfrey show who goes, "Oh, they're putting down black people" is going to fuckin' take one of these guys at the bus stop home and feed him and take care of him and let him babysit the kids? They ain't gonna be near the guy!

'I don't think every black person is a nigger. I don't care. I consider myself kinda green and from another planet or somethin', you know? I've never felt I fit into any group, so to speak. A black person has this three hundred years of whatever on his shoulders. OK. But I ain't got nothin' to do with that. It bores me, too. There's such a thing as too sensitive. You can watch a movie about someone blowing the crap outta all these people, but you could be the most anti-violent person in the world. But you get off on this movie, like, yeah! He deserved it, the bad guy got shot.

'Something I've noticed that's really weird about "One in a Million" is the whole song coming together took me by surprise. I wrote the song as a joke. West [Craven; co-lyricist of 'It's So Easy', amongst other GN'R songs] just got robbed by two black guys on Christmas night, a few years back. He went out to play guitar on Hollywood Boulevard and he's standing there playing in front of the band and he gets robbed at knife-point for seventy-eight cents.

'Coupla days later we're all sittin' around watching TV – there's Duff and West and a couple other guys – and we're all bummed out, hungover and this an' that. And I'm sittin' there with no money, no job, feeling guilty for being at West's house all the time suckin' up the oxygen, you know? And I picked up this guitar, and I can only play like the top two strings, and I ended up fuckin' around with this little riff. It was the only thing I could play on the guitar at the time. And then I started ad-libbing some words to it as a joke. And we had just watched Sam Kinison or somethin' on the video, you know, and I guess the humour was just sorta leanin' that way or somethin'. I don't know. But we just started writing this thing, and when I sang "Police and niggers / That's right ... " that was to fuck with West's head, 'cos he couldn't believe I would write that. And it came out like that.

'Then the chorus came about because I like getting really far away, like "Rocket Man", Elton John. I was thinking about friends and family in Indiana, and I realised those people have no concept of who I am any more. Even the ones I was close to. Since then I've flown people out, had 'em hang out here, I've paid for everything. But there was no joy in it for them. I was smashin' shit, going fuckin' nuts. And yet, tryin' to work. And they were going, "Man, I don't wanna be a rocker any more, not if you go through this". But at the same time, I brought 'em out here, you know, and we just hung out for a couple months – wrote songs together, had serious talks, it was almost like being on acid 'cos we'd talk about the family and life and stuff, and we'd get really heavy and get to know each other all over again. It's hard to try and replace eight years of knowing each other every day, and then all of a sudden I'm in this new world. Back there I was a street kid with a skateboard and no money, dreamin' 'bout being in a rock band, and now all of a sudden I'm here. And it's weird for them to see their friends putting up Axl posters, you know? And it's weird for me, too. So anyway, all of a sudden I came up with this chorus, "You're one in a million", you know, and "We tried to reach you but you were much too high".'

So many of your lyrics are littered with drug analogies. Is that a fair comment?

'Everybody was into dope then and those analogies are great in rock songs – Aerosmith done proved that on their old stuff, and the Stones. And drug analogies – the language is always like the hippest language. A lot of hip-hop and stuff, even the stuff that's anti-drugs, a lot of the terms come directly from drug street-raps. 'Cos they're always on top of stuff, 'cos they gotta change the language all the time so people don't know what they're saying, so they can keep dealing. Plus they're trying to be the hippest, coolest, baddest thing out there. It happens. So that's like, "We tried to reach you but you were much too high" – I was picturing 'em trying to call me if, like, I disappeared or died or something. And "You're one in a million" – someone said that to me real sarcastically, it wasn't like an ego thing. But that's the good thing, you use that "I'm one in a million" positively to make yourself get things done. But originally it was kinda like someone went, "Yeah, you're just fuckin' one in a million, aren't ya?" and it stuck with me.

'Then we go in the studio, and Duff plays the guitar much more aggressively than I did. Slash made it too tight and concise, and I wanted it a bit rawer. Then Izzy comes up with this electric guitar thing. I was pushing him to come up with a cool tone, and all of a sudden he's coming up with this aggressive thing. It just happened. So suddenly it didn't work to sing the song in a low funny voice any more. We tried and it didn't work, didn't sound right, it didn't fit. And the guitar parts were so cool, I had to sing it like HURRHHHH! So that I sound like I'm totally into this.'

It certainly doesn't sound like you're pretending on the record, though, does it?

'No, but this is just one point of view out of hundreds that I have on the situation. When I meet a black person, I deal with each situation differently. Like I deal with every person I meet, it doesn't matter.'

Have you taken any abuse personally from any black people since this whole controversy first started raging?

'No, not actually. Actually, I meet a lot of black people that come up and just wanna talk about it, discuss it with me because they find it interesting. Like a black chick came up to me in Chicago and goes, "You know, I hated you cos of 'One in a Million'." And I'm like, "Oh great, here we go." Then she goes, "But I ride the subway . . ." All of a sudden she gets real serious. She says, "And I looked around one day and I know what you're talkin' about. So you're all right." I've got a lot of that.'

What about from other musicians?

'I had a big heavy conversation with Ice T [former member of hard-line LA rappers NWA: Niggers With Attitude or, alternately, No Whites Allowed]. He sent a letter, wanting to work on "Welcome to the Jungle" 'cos he'd heard I was interested in turning it into a rap thing. He wanted to be part of it. Anyway, we ended up having this big heavy conversation about "One in a Million", and he could see where I was coming from all right. And he knows more about that shit than most.'

At last the grisly subject of 'One in a Million' is allowed to drop. Axl lights another cigarette, unzips the top from another can of Coke, rubs a tired eye with the back of a thumb, and the conversation drifts towards the next Guns N' Roses album.

'There's, like, seven [finished] songs right now, but I know by the end of the record there'll be forty-two to forty-five and I want thirty of them down.'

A double album then?

'Well, a double album or a single seventy-six minutes or something like that. Then I want four or five B-sides – people never listen to B-sides anymore – and that'll be the back of another EP. We'll say it's B-sides, you know. Plus there should be four other songs for an EP, if we pull this off. So that's the next record and then there's the live record from the tour. If we do this right, we won't have to make another album for five years!'

Why wouldn't he want to make another album for five years?

'But it's not so much like five years to sit on our asses. It's like five years to figure out what we're gonna say next, you know? After the crowd and the people figure out how they're gonna react to this album.'

What kind of direction do you see the band taking on this next album? Do you plan to expand your usual themes somewhat, or are you sticking pretty much to the sleazy half-world undercurrents of the first album for inspiration?

'This record will show we've grown a lot, but there'll be some childish, you know, arrogant, male, false-bravado crap on there, too. But there'll also be some really heavy serious stuff.'

It's been such a long time since the release of *Appetite for Destruction*, and what with everything that's gone down in between, do you sense the possibility of a backlash building up in time for the new album?

'It doesn't fuckin' matter. This doesn't matter, man. It's too late. If we record this album the way we wanna record this album, it could bomb, sure. But five years from now, there'll be a lot of kids into it in Hollywood. Ten years from now, it'll be an underground thing like Aerosmith and Hanoi Rocks. The material has strong enough lyric content and strong enough guitar parts, you'll have no choice, it'll permeate into people's brains one way or another. If the album doesn't sell and be successful, someday in ten years from now someone's gonna write a record and we're gonna be one of their main influences, and so the message is still gonna get through. Whatever we're trying to say and the way in which we try to say it, we pay attention to that. If we get that right, the rest just takes care of itself. There is an audience for what we're saying that's goin' through the same things we are, and, in a way, we are leading.'

How conscious are you of the role as 'leaders', in terms of your position – both critically and commercially – at the forefront of modern rock music?

'It's been ... shown to me in a lot of ways. I didn't want to accept the responsibility of it really, even though I was trying, but I still was reluctant. Now I'm kind of into it. Because it's like, you have a choice, man, you can grow or die. We have to do it – we have to grow. If we don't grow, we die. We can't do the same sludge; I'm not Paul Stanley, man! I can't fuckin' play sludge, man, for fuckin' thirty years. Sludge, man. It's sludge rock.

'That's one of the reasons why 1989 kinda got written off. We had to find a whole new way of working together. Everybody got successful and it changed things, of course it did. Everybody had the dream, when they got successful they could do what they want, right? That turns into Slash bringing in eight songs! It's never been done before, Slash bringing in a song first and me writing words to it. I've done it twice with him before and we didn't use either of those songs, out of Slash's choice. Now he's got eight of 'em that I gotta write words to! They're bad-assed songs, too.

'I was working on, like, writing these ballads that I feel have really rich tapestries and stuff, and making sure each note, each effect, is right. 'Cos whether I'm using a lot of instrumentation and stuff or not, I'll still write with minimalism. But it has to be right; it has to be the right note and it has to be held the right way and it has to have the right effect, do you know what I mean?'

I didn't know you were such a perfectionist.

'What people don't understand is there was a perfectionist attitude to *Appetite*. There was a definite plan to that. We could have made it all smooth and polished. We went and did test tracks with different people and they came out smooth and polished. We did some stuff with Spencer Proffer, and Geffen Records said it was too fuckin' radio. That's why we went with Mike Clink; we went for a raw sound because it just didn't gel having it too tight and concise.

'We knew what we were doing, and we knew this: we know the way we are onstage, and the only way to capture that energy on the record, OK, is by making it somewhat live. Doin' the bass, the drums, the rhythm guitar at the same time. Getting the best track, having it a bit faster than you play it live, so that brings some energy into it. Then adding lots of vocal parts and overdubs with the guitars. Adding more music to capture . . . because Guns N' Roses onstage, man, can be out to lunch! But it's like, you know, visually we're all over the place and you don't know what to expect. How do you get that on a record? That's the thing.

'That's why recording is my favourite thing, because it's like painting a picture. You start out with a shadow, or an idea, and you come up with something and it's a shadow of that. You might like it better. It's still not exactly what you pictured in your head. But you go into the studio and add all these things and you come up with something you didn't even expect. Slash will do, like, one slow little guitar fill that adds a while different mood that you didn't expect. That's what I love. It's like you're doing a painting and you go away and come back and it's different. You allow different shading to creep in and then you go, "Wow, I got a whole different effect on this that's even heavier than what I pictured. I don't know quite what I'm onto, but I'm on it", you know?'

You're using Clink again to produce the new album, and you're recording in the same studios you made *Appetite* in. Are there any ingredients you plan to add to the recording that you didn't use first time around?

'Yeah. We're tryin' to find Jeff Lynne.'

Jeff Lynne? Leader of '70s monoliths Electric Light Orchestra – ELO – last seen hobnobbing it with the Traveling Wilburys?

'I want him to work on "November Rain", and there's like three or four possible other songs that if it works out I'd maybe like him to look at.'

As an additional producer to Clink, or to contribute some string arrangements, or what?

'Maybe some strings, I don't know. 'Cos this record will be produced by Guns N' Roses and Mike Clink. I might be using synthesiser – but I'm gonna say I'm using synthesiser and what I programmed. It's not gonna be like, "Oh, you know, we do all our shows live", and then it's on tape. That's not gonna be the thing. I mean, I took electronics in school. It's like, I don't know shit about synthesisers but I can take a fuckin' patch-chord and shape my own wave-forms and shit, you know? So now I wanna, you know, jump into today. I've never had the money to do it before. Maybe someone like Jeff Lynne can help me. It's a thought.'

This song, 'November Rain', I read somewhere that you said if it wasn't recorded to your complete satisfaction you would quit the music business.

'That was then. At that time it was the most important song to me.'

Were you serious, though, when you said you'd quit the music business if it wasn't done right?

'Yeah, that's the fuckin' truth, all right. But the worse part of that is, like, if you wanna look at it in a negative way, I've got four of those motherfuckers now, man! I don't know how I wrote these, but I like 'em better than "November Rain"! And I'm gonna crush that motherfuckin' song, man!

'But now I've got four of 'em I gotta do, and they're all big songs. We play them and we get chills. It started when I came in one day with this heavy piano part, it's like real big, and it fits this bluesy gospel thing that was supposed to be a blues-rocker like "Buy Me a Chevrolet" by Foghat or somethin'. Now it's turned into this thing, like, "Take Another Piece of My Heart" [by Janis Joplin] or somethin'.'

I'm still mulling over the giddy prospect of Jeff Lynne working on the next Guns N' Roses album. Why him? Were you an ELO fan?

'Oh yeah, I'm an ELO fanatic! I like old ELO, *Out of the Blue*, that period. I went to see 'em play when they came to town when I was kid and shit like that. I respect Jeff Lynne for being Jeff Lynne. I mean, *Out of the Blue* is an awesome album. So, one: he's got stamina. And two: he's used to working with a lot of different material. Three: he's used to working with all kinds of instrumentation for all kinds of different styles of music. Four: he wrote all his own material. Five: he produced it! That's a lot of concentration, and a lot of energy needed. Hopefully, I would like, if he's available, to have him. He's the best. But I don't know if we can get him or not.'

You'd work with him just on certain tracks?

'That's what I'd like to start with. I mean, who knows, maybe him and Clink will hit it off just great, and everybody'll be into it. If it works, then great, welcome to it, you know?'

Silence reigns for a brief moment, Axl's attention turned suddenly to the low distant hum of his hi-fi, which has been spinning taped music throughout the conversation, his gaze frozen between the ashtrays and magazines littered on the table before us, a pinched little smile creasing his lips. I ask who it is we're listening to.

'Cheap Trick, *In Color*, featuring Rick "The Dick" Neilsen,' he says. 'What a fuckin' asshole! I love Cheap Trick, too. It's kinda funny now, 'cos I listen to it and just laugh at him.'

Why? What happened?

'There was a thing in *Rolling Stone* where he said he fuckin' decked Slash! He didn't deck Slash! Do you think anyone is gonna fuckin' deck Slash when Doug Goldstein [GN'R tour manager] is standing right there between them? It's not gonna happen.'

Why does everybody want to tell the world they beat up one of Guns N' Roses?

'Because Guns N' Roses has this reputation for being bad, you know, the new bad boys in town, and so, like, hey, man, it perpetuates down to fuckin' Rick Neilsen wanting to get back in good with the youth market by claimin' he's badder than Guns N' Roses, you know? If he had any real balls, he'd apologise to Slash in the press. Not in person; he can come up to me and say he's sorry all he wants, it doesn't mean shit till he says it in the press.

'Now Bowie's a different situation, because Bowie hasn't talked to the press about our bust-up. So Bowie can apologise to me, and then when they see photos of me and him together they'll go, "Fuck, we tried to start a war and look at these guys, they're hanging' out!" Ha! That's cool, you know? Like Jagger was supposed to have told me off and the next thing you know I'm onstage singing with him – that fucked with a lot of 'em. I mean, it's either somebody kicked our ass or it's how some chick is scared I'm gonna come kill her cat. I mean, I could make a joke about it, but . . .'

Speaking of bad boys, did you get to meet Keith Richards when you supported the Stones?

'I got to meet him and talk to him for a little bit. I just kinda watched the guy. Basically, I told him I gotta go shopping, 'cos he has the coolest coats in the world. He just loved that. And I asked him about Billy Idol rippin' the idea of the *Rebel Yell* album off him, kinda joking. And he goes . . .' [Adopts the tie-dyed Cockney again], "Stole it off my fucking night-table, he did!" Hahaha! I thought that was great!

'It's like, I met John Entwistle from The Who, man, and I said I'd always wondered about these rumours about "Baba O'Riley", you know. Like for the keyboard parts they went and got brainwaves and then programmed 'em through a computer, you know? So I asked Entwistle, and Entwistle's annihilated out of his mind, right? He's in his own little world, and he looks at me and goes: "Brainwaves? What fuckin' brainwaves? Townshend's got no fuckin' brainwaves!" He sniggered.

'Then I asked him about the time he was supposed to have shot up all his gold records, and he said, "I'll let you in on a secret, mate. Those were all Connie Francis's gold records, I fucking stole 'em!" I said, "Wow, OK, I've had enough of this guy. I can't deal with him anymore!" He was just fuckin' lit and ready to go.'

You seem very settled at the moment, relaxed, not a bit like your image.

'I'm happy to kick back tonight and sit around jawing, because today everything is under control. Tomorrow – wait and see – it's fuckin' over! Something will come up. There's only one thing left, and that's this damn album, man. That's it. I mean, we may do another record but it's like, Guns N' Roses doesn't fully function, nothing ever really happens, to its utmost potential, unless it's a kamikaze run. Unless it's like, this is it, man! Like, fuck it, let's go down in fuckin' flames with this motherfucker! That's how we are about the record, everybody's like, we're just gonna do this son of a bitch.'

The hour, as the prophet sang, is getting late. We wind up with the obligatory, 'What now?' questions, Axl casting a slant-eyed glance into the immediate future for himself and his band.

'The main thing about the next record is this is our dream, to get these songs out there into the public. Then once we get out there we'll fight for them with the business side and stuff. But at this point that's not what's important. What's important is the recording of the songs. If the business comes down really hard on us in a weird way, then we'll make our choices – do we wanna deal with this, or do we not wanna fuckin' deal with this?

'The record will sell a certain amount of copies the minute it comes out anyway, and we could live off that for the rest of our lives and record our records on small independent labels, it doesn't matter. I mean, that's not in the plans, but, ultimately, it just doesn't matter, you know? It's all down to what we want to deal with. Do we wanna be giving everything that we feel we have inside of ourselves, to do the shows, to our top potential? Yes, we do. But I don't choreograph things. I don't know when I'm gonna slam down on my knees or whatever. It's like, you have to ask yourself, do I wanna give all that, and have someone fuckin' spittin' in my face? Does it mean that much to me? No! I dig the songs. If you don't want 'em, fine. But I don't have to give them to you.'

I know you've often threatened it, but if you wanted to, could you really leave all this behind? The band, your career in the music business – not just financially, but emotionally, artistically?

'If I wanted to badly enough, sure. This is all right, in bits and pieces, but whether it'll take up all the chapters in the book of my life, I don't know. I would like to record for a long time. I have to make this album. Then it doesn't matter. This album is the album I've always been waitin' on. Our second album is the album I've been waitin' on since before we got signed. We were planning out the second album before we started work on the first one! But as much as it means to me, if it bombs, if that happens, yeah, I'm sure I'll be bummed business-wise and let down or whatever, but at the same time it doesn't matter. It's like, I got it out there. That's the artistic thing taken care of. Then I could walk away.'

What about the money, could you walk away from that?

'I'd like to make the cash off the touring, and then I'd like to walk away knowing that I can support my kids, for whatever they want, for the rest of my life, you know? And that I can still donate to charities. I'd like to have that security. I've never known any security in my whole life. The financial aspect is just to get that security. If I have that in the bank I can live off the interest and still have money to spend on whatever – including, top of the list, the welfare of my own immediate and future family.'

Last question. First question. Same question, in fact, I've been asking for the last couple of years.

'When will the album actually fuckin' come out?'

I nod. He doesn't.

'It's taken a lot of time to put together the ideas for this album. In certain ways, no one's done what we've done – come out with a record that captured that kind of spirit, since maybe the first Sex Pistols album. No one's followed it up, and we're not gonna put out a fuckin' record until we're sure we can. So we've been trying to build it up. It's like, it's only really these last couple of months that I've been writing the right words. Now suddenly I'm on a roll, all the words for Slash's songs are there. But it's taken this long to find 'em.

'I just hope the people are into it, you know? I think that the audience will have grown enough, though. It's been three years – they've gone through three years of shit, too, so hopefully they'll be ready to relate to some new things. When you're writing about real life, not fantasy, you have to take time to live your own life first and allow yourself to go through different phases. Now I think there's enough different sides of Guns N' Roses that when the album is finally released no one will know what to think, let alone us! Like, what are they tryin' to say? Sometimes even I don't fuckin' know . . .'

CODA

Axl would eventually fall out with everyone: me, Vince Neil, his first wife, his many managers and record company, eventually even his whole band, leaving him to soldier on alone, the sole original member. He also lived up to his prediction-cum-threat in his interview with me to 'walk away' from it all after the twin *Use Your Illusion* sets were finally released in 1991. Indeed, it would be seventeen years before he finally felt confident enough to release the next so-called Guns N' Roses album, *Chinese Democracy* – actually, a pretty good piece of work, if hardly a legitimate GN'R album – which arrived to great fanfare in November 2008 but spectacularly failed to live up to the hype. The album seems now to be all but forgotten, even by Axl, who only released one single from it, made no promotional videos to back it, and singularly failed to tour and/or commit to any product-promotion whatsoever.

As I write, a year on, the hot rumour is that the original five-man line-up will be returning to the road sometime next year. But like the man said, believe it when you see it, suckers. In the rock world there is 'crazy' – Ozzy Osbourne, Lemmy, et cetera – and there is *really* crazy – Syd Barrett, Kurt Cobain, et cetera.

And then there is W. Axl Rose. Even he doesn't know what he'll do next.

LINDA PERRY, 1992

After I left *Kerrang!* at the end of 1991, I did so ostensibly to get into management. I had found the new Def Leppard – called Cat People – and I was going to use them as my ticket out of rock journalism and into something much more interesting and, yes, lucrative. Unfortunately, my timing could not have been worse. As one well-known London agent later put it to me: 'The trouble is, we're having enough trouble keeping the old Def Leppard going, let alone getting behind the new one.' Instead, the rock business was now focused on a new musical phenomenon: grunge. Laughed out of the A&R offices of Sony, messed around no end by the likes of EMI and Polydor, 1992 was absolutely not the year to try and get a band not sporting goatees or plaid shirts off the ground. A year later the new Def Leppard had gone the way of New Coke and I was back trying to scrape together a living from writing about the bands that had weathered the grunge storm, which is how I found myself working for a short-lived so-called 'adult-orientated' mag called *Rock World* – a sort of before-its-time *Classic Rock*. If there was an upside – apart from being able to pay the rent – it was that it put me in touch with a whole new generation of rock artists I would never have gotten around to otherwise. In the 1980s, I knew them all. Here, in the '90s, it often felt like I knew no one. That was certainly the position I found myself in when I came to interview 4 Non Blondes and their charismatic singer Linda Perry.

Interview with Linda Perry, first published in Rock World, *August 1992.*

Shooting a straight line somewhere between the Pretenders and Pearl Jam, with just a dash of Janis Joplin mixed in for bad measure, 4 Non Blondes are fast becoming this year's – pardon me – summer smash sensation. That's radio-speak for new-band-has-BIG-hit-single. The tune in question, 'What's Up?', you will doubtless have been bored to death with by now. The first 4 Non Blondes single and already a hit of capital 'H' proportions in America, where the band are from, all through June and July it has been roving relentlessly across the beaches of Britain, Spain, France, Greece, Italy and every other coastal resort this side of the equator. It doesn't matter whether or not you liked it the first ten times you heard it. By the time you get through your next fifty listens, like it or not, you're hooked.

'I think the reason "What's Up?" is doing really well right now is because it's very familiar but it's very new as well,' says Linda Perry, the singer, acoustic guitar player and main songwriter in 4 Non Blondes. 'People can touch it, people can relate to it, people have been there before, they know exactly what's going when I sing "... what's going on?"'

Perry says that when she finished writing 'What's Up?', she was so convinced she must have subconsciously pinched it from somewhere else that she didn't want to take it to the band. 'Then Christa [Hill-house, bassist and band founder] heard it one night, she said: "You're crazy, that's a great song, why haven't you brought it to the band yet?" So I brought it in very kind of tentatively, and now it's the song that's really helping us to take off.'

The butch voice is what makes it for me.

'I think there's something about the voice which is familiar but hard to place,' she shrugs. 'People ask what my influences are. I say everything and everyone I've ever heard. I ask them what they think and they come back with everything from Janis Joplin to Joe Cocker, to Geddy Lee.'

The debut 4 Non Blondes album, *Bigger, Better, Faster, More!*, just released on Interscope and produced by David Tickle (Prince, Peter Gabriel, Police), is just as insistently euphoric. Again, it's not until you've made an effort to play the album more than two or three times that its true power begins to show itself. But tracks like the bustling, neurotic 'Train', the bristling, jazzy 'Spaceman', the ditto 'Drifting' and the double-ditto Primus-esque 'No Place Like Home' all confirm that here is not another Lita Ford, my rude dude-type friends (not one single girlie pout on the whole damn album). This here is something else again.

'I love women with balls,' says Perry. 'Women with balls that go out there and do it and don't be the typical woman in high heels and showing their titties all over the place. I'm very aware of that, too. It's something I miss. As a female rock fan I *miss* Janis Joplin. I miss Patti Smith, I miss that dimension in modern rock music.'

Linda Perry was born in Massachusetts but always tells people she's from Brazil. 'My background's Brazilian and it just sounds better.' Raised in San Diego, she says she's been into music as long as she can remember. 'There are pictures of me as a little kid wearing a big hat and carrying a whompin' big guitar.'

An acknowledged troublemaker at high school – 'I got straight Fs in everything except P.E.' – she dropped out for good when she was sixteen. 'I did the kid thing, took acid, played hide-and-seek in the park at 5.00 a.m., lived with friends.' When that, in her own words, 'grew old', she packed up her things into one small carrier bag and drove to San Francisco with nothing more in mind than 'just getting out of where I'd been already'.

Perry hadn't planned to stay but 'I went over the bridge and the city just went through my heart'. She started gigging around SF, doing solo acoustic gigs and 'this enormous voice started coming out of my mouth that I had never heard before. I thought, wow, maybe I've got something here ...'

Ironically, only guitarist Roger Rocha is a true blue Bay Area native. The grandson of famous American abstract expressionist painter Clyfford Still, and the only man in the band, Rocha says it was the 'integrity of the songwriting that hooked me immediately. I was blown away by the honest sound they have. It really gave me the chills.'

The other Non Blondes, Hillhouse and drummer Dawn Richardson, eventually arrived from Arkansas (via Oklahoma), and Pasadena (via LA), respectively. All are talented instrumentalists that Perry describes as 'my best friends, at this point'. She goes on: 'I was worried when we first got together that we might just be band-pals, you know, and nothing else. But recently it's been made clear that we're all in this together like a family. It's the closest relationship I've ever had with anybody, that's for sure.'

They got the name they say while sitting on a park bench one afternoon in the ultra-yuppie North Beach area of SF. 'This family came walking by – six-year-old blonde boy in a sailor suit with his blonde mum and dad,' explains Hillhouse. 'Next to us there's a trash can with a piece of pizza lying on top and the kid wanted to pick it up. The mom said, "No, it's probably dirty, what with the pigeons and the people." And she was looking right at us! We were Non Blondes!'

The first 4 Non Blondes rehearsal was set for 6.00 p.m. on 17 October 1989. The San Francisco earthquake hit at approximately 5.15 p.m. the same day. It was an auspicious beginning. To begin with, like everyone else they dragged around the clubs, scrounging supports and occasional headliners – the Paradise Lounge, DNA, Slim's, and the Warfield Theater were all regular Non Blonde hang-outs in the early days. Then a demo of 'Dear Mr President' (a finished version appears on the album) became a regular on local SF alternative radio and before you could say 'Bill Graham's dead', they were signed to Interscope.

It sounds like quite a ride but Perry says she already has her sights set on something bigger, something better . . . faster . . . well, you get the picture. Take it, Linda: 'For me personally there's a lot more I want to do than sing in a band. Singing in a band is just the first step in fulfilling those plans, you know? I want to produce, I wanna write songs for other people, I wanna write commercials, I wanna have my own studio one day, possibly my own record company. These are my fantasies, and being a singer is one step closer to all that. Right now I love singing, I love entertaining, I love people watching me, I love attention, so . . . I don't know. It's a great release and it's the only thing I really know at this point.'

What do you think it is that people like about 4 Non Blondes particularly?

'I don't know. The record industry already wrote the history of music, and they're just waiting for somebody to do something just a little bit more special so that they can fill in the blanks that are already there in their minds. Everything is already so labelled, everything is so familiar, the format is already in place, you know – not just in music but in life, too, I think – that it's hard to know exactly why any of 'em like anything!' She snorts with derision.

She says the audiences they attract are 'a real heavy crossover between, like, these black hip-hop guys, total rednecks, rock and rollers, foreign exchange students, Asians, everybody, you know – forty-four-year-old mothers with three kids, the sixty-year-old grand-pas – I've never seen such diversity amongst the crowd as you get at one of our shows. Our music has no prejudice, you know? We're really lucky, I think. We really stumbled across something and got lucky. It's as simple as that.'

By the time you come to scroll through this, 4 Non Blondes will have begun their first ever swing through Britain and Europe, sup-porting Neil Young in London with Pearl Jam, and kicking out with a handful of dates in their own right. Excited about that?

'Shit, man. Of course!' She laughs. It's a big, uproarious sound, like her singing. 'Wouldn't you be? I mean, Neil Young is not even one of my favourite artists but he's one of those guys like the Rolling Stones, the Beatles, you know, he's like one of the guys who started all this mess. And Pearl Jam, I love Pearl Jam. When we heard we were, like, no way! We're not going on tour with Neil Young and Pearl Jam!' More wheezy giggles.

Strange how the '90s looks just like the '60s reversed, isn't it?

'I think it's great. There was a time where I was being scared of the music that was going on. I did not like the music of the Eighties much at all. Now it's our turn, man, and I'll tell you this: we intend to make the most of it. Fuck, yeah!' More noisy, hoarse laughter. 'Me and Christa and Dawn are not the average women and Roger is definitely not the average man. I mean, I know we're gonna be Number One in Billboard, I know this band is going right to the fuckin' top, man! But we're very down-to-earth. Yes, some of us are women, but let's not make it into a big fuckin' deal, you know what I mean?'

One day, though . . .

CODA

When Linda Perry talked to me back in 1992 about writing for other singers – specifically, strong female artists who relied on more than just 'high heels and showing their titties all over the place' – I could not really imagine the type she was talking about. Don't forget this was a pre-Christina Aguilera or Pink world; a time and place when even a 'strong female artist' like Madonna was still largely pedalling sex to sell her music. (Some would argue she still is.) But things did change and Linda did go on to become a great writer of other people's songs – I'm thinking here of 'Beautiful' for Christina, 'Get the Party Started' for Pink and Gwen Stefani's 'What You Waiting For?'. What's more, she kept her promise about starting her own record company, too, signing and distributing James Blunt in the USA. All of this makes her just about the most talented and enterprising rock person I have met, not least compared to poor old Madonna – still feeling obliged to 'show her bits', so to speak, into her increasingly queasy middle-age.

DAN REED, 1993

Hard to fathom now, perhaps, from this perspective, but Dan Reed was once the future of rock 'n' roll; or – more accurately – one of its very definite possible futures. In fact, his then unusual blend of rock and funk, black and white, wah-wahs and synth-boards, was positively out of step when it first surfaced in the mid-1980s. Sure, we'd seen Hendrix and Sly Stone – not to mention several others, not least Prince, who was obviously a huge influence on Reed – take that blend and do something magical with it years before. And we have certainly seen it done several times and in several zillion crazy ways since. But rock in the '80s was no longer about melting pots; it was pure demographics and Dan Reed and his band the Network didn't so much cross several of them as confuse their potential audience into the bargain. Such was the banal, one-dimensional state of affairs in the newly niche-drive decade they happened to find themselves trying to strut their stuff in.

It really looked like they might make it, though. Dan was pretty enough to attract the attention of the girls, and his band was tough enough to pass muster with all but the most ardent of metal-freak boys. But then he went and spoiled it all by doing something stupid like shaving his head bald. These days, of course, that is not such a big deal. Nor might it have been back then had his name been Ozzy Osbourne or Kerry King from Slayer. But Dan losing his luxurious locks was like Bob Marley wilfully cutting off his. It seemed more an act of self-harm than self-expression. Certainly it did nothing very positive for his career, as we shall see . . .

Interview with Dan Reed, first published in Rock World, *March 1993.*

In the lexicon of popular music, few names invite such a wide and contradictory variety of reactions as that of Dan Reed. To some he is the black/white minstrel whose radio-friendly melting pot of rock, funk and p-o-p paved the way for the likes of Lenny Kravitz, Faith No More, Extreme, Red Hot Chili Peppers *et al* to become a part of this generation's collective consciousness, its airwaves and its grooves. To others he is no less than the Black Bon Jovi, a singles swinger in album-length clothing whose career deservedly died a death after Pearl Jam and Nirvana and all those other funny-looking beards started messing up the place. And to still others, these days mention of the name Dan Reed excites merely a one-syllable question followed by a blank stare and a swift change of subject: '*Who?*'

You remember, though: released two albums with his band, Dan Reed Network, in the late Eighties: the self-titled, good-not-great *DRN*, in 1987, and the much punchier if still not totally titanic *Slam*, in 1989; got described variously as a raunchier, rip-it-up Prince or a shinier, more techno King's X; toured with the Rolling Stones and shared magazine covers with Jon Bon Jovi.

Then went mad and shaved his head.

Oh yeah . . . *that* guy.

'Hey, I'm aware of it, you know,' Dan Reed remarks wistfully of his own epigrammatic fame. 'But I never promised to make things easy for myself.'

Reed is in New York to promote *Mixin' It Up*, the just-released sixteen-track compilation album of the best moments from his zig-zagging, three-album career. No longer bald, he admits his hair will probably never return to the female-envying, arse-length it once achieved. These days, it barely reaches his tattooed shoulders. 'This way the length of my hair isn't an issue any more,' he chuckles self-consciously.

The first official Dan Reed Network release since the disappointing

The Heat album sunk without a trace two years ago, *Mixin' it Up* is intended to assure the world of two things, Reed tells me. Firstly, that the Network have not disappeared; that they are, in fact, returning for some British and European dates to coincide with its release this summer. And secondly, as he puts it, 'to prove to people that have never really heard our music yet that whatever else we may be known for, mostly it's because we've got a lot of good songs. Some of my favourite tracks of all time are on this album,' he adds without blushing.

Certainly, *Mixin' It Up* covers all essential DRN bases – all the solid-gold heavyweights like 'Make it Easy', 'Tiger in a Dress' and 'Lover'. Plus a remixed 'Stronger Than Steel', a re-recorded 'Long Way to Go' featuring Extreme's Nuno Bettencourt on a nice, mince-free acoustic guitar, 'Rainbow Child', the great hit single that never was … Right down to guff like the dreary 'Rock You All Night Long' or the simply babe-noxious 'Baby Don't Fade'. I made a list of Good Tracks vs. Bad Tracks and the Good beat the Bad eleven-to-five. That may not sound like much of a wipe-out, but it's at least five more GTs than I remembered from my days of whamming to *Slam*.

Dan Reed takes this philosophically. 'I say if the critics are positive, great; if they're negative, great, too. I try not to let either viewpoint affect the way I go about my work. Basically, I've learned not to give a fuck.'

But if that was strictly the case, why bother to release a Best Of like this in the first place? Why not just up the ante and release a brand new fully fledged DRN album?

'Good question … if I'm truthful I have to admit that I think a lot of people do need reminding of who we are. We did have one foot in that sort of pop-metal grave, and rightly or wrongly a lot of that just got swept away by the whole Seattle thing.'

Hmmm. I thought that happened when you shaved your head that time.

'Yeah, well, you could be right.' Another dark chuckle.

Do you look back on that whole episode as a mistake now?

'No, no, I don't. As a career move, I can't say it was the *right* thing to do, it was just the *me* thing to do.'

Did you just have a freak-out one night and do it, or were you tripping, or what?

'Well, it wasn't a drug experience, but it was certainly a visionary type thing, yeah. It was my way of trying to bust out of this teen-hero kind of deal that I felt was obscuring the music, obscuring us as people, everything. But what I was going through naturally then is kind of like what the music business is naturally going through now. I just thought, hey, if I can't make it without having long hair, maybe I just don't wanna make it,' he shrugs.

Maybe. Reed spent a year as a slaphead. He says the most instructive thing he learned from the experience was that it doesn't matter what your appearance says about you to others, it rarely matches how it is you actually see yourself.

'Oh man, I got attacked on the street for being a racist skinhead pig! Me! I got people coming up and confessing all these crazy things that are going through their heads because they thought I looked like a monk or something.' He shakes his own head. 'And not just on the street. In the press, I went from being perceived as this sex symbol to being this out-and-out weirdo.'

Two years ago he formed his own production company, specialising in anything from film and video soundtracks to TV commercials for Nike. This September, he is directing and producing a video special with Nuno Bettencourt. But Reed fights shy of discussing these projects overmuch. He'd rather tell you about his acting assignments. Last year he cropped up as a Chinese club owner in 'one of the more wild and sensual scenes' in *Lake Consequence*, a film made by the same team as *9½ Weeks*, and this autumn he pops up again in *Even Cowgirls Get the Blues*, in which he says he plays 'another weirdo; I was typecast!'

He also has plans to write, star and direct a film of his own called *The Ocean*, about a Native American who travels across the country to see the ocean and 'discovers the truth about the real sub-culture of America'. But like the man said, that's all for the wide blue who-knows-when and meantime this is the pearly-round now.

'We'll definitely be playing some of the new songs on these European dates. My favourite so far is one called 'Rattle of the Simple Man'. It's from this 1953 film about this kind of Ghandi-like figure who they say 'makes a lot of noise by being simple'. I like that idea, that hopefully someday we'll all be able to dance to the rattle of the simple man . . .'

CODA

The Dan Reed Network never made another album of entirely original material, their career already having effectively ended by the time Dan spoke to me for this piece. Was it just the hair thing? No, although that didn't help – alienating his management and record company, not to mention killing off the band's female fan-base overnight. My hunch is that Reed just wasn't cut out for stardom. You can be the most fabulously talented musician in the world – and I've met many musicians no one else has ever heard of who might fit that description – but that doesn't make you star material. Dan was one of those guys who looked like a star, sang and played like one, but ran frightened from the spotlight at the first chance he could. Since then, he has appeared occasionally on album – usually in partnership with others, such as Extreme guitarist Nuno Bettencourt – and he has acted in small things. What else he does, or how he does it, I have no idea. I hear he does these 'Evening With ...' things occasionally, but he never did get the right haircut again ...

HENRY ROLLINS, 1995

The brief I was given for this story was very simple: ask him if he's gay. With his bulging biceps, head-to-toe tattoos and granite jawline, Henry Rollins was already acknowledged as a certain kind of gay icon. Behind that tough-guy facade, though, was there a feminine side just bustling to get out and start sashaying around? Having met Henry before, I rather doubted it. Or if there was, I certainly doubted whether he would be prepared to reveal it to me in the middle of a tape-recorded interview. Still, you never knew. Maybe I would strike lucky. Or maybe just get a fist to my own jawline for my trouble.

As it turned out, Henry was more than happy to discuss that side of things, although he was rather forceful in his complete denial – key word, you can't help feeling still – of any so-called feminine side. Ultimately, it doesn't matter, of course. Back in 1995, however, such things could grip the imagination of an editorial office more than you might healthily be able to imagine.

Interview with Henry Rollins, first published in RAW, *April 1995.*

Henry Rollins and I are seated in a top-floor office above the Paris club where the Rollins Band will be appearing later tonight. Outside, temperatures are nudging the nineties. The French version of air-conditioning – a fan and a small open window – is full on, but we're both sweating profusely. It's just man-to-man stuff here, eyeball to eyeball. We get straight into it . . .

Even if you're unable to name one of his songs, you all know who Henry is. The muscles, the tattoos, the permanently furrowed brow. It's an intense image. Henry Rollins looks like a heavy guy, talks like a heavy guy, probably is a heavy guy. But what about the other, more reflective side? What about the feminine side of Henry Rollins?

'Huh,' he scoffs.

Don't all men have a feminine side?

'Well, I've always had a problem with that whole like, "Oh, show me your feminine side." I'm a guy. I don't have a feminine side. I've got a dick, therefore I have no feminine side. OK?'

He will concede, under pressure, that he has 'a more reflective side'.

'I couldn't get to where I've got playing this music if I was insensitive. That's why I do spoken-word gigs. That's why I do books. I just don't understand the thing about some feminine side. It sounds like some guy trying to get laid.'

Sometimes, staring at yet another picture of Henry Rollins looking like a puffed-up bullfrog, I am reminded of the end of *The Wizard of Oz*, where they discover that the wizard is just a little old man hiding behind a big, frightening screen. With his military haircut and his bricklayer's arms, Henry Rollins throws up a pretty big screen to the world. What lies behind it?

'Fury!' he scowls. 'Rage! Boiling blood! Passion! Just getting up in the morning and wanting to break something, but going, "Oh no, no, no. I'm not gonna break that computer. Let's see what we can do with all this energy and channel it into something positive, like a song or a good workout." I don't go out and mug people. I go out with a silly little microphone and get it out in a confined area at eight o'clock every night, and I stand in my own sweat and do it.' If Henry didn't do these things, 'I'd probably be a very frustrated ugly American with a bad job, one of millions. Just like I was before I joined Black Flag.'

Rollins joined Black Flag in 1981. He was twenty and, 'working forty to sixty hours at an ice cream store. I'd go eat at the same hamburger place every night, and I would be so infuriated by life I would just walk around waiting for someone to mess with me. Some Marine, some biker, whoever, to come up to me so we could get into it.'

He didn't pick on the small fish then?

'Back in the old [Washington] DC days we used to get into it with all manner of people, frat boys, jocks from local universities, whoever was around,' he says, deadpan.

Wasn't he ever frightened?

'Yeah. But you have so much fury when you're young. This was when I was eighteen or nineteen. Sex and violence are pretty close to each other. I didn't know many girls; I only had sex once before I joined Black Flag, and I was twenty then. But I still had all this testosterone. I didn't have to sleep at night, I could just go through the night and go right to work the next day. Burning all the time. Sitting in an air-conditioned room, sweating. Never mugged anybody, though. Never went, like, gay-bashing, never hit women.'

All that 'petered out', says Henry, 'when I turned about twenty-one and I got a little more sensible. The last fight I got in was just a couple of years ago.'

Do you find you get more respect because people know you could do them serious damage if they crossed you?

'I like being physically solid for many reasons. One of those reasons is so there's a definite presence in the room. But that's about twenty per cent of the reason why I'm so into the weights. There's a lot of compromise in life. There's just a lot of, "OK, I'll tone it down because I don't wanna get this guy pissed off." There's a lot of that in my life. With weights, there's only truth.'

What makes Henry lose his cool? He doesn't have to think long. His muscles visibly tense as he recounts the story of two fans who grabbed him as he came offstage in Italy a few nights previously.

'They were like, "We have travelled from Sicily", and I was like, "Look, I've just finished playing, you've got to give me a minute." What I wanted to do was grab this guy and start smashing his face into the floor. Like, "Did you see what I just did? Who the fuck are you coming talking to me! I'm on a planet that you'll never see and you want me to sign some fucking piece of paper?" I just wanted to, like, hear cartilage snap! But instead I just went like, these guys don't know. They just like the band.'

Before the interview, I overheard Henry talking about going to New York that weekend, 'for fun'. This is the man who has to put the word 'fun' on his computer, otherwise it doesn't happen.

'Yeah, unfortunately,' he nods.

So what does Henry Rollins do for 'fun'? Well, he goes to New York, 'My favourite city to hang out in', where – believe it or not – he likes to go to the World Gym on Lafayette Street, in Greenwich Village: 'I'll get two great workouts. It's a great gym, man. It's got everything.'

And away from the gym?

'I'll go to Tower Records, walk around at night, smell the smells, see the sights, do some thinking, hit a few bookstores . . .'

Alone?

'No, a friend of mine, a girl, is flying in to meet me. We see each other twice or three times a year. She's really cool, I've known her for a little while. And we'll have some fun . . .' He pauses to chuckle. 'And then I'll go on tour.'

The fact is, Henry just can't leave the store to mind itself for a minute. Later, he admits he has actually set up a couple of 'informal' meetings during his weekend off in New York.

Despite the sudden increase in wealth he has enjoyed over the last two years, Henry still lives in a small two-room apartment in LA. He doesn't even own a car. He rides his bicycle to meetings: 'I can fit all the shit I own in a couple of garbage bags. My accountant begs me to spend money on myself. "How about a brand new couch?" But I can't do anything with a couch.'

Furnishings *chez* Henry are a spartan affair: 'I've got a futon I sleep on, and I got another futon for when someone comes over . . . a computer, a big stereo and a TV, which I watch videos on.'

Henry makes a good living selling the popularly received image of something of a new wave Arnie or Sly. Between stints as a futuristic headcase on the set of the movie version of William Gibson's cyberpunk novel *Neuromancer*, Henry does voice-overs for Gap and Nike ads. 'Rambo missions', he calls 'em.

'I love sweet-smelling corporate dollars. I think it's the biggest coup; voice-overs for Gap, one hour's work, $9,000. I run back to my office, "Boys, I got the money for the new printer!" We got some more money from somewhere else, guess what, now we get to do another book. This, to me, is punk rock, but grown up. To be self-sufficient and keep putting out books and CDs and videos of your own stuff and other stuff by artists you genuinely admire. Putting your money where your mouth is. So when I walk away from it I wanna leave behind a small canon of work where you can go, "Yeah, that guy gave up everything he had for it. There's a lot of integrity there, a lot of musical honesty, and he gave it all and then he quit."'

And what about love? Is Henry doomed to walk the bootleg record stores and gyms of this world alone?

'I loved a woman once,' he says, straight-faced. 'It was four years ago, and . . . she dropped me – you know, big deal, it happens to everybody. But I've never found anybody that did that to me ever again. Ever since the death of my friend Joe [Cole – shot dead on the doorstep of the apartment they shared at Venice Beach] I've become extremely withdrawn from any real intimacy with women. Where I used to be able to get more intimate with a woman way more regularly, now it's, like, impossible. I just don't have anything to say. I've given myself to work for so many years, now, I really lost the art of being close to anybody. I have, like, no really close friends. I've been so solitary that a lot of people I think I'm gay,' he adds, brightening.

Henry has been a well-known icon on the gay magazine and video scene since his Black Flag days.

'Oh yeah,' he nods enthusiastically. 'I don't have a problem with that. Some guy thinks you're hot-looking, well, then you've got good taste in men, you know what I mean? But I've never had a homosexual encounter. I'm not interested. It's just, these days, I'm alone a lot. And it must be how I like it. It must be. Because it's how I end up every night, usually.'

We both smile, but I don't think either of us can remember what the joke was any more.

CODA

Although I never met Henry again, I continue to admire him from afar. In many ways, he's the kind of guy I almost aspire to be: independent, hard-working, a reader, a writer and a health nut; an honest performer. I just don't have the same dedication. I'm also rather partial to good red wine and being a father to several children. And although I, too, enjoy my own company, one can't help looking at Rollins as a fairly lonely figure. He'd still say that's his choice: that he prefers it that way. I say he'd soon change his mind if the right woman (or whatever) came along . . .

MOTHER LOVE BONE, 1994

I'd said sad goodbyes to musicians before, of course: Bon Scott, Philip Lynott, Steve Clark, all of whom I'd known a little or a lot. But for some reason the death of one I'd never even met, let alone gotten to know – Mother Love Bone singer Andrew Wood – filled me with more sadness and regret than any of the others. Perhaps because his story was so poignant: over before it had barely begun. Perhaps because I saw echoes of one of my own previous lives in his tale – that of the joke-a-minute junkie who pays too heavily for the simple errors of an over-zestful, over-fantasized youth. Perhaps, also, I can't help thinking now, because his passing, in metaphor, paralleled the end of the kind of non-ironic rock I had spent the 1980s chronicling, the self-inflicted death of which – through overindulgence, through arrogance, through the natural order of these things – had now made way for what was still, at the time of this story's writing in 1994, seen as the antidote to all of that: grunge. In Wood's case, most specifically, to Pearl Jam, the second-best grunge band of the time. For if the iconoclastic, throw-the-baby-out-with-the-bath-water Nirvana were the Sex Pistols of grunge, then earnest Pearl Jam, and their painfully self-conscious, endlessly soul-searching singer Eddie Vedder, were The Clash. Whatever; researching and writing the following story affected me far more deeply than anything else I had ever written for a magazine, up to that point.

The story of Pearl Jam is not merely the story of how guitarist Stone Gossard and bassist Jeff Ament found the perfect singer for the songs they wanted to write. More profoundly, it's the story of how they lost the perfect singer. When Green River, their original band, had split up on Halloween 1987, neither man was sorry to see the back of singer Mark Arm. Mark had been talented, but his stringent pro-punk ideals would always put him at odds with Stone and Jeff's more rock-steady groove.

So, while Mark turned to his erstwhile guitar partner and co-founder of Green River, Steve Turner, for inspiration in a new band they christened Mudhoney, Stone and Jeff recruited the twenty-two-year-old singer of another Seattle combo: less popular glamsters Malfunkshun. Hitting even the tiniest of backroom stages in white-face, glittery jackets and spray-painted gold motorcycle boots, yodelling 'Helloooo Seattle!' and camping around like Freddie Mercury's long-lost younger sister, Andrew Wood appeared to be the answer to Jeff and Stone's most weed-ridden prayers. On the surface, at least.

'I've been training for this all my life; I've always been a frontman,' Andy told Seattle's local music paper, *The Rocket*, in January 1989. 'I remember when I was nine or ten, I'd wait till my folks were gone, then I'd put Kiss's *Alive!* on really loud and I'd use my bed as a drum riser and a tennis racket for a guitar. At the end of the album, I'd smash my tennis racket – my guitar – start the album over for the encore, and walk out onstage with a brand new guitar. You should have seen it! The Andy Wood Band! We were really big in the Seventies!'

Andrew Wood, the star that died before it could be born, came into the world on 8 January 1966, the youngest and most naturally outgoing of a family of three boys. His father, David, was a naval officer, and the Wood family moved incessantly throughout Andy's childhood – Mississippi, Washington, Maine, even West Germany for a brief spell. Finally, in 1978, David Wood found himself stationed on Bainbridge

Island, one of several small residential dots just off the coast of Seattle. Now divorced, Toni and David Wood had married when they were barely out of their teens. Unable to cope with the lonely life of a naval spouse, more a big sister than a mother, Toni would later blame herself for the history of drug dependency that all three of her sons – Brian, Kevin and Andy – would succumb to in later life. Growing up being allowed to do pretty much as he pleased, Andy Wood spent his teens hanging out with a circle of like-minded young Bainbridge tykes, passing around joints and indulging in 'beer and keg' parties at the home of his best friend, Regan Hagar.

Kevin Wood recalled the night in 1977 he took his baby brother to see Kiss at the local Coliseum: 'The opening act was Cheap Trick [and] right after the set Andy turned to me and said, "Yeah, I want to be a rock star." I looked at him and said, "Yeah, I want to be a rock star, too", and that was pretty much it from then.'

Andy would be the outrageous singer; Kevin his trusty co-conspirator and guitarist. When Regan Hagar revealed that he had begun taking drum lessons, Malfunkshun stopped existing solely in the frenzied imaginations of the star-struck Wood brothers and became something like a real band. A connoisseur of masks and a skilled mimic, it wasn't long before Andy had invented a whole new persona for himself. In future, he told his bandmates, he wished to be known on stage as L'andrew. All the flyers for Malfunkshun's earliest gigs contained the immortal line: 'L'andrew, mythical love child from Olympus, now resides in Seattle where he fronts a band called Malfunkshun.'

Of course, L'andrew and Malfunkshun wouldn't play just any old rock 'n' roll. Andy decided they would play something called Love Rock, the most important component of which was something called 3-Power: 'A symbol of the trio's spiritual unity,' he would declare without blushing. 'We had a mission to spread the word of love,' Regan Hagar explained, wryly, years later. 'We were the odd eccentrics because of that, the opposite of all the bands that were all heavy and Satanic.'

Andy admired and adored the pop showmen who knew what it meant to be glamorous, no matter how unpromising their sur-roundings – Freddie Mercury, Marc Bolan, David Bowie, Prince, Elton

John – these were the stars Andrew Wood aspired to emulate the trajectories of. No stage was too small, no venue too modest for L'andrew the Love Child.

But what made Malfunkshun big is, as they say, what kept them small. The only recording they ever released, a home-made contribution to the same *Deep Six* compilation that Green River first appeared on in 1985, entitled 'With Yo Heart (Not Yo Hands)', was, Andy confided all too eagerly to *The Rocket*, about taking heroin and catching hepatitis.

That summer, Andy had begun seeing a lot of a new girl who came from Seattle; it's generally assumed that it was she who first introduced Andy to the dubious pleasures of mainlining cocaine and heroin. Not yet twenty, Andy's shooting habit was soon so out of control that he had track marks up both arms. Worse, he had contracted a severe case of hepatitis after injecting heroin with infected syringes: 'dirty needles'.

Alarmed at the sight of his son – Andy's eyes and skin had turned a sickening bright yellow – David Wood checked him into the casualty department of nearby Cabrini Hospital, where he also underwent his first professional drug detoxification programme. 'Andy had a very giddy charm,' Stone Gossard remembered. 'He was always so funny, so disarming, that it was hard not to like the guy.' But, he hinted, there was a dark side, too.

When Gossard and Ament emerged from the wreckage of Green River and started looking for a new singer, Wood heard their call and immediately left Malfunkshun to join their new band, Lords Of The Wasteland, which also featured guitarist Bruce Fairweather. To begin with, the drummer in Lords Of The Wasteland was going to be Regan Hagar. But that was always more Andy's idea than Regan's, and soon Jeff and Stone were calling on another well-known Seattle scene-stealer, Greg Gilmore, who had drummed in Ten Minute Warning (featuring a teenage Duff McKagan). Andy felt bad about leaving Malfunkshun. It meant leaving Kevin behind. But Green River had been the most well known of the bands then crowding the increasingly self-conscious Seattle scene, and Andy wasn't about to pass up his chance to become even better known. He swore to Kevin that once he was a big success, he would return to help get his brother's career off the ground.

With the arrival of Greg, the Lords Of The Wasteland soon had enough original material to start bothering other people about it on a stage somewhere. They even had a new name: Mother Love Bone. It came from Andy's lyrics to 'Capricorn Sister', one of the first songs he and Stone wrote together. Oedipal and, in the wrong mouths, quite perverted, it fitted the music like a glove; rings worn on the outside, natch. 'Any word Andy liked, he'd work into a lyric in some strange way,' Stone reflected. 'He's absolutely one of my favourite lyricists of all time.'

Once he'd got used to his new surroundings, Andy's performances with Mother Love Bone started to take hold. He left behind the white-faced mewl of L'andrew and became, in his words, plain Andy Wood, 'world's greatest rock 'n' roll frontman!' Rooted in the 1970s with its blue-eyed funk-edge, roaring big-gig guitars and bitchy glam vocals, Mother Love Bone's best live performances were the ones where Andy pranced around in a ripped fur coat, huge lollipop shades, his long blonde hair – not cut since 1981 – poking out of oddly shaped hats.

'Andrew Wood had so much presence on stage,' says Kate Ellison, Music Director and Local Music Co-ordinator of Seattle radio station, KXRX, who remembers her one and only glimpse of Andy Wood and Mother Love Bone vividly: 'He had the audience in the palm of his hand. People were just awestruck by him.'

As word got out about the extraordinary new band that was swinging 'em in Seattle, the group began what Andy laughingly referred to as 'the restaurant tour of Seattle' as first Geffen, then Island, Capitol, A&M, Polygram and Atlantic Records all actively sought out the signatures of the band. The man whose calls they finally returned was Michael Goldstone, newest gun in the Polygram A&R department, with whom Mother Love Bone signed a lucrative seven-album deal on 19 November 1988. The band had played fewer than a dozen gigs when, over Thanksgiving weekend, November 1988, Mother Love Bone began work on their first EP at Seattle's London Bridge Studios.

With the steadying hand of former AC/DC producer Mark Dearnley on the faders, the tracks on *Shine* paid homage to everyone from T.Rex ('Capricorn Sister', 'Half Ass Monkeyboy'), to the Red Hot Chili Peppers ('Thru Fadeaway'), and early Hanoi Rocks ('Mindshaker Meltdown'). But the stand-out cut was the eight-minute-plus Wood opus 'Chloe Dancer/Crown of Thorns', with Andy's cigarette-stung vocals wafting from a twilight soundscape of piano and guitar. 'You ever heard the story,' the love child drawls, 'of mister faded glory? They say he who rides the pony must someday fall.'

Released in March 1989, when they embarked on a gruelling forty-date US tour, opening for Dogs D'Amour, *Shine* sold nearly 25,000 copies – enough to encourage Polygram to put the band back into the studio for their first album. The only fly in the ointment remained Andy's unpredictable nocturnal habits. After his recovery from hepatitis in 1985, he had stayed away from anything heavier than weed or wine for almost a year. Then slowly, for no reason he could name, he got back into it. A girlfriend from those days, Wendy Watson, claims that Andy would drive over to her apartment, phone a dealer and arrange to have the smack delivered like pizza. Andy would cook it up in the spoon in front of her, but would always turn his back when he came to actually take the shot. He always made Wendy cross her heart and promise not to tell anyone she'd seen him.

Mother Love Bone spent the late summer and early autumn of 1989 recording their first album, *Apple*, at the Plant in Sausalito, San Francisco. However, while everybody was excited by the sounds that were emanating from the giant Plant speakers, it was during the *Apple* sessions that it became apparent Andy was up to his old tricks. When they returned home Andy was once again persuaded to enter a drug rehabilitation programme. With the album finished and tour dates being finalised, the band needed their flamboyant frontman in good shape to make the thing catch fire, and through much of November and December 1989, Andy Wood was incarcerated in Valley General Drug Recovery Center, in nearby Monroe.

During his thirty-day stay there, Andy took to documenting his painful personal struggle with his cravings and emotions, filling pages and pages of a red spiral notepad with nightmarish poems and jagged, surreal lyrics. He was a man 'angry too long'. A man who had 'locked emotions'. He confessed that he sucked his thumb while he wrote his songs, and that now he toiled in 'toxic shame'. He saw his rehab programme as 'a new way to show love and a new way to feel', as a way of finally being able to 'pull off the mask' of his addiction.

The most important relationship in Andy Wood's short but special life, after Mother Love Bone, was with his live-in girlfriend, Xana LaFuente. His 'dream girl' is how he described her to his friends. Dark eyes; even darker hair; the body of a cat. A bundle of camp energy, Andy both delighted and dismayed Xana. She loved him and believed him when he told her how he was going to take Love Rock to the top of the charts. But she deplored his drug abuse. It wasn't enough that he wanted to be drunk and stoned all the time; Andy always wanted to take things further, scoring coke and eventually heroin, then snorting or injecting it in front of her. Then, when the gear was gone as he was coming down, he'd beg for Xana's forgiveness. 'You're my only friend,' he would weep pathetically. 'The only one I can talk to. I want to stop! I don't know what to do!'

'Go ahead,' she screamed at him once. 'Do it in front of me! Show me how sick you are!' So he did. Not just once but several times that night, repeatedly plunging the needle into his arm and watching, hypnotised, as the syringe filled with blood.

Andy's first show straight for more than a year and practically his last-ever appearance on stage with Mother Love Bone was at the tenth anniversary party for *The Rocket*, held at the Paramount Theater on 29 December 1989, just a week after he left Valley General. The impressive line-up included the Fastbacks, the Posies, the Walkabouts, and the Young Fresh Fellows. And although still physically weak, Andy positively glowed on stage, making up lyrics as he went along, whipping the audience and himself into a genuine fury.

Then, two weeks before *Apple* was due to be released, a strange thing happened. It was around 10.30 p.m. on Friday, 16 March 1990, when Xana returned home to the apartment she shared with Andy. She had not expected to find him home, but his car was parked outside.

He was supposed to be meeting the band's new tour manager – himself a 'recovering addict' who specialised in road-managing musicians also in recovery – at his manager's office. But Andy had cried off at the last minute, claiming he was too ill to make it and suggesting they reschedule some time the following week. Instead, Andy took a drive out to First Avenue and Pike Street – a well-known local hangout for prostitutes and dope dealers – and bought himself some heroin. Despite his weekly sessions with a therapist, despite attending meetings with Narcotics Anonymous and Alcoholics Anonymous, Andy

Wood had relapsed after exactly 116 days of being clean and sober.

The apartment was strangely quiet as Xana closed the door behind her. The lights were on, but there was no music or TV blaring; unusual for Andy. For a moment she thought maybe he had gone out after all. When she walked into the bedroom, she found her boyfriend lying face-down on the bed, apparently asleep. Xana tried to wake him. When she noticed the blood oozing from his lips and the blue-tinge of his expressionless face she ran to the phone and called for an ambulance. Thirty minutes later, Andy's comatose body had been rushed to nearby Harborview Medical Center.

For all his vivacity and apparent street-wiseness, Andy Wood had fallen for the oldest trick in the book: filling the spoon with the same amount of heroin he had the last time he'd taken a shot four months before, at a time when his smack habit was so severe he was shooting up three or four times a day just to feel 'normal'. The effect of the powerful opiate on his newly rehabilitated metabolism was instant. For three days Andy lay in a coma, close to death. His brain had been starved of so much oxygen before being admitted to hospital, doctors told his horrified family, that they estimated that if Andy did ever regain consciousness – a one in a million chance – he would, in all probability, be little more than a vegetable.

After spending the 'longest weekend of our lives' at their stricken son's bedside, Toni and David Wood reluctantly gave their permission to have the life-support systems switched off, on the afternoon of Monday, 19 March 1990. As a strangely touching mark of respect for the half-world life their son had chosen to lead, the lights were lowered in the hospital room where he lay, the way Andy always liked them to be when he was relaxing or making music, and a cassette of Queen's *A Night at the Opera* was played on a portable ghetto-blaster. Everybody in the room – his family, his band and his girlfriend – stood around his bed holding hands, and cried as the doctors discreetly pulled the plugs. Andy Wood – 'world's greatest rock 'n' roll frontman' – was just twenty-four years old.

Almost a thousand people, mostly fans, attended a memorial service held for the deceased singer the following Saturday evening, 24 March, at the Paramount Theater, Seattle; scene of so many of Andy's real and imagined triumphs. David Wood gave a brief but moving eulogy to his son's memory. Friends still insist that Andrew Wood was simply unlucky. 'There was a great deal of pressure on Andy,' Xana pointed out. 'He had me counting on him for things. He also had the band counting on him to stay sober.'

'He was never a junkie,' said Regan Hagar. 'He liked getting high because it made him float that much higher, maybe, than life already did. And he really did like to float.' David Wood disagreed. Barely able to speak through his grief at the Paramount, he said the best thing Andy's bandmates could do was to find themselves a new singer. 'But whatever you do,' he sobbed, 'make sure he's not a junkie.'

'The only thing about drugs and rock 'n' roll that I ever really knew for sure about and noticed and understood was back when guys like Andy were getting into it,' said Soundgarden vocalist Chris Cornell, whose apartment Andy had crashed at for months when he first moved to Seattle. 'I've seen a lot of guys in music doing it because they thought that was part of how you became a rock star. That's definitely why Andy started doing drugs. He was that guy and that's all he wanted to be.'

So was his death inevitable, then? Stone Gossard didn't think so. 'Everyone was aware that Andy had a drug problem. He had been fighting it for as long as we knew him – he just broke down. Sometimes you break down and get bad heroin – and that's it. Andy always knew he was an addict and it was never anything that he thought was cool. He really felt ashamed of it – it wasn't very glamorous.'

On Tuesday, 27 March, the King County's Medical Examiner's Division announced that the death of Andrew Wood had resulted from an acute and accidental overdose of heroin. There were no suspicious circumstances involved, they added. Dying, it seems, like singing and writing, was one of those rare things Andy Wood could do all on his own, and still draw a crowd. The irony would no doubt have brought a smile to his eternally surprised face.

'As far as coming to terms with Andy's death, I don't really know if I have yet or not,' said Jeff Ament in an interview nearly three years later. 'I miss him a lot, and think about him all the time. But at the same time, I feel he might even be better off and a lot more happy where he is than he was in real life. I think he suffered a lot. In some ways, I can't help but think that, whether it's sick or not.'

When Andrew Wood died, so did Mother Love Bone. 'It wasn't openly discussed right away,' said Stone. 'When your friend is lying there in a coma you're thinking a million thoughts. But what we stood for is on [Apple], and I'm certainly not going to try and recreate what made us great with some other singer. I'm not into it. When something is over, you've got to let it die.' Or as The Rocket's Editor/Publisher, Charles R. Cross, says today: 'Mother Love Bone was a great group that gained a lot of local attention ... but a lot of that was Andrew Wood. It wasn't like anybody saw Mother Love Bone and talked about any of the other guys in the group.'

From a fan's-eye-view, the sad part is that Apple, when it was finally released in July 1990, proved that beneath the spangled attitude and low-slung guitars, Mother Love Bone were more than capable of wringing fresh ideas from the heard-it-all-before grunt-speak of hard rock. Tracks such as the thrillingly self-parodic 'This is Shangrila' (with Andy turning the room cold as he begs, 'Doncha die on me, babe') or 'Holy Roller' (with its humorous 'Love Rock' rap tacked onto the end) were shameless knee-tremblers, the lyrics squeezed out in heart-shaped thought bubbles and blown into infinity with a wave of the hand. But where the love child really excelled was on slower, more enigmatic tracks such as the mournful 'Man of Golden Words' or the grandiose 'Bone China' – 'Andy's Bolan tribute,' according to Jeff. And, of course, 'Crown of Thorns', here regretfully shorn of its original 'Chloe Dancer' prelude, but still undeniably Andy and Mother Love Bone's greatest moment.

CODA

The 'What if?' game is always a fruitless challenge, of course: what if my uncle had tits, would he be my auntie? Nevertheless, in this case it's worth asking: what if Andy Wood hadn't died? Well, there would have been no Pearl Jam, obviously. But then what? There were plenty of other contenders for the crown of boo-hoo grunge self-pityists, from Wood's pals in Soundgarden, to Stone Temple Pilots and Alice In Chains. What of Mother Love Bone, though? Would they have managed to make an impact, or would they, too, have become subsumed in the goateed tidal wave that ensued just a year after *Apple* was released? Considering the fate of Queensrÿche – fellow Seattle avant-metallists who did manage to have two multi-platinum albums before the grunge tsunami hit and the world completely forgot there had been any Seattle bands before Nirvana – I think it's fair to assume that whatever fame the would-be stardog might have achieved, the band would have been washed away. A great pity. One only has to look at the success enjoyed a decade later by a band like the Darkness to imagine just how loved Mother Love Bone might have become if the time, and not just the place, had been right.

KING'S X, 1994

King's X was one of those great discoveries you get to make once in a while as a rock journalist – a truly great new band who simply can't fail to make it once the rest of the world gets to hear about them too. So it was that I persuaded *Kerrang!* to put them on the cover in early 1988, at a time when they were about to release their first album, *Out of the Silent Planet*. And for a while there it looked like I was absolutely right. Everyone who heard it fell under its spell. Like Hendrix might have sounded if the Experience had been a real band and not merely an overqualified, if wonderfully talented, backing group.

When the second King's X album, *Gretchen Goes to Nebraska*, was released the following year, it was the same thing: great reviews, more front covers, yet more people proclaiming them as the Next Big Thing. It was the same – but different – when in 1990 the third X album, *Faith, Hope, Love* came out. Again, I was the one providing the copy for the by now obligatory cover story, only not even I was convinced anymore that the group were on their way to stardom. Indeed, I was almost certain they were not. Not because of the music, which simply got better and better. But because they were ... well, let's say ill-advised by their then manager, a well-meaning if a little too serious 'born again' Christian named Sam Taylor, whose idea of musical democracy – allowing each member to carry the lead vocals on various tunes, giving them all a fair share of the songwriting – did them no favours in terms of focusing their talents towards success, certainly not '80s-style success, which is all there was back then.

In fairness, it should also be pointed out that the band did themselves no favours either by a) allowing this to happen, and b) being too damn nice for their own good. King's X was one of those rare groups that always performed onstage with smiles on their faces. Like, shucks, aren't we lucky to be here. This at a time when legendary non-smilers like Metallica and Guns N' Roses were beginning to rule the rocking world.

This story comes in a few years later, after Taylor has gone and just as the group realise their mistakes and are now trying to rectify them, in time to fit in with what had actually become the Next Big Thing instead: grunge.

Interview with King's X, first published in RAW, *January 1994.*

Doug Pinnick shrugs his lean shoulders and studies the space about a foot in front of him. 'I hate to use the word "mistake",' he grimaces. 'But for me, personally, there are a whole lotta things that I wanted to do with this band that, for a long time, we just couldn't get to. I don't even remember doing the fourth album. I listen to the record and . . . well, I don't listen to the record, to tell you the truth. I don't play it. I don't play the third album, either. I think back and all I have is a horrible feeling of being just totally boxed in by what I was starting to think the image of King's X must be.'

He makes a steeple with his long, calloused fingers. 'But *Dogman*, I am truly excited about. The other records, I always felt there was something missing. I don't care for them now. I can't listen to it . . . This album, I play it all the time, I love it. This is how I feel. This is what I want to say.'

Well, it had to happen one day. As little green apples will some day be munched or left to rot, we're all forced to grow up and stand on our own two feet sooner or later. In the case of Pinnick and his ahead-of-their-time group, King's X, despite a talent recognisably both prodigious and glorious in its scope – although somewhat limited up until now in its direction – it was never gonna be sooner. At least, not while their former manager, producer, occasional co-songwriter and self-proclaimed 'fourth member' Sam Taylor was still leading the way. A devout neo-Christian and an accomplished musician and studio engineer in his own right, who had gained his experience of the business end of music while working for ZZ Top in the early 1980s (Taylor has always claimed it was he that first introduced Billy Gibbons to synthesisers, an experiment that led to the Top's multi-squillion-selling *Eliminator* album), Taylor had held sway in the King's X camp for five years, conducting business meetings like Bible-reading classes and reacting to any intrusion from the outside world like a worried lioness shielding her cubs from danger.

When I first met King's X six years ago, just prior to the release of their first album, *Out of the Silent Planet*, all three members of the band – bassist/vocalist Pinnick, guitarist/vocalist Ty Tabor and drummer/vocalist Jerry Gaskill – were clearly in thrall of their solemn-faced leader. 'I am the mirror the band hold up to themselves,' Taylor announced grandly on more than one occasion, and all three would dutifully nod their heads. Clearly, back then, there was Sam's way or the highway. Nevertheless, they did record those first two, still iridescent King's X albums together – their critic-slaying debut in 1988 and the following year's equally astounding *Gretchen Goes to Nebraska*.

'So what happened to the "fourth member"?' I ask, when we meet again around a long table in a boardroom at the London offices of their record company, just before Christmas. 'Only you would ask that,' smiles Pinnick somewhat self-consciously, still shaven-headed at the sides, but where there used to be the punk brush, there are now thickly coiled black locks.

Although reluctant to get into the detail, they let it be known that whatever the specific reasons for Sam Taylor's departure from the set-up, they certainly weren't all musical. 'All of the real reasons are extremely personal,' confesses Pinnick. 'The truth is, I was just kind of lost in that period,' he says of the last two King's X albums, 1990's overambitious *Faith Hope Love* and their last, glib, eponymously titled effort, released to barely stifled yawns eighteen months ago. 'Lyrically, it didn't have a lot to say for me, I was just lost.'

And now he's found. The most immediately detectable change on *Dogman*, possibly the best King's X album yet – particularly on tracks such as 'Don't Care', 'Pretend', 'Black the Sky', 'Cigarettes' or the fifty-one-second-long 'Go to Hell' – is the arrival of unmistakably . . . well, darker, more cynical elements to the new material. Frankly, I'm a little shocked. Didn't this used to be the band that came on stage grinning from amp-to-amp and harmonising about the 'Power of Love' in a place called 'Summerland', where we would all live 'In the New Age' happily ever after with 'Goldilox' – or something?

'All of the lyrics that I wrote on this were things I went through last year,' explains Pinnick, who handles all the lead vocals on the album – another first. 'I don't want to go into it, but I went through some real heavy trauma. It had nothing to do with Sam,' he assures me before

I can ask. 'It's just finding yourself inside. Those songs were therapy.'

Tell me if I'm wrong, I say, but one track, 'Fool You' – a moment of unsweetened realism that revolves around the joyously paranoiac epithet: 'Don't believe anything / I'll be your everything / They will all try to / Fool you' – sounds uncannily like it was written for Sam Taylor.

Silence.

'Well, you said to tell you if you were wrong,' Gaskill eventually chuckles softly.

'I would say that it mostly stems from the fact that we were in a different situation,' reasons Tabor. 'You know, we can pretty much do what we want to do now. Just us three. Without being inhibited about what anybody else thinks about it.'

You mean, in the past, Sam might have discouraged you from expressing your darker side?

'I don't think it was discouraged by anyone,' says Pinnick. 'For me, the dark side was one that I suppressed because I didn't want to share those feelings with anyone. I wanted to share this other side of the way I think. But for whatever reason, this year, I've exhausted that whole "love" side. There's another side to me and to King's X, I think. We've been branded the nice guys of rock 'n' roll and all that – but there's the other side, too. We're assholes – just like anybody. I can just as soon give somebody the finger as shake their hand.'

He looks at me.

'We're just not the same people anymore,' he says and I believe him. Calling the new album *Dogman* is merely another way King's X have chosen to dramatise and distance themselves from what they feel quickly became the staid goody-who-cares image of the band.

'Originally, the track itself was called "Good Man",' explains Tabor, who wrote it. 'It was a confusing song about how do I become a good man. But the connotations of having "Good Man" as the title was so dorky. "Dogman" was more appropriate to what the real feelings are than anything, even though – at the time when we came up with it – it was almost a joke.'

Dogman, the album, took just six weeks to make.

'We wrote all of the songs on the first day,' boasts Pinnick. Producer Brendan O'Brien, who has recently worked his fingers to the platinum-plated bones with the likes of the Black Crowes and Pearl Jam, was, he insists, the key. 'He was such a joker,' grins Tabor. 'A complete lunatic – I was always laughing my head off. It was almost as if we were going into rehearsals here and there and just really taking it easy.'

Apart from their obvious commercial needs – 'If this one doesn't happen, there might not be another one,' Tabor cheerfully confides – more than anything, King's X want this album to succeed just to prove to themselves that they can do it. To reaffirm their own faith not just in the music but in themselves, too. Back in 1988, King's X was a rare bird indeed – nothing like the Mötley Crüe/Def Leppard scarves-around-the-mike, put-your-bums-in-the-air school of hair metal. King's X was a heavy rock band that actually wrote songs about real things. They were so far ahead of their time they had come full circle up to the 1960s again, when rock music still mattered; when it could, literally, make you kiss the sky. Jerry Gaskill was the first person in a rock band to sport a goatee since 1971; Ty Tabor was the first guitarist to wear his glasses on stage since Elvis Costello threw away his contacts. And of course, Doug Pinnick was the first black man to convincingly front a white rock band since the great Philip Lynott strode the magic boards.

And yet, talk to their accountants and they will tell you that – for all the hype and the critical back-slapping – the biggest-selling King's X album to date was their third, *Faith Hope Love*, which notched up slightly fewer than 250,000 sales worldwide. Lars Ulrich of Metallica wouldn't get out of bed for those kind of figures. Add another zero and you still wouldn't be talking the same ball park as a Pearl Jam, or even a Soul Asylum, for dog's sake.

'It used to bother me,' Pinnick admits. 'But … people make their mistakes, they make their decisions. That's just the way it is. Ultimately, it's up to the people what they like and what they don't like.'

I wonder if, as practising Christians, they ever wonder whether they aren't doing something wrong? Do they ever suspect that there is something that life – that God, perhaps – is trying to tell them?

'I think about that all the time,' says Pinnick, his voice not much above a whisper now. 'For years and years and years, that has always gone through my head. As for the Christian aspect, I question every-thing right now. I don't know what I believe, just that I have to be honest.'

But how did they resolve their lack of success with their faith in a Christian God when so many apparently 'undeserving' cases seem to hit the top of the world's charts, no prayers said at all?

'I see a lot of things that I just can't agree with,' Pinnick says. 'Everything I've done hasn't worked. I believe in God; I've got to, I look around and I know something's going on. But all the other stuff . . . I just feel that we did a lot of wrong things. We could have branched out. Like, if Ty wanted to play on an album with someone else, he wasn't allowed to do that.'

He throws me those lonely brown eyes again.

'Now we're free. I can get onstage with Pearl Jam and sing without walking off with the management saying, "You shouldn't have done that because that's bad for your career."'

He shakes his head clear and conjures up a smile.

'I consider us very lucky, too, you know. We still have a career. We've still got five records, still got a chance to get out there. No one is slagging us yet. We haven't sold ten million records but we've still got it going on. It's very exciting.'

Check out *Dogman* and discover just how much.

CODA

As I suspected at the time, the release of the *Dogman* album didn't do enough to fully revive the career of King's X. It seems there is only ever one window of opportunity when it comes to success and the band had singularly failed to climb through it when they had their chance. Not that this has stopped them making beautiful music together. They are still out there on the internet and in the theatres and clubs; still enjoying great respect in that half-world of name-recognition and word-of-mouth success that guarantees them their own kind of mini-legend, if not the kind of massive record sales the groups that have acknowledged their influence, such as Pearl Jam, continue to enjoy. From this perspective, it might even be said that they were so far ahead of their time that they are only now really maturing into the kind of underground heroes their shadowy music and deep philosophical – and religious – lyrical stances deserve. I wish them well, always.

NIRVANA, 1994

It seems more shocking now, I think, looking back, than it did even then, the way death stalked the Seattle grunge scene. I have to confess, though, that at the time I wrote the following piece, my sympathies for Nirvana's Kurt Cobain were all for the undeservedly broken band he had left behind, and, most of all, for the tiny, daddy-eyed daughter who would have to grow up without him. Like all suicides, but particularly his – being so famous, so rich and successful – I saw the whole thing as an unforgivably selfish act committed by a self-pitying junkie. Not that much of this comes across in the finished article. By then, we were all jumping aboard the bandwagon and this was a cover story for *RAW* intended to shore up its creaking circulation, not offer actual insight into what was, after all, a deeply tragic, nightmarish event. Never mind the music, here's the bollocks. Beautifully wrought bollocks, though, obviously, with many a long night at the laptop spent sweating over getting the shocked tone just right ...

Nirvana article, first published in RAW, *August 1994.*

If the Seattle scene took off in earnest with the leering, ironic challenge of Kurt Cobain's best-known line from Nirvana's best-known hit, 'Smells Like Teen Spirit' – 'Here we are now / Entertain us' – it surely ended the afternoon the singer balanced a six-pound Remington Model 11 20-gauge shotgun between his legs, carefully placed the end of the double-barrel into his mouth, closed his eyes, and pulled the trigger.

Beside him Cobain had arranged a few personal effects – the plaid hunter's cap with ridiculous earflaps he sometimes wore to disguise himself, his driver's licence, credit cards, and the old cigar box he kept his drug paraphernalia in – all the outward signs of his public identity and the face he had made famous to the world. It was as if he wanted the world to know that he really didn't need it after all. That he simply refused to do an encore.

Why? Because Kurt Cobain, like his music, was the sort of person about whom anything you said could be countered with its opposite, and both statements would probably be true. There seemed to be not a single issue in the Nirvana singer's short, tragic life that he wasn't agonisingly ambivalent about. For Kurt, the talent to write, play guitar, and sing some of the most affecting rock anthems for a generation was both a blessing and a curse. The most famous rock star in the world, he recoiled in horror at the attention he received wherever he went.

Marriage to Hole singer Courtney Love was always of the love/hate variety, too. 'They were totally in love. You couldn't separate them,' recalled photographer Michael Levine at the time of his photo-shoot with the couple for their joint front cover of *Sassy* magazine (the US equivalent of *Smash Hits*) in 1992. 'I'm married / Buried', Kurt would scream on Nirvana's very next album, *In Utero*, released a year later. Kurt was, by common consent, an attentive, loving father, yet even that simple pleasure was somehow sullied for him by a deep foreboding over his daughter's almost preternatural physical resemblance to him. And, finally, as we now know, Kurt was unable to decide on the fundamental question of life itself: to stay or go? To dig in and take it, or fuck the whole deal off? Given the unrelentingly bleak demeanour that endured throughout his last days, the fact that he settled for the latter option should have come as no surprise to those that knew him best.

The morning after Kurt Cobain's mutilated body was discovered, the *Seattle Times* ran a full-colour, page-one photo of the scene – 'as dirty a stinking drug box as I've ever seen,' according to one of the police officers present – zooming in its tabloid eyes one last time on the motif baggy jeans and dirty trainers, one tatty pyjama-sleeve ending in a porcelain-white clenched fist. All journalists are ambulance-chasers, in the sense that there's no news like bad news, but the unmitigated glee with which the media fell upon Kurt Cobain's suicide has more than a little to do with told-you-so sanctimony. Proof positive that the path to oblivion is crowded with loser musician types; that there was something rotten buried at the bottom of the grunge garden after all. But then, witnessing the distressing haste with which Nirvana's contemporaries jumped aboard the nowhere-train (Soundgarden refusing to speak to anybody and trashing the dressing rooms on their UK tour; Pearl Jam cancelling immediate plans to tour amid floods of 'Eddie's next' innuendos), who knows, maybe they had a point.

No doubt the reasons for the overriding depression that beset Cobain could be traced back to the emotional upheavals of his child-hood. Kurt's parents broke up when he was eight and the battle for custody was ugly. On the walls of his bedroom he wrote the words: 'I hate Mom, I hate Dad, Dad hates Mom, Mom hates Dad, it simply makes you want to be sad', and drew a picture of a big question mark over it. 'I used to try to make my head explode by holding my breath, thinking if I blew up my head, they'd be sorry,' he told one reporter.

But the punk ethos he followed – that to get to the top you have to aim for the bottom, rigidly rejecting the fake, the dishonest, the greedy and the hypocritical – was as compellingly imbued in the musical outlook of the other key movers and shakers on the Seattle circuit. So what happens when you become popular? When friends used to tell Kurt how much they liked his paintings (always more than just a hobby), he would immediately rip them up and start again. But it simply wasn't possible to tear up nine million existing copies of *Nevermind*, so what then? Are you still legitimate? Is your work still good, or have you sold out? Typically, Kurt didn't hang around long enough to find out. Now it looks like Eddie Vedder will have to do it for him.

'After I reached my teens, I decided I didn't want to hang out with anyone,' Kurt once said. 'I couldn't handle the stupidity.' Who can? Since Cobain's death, nobody is pretending that Seattle is a cool town anymore. According to friends, Courtney won't even go near the place these days. 'She's afraid,' said one close friend who asked not to be named. 'Seattle is Heroin City, and Courtney's afraid that if she even goes near the place she'll be sucked into it, too.'

The recent OD of Hole bassist Kristen Pfaff – found dead in her bathtub – was seen as another warning. Kristen had planned to leave Seattle for the same reasons as Courtney. She just didn't move quickly enough. Even official police statistics would appear to back up this grisly theory. Heroin-related deaths in Seattle were sixty per cent higher in 1993 than twelve months before. Senior staff at Geffen Records in America, who have both Nirvana and Hole on their label, are said to have become so inured to the idea of their artists 'dropping off like flies' that they recently sent a joke press release around their LA headquarters that read, in part: Geffen Records regret to announce the death of (insert name) of (insert name of band) who played (insert instrument), et cetera. When Courtney caught sight of it by accident one day, she told the Geffen execs they were 'sick'.

It seems the only people left who still think the Seattle scene exists are bonehead perps like Robert Sceeles, the whacko who recently showed up at Courtney's LA abode in a red Porsche with the word 'Nirvana' spray-painted across the hood. At first he told a questioning security guard that he merely wanted to give Courtney the car. When the grim-faced guard tried to send him on his way, he yelled, 'I don't care if I die tonight! I want to see Courtney!' An anti-harassment suit has since been served on Sceeles while police wait to see what he might try next.

And the beep-beep of the cash register goes on. Geffen are about to make an album out of Nirvana's neo-legendary *MTV Unplugged* session (including unbroadcast outtakes); Pearl Jam are ready to release a new album that, according to sources, will be 'their best yet'; Soundgarden are currently the most famous hermits the world over, playing the biggest and best-known arenas, selling squillions of CDs, records, tapes, videos, T-shirts, baseball caps turned backwards, you name it – and hating every minute. They say.

And the rest of us? Well, it's not just the big boys who are cashing in. In the shop below the office in which I write this, there are an abundance of 'Steady Eddie' and 'Courtney Killed Kurt'-type T-shirts. Nothing in rockdom sells better than premature death. But the killer, must-have T-shirt to end them all is the one currently available in the Washington area with Kurt's suicide note printed on it, including those paragraphs not read out by Courtney at Kurt's anodyne public memorial in Seattle last April. Only Courtney, the medical examiner, the police and Kurt's family had copies, so how the makers of the shirts – Grunge Enterprises, would you believe? – have obtained a copy remains a mystery. According to an official from Nirvana's management office, it's 'The sickest, lowest and most pitiful thing I've ever heard of'.

As for the ghost of Kurt Cobain, he had begun speaking privately of a life without Nirvana for almost a year before his death, threatening to quit, by one insider's estimation, 'at least ten times'. The same restless energy and inability to merely follow trends that drove Nirvana to the tremulous peak of its artistic and commercial success in the space of two albums, was what was now urging him on to do something new. Soft, then loud, then soft again – that was how Kurt sarcastically described the typical Nirvana song to friends. Indeed, Kurt's first-choice title for the *In Utero* album was *Verse Chorus Verse*. Nirvana had become boring; too formulaic. Worse, the other band members were far too 'normal' – at least in Kurt's eyes.

When Nirvana kicked off 1994 with a show at the Seattle Center, Kurt introduced 'Smells Like Teen Spirit' by saying 'We have to play this song next – it's in our contract. This is the song that ruined our lives and ruined Seattle and ruined your lives, too.' The European tour, which followed, was a disaster. Kurt was convinced that Courtney was having an affair with her former boyfriend, Smashing Pumpkins singer Billy Corgan, something Courtney continues to deny, although she'll admit that Corgan had begun calling her on the phone regularly again.

Last week, a UK tabloid ran pictures of Love and Lemonheads leader Evan Dando kissing on a bed in a hotel room, claiming that the pair are now a couple.

Whatever the truth of the situation, there's no doubting that in Kurt's mind the threat of betrayal had bared its teeth yet again. That and the fact that he and Courtney were increasingly worried by the threat of having baby Frances taken away from them and placed into care if they didn't clean up their act were more than enough to pull the final rug from beneath Cobain's feet. When, on the night of 3 March, while 'resting' in Rome – following the cancellation of dates in Germany – Kurt sent the bellboy to the local pharmacy to fill a prescription for the powerful tranquilliser, Rohipnol (related to Valium), and also asked for two bottles of champagne, there was nothing careless about his actions. Kurt planned to take his own life. Viciously downplayed at the time as the overindulgence of someone merely trying to secure a good night's sleep, the truth is that Kurt, an experienced drug user, had swallowed more than fifty pills that night, plus most of the champagne. A suicide note, the first of two he would eventually write, was found nearby. 'I believe firmly in revenge,' Kurt once said. He may have screwed up that first attempt at killing himself, but that didn't mean he thought he'd been saved. It merely underlined his determination to do the job properly next time.

The fact that when Kurt pulled the trigger on his own life he also managed to take Nirvana, probably Hole, and even possibly Pearl Jam with him, would not have mattered to him. Indeed, the thought that he might have single-handedly burst the grunge boil with one last 'follow that' anti-everything blast of hate might even have been an incentive to do 'the unthinkable'. Ultimately, reading the cards as best you can, the sudden suicide of Kurt Cobain and the slow subsequent death of the Seattle scene had perhaps been on the agenda from the very beginning.

Life, death, rebirth – Kurt Cobain had an almost obsessional interest in what might be deemed 'foetal imagery'. The covers of both *Nevermind* and *In Utero* abound with visions of babies in strange surroundings; of innocence hurtling towards corruption. The naked dolls he used to collect and dissect and the absurd frocks he sometimes dressed up in onstage and in photo-sessions, testified to Kurt's conviction that, for him at least, the innocence behind who he really was and what his music was about had long been expunged from the equation. This was not the beginning of anything, just possibly the end of everything.

Elsewhere in Seattle, the emotional fall-out that has followed the grisly end of Nirvana continues to shroud everything the city's other main bands – Pearl Jam, Alice In Chains and Soundgarden – attempt to do. As this issue of *RAW* went to press, the shattering news of Alice In Chains' withdrawal from their US summer tour, which included a prestige support slot on Metallica's dates and an equally prestigious appearance at the Woodstock II festival, came in. A bleak management statement ran in full: 'Alice In Chains have withdrawn from the Metallica summer tour as well as an appearance at the Woodstock '94 festival. This decision is due to health problems within the band. Alice In Chains apologise to their fans, and appreciate their support and concern. The band hope to resolve this situation in privacy. The members look forward to returning to the recording studio in the fall.'

They couldn't really spell it out any plainer, could they? The band's drug problems have been well documented, not least on their 1992 album, *Dirt*. *RAW* understands from close acquaintances of the band that vocalist Layne Staley has fought a long battle with hard drugs and heroin addiction, which have caused real problems with Alice In Chains' touring and recording schedules. Now, the band have asked to be left in peace to resolve their problems. Some stories from the USA suggest that Staley is on a last-chance ultimatum. Sort it or leave. It appears sad but true that Alice In Chains' current problems are extremely serious. The band aren't prepared to elaborate any further on their statement, and neither are their management or record company. Read between the lines.

For Eddie Vedder, his problem isn't drugs, his problem isn't dying. Eddie's problem is living. In common with Kurt, whose death has affected him deeply, Eddie's ideal gig would probably be with a band such as Fugazi, who he greatly admires – low-profile national chart-wise, but big cheeses within the indie rat-trap. But where Kurt confessed to his official biographer Michael Azerrad that, 'It's sad to think what the state of rock 'n' roll will be in twenty years. It's already so rehashed and so plagiarised that it's barely alive now. It's disgusting.'

Eddie still likes to believe that, 'When it comes down to it, you can't turn your back on what's happening. You have to do something. Jesus knows, it's tough, because you never really know if what you're doing is going to have any effect. But what's the alternative? I didn't get into this to end up as a face on a fucking billboard. All I ever wanted to do was play music, simple as that. I don't need all this other bullshit. But you can't afford to think about it too much; it'll just fucking kill you.'

Pearl Jam guitarist Stone Gossard, who also played in Mother Love Bone, says his own outlook on drugs has changed dramatically since the death of singer Andy Wood. 'When one of your closest friends dies, you have these feelings about your own limitations as a human being. It's frightening. At the same time, it makes you confront things in your own life. The whole process has been one where it's made me say, "Fuck, if that's gonna happen to me". That's the main thing. Apart from the total tragedy of losing my best friend.'

'A fucked-up person who's had bad things happen can relate to me because he sees someone else who's fucked up,' says Eddie. 'But they don't understand, at that bottom level, we're both fucked up. And whenever you do have answers, it's at 3.30 in the morning, and you're alone and you can't find a piece of paper. I don't want to be Bono. He sang about issues in songs and suddenly people were turning to him for answers. But I can't kick back and sing about how life is good and everything is good while all I see is tragedy all around me, to the point where I could easily let it catch me in a downward spiral and suck me under. I walk up onstage with a lot of baggage, and you gotta sing it as hard as you can, just let it out. I'm not singing for myself anymore.'

Too long in the tooth for the usual all-for-one, one-for-all band mentality, Pearl Jam are caught between humouring Eddie's more indulgent eccentricities and respecting his unquestionably high ideals. The band are currently refusing to tour following a dispute with US ticket agents Ticketmaster, who, the band claim, are keeping prices artificially high. In many ways, like Kurt, Eddie is the outsider in his own group. 'Eddie's not really close to anybody in the group,' says one acquaintance. 'His best friend in Seattle is probably Matt Chamberlain from the New Bohemians.'

One of the last dates Pearl Jam played before disappearing from sight was at the Ritz in New York. Afterwards, the record company held a huge party for the band. Eddie didn't show up. Instead, he spent the entire time locked away in a back room talking to his friend Henry Rollins. 'He was just letting it spill out,' says Henry, reluctant to say more. 'The madness that surrounds that band, that surrounds him is just . . .' he shrugs and smiles a weary smile. Not even Henry knows a bad enough word to describe that scene.

'Everyone says, you've got to expect it because you put yourself out there,' Eddie said recently. 'So maybe I won't put myself out there anymore. Maybe I'll just quit. It doesn't matter.'

Will Vedder quit? Perhaps the Ticketmaster row and the balm of making some new music, recording a new album away from the glare of the spotlight, will give Vedder the space he so desperately needs. With Cobain's death, the torch passed to him whether he wanted it or not. Now it looks sure that he'll carry it away from Seattle. That scene died when Kurt did, and no one wants the mess that's left behind.

On the cover of the Nirvana rarities album, *Incesticide*, is a painting by Kurt depicting a crying baby reaching out for a shadowy parent whose back is turned and whose expression is cold and blank. You notice the baby's head is cracked open like an egg. It could be a depiction of the Seattle scene right now. In despair and with the top of its head missing . . .

CODA

Fifteen years and who knows how many lifetimes later since this story was chiselled out, I feel rather differently about things. As a piece of writing, I see it as one of my better works of craft from those days – like a watercolour you once did at college that has somehow survived the intervening non-college years surprisingly well. The stuff that doesn't survive can often be the most fun, so far away are those days and nights now. But this one's different. Yes, it was a long, long time ago, but it still means ... something. As my own doctor later remarked, 'Having worldly wealth is no protection against the effects of deep depression.' Quite so. Unfortunately, rock star deaths are always measured in exactly those terms – the death not of an unfortunate human being, but of a rock star. How dare they throw away opportunities that most of the rest of us would have given almost everything to enjoy, as though that actually had anything to do with it.

BLIND MELON, 1995

At the time of this interview I thought I was doing Blind Melon a bit of a favour. Yes, they'd just had a minor hit in 1993 with 'No Rain', but they were still barely known outside America, beyond the neo-grunge crowd. As it turned out, they were also doing me a favour, helping me to get with it in terms of the new post-1980s rock reality. I was still wearing pointed high-heel Chelsea boots at the time of the interview with their singer, the soon-to-be deceased Shannon Hoon. Thankfully, I was paying attention to a lot more than just their music, nice though it was. Having stuck out like a sore thumb, after writing this piece I invested in a pair of Doc Martens, had a 'proper' haircut and faced up to the fact that those days were gone and I was no longer twenty-seven. Shannon's up-all-night vitality, his dirty-fingernailed sincerity and devil-may-care attitude to that fuck-around bitch success – all, as you will see, gloriously on the record – was so unlike the studied un-cool of so many of the Eighties stars I had made my name traipsing around with, it was reality-check time. For me, for all of us who had lived too long, at that point. Like punk, grunge really had effected a ground-zero mentality and I was determined to survive the aftershocks as best I could.

Of course, Shannon *was* still twenty-seven, and what I had been too self-absorbed to realise was that he was going through his own deep confusions. He was still at that age when you are invulnerable; when you still know the score better than anybody else, not least the thirty-something Limey with the metaphorical hunch and not-so-critical squint. He hadn't realised yet that he was only made of flesh and blood; that the nights may be long but that life is short. He would find out sooner – much sooner – than either of us could possibly have even joked about when we talked for this piece.

Interview with Shannon Hoon of Blind Melon, first published in RAW, April 1995.

Shannon Hoon calls me late because, he says, 'I'm having difficulty with my pregnancy.'

Uh . . . come again, dude?

'I think I'm giving birth to a St. Bernard!'

It is a beautiful morning in Southern California. City of earthquakes and OJ. City of lost angels. We are all blind in the melon-shaped sky. We start again . . .

'I'm sorry, I've been up all night,' he says, sitting up in bed, shaking the sleep out of his hair. 'I had some friends that I was playing with that ended up keeping me up all night.'

We begin with the new single, 'Galaxy'. Upbeat and salty, it is not the catchy follow-up to 'No Rain' your mum might have preferred, but it will please the purists no end. Short, sharp, not necessarily straight to the point, 'Galaxy' works its spell best after a few listens. Like all the best records in your collection.

'New Orleans, that's the place. We made the record there and I think that had everything to do with how it all ended up sounding. Really, at no point did we even consider making a single. We were there to make this one, long record that wasn't just about one song or whatever. But was about a state-of-mind, or a state-of-place that was whole. It's very hard for me to think of any song off this record on its own. To me, they all belong together. We put a lot of thought into the sequencing. It's like chapters in a book. That's how they were written and that's how they sound best, when they're all played together like that.'

He tells me the new Blind Melon album is going to be called *Soup*. 'I think so, anyway. That's what it was the last time we discussed it,' he smiles. His speaking voice is very much like his singing one; high and dreamy. A happy, baffled voice. Most of the time, anyway. Talking about some of his favourite moments from the new album, his voice drops to almost a whisper as he relates the story behind a track he wrote with Melon drummer Glenn Graham called 'Car Seat (God's Presents)'.

'There was a big story in the news here about a lady in South Carolina who drove her car into a lake and drowned her children. She told the police that someone had car-jacked her and made off with the kids. Then it came out that she had been having an affair with a guy who, basically, didn't want the kids, so she decided to get rid of 'em.' The eyes go round with wonder. 'She brutally murdered her own children. One of them was, like, eight months old, and the other one was two years old. But she rolled the car into a lake with the children still alive and it wasn't discovered for five or six days.'

And when it was?

'The lady was charged with murder.'

Silence.

'Anyway, that's what the song is about. I know it's a kind of grisly subject matter, but at the end of the song I try to resolve it, or give it some kind of deeper meaning, I guess, by reading this poem I discovered by my great, great grandmother.'

When Shannon inherited his great, great grandmother's personal journal, he was amazed to discover that she had composed 'hundreds of these really amazing poems'. Over 100 years old now, the pages, he says, 'are so dry and old they would break in your hands if you weren't careful. You'd have to see it to know what I mean, but it's bound in this old leather and you put your hand on it and you can just feel this aura kinda emanating from it. So at the end of the song, "Car Seat", we were in New York mixing and I went to a pay-phone one night, called 'em up and read 'em this poem that my great, great grandmother wrote. It was 11 February 1995, and the poem was dated 11 February 1884, so it was exactly one hundred and eleven years from the day she wrote it, and I read it down the phone and they recorded it at the studio, and that was how we used it on the album.'

A sudden breath, then another rush of words.

'It's a poem called "God's Presents", because she truly believed that children are God's gifts to the Earth, you know? So I read it in this pay-phone, barefoot on the streets of New York in the middle of winter, and it felt right.'

Children, of course, are very much in Shannon's mind right now as his girlfriend is seven months' pregnant with the couple's first child. He says that the doctors have already told them it's going to be a girl and that they have named her Nico Blue. Shannon is already the jealous father. 'I'm telling you, man, if anyone – ANYONE! – tries to hurt my daughter or come near her . . .' He shakes his head then laughs. 'It's true, I can't help it. I'm a sad case, man.'

His tousled thoughts turn back towards the new album.

'Like I say, it wasn't just about recording the songs the way they were meant to go. It was kind of letting things take their own shape,' he muses. 'The aura that surrounded a take was more important than if someone played or sang the notes right, you know what I'm saying?'

Ride on.

'New Orleans is just a city that enhances every kind of . . . madness,' he cackles. 'They say the Devil was born there and I'm not too sure he wasn't born in the room I had to sleep in! It brought the werewolf out in me, man! That city will clean your pores, man. Let's put it that way!'

Soup was produced by Andy Wallace, the man who also brought the best out of Faith No More in the studio. 'Andy was a psychiatrist as well as a producer,' Shannon reckons. 'There was an eight-foot groove in the floor behind his producer's chair, where he would slide back constantly and go "Whoa!" at some idea one of us had. But by the end of it we all understood each other real well. Real well . . .'

The direction the new album would take was defined early on after the band abandoned plans last summer to release an EP of what Shannon now calls 'loose, jammed songs written on-the-spot, on the road, using anybody and everybody that happened to be wandering by at the time'. Christened *The Mammoth Sessions*, the EP was characterised by its essentially non-studio vibe – doors slam in the background as the band play, people talk quite unaware that anything else is taking place, trombones wail, swordfish fly . . .

'It kinda got carried away,' Shannon admits. 'We just kept recording, kept writing songs, kept going until we didn't know why any more.'

It still hasn't seen the light of day, though.

'In the end, we decided that rather than have sex with half a hard-on, we'd just wait till we had a full one. I'd like to describe it a little less disgustingly, but ever since someone said that to me, it's how

I always think of it. But it will eventually surface, maybe through our fan club. I'm not sure yet. But it'll come out one day, one way or another. For those who want to go to the effort of getting it, you know what I'm saying?'

One of the pivotal moments on the new album is a track called 'St. Andrew's Fall'. Once again it was inspired by a real-life tragedy, but one witnessed first-hand this time by all the members of the band.

'One night, we were playing in Detroit at this old church that had been converted into a music hall, called St. Andrew's Hall. And after the show, we were standing up in our dressing room, and it had these windows so you could look down and see all the people leaving the club. And I was standing there looking out, when I noticed all these people beginning to congregate over on the corner. We were arguing about a monitor mix or something stupid from the gig, I don't know. But my attention was caught by all these people on the corner. I thought, man, is there a fight going on or something? What's going on? Then I see someone point up, and I look up and there's this girl on the edge of the building, twenty floors up! It wasn't someone from the show, it was a hotel next door to the club. I was like, "Holy shit, you guys, there's a girl up there!" We had the most horrific view of this.

'There's about two hundred people all watching by now, and of course you get all the heartless ones that start heckling and screaming at a time when you should really understand that someone for what-ever reason is deliberating life and death here. It was unbelievable. There were people yelling "Jump!". I thought, my God, what's going on here?'

And did she?

'All of a sudden there was this dead calm, and that girl stood up and she jumped, and we were all standing there. And I mean it seemed like it took forever for her to fall. It was one of those situations where you don't want to look but something in your mind makes you watch and will not let you take your eyes off it because you're going to learn something from it. I mean, not only did I learn that monitor mixes were irrelevant to life, it just ... phooosh! Nobody was able to say a thing for like the next three hours. We just got into the van and drove.

'Rogers [Stevens, guitarist] had actually left the hall where we were playing and he was down on the street when it happened. It was something that really scarred all of us. She was just twenty-six, and no one knew why she jumped. She took her secret with her. They thought she might have tested positive for AIDS, but she wasn't. She wasn't pregnant, she had a job . . . she just suffered from depression. It could have been anybody. It was really sad. And that's what "St. Andrew's Fall" is all about.'

We sit there thinking it over. You will be able to hear 'St. Andrew's Fall' for yourself when *Soup* is released on 19 June. Ditto the 'Galaxy' single. Whatever, both will be worth the wait.

And then?

'It begins again!' he howls. 'It' being another prolonged bout of serious road-work which, says Shannon, will 'definitely' include UK and European dates as early as this summer. Does he mean a proper tour or some festival appearances?

'I mean, both! But we're gonna start with some outdoor stuff, I think. Some festivals in Europe and maybe Reading in England. I like outdoor festivals. You can feel the grass underneath you.'

He still walks almost everywhere barefoot.

'I wouldn't know how not to anymore,' he shrugs. 'But you should see the second toe along from my big toe, man, it's like a fuckin' claw! When I'm down I sometimes think I should cut it off and send it to somebody.'

Oh yeah?

'Sure! Next time, I'll do it! Would you like me to send it to you?'

Only if you sign it first.

'You're sick!'

You're not?

'Heh heh heh . . .'

CODA

Shannon Hoon overdosed and died a few months after this piece was published. There had been a show in Houston that had gone badly and Shannon, by then a self-confessed cocaine addict, who had recently checked out of rehab, had used it as one more excuse to get as far out of his head as he could and still come back – except this time he didn't quite manage it. Ironically, Blind Melon was due to play a show in Hoon's – and the Devil's – beloved New Orleans the very next day. More tragically, considering his words above, he left behind a baby daughter, who the band later named a compilation album after – *Nico*. Opening track: a version of the old Steppenwolf number, 'The Pusher'. Not funny. Beyond sad. Needless to say, although they have regrouped in more recent times with a 'new' singer, Blind Melon disappeared not long after.

DEICIDE, 1995

I'd worked with Ozzy Osbourne and Black Sabbath for years. I'd been there when Ronnie James Dio invented what is now known as the 'Devil's horn salute' – actually Ronnie's way of carrying on Ozzy's tradition in Sabbath of flashing peace signs, but done a little differently to denote the fact he was now replacing Ozzy in the band. And of course I'd known my fair share of genuine evil-doers along the way. (Not all of them rock stars, by any means.) But I had never met anyone before like Deicide's Glen Benton. I mean, the guy had an upside-down cross branded into his *forehead*. And claimed he would commit suicide onstage at the age of thirty-three.

It was for this reason, much more than his music – I couldn't name you a single Deicide song, then or now – that I actually wanted to meet and talk to Benton. Could he be for real? Yes, actually, he could. Not only that, but he was clearly intelligent. Even more fascinating, he seemed to know what he was talking about in that way that people absolutely obsessed with their subject seem to know more than anyone needs to about what they're obsessing about – in Glen's case, the evil of Christianity; the certainty that Satan already ruled the world; and his own self-appointed mission to bring down the walls on the whole shitty deal. Or something. It didn't really matter to me. I just loved meeting and interviewing characters, and Glen certainly was one. Now read on, oh ye of little faith.

Interview with Glen Benton of Deicide, first published in RAW, *May 1995.*

When I first met Glen Benton, frontman of death metal's most determinedly evil sons, Deicide, he and the band had completed their much-touted third album, *Once Upon the Cross*, and were now preparing for a full worldwide release on Roadrunner Records in the spring of 1995. Speaking to me at Florida's Morrisound Studios, where he was putting the final touches to the mix, the man with the upside-down cross burned into his forehead explained how Deicide's fans could expect an album that 'harks back to the band's first album [*Deicide*], in terms of density and weight', but with the straight-faced proviso of 'some extremely ... catchy moments. We've been evolving,' he added with one of his trademark pitch-dark chuckles.

Working once again with producer and long-time cohort Scott Burns, 'almost all' of the music was written by drummer/multi-instrumentalist Steve Asheim, with Glen supplying lyrics and arrangements. The full tracklisting, although not as yet arranged into any particular order, was as follows: 'Once Upon the Cross', 'Christ Denied', 'From Behind the Light Thou Shalt Rise', 'Kill the Christians', 'When Satan Rules This World', 'Confessional Rape', 'Trick or Betrayed', 'To Be Dead', and 'They are the Children of the Underworld'.

Glen talked me through the album. First of all, the title track, 'Once Upon the Cross'. 'It's about how some people think that Christ didn't actually die on the cross,' he deadpanned, referring to his favourite hate-figures: Christians. 'I hope he did die,' he added.

Indeed, at least two more of the tracks – 'Christ Denied' and 'Kill the Christians' – were about Glen's immense distaste for the Christian religion. 'I like realism; I like truth,' he insisted. 'Neither of which the Christian religion offers me. Instead I am offered lies and deceit, violence and corruption, and this offends me deeply.'

As an aside, Glen describes his arch-enemy in the US media, Denver Christian Rock DJ Bob Larsen, as 'one of the most pathetic, evil-hearted assholes' he's ever seen. 'He's never actually agreed to meet me and talk about this man-to-man,' Glen huffs. 'But I've tried to get to him a couple of times. He's always surrounded by security guards, though, wherever he goes. That's how much he's loved,' he spits.

Nevertheless, Glen admitted that 'every member of Deicide is licensed to carry a concealed weapon. When you've had as many death threats as we've had, you'd be stupid not to take some of it seriously. I carry a handgun with me everywhere, and I have a 12-gauge shotgun that I carry in my truck.'

How much of this anti-Christ stuff was just to grab attention, though?

'I hope as many Christians as possible are disturbed by what we're doing,' he said without missing a beat. 'If my truth brings attention on their lies, I have accomplished something. But that's just one of the reasons,' he added enigmatically.

Controversy had already begun to rage in the USA over the proposed sleeve artwork for the new album. An extremely lurid crucifixion scene designed for the band by English cult artist Trevor Brown, elsewhere on the inner sleeve, the body of Christ was depicted being disembowelled on an autopsy table.

'They wouldn't have minded so much if it had been some stupid cartoon monster with his guts spattered everywhere,' Glen reasoned. 'But because it is not at all cartoon-like – it's very, very realistically done, very vivid – they find it hard to swallow. I think it is extremely beautiful. The ideas come from a very deep place, but the image is true.' Glen insisted that, come what may, 'the artwork will be used. I will not let them deny us.'

What about 'When Satan Rules This World' and 'From Behind the Light Thou Shalt Rise' – are they about waiting for Satan to come, or the fact that he's already here?

'It's saying that Satan already rules this world,' he said. 'It's also about Jehovah's Witnesses that come knocking on your door peddling their lies, selling you their evil. The opening line of that one is, "Open the door / Jehovah, you whore . . . "'

Then there's 'Confessional Rape' . . .

'It's about your friendly neighbourhood priest who likes luring little children into places of sickness and perversion,' Glen explained matter-of-factly. 'That's the plot, anyway. The deeper message is that Christianity is one of the most violent and terroristic movements the world has ever seen. And of course, one of the most hypocritical, too. I mean, I wake up every morning with an erection. Are you telling me a priest *doesn't*? Or that he doesn't pull his pud once in a while? Yet they tell your children they'll go to eternal damnation if they do the same thing. This, I believe, is true evil.'

The lyrics to 'Trick or Betrayed', he said, were based on 'my thoughts on the Bible. That book is one of the biggest hoaxes ever perpetrated on mankind and it's about time it was exposed for what it is. A sick joke.' The lyrics to 'They are the Children of the Underworld' come from a very different kind of book. Based on the ancient text of one of the many black magic volumes Glen has collected over the years, sadly I was unable to keep up with much of his explanation of the lyrics. Something to do with 'the Seven Offspring of Anu, who have no name', but who were apparently there 'when the Earth was created'.

And, lastly, there is 'To Be Dead', Glen's grim prognosis for his own future.

'The title is self-explanatory, really. People talk about a life after death, but they're thinking of Hollywood,' he shrugged. 'All I know is, I have to go real soon. I've spent a lot of time thinking about it, putting myself into that place, and I think I know what's coming now. The opening line is, "To be dead / Is to always dream ... "'

Was he serious? Did he really believe that he's going to die soon?

'My number is coming up,' he intoned solemnly. 'Sometimes you are allowed to know these things, but most people don't want to know so they reject the information. I accept it.'

But not before April, because that's when Deicide would return to the UK for a series of live dates.

'It's all being arranged right now, so I don't have any dates for you yet. But the album will be out by then and so will the single.'

Single? Which track?

'We're not sure yet. But our record company tells us they think we've got a few really good catchy singles on this album, so there could be two or three.'

The mind boggled for a moment at the frankly nerve-jangling

prospect of Deicide spreading their own peculiar mist all over the *Top of the Pops* studio. Was he joking?

'I never joke about these things,' said Glen Benton. 'I take this stuff very, very, very seriously. This is a serious world we live in.'

And getting more so all the time . . .

When we spoke again a couple of months later, during the band's tour of Europe, Glen was already showing his, er, impatient side after being told that the band's new album, *Once Upon the Cross*, had not actually been released in time for the tour. 'How is anybody expected to appreciate what we're doing if no one has even heard the album yet?' thundered the clearly distraught vocalist – not unreasonably, under the circumstances.

The delay apparently stemmed from the unforeseen refusal of their record company's usual distribution outlet to print up copies of the controversial sleeve of the new album – a lurid Christ nailed to the cross with his innards exposed – on the grounds that it was 'blasphemous'. However, when Glen was then informed that the band's final gig of the tour, in Katwijk, had been cancelled by the local city council on 'religious grounds', Glen's mood went from bad to ballistic in no time at all.

'But we played there before and we had no trouble!' he protested.

But this concert was to have been part of the city's Easter Festival weekend, and the church objected strongly to what they described as the – you guessed it – 'blasphemous' nature of the *Once Upon the Cross* artwork.

'It is not I who is the emissary of evil, it is THEY!' he thundered when I broached the subject. As a result, he refused to do any more promotional interviews until his record company, Roadrunner, had booked him onto the first flight home to Florida the next day. Flight eventually booked, Glen reluctantly agreed to simmer down and get some of his scheduled interviews done. Big mistake. First on the list was a telephone interview with the only radio show in Holland that plays any metal, and therefore one of the only stations in Europe where you might actually hear the occasional Deicide track.

Expressing his disappointment at the cancellation of the band's Katwijk show, things were going well until the interviewer began to question Glen about rumours that animal rights activists in Britain had threatened to set off a bomb at one of his shows if Deicide ever tried to play in the UK again, and that this was the reason why the band had not scheduled any UK shows on this trip.

Glen began to get that tell-tale facial twitch he gets just before pressing the mental button marked 'nuclear'. 'Bullshit!' he told them, and other expressions of (unprintable) disbelief. Ignoring the irritation in Glen's voice – always a dicey option – the interviewer pressed on. Reflecting on an incident reported in the USA, where it was alleged that two teenage boys sacrificed a neighbour's dog – ostensibly 'in honour' of Deicide – Glen was asked if he felt proud that children sacrificed animals in his name.

Glen launched the rockets. 'Why don't you READ THE FUCKIN' LYRICS?' he roared. Glen was here to talk about his music and not anything else, he said.

Unperturbed, the Dutch interrogator ploughed on. Would Glen approve of radio stations sacrificing musicians in favour of better music? Glen, however, took this very seriously indeed. He asked who would be the first musician they should sacrifice: 'Me, maybe?'

'Yes,' said Dutch Radio. 'You.' They say you could hear the explosion a mile away and the interview was hurriedly curtailed, Glen flouncing off into the ever-darkening night, his Deicidely deeds to perform . . .

What next for Satan's little helper? Certainly not a job at MTV. They won't even consider playing any Deicide videos any more. Apparently, in-house MTV metal VJ Vanessa Warwick says she finds them 'blasphemous'.

Hmmm. If all else fails, we hear you've got a couple of mean hooves on you, Glen – how about a swift transfer to Manchester United? We hear they might be looking for a 'killer Number Seven' to replace that other close associate of the Dark Side and well-known sacrificer of sardines, 'Evil' Eric Cantona.

On the other hand, this could all be getting very silly . . .

CODA

Even after reading this piece again I'm not entirely sure I know what Glen was getting so worked up about. Well, I do, but neither of us are as young as we were then and I can't help feeling he must have got over it by now. It goes without saying that he didn't kill himself when he got to thirty-three – in 2000 – apparently describing suicides as 'cowards and losers'. Less inevitably, it seems he is still working and recording with Deicide, with whom he's put out over a dozen CDs and DVDs over the past fifteen years. I doubt he and the rest of the band still carry concealed weapons, though – if indeed they ever really did. Still, you've got to admire him, in one way. What would rock music – the loud, insanely heavy kind – be without people like Benton? More to the point, what would people like Glen do if they didn't have heavy metal to invest their energies in?

STONE TEMPLE PILOTS, 1995

Somehow, by 1994, I had become the 'grunge writer' on *RAW*. It hadn't been intentional; it was just the way the whole world was going then. I had never been much interested in interviewing new bands that hadn't done anything with their lives and careers yet; always enthralled by those that had. I was a story-junkie, a details-freak, and the big boys either riding high in private planes or pretending they hated every minute of life in the back of the limos were the ones where the good shit could be easily found. Slowly then, just as I had with Bon Jovi, Def Leppard and Iron Maiden in the 1980s, I had begun collecting the set in the '90s: Pearl Jam, Soundgarden, Nirvana . . .

The one that really fascinated me, though, was the band that was always routinely portrayed in the rock press as the great grunge pretenders: the Stone Temple Pilots. As far as I could see, their hideous crimes consisted solely of not coming from Seattle but from Los Angeles (still, then, the greatest city in the world, for me). Oh, and the fact that their singer, Scott Weiland, sounded a little like Pearl Jam singer Eddie Vedder (who sounded a little like Tim Buckley, but no one ever pulled him on it, presumably because most *NME* writers then had never heard of Tim Buckley).

So I was looking forward to this one. If only Weiland and the band had felt the same about me. Even after I fixed them up with some hash they kept their distance, waiting to see what I would eventually write before committing themselves to actually looking me in the eye on any sort of regular basis. When I brought Weiland a little gift to our interview – my own dog-eared copy of Nik Cohn's novel, *I Am Still the Greatest Says Johnny Angelo*, thinking that would get his attention, let him know I was Different From The Rest – it barely registered more than a flicker of interest from the singer. Well, more fool me . . .

Interview with Scott Weiland of Stone Temple Pilots, first published in RAW, *November 1995.*

I had just spent a week following the Stone Temple Pilots around on their autumn tour of the UK. From Glasgow to Nottingham to . . . wherever. Every day of the tour I was told to get ready for my interview with STP singer Scott Weiland but come the appointed hour, come the bullshit excuse from band manager Steve Stewart. Scott had a cold; Scott was busy; Scott's head was 'not in the right place'. What really made it weird, though, was that I was staying in the adjoining room to Weiland at one hotel and I could hear him through the walls, yelling and cursing, followed by what sounded like loud weeping. Jeez, I thought, what's up with this guy? Yes, he had been badly portrayed in the press as a grunge bandwagon-jumper. But so had Pearl Jam's Eddie Vedder and he wasn't . . . Actually, no, scrub that. Vedder had been done in by the bad press he got and was now refusing to do interviews at all; refusing even to help his band make videos anymore. Maybe I could understand where Weiland, whose band had been compared to a poor man's Pearl Jam, was coming from – or going to – after all.

Then, when we finally got back to London, I got a call at home asking me to meet up with Scott at his hotel. He's finally ready to talk, they said. Having been there so many times before, though, I turned up later that day with zero expectation that he would actually keep his word this time and sit down with me. Except he did! Turning up in an ankle-length black leather trench coat he told me he'd just bought that afternoon from Kensington Market, he added that he'd have to be 'kinda quick' as he was meeting his wife, who'd just flown in from LA, to take her to a movie. 'Which movie?' I asked nosily. 'The new Quentin Tarantino,' he said. '*Pulp Fiction*.' Oh, I said; that's cool. I heard it was quite good. 'Yeah,' he said.

So we sat together in the coffee shop of his hotel, where other nearby guests bothered us not at all. He may have sold three million copies of his latest album, *Purple*, with his band Stone Temple Pilots but that don't mean shit, daddy, here in the UK, where most people don't even know what Eddie Vedder looks like. But hey, let's not go there – yet – right? Besides, fame and wealth was never the whole deal for Scott Weiland anyway. 'Money isn't really an issue; that's all relative,' he says. 'There's security in the fact that we can own a home, but that's it. I spend more money eating out than I used to, but I still buy pants and shirts for $1.25. There's other elements of success that are far more confusing, like the idea of celebrity. That's such a misconception. Unfortunately, people think that a public person is always a public person, and that you have these responsibilities to other people because you influence them. But the only thing we feel ultimately responsible to is music.'

What was his take on the death earlier this summer of Kurt Cobain? He lit a cigarette. Kurt was, he says, 'one of the three people I admired more than anybody in the last fifteen years of rock or pop or whatever you want to call it. The other two would be [ex-Jane's Addiction, now Porno For Pyros frontman] Perry Farrell and [R.E.M.'s] Michael Stipe, probably.'

Pressed for his feelings on the day he heard Kurt had taken his own life, Scott is extremely reticent to be drawn too far.

'I don't like how certain people used the situation to elevate themselves to a certain . . . likeness of the same situation.'

He asks for the tape-recorder to be turned off for a moment then goes into a tirade against a well-known British band that managed to clamber aboard the cover of an even more well-known British music weekly by dint of their own cloudy views on 'the truth' behind Cobain's sad, mind-fucking suicide. 'I don't think anyone could have stopped it,' he is saying as we turn the machine back on. 'I've heard people say he should have had someone there to take care of him but from what I've been told, he was pretty determined to do it.' A pause, then: 'You want to know how I felt when I heard he was dead? I was sad. I was just really, really . . . sad.'

Were you surprised?

Long pause.

'Yeah. Actually, I was surprised. I really was.'

Dead junky, all right, you could see it coming. But a gun in the mouth?

'The experiences of how drugs can affect your mind, I understand that kind of pain, you know. But ... I dunno. I can't say I wasn't shocked. I found it extremely shocking.'

And now?

'I dunno. We were on tour with the Meat Puppets this summer and they had spent some time with Nirvana, playing on the *Unplugged* thing and playing with them on tour. And they told me that they'd noticed this, er, this really deep sadness in Kurt.' His eyes clamber the walls for the words. 'I think there are times when we all have a hard time getting out of the darkness, the haze, the fog, whatever you wanna call it. Sometimes it seems like there's no light at all, I guess. But I have no right to try and analyse this. The whole thing is just ...'

He looks away, shakes his head.

'I would have hoped that the daughter and wife would be one of those, like, grounding sort of forces. With me, it's like, you know, I had my wife flown out to London because I've been feeling low and depressed lately. And within twenty-four hours, you know, I feel alive and ready to participate. She's a beautiful person.'

Maybe Courtney Love wasn't the home-loving kind. He nods his head.

'Her thing was counter-productive upon him completely. I mean I know her, I've hung out with her and stuff,' he begins, then remembering the tape is rolling again, changes his mind and refuses to say more.

People say, if you're so disenchanted with it all, why don't you just stop?

'But that's what I do. Music is what I do! What am I supposed to do – sit around and fucking chop wood? It's really not a choice, you know?'

Would he rather sell fuck-all and be loved by the critics (like the Meat Puppets and Fugazi, et al)?

'Well, not really, because I don't think success or lack of it makes the work itself any more substantial or insubstantial. It's just an old-fashioned perspective.'

Had he ever considered suicide?

'Sure.'

Because of the band, or because of something more personal?

'There isn't anything much more personal for me than music. The first time I started singing with a band I suddenly realised why I had never felt at home in the shower with the big fat jocks that thought about nothing except football and getting into High School girls' panties.'

But music in itself isn't enough, is it? Otherwise you wouldn't be so miserable all the time.

'You can get to a point where the music's not worth all the rest of the shit, and you decide to fold, or you can decide to try and enjoy at least the positive aspects. I think that's where we're at right now. I think the making of *Purple* was a rebirth. It gave us a chance to live again and start to enjoy things, instead of feeling like trapped animals.'

It was all down to 'a basic lack of respect', he says. A 'blanket of the wrong kind of recognition. I don't think there's any fucking musician or entertainment artist that doesn't pay attention to the music press, although most of them will deny it till their death bed, as they do. That could have influenced some of our peers that we hadn't yet met or hadn't yet played with. There might be certain bands, whatever, that we had admired and loved and had these desires to play and perform with, to write with or whatever, and there were certain people within that elite realm of alternative godliness that had these predisposed ideas and notions of what we were, what we were about, before they even, you know, gave us a chance. And that really fucked with us a lot. We were a band of people that had a lot of confidence in the songs that we wrote and so at first we were able to say, "Fuck you, fuck you, fuck you". Then after a while it started running on us and we were thinking like, "Maybe they're right", you know, maybe there really was something wrong with what we're doing. I know that we really didn't believe that, but I mean, you start to wonder and so we took some time off and didn't really do anything.'

This was when they seriously considered jacking it in.

'It was like, "Well, what are we going to do?" Fucking, you know, go away and chop wood because some snotty critics want us to piss off and die? And so, we started to get together and write songs.'

Did you start to feel self-conscious in front of each other?

'Yes, we did; it was really strange. It was a bit like making love to a woman that you've made love to for many years; you suddenly turn the lights down and put music on, have a little wine . . . but there's no way that's going to work. It has to be real. If you feel guilty over something, you're holding back on your loved one and you're not cutting to the chase on what the problem is and . . . and nobody talks to the other. And then you try to have sex and you don't make the connection at all. That's what it was like. It was like fucking, or even worse, masturbating. But it was because everyone was ready to go into their own trip.'

He admits that he and STP bassist Robert DeLeo 'had a showdown during this period . . . It was really very sad, especially as we'd been such close friends for a long time – I knew that he was saying to our manager all the time, "I don't think I'm going to make another record, I don't think I want to be in this band anymore", and it's like . . . 'cos I knew that if one of us left this band it just wouldn't be the same band.'

What about Scott? Had he thought about leaving the band?

'No, I . . . see, I had faith, for one thing. Robert and I are like complete polar opposites. He chooses to live his life one way, and I choose another. And either we get on really well together, or, like, not at all. It's probably why we work so well together.'

So at this point did you start to feel a little more optimistic?

'Oh, yes! As far as musically, definitely! I was still really upset with the way the vibe of the band was going. But I knew that part of that was up to me to change things. So I decided to get my head straight again after we made the record, which was completely, artistically satisfying and very therapeutic.'

He still refuses to specify, but word is the juice count ran mighty high for a while there.

'I don't like getting into specifics,' he eyes me. 'But I was sick, yeah.'

Strange that you have this fantastic, exciting record, yet in a way – because of your experiences with the first record – you had to wait to see if it was all right to get excited about it.

'I didn't have to wait to be told. I knew we had something hot,' he says defiantly. 'I think that may be part of the deal – we've never needed good reviews to sell records. I think the critics feel left behind sometimes.'

Where were you exactly when you heard that *Purple* had gone straight into the US charts at Number One?

'I knew exactly what time of day it would be announced as being top of the charts. I was at home with [wife] Janina. I had actually been warned that it might go in that high. The single had come out, "Vasoline", and people were like going crazy over it. And so there was some talk about the album, but ... It was like Christmas Eve. I was waiting around like a ten-year-old child, and I got a call from our manager and he said, "Congratulations, you've got a Number One record".'

He smiles for the first time all day.

'Within an hour the record company had bottles of champagne littered all over the house. I put it in the closet with all the others. It's great, 'cos I can have a party once a year, and people will think that I'm this lavish host.'

Getting to Number One, that still has that ring, that oomph to it.

'Oh, yeah! There's no better than that. Even the most cynical of people can't contain themselves when they hear that. On one level it's kind of silly, it's like relating it to a sporting event or something, but still, there's always this certain, like, mystery associated to going to Number One and its surrounding excitement. Who can help but get caught up in it?'

Are you a democratic band?

'Yeah, although people's ways of arguing are very different. Some are better at it than others. With some you have to not only wait for catchphrases or smart words, but also sharp projectiles – sharp glass on the dressing-room floor!'

He could have been describing the scene I witnessed backstage at the band's first Brixton Academy show.

'It was [guitarist] Dean [DeLeo]! Anyway, we had a discussion about politics and who are the oppressed and who is the oppressor. And what kind of propaganda is thrown out to other countries to lead them to believe that one is the country oppressed and the other is the oppressor.'

Beats arguing over dope, I suppose.

Already 1995 looks like being another busy year for the band. The plan, still being modelled when Weiland and I talked, was that they return to the studio as early as February to bang out their next album, at least six songs for which have already been 'sketched out', with a view to having the finished product on the street as early as May.

One new song is said to concern his father. Weiland says his first musical memory is of driving around in his father's Chevvy pick-up, listening to Hank Williams on the car radio. His father was a big country-and-western fan who taught his son how to yodel. Listen to 'Creep' from the *Core* album, and you can still hear Scott's father's influence at work.

After his parents divorced, Scott's natural father had another son, just nine months younger than he; they would stay together every summer. But when Weiland was just eleven years old, his stepbrother was hit by a car while playing in the street, and died. After that, the summer visits petered out. No coincidence, then, perhaps, that he once confessed that the song he most wishes he had written is Jane's Addiction's 'Had a Dad'. When his father actually showed up backstage on the band's US tour last summer, it was the first time Scott had seen his real father in, by his own estimation, 'seven or eight years'.

'After all these years of denying I had this other life, seeing him, and hearing him say that he is so proud of me, triggered these emotions that I had never dealt with. I completely broke down and didn't know why I was hysterical.'

Another of the new songs is said to reflect the singer's troubled upbringing as a Catholic, and the way he blames this for filling him with an eternal sense of shame about his (according to the Church) 'unconventional' sexual desires. He admits to having his first orgasm at the age of twelve when he and another boy from school built a dugout in a hay bale inside a barn they used to play in, and began fooling around with three young girls. Young Scott claimed that he knew exactly what he was doing, but his classmates at school decided that, in reality, their red-haired buddy was something of a pervert.

'After that barn incident I was made to feel very guilty,' Scott recalled years later. 'That destroyed me. I thought, "I'm a complete freak. I have this bizarre sexual appetite which has completely ruined my chances of ever being part of this whole thing that I was not part of before."'

A married man still in the bloom of a long-term relationship, Scott claims he has always looked down on the groupie scene.

'We don't really have any groupies – I don't think anybody in the band could just walk up to somebody and use who they are to manipulate them into taking their clothes off.'

Or, as Dean DeLeo says: 'This is the Nineties, man. Sex, drugs and rock 'n' roll went out a long while ago. With everything going on these days, it's masturbation, crack and Madonna.'

And, of course, as on both previous STP albums, there is expected to be at least one song about Janina Castaneda Kent – or Mrs Weiland to you, chief. There are probably hundreds of Scott's lyrics that deal with his longstanding relationship with the beautiful Janina, although he will only ever admit to two: 'Loungefly' (written as his way of saying 'sorry' for all the times in the days when the band was still called Mighty Joe Young and Scott would borrow money from her on the pretext of needing something for the band, then head straight to the nearest bar) and 'Still Remains' (simply an open declaration of love: 'Take a bath / I'll drink the water that you leave').

And yet, clouds still hover menacingly at that musty interface between rumour, innuendo and cold, hard facts. The nastiest and potentially most band-splitting rumour recently concerned the DeLeo brothers, who insiders claimed were considering suing Weiland over the publishing rights to some of the songs.

'Absolutely not true,' said Steve Stewart when I put it to him. 'I have no idea where that comes from. I mean, they're together every day at the moment, writing new songs. It's hard to imagine they would be doing that if they were arguing over who owns existing songs,' he points out, not unreasonably. 'This stuff about Robert and Scott not getting on is old.'

Maybe. But then Robert and Scott are like chalk and cheese. Where Robert is relaxed, groomed, certain of what he likes [1940s fashion and 1990s music] and what he doesn't like [anything else], Scott is neurotic and insecure; loud and over-concerned. Possibly the only thing they really have in common is their determination not to let the hysteria – positive and negative – that surrounds everything STP do or don't do, get to them. For a time Robert lived in his car, parking outside friends' homes, while working occasionally as a counter clerk in places like Orange Julius. Up until recently, in a doomed bid to keep his feet on the ground and not fall for all the 'rock star bullshit', Weiland drove a 1986 Nissan pick-up truck.

As Scott told another interviewer, 'You have to keep in mind why you're doing this. Keep it like it was when you'd pick up a tennis racquet and play air guitar in front of the mirror.'

One thing we can be certain of is that the new Stone Temple Pilots album will again be produced by Brendan O'Brien.

'Brendan is such a catalyst, to playing us off each other and being like a mediator,' Scott tells me. 'As well as being a great producer, he's a psychologist as well – or should be. I can imagine what it must be like working with a band like the Black Crowes and those egos!'

Although they originally expressed a desire to have an album out 'by the summer', the only thing they are really determined to do now, they say, is take their time. Steve Stewart has vowed not to let anyone near the studio until the thing is completed, to make up for the under-the-microscope atmosphere surrounding *Purple*.

'I can see this next one having a few more issue-driven songs than *Purple*,' says Scott. He's thinking, he says, of one idea in particular to do with war. 'I think years ago things were more black-and-white. The reasons to fight a war or the reasons to protect yourself seemed to be more clear-cut. Until people in the modern world started realising just how much money you could make from waging war and then all of a sudden you get people who run corporations saying, well, if we can influence global policy or international policies and start a conflict and make another thirty-five billion dollars, let's do it! So war is dirty now. War is dirty; it's always been nasty but now it's not even Saint Joan of Arc versus Evil anymore.'

It's funny how people had never heard of Kuwait until suddenly they were concerned about the 'gold in the ground' (oil fields). 'Oh, yeah. When Janina and I were on our honeymoon, in Greece on the island of Santorini, we hit this little artist village that was this old ransacked tomato factory that had been turned into a little artists' hole. It was right on the water. We would go out and have coffee with them, smoke some hash and just talk, went swimming – right in that beautiful water. People from all over the world. There was this guy from Yugoslavia, Sean was his short name – his real name was something I could hardly pronounce – plus a couple of people from Italy, United States, Australia. A sort of little commune.'

Did they recognise you?

He shrugged.

'Um . . . I said I was a musician. I was an artist. And that was it. I was equal to them. I was another person who made a living, writing words down – which seems like such a stupid thing.'

It can certainly get you into a lot of trouble.

'Yes, bizarre thought. I was speaking to Chris Kirkwood, the bassist from the Meat Puppets. We were talking about the fact that we know that there's gotta be this huge FBI file on us. The FBI keeps files on people and public figures who speak openly about anything at all. All the true evils support our government!'

And on that thought we will leave it. For now. Scott Weiland and the Stone Temple Pilots might not change the world, but they so desperately want to change and progress as people, you sense they might just make some of the best records you'll ever hear. Or die trying.

Scott says the band will also donate a song to the educational project *Schoolhouse Rock!* (due out Summer 1995) and will no doubt continue to draw crowds wherever they play. The last time I saw Scott Weiland he was standing in the middle of the dance-floor, gyrating like a stoned go-go dancer at a post-gig party for the band after that first London show. Dancing with Janina to Abba's 'Gimme! Gimme! Gimme! (A Man After Midnight)', his gig over, his shirt loose, his head completely bald, he actually looked happy. Earlier at the party, when I asked why he did it (shave his nut), he just smiled serenely and said, 'I wanted to look more like Madonna.'

So now you know.

CODA

A few days after our interview, Scott Weiland had shaved his head completely bald. Interesting, I thought. R.E.M.'s Michael Stipe had just unveiled his own newly shaven bonce in the then-current 'What's the Frequency, Kenneth?' video. Three months later, I had also shaved my head completely bald. Like Stipe, my hair was already thinning; shaving it off was the only way I could see to keep some dignity. Unlike me and Michael, Scott shaved his off because he wanted to make some sort of statement. About what, I could only guess – pressures of fame, insistence on private personal concerns over public perception and popularity? Just feeling, you know, fucked up? Don't know. But fifteen years later, Weiland appears to have moved on very little. His hair is back and he's even skinnier now than he was then, but the stories of drug busts, abandoned spells in rehab, relationship breakdowns and arrests by police have piled up with depressing regularity ever since. Along the way, he did make two very good albums with Velvet Revolver – the post-Guns N' Roses band formed by Slash and Duff McKagan. As I write, however, Scott is back in a re-formed line-up of STP, still refusing to come out of his hotel room some days; others, probably wishing he could be left alone to watch a movie with his wife . . .

WILDHEARTS, 1995

The only British rock band in the mid-1990s to offer any serious challenge to the near-hegemony of the new grunge-generation of US rock bands was the Wildhearts. Fronted by former Quireboys guitarist Ginger (real name: David Walls), the Wildhearts were a huge surprise on a number of levels. Having known Ginger well for some years before as the most out-of-it, eyes-hidden-behind-his-hair one in the Quireboys, a band known internationally for their ability to empty any bar before lunchtime, to discover that beneath that shoddy, apologetic exterior was one of the most extraordinary talents this country has ever known was like finding treasure at the bottom of the toilet bowl. You can't quite believe what you're seeing, you just know you're going to have to get up to your armpits in shit and get hold of it.

So it was that I tagged along for one of their then-frequent *Top of the Pops* appearances in the summer of 1995. Ginger may now have been leading one of the most original-sounding – like the Beatles meets Metallica – bands of its era, but that didn't mean he had changed his own personal habits none. He was still drinking – obviously – still asking awkward questions of anyone bold enough to try to actually interview him. Still firing and hiring band members like there was no tomorrow, which for Ginger there really wasn't. And I still wasn't sure how he did it, or for how long he'd be able to keep it up. I could only stand back and admire . . .

Top of the Pops is recorded at Elstree Studios, in Hertfordshire, every Wednesday evening. It is the same BBC studio where they record *Eastenders* and as we drive through the studio gates, Ricky Butcher, the manic mechanic, is being chauffeured away, smoking a cigarette and peering into our car to see if he recognises anybody. He doesn't. Parking, Nigel from the video shop passes by on foot, and looking pensive. It's funny. I never knew how close rock 'n' roll Shangri-La was to Albert Square. I half expect to find the Wildhearts propping up the bar of the Queen Vic.

'Nah, they don't sell real beer, just coloured water,' Wildhearts mainman Ginger wrinkles his nose. 'Besides, we've got our own port-able pub, haven't we?' It has just gone 3.00 p.m. and the band's record company minder has just returned from his second beer-run. A large plastic dustbin full of (very) cold beers seems to follow us everywhere.

We meet up outside on the *Top of the Pops* lawn, where the band appear to have been enjoying lunch – one large pizza and one large bottle of tequila (now empty). It's one of those brilliant English sum-mer's days. The sun gets in your eyes and the sky just sits there thinking. Strange birds tweet merrily in your brain. This is the fourth time the Wildhearts have done *TOTP*. Their first time was with 'Caffeine Bomb' (Number Thirty-One in February 1994); their second with 'Geordie in Wonderland' (also Number Thirty-One, January 1995). And then there was last week's appearance with the new 'I Wanna Go Where the People Go' single. Billed as a *TOTP* exclusive, it immediately leapt into the charts at Number Sixteen. Hence, this rare opportunity to witness Ginger and crew on *TOTP* two weeks running.

It's unusual to find the show giving such devoted attention to an out-and-out rock band. But then the producer of the show, Ric Blaxill, is such a fan of the Wildhearts that he actually got up and pretended to be the second guitarist last week, prancing around in a black bobble-hat and cross-shaped guitar. 'Ric is just a huge fan of the band; I once caught him strutting around his office, playing air guitar to one of their records,' one of the production staff confides at one point.

Blaxill is unabashed. 'I've always been a Wildhearts fan,' he tells me. 'Going back to when I was the producer of the *Breakfast Show* at Radio One, I got "TV Tan" playlisted there. And *Top of the Pops* was so unfriendly to guitar bands in the past, when I got here, I thought, right, if there are any bands out there that are guitar-oriented but are brilliant, let's have 'em on. Hopefully, people will see the Wildhearts on *Top of the Pops* and it will spawn a new generation of rock bands.'

There will be no need for a repeat performance from Ric this week, however, as the band have their new guitarist in tow this time: former Senseless Things mainman, Mark Keds. A friend of Ginger's and a committed Wildhearts supporter for some time, this is not actually Mark's first appearance on *TOTP* with them: he joined them for that lone 'Geordie in Wonderland' performance, when they were also accompanied by ex-Wolfsbane member, Jess Hately, on mandolin.

Although Keds didn't audition for the job – vacant since the acrimonious departure last year of CJ – as bass player Danny McCormack remarks, 'You can learn music, but you can't learn personality. I mean, Mark's a good bloke, isn't he?' And a talented one. He's been at Number Sixteen before, when the Senseless Things got there in 1993, with 'Easy to Smile'. He also now knows how quickly the buzz can fade. It was the last time the Senseless Things ever did *Top of the Pops*.

Keds joined the Wildhearts, though, he says, not for another chance to appear on the nation's oldest teen-prog, but 'because I really like the album. I've always known how talented Ginger is, so the idea of working together isn't so strange, really.' The Senseless Things had quietly broken up last January. 'We didn't tell anybody because we wanted to get going with something else first,' he shrugs. 'Then this came along.'

Keds admits he wasn't sure at first if it was the right thing for him to do.

'I've been working in the studio, and I wasn't sure if I wanted to go on the road for a long time, which is what joining this band means.'

He says he literally made up his mind yesterday evening.

'A decision had to be made and I couldn't do it, so I got out the cards. I cut them and pulled one out at random. I decided that if it was a ten or under, the answer was no. A picture card or ace, and I was in.'

And?

'I got the ace of spades.' He eyes me seriously for a moment. 'I'm not joking. That's what happened. I mean, how could I not do it after that?' How long it will last, though, nobody knows. He yawns meaningfully. 'What did Ginger say when you spoke to him?' He said to ask you. 'Ah, well . . .'

What Ginger actually says is that he knew Mark was the man for the job, 'the day I met him. But it's like getting married or falling in love – you want to have a night on the town first. It was a similar thing with my girlfriend.' He squints at me through his pink John Lennon specs. 'We'd been going out for ages before we both realised we were in love. Suddenly it was . . . obvious.'

Ginger and I sit sipping cold ale on the hot grass, he waxing wise, me ear-wigging, everything as per. Talking about the current escalating success of the band, he says: 'I mean, honestly, I can't really figure it out. Now suddenly, it's our time. The band is back, and the whole personality thing is back in fashion. You know, if you're going to be boring, hopefully you ain't gonna work in the Nineties. And this band is anything but boring. So it was one of those done things that was sealed before we even got the envelope.'

TOTP apart, Keds will make his live debut with the band at a string of UK dates hurriedly being put together for late June, followed by a headline appearance at this year's Phoenix Festival, in July, with the Senseless Things bidding a fond adieu below them on the bill. Mark will play with both bands.

'We've got a lot of wasted time to make up for,' says Ginger. 'We haven't really toured at all for the last nine months. The trouble is, if you're sitting around on your arse, you can draw some comfort from it. It's dangerous, it's like a lazy, lethargic cancer sets in. You don't really want to do much more than what you're doing, which is sitting around on your arse, drinking, taking drugs. So we just thought, well, fuck it, let's stop all that shit. So we've cleaned ourselves up – a bit. And we're gonna get out and do what we haven't been doing for a while.'

He's obviously itching to get back out there.

'It's like after working all this time, God's just gone, "OK, there's a break for you." Like, we've tried hard, we haven't given up our values or compromised ourselves, we haven't sucked cock to get here. We've done it all our own way, and it's paid off. People have finally realised, they don't only break computers and burn hotel rooms, they actually write good songs as well. I mean, we've been offered the keys to the fucking kingdom before, we've been offered the world, if we just do it this way, or just do it that way, or if we just take this much shit. But we've always said, we'd rather not do anything than do things someone else's way. It's gotta be our way, no matter how big or small.

'So now we feel like the most proud band in the world, because we've done it all our own way. Some bands come along and have a Number One with their first album, and good luck to them. But I feel a bit more proud of this because we've had a lot of shit and we've sailed through it. We found the light at the end of the tunnel and just followed the fucker. Just blindly, like a load of mad fucking sperms, just followed the light . . .' His eyes are suddenly very far away. 'I always had a feeling it would feel fuckin' good. And, you know what? It fuckin' does,' he grins like a crow.

With or without the charts, though, the Wildhearts have already become a massive influence in British rock in the Nineties. 'It's the attitude they like, probably,' says Ginger. 'Not putting your cock and balls on the table for success. If we can instil that kind of self-respect in young bands, well, glad to be of service. Most bands don't have any say in their videos, or get involved with the artwork for their albums. Next thing they know, they're big, they're on *Top of the Pops*, and they don't know why. They haven't got any values in the band. Just to have hits and do what they're told.'

Ginger says he is particularly proud of the fact that the Wildhearts have got to Number Sixteen in the charts without putting out their singles in the usual multi-format fashion.

'It's a rip-off,' he says. 'Vinyl, cassette or CD, with us you get the same tracks every time. That way they buy it once, not four fuckin' times. So if we're in the charts, you know it's for real. There's none of this different mixes and different B-sides crap. I think bands that allow themselves to be prostituted like that really should be ashamed of themselves. They should be hung by their fuckin' balls.'

I ask what happened in New York: first the band were relocating for good, next they were back in Britain.

'The first couple of weeks were great, the second couple of weeks were shite,' he frowns. 'As soon as we started all living together in this one room in Brooklyn, it went to pieces. I read that letter you printed in *RAW*, if that's what you mean,' he says, referring to a blistering missive from someone signing themselves Rob Zombie's Dreadlocks, accusing the band of deserting their British fans for the lure of the Yankee-dollar. Ginger was clearly not amused: 'These little shitbags won't even put their fuckin' names on the letters they write!' he cries. 'Well, Rob Zombie's Dreadlocks, come and talk to me about it, 'cos I'd love to talk to you, Rob Zombie's fuckin' Dreadlocks!'

Isn't that a strand of the same sentiment you were tapping into, though, when you wrote 'Turning American', from the very first Wildhearts EP, *Mondo Akimbo a-Go-Go*?

'No. It's a resentment of people doing well. It's not just focused on America. It's focused on anything people can collectively moan about. That sad little cunt that wrote into *RAW*, he really fuckin' pissed me off that guy, because he didn't have any basis for what he said. Nobody said we were going to America and never coming back. What really upsets me is that we might have fans that fuckin' stupid. Most Wildhearts fans, I get letters from them, I hear from them, and they're a really cool bunch of people. They want to get off their arses and do something. But you don't get too many letters in magazines from them because they're too busy doing something else. It's only the sad little cunts in the house with nothing better to do. He hasn't even read the lyrics. "Turning American" has got fuck-all to do with living in America. You silly little cunt! I bet you don't even go to the fuckin' pub, let alone America!'

The smile is back but you can tell the rant isn't over yet. Not in this lifetime.

'Tell Mr Rob Fuckin' Zombie's Dreadlocks that we don't need his support and understanding. And his mother's got a beard! And she came to our last gig and Danny fucked her! That's right, Mr Rob Fuckin' Zombie's Dreadlocks, DANNY FUCKED YOUR MOTHER!'

Identified early on as one of the ones Least Likely To, Ginger hates to be underestimated. Kicked out of the Quireboys – who were then on the verge of major chart success – for his drinking and general untogetherness, unable even, as he puts it, 'to get into the Marquee for free, after playing there about nine fuckin' times!', some people don't like to say I Told You So but Ginger, perhaps understandably, is not one of them.

'I heard the rumours. I was a heroin addict. I was gonna drop the Wildhearts into my own personal hell. And this was from people I had respect for. This from friends! Now every single one of those friends that tries to get back with the band, I can turn around with my hand on my heart and say, "Fuck you!" And it's a great feeling. Tell the cunts to fuck off,' he says. He is not smiling. 'I'm not for pushing it in anyone's face. But if any of them come crawling, I shall say, "You weren't there when I needed you, I don't need you anymore!"'

We watch the rehearsal. Ginger plays the drums, Ritch pretends to sing. The camera guys rehearse knocking people out of the way. I eavesdrop on a conversation between Jimmy Nail, who is also on the show, and Ric Blaxill. 'I heard about you and them Wildhearts last week,' Nail says in his broad Geordie accent. Ric smiles, 'Oh, yes?' but looks edgy. 'Aye. You'll be fuckin' touring with them next!' the big man admonishes him. 'Yes,' Ric smiles. 'You wanna watch yourself,' Nail tells him, then turns away. The Wildhearts finish and Jimmy goes through his paces. Not bad. He plays, he sings, and he's just sold a million albums.

Over on the stage the Wildhearts have just vacated, Björk and Skunk Anansie ready themselves for their rehearsal. We're in a much smaller room than you might imagine from watching at home and it's a novel experience seeing so many different artists doing their giddy stuff in such a dark, small space. Do your single and piss off. It's still the best show there is.

Outside in the corridor, the Wildhearts are having their photograph taken. These are the first pictures they have done with Mark in the band. They do their best in cramped circumstances to throw the camera some attitude. Further along the corridor, behind them, members of Oasis are sidling into the studio for their turn. 'Eh up, lads, nice pose!' Oasis singer Liam Gallagher calls out. 'Nice straight backs now!'

At first it is unclear whether Liam is being sarcastic or just trying to be friendly. But the look on Ginger's face, as he turns around and glares at him, says that none of this is funny. The two singers eye each other expressionlessly, Liam poised at the door of the studio staring down at us, Ginger – the photo-session forgotten – staring back at him, hard.

For a moment, it looks like it's about to go off. Then Liam ducks inside the studio and Ginger turns wordlessly back to the camera. Later, I discover that on the previous week's show, Ginger had wandered uninvited into the Oasis dressing room, in search of a drink and the chance to say hello. Liam took one look at him, then turned to one of his security men and said he wanted Ginger out of his dressing room now. Ginger was swiftly shown the door.

Maybe it's like a mods-versus-rockers thing, I dunno, but it's a shame because to the non-committed, there's very little difference between the music of the Wildhearts and that of Oasis. Good lyrics, strong melodies, great guitars, true spirit, real commitment. Just different haircuts. And the fact that Oasis don't move on stage, whereas the Wildhearts never stop. So what's the problem? Ginger can't tell me because there is no problem – in his mind. And Oasis won't tell me because if you're not seen to be with them, you're against them.

Danny and I stand there and watch them rehearse. 'I think they're a great band,' he says. 'Great band, great bunch of blokes. We all get on great together.' Danny is clearly pissed.

The programme itself, in case you missed it, was a cracker. The Wildhearts opened the show; Oasis finished it. In between, me and the rest of the kids hopped from stage to stage watching Björk, Skunk, Jimmy and the rest with our mouths open and our botts pumping. I didn't know what it meant and I didn't care. Ginger, of course, is different. He not only knows what it means, he cares too. A true weirdo.

'Rock music is the greatest because it's live, it's not tapes, and it could fuck up at any moment,' he tells me at one point.

A bit like the Wildhearts, you mean?

'A bit like life,' he retorts, then catches himself being too serious and laughs it off.

Cue title music. Roll credits. Grab zapper . . .

CODA

I'm pleased – relieved – to say that Ginger and the Wildhearts are still going strong. They've had their ups and downs – god, have they had their ups and downs – going through, at last count, something like fourteen different line-ups, even splitting up for a spell in the late 1990s. But you'd need a silver bullet to kill off someone like Ginger and thankfully no one's thought to load their critical pistols with one yet. If anything, the new web-driven era of MySpace pages and downloadable tracks has benefited them. Ginger and the Wildhearts were always about taking the path least trodden – and making sure that no one else can possibly follow, by setting fire to the trail they've left behind them. Exactly the sort of band I once dreamed all bands were like, back when I started writing seriously – if that's the word and it probably isn't – about this stuff. Long may they – and it – drive the rest of us round the fucking bend and back again.

GUNS N' ROSES, 1994

The following piece is chiefly interesting now for the bizarre Q&A at the end between myself and Slash and Duff. The first half of the story became a sort of template for a great many similar such tales I would be required to write over the next few years, as fascination with the story of Guns N' Roses began to outstrip and then overlap any chance of something new to say about them. For those of us that were there, the meaning of those days continues to be dissected in books (including some written by me), TV programmes, magazine and newspaper articles and various other new media guises.

For me, personally, however, the chief reason I am now fond of this piece is for the section at the end that reports verbatim a radio interview I did with Slash and Duff one drunken New Year's holiday at the start of 1990. The radio interview was never broadcast – for obvious reasons, once you read the transcript – but it may just have been the most entertaining piece I ever did for that medium. Anyway, it still makes me laugh. It's also a strange kind of insight into the real personalities of Slash and Duff, both of whom – like all of us – have changed a great deal in the past twenty years. Although not so much that their contribution here doesn't still ring true, bless them ...

Guns N' Roses article, first published in RAW, *December 1994.*

It had been a strange, ghostly kind of Christmas for the members of Guns N' Roses; a time of celebration, only no one could remember exactly what it was they were supposed to be celebrating. 1989 had been a dog, and no argument allowed; the arse-end of a worryingly downward curve even their closest friends had feared the band would not be able to pull out of in time to save themselves from the kind of ignoble end the much-despised rock press had been predicting for them since the release of their first all too aptly named *Appetite for Destruction* album, two-and-half-years before.

The massive and – whatever they say now – even more massively unpredicted success of *Appetite*, and a world tour that took them away from home for the weirdest part of two years, had left the band, on their return to Los Angeles at the end of 1988 – as Slash wearily put it – 'richer in one way, poorer in others'. A year on, they had roused themselves from their collective torpor just once: an aborted attempt at recording material for a follow-up album, over three listless, bad-tempered weeks in Chicago during the summer, for which Axl and Izzy hadn't even bothered to show up. And now, despite four shows supporting the Rolling Stones at the 70,000-capacity LA Coliseum in September, outside of the Top Forty, as far as the rest of the world was concerned, Guns N' Roses had all but vanished off the face of the earth.

Newly made millionaires, the truth was that they didn't know how to adjust to the experience; the sudden adulation, the unexpected bitterness and subterranean jealousies, the bullshit that being famous, even more than being rich, brings down on your head, wherever you go, whatever you do, even among your friends and family – sometimes *especially* among your friends and family. Old friends become lost; new friends become best. Band friends become business partners. 'It's just fucked,' Slash shook his head by way of explanation whenever we talked about it. 'The whole thing's just fucked,' he would repeat, pulling his hair down further over his eyes. Or as Duff told me, his pink, unshaven face scrunching up into a tight little ball of indignation, 'Before we did *Appetite*, we were down, no money, going through all this shit. Now it's like a whole different bunch of shit to deal with. You got people who want to sue you, you got people that want to fight you, you can't go to clubs . . . It's a horror having to deal with shit like that all the time, man! It's a horror.'

And of course, the drugs didn't help, either. Not so much the fact of drugs – Guns N' Roses had always been a drug-conscious band, as a cursory scan of their lyric-sheets would quickly testify – more the sheer quantity and choice of drugs they were imbibing on a day-to-day basis by 1989. Gone were the 'recreational' weed-and-wine highs of '85 and '86. Cocaine and heroin were now the popular drugs of choice amongst the Gunners' inner circle. Even Axl, who had always complained of unsettling experiences on anything more strenuous than a few tokes and a couple of beers, went on record as saying that an occasional 'lost weekend' on smack was not entirely out of the question for him these days.

But Axl was a dabbler; a dilettante when it came to committed drug abuse. The real culprits were Slash, Izzy and Steven, all of whom had dabbled with heroin, on and off, since the earliest days of the band's success. Now, in 1989, with nothing better to do and all the dollars they needed to do it with, all three had become seriously addicted. It was an intolerable situation. As Duff said, 'It would mess with the band; guys wouldn't show up for rehearsal; guys would come to gigs all fucked up.'

Something had to be done, and, as always, Axl had been the one to finally do it, taking things into his own hands by announcing, mid-set from the stage of the LA Coliseum the first night they opened for the Stones, that he was leaving the band because, he said pointedly, too many members of the band had been 'dancing with Mr Brownstone' – a thinly veiled reference to the harrowing excesses that now threatened to pull apart not just the band's career, but also the lives of most of the individuals in it. Like the boy who cried wolf, nobody was really sure if Axl would carry out his threat – he had made it so many times before when he felt the others weren't 'seeing things right'. But then, nobody was really sure he wouldn't.

'He's about crazy enough, I think, yes,' was manager Alan Niven's terse comment at the time. In the end, after extracting firm promises from Slash, Izzy and Steven that they would all clean up their acts immediately after their stint with the Stones was completed, Axl had returned to the Coliseum stage the following night. What's more, miracle of miracles, it appeared that at least two-thirds of the woozy trio – Slash and Izzy – had taken Axl's words to heart enough to really do something about it this time, checking themselves into professional rehabilitation centres in LA soon after.

The odd man out remained Steven. Thoroughly unrepentant, con-vinced that the others neither would, nor could, keep up a 'straight front' for long, Steven went right on doing what he'd been doing all through the Christmas holidays, hidden away at his big, empty house (he hadn't gotten around to buying any proper furniture for it yet) buried in the steep, brown, snowless Hollywood hills. That year, Christ-mas had come too quickly for all of Guns N' Roses. Like Steven, Izzy had barricaded himself away from the outside world – although for entirely opposite reasons. Izzy was still in early rehab-mode and far too nervous of falling off the wagon to stick his head outside the door now, of all times, with the world red-nosed and shit-faced.

Meanwhile, the others spent Christmas Day alone with their respect-ive wives and girlfriends, pretending it was a day, a time, like any other. But even that festively mellow occasion had not passed by without incident. 'Man, I just had the worst Christmas!' Duff complained to me loudly when I bumped into him at a party on New Year's Eve. He told me that he had just split up with his wife, Mandy, following a bitter row that had broken out between them on Christmas Day. 'She told me she hated me and I told her to get out and she did. It was the shittiest fucking Christmas I ever had,' he shook his head dolefully. Duff and Mandy had been together for two years, married for most of that time.

Slash's relationship with his girlfriend, Sally, a pretty, dark-haired creature from Chicago with vaguely Oriental features and large cow-eyes, was somewhat less established, however, and the poor dear had been dismissed and sent back to Chicago within hours of Slash's dis-covery of Duff's predicament. It seemed like a drastic measure, but Slash didn't think so, and neither did Duff. The two of them had spent most of the subsequent week between Christmas and New Year hanging out together, either up at Duff's house 'getting wrecked' or cruising the clubs in a chauffeur-driven, tan-coloured limousine, two wasp-waisted, honey-pot blondes who knew when to keep their mouths shut in tow.

Slash's recovery from heroin addiction was – remarkably, given how deep and dangerous a hole he had apparently dug himself – almost instantaneous. Once he'd made up his mind to quit, he appeared to just shrug it off. I hadn't seen him so self-assured since the pre-Platinum days of smoky Marquees and half-filled Apollos. As Duff, who never got into anything outside of his vodka bottle with any sort of regularity, was quick to reassure me, Slash was 'really fucking happening right now. You look at him and think, well, here's this totally fucked-up guy, but he's not! He's strong, man! Stronger than you think.'

The day after New Year's Day, 1990, Slash and Duff came by the place where I was staying in Los Angeles with my girlfriend and we attempted to record an interview for a show I was presenting in those days for Capital Radio, in London. I'll never forget my producer's face after he'd spent a whole morning trying to edit the tape I brought back into a shape fit to broadcast. 'That's probably one of the most surreal interviews I've ever listened to,' he told me, his eyes glittering. 'And I can tell you right now there's absolutely no way you're going to put that out on this station! Every second word is "fuck", they can't remember the names of their own songs, and the lot of you sound as though you're completely drunk!'

'We were; it was Christmas!' I protested, but to no avail. Listening back to it now, five Christmases later, it's not hard to understand why that particular interview never got broadcast. They'd have sacked me. But they'd have hung my producer by his balls from the top of the Euston tower! (See transcription below.)

And Axl? Well, as usual, Axl was being mysterious over what his plans were. There was some talk that he had spent Christmas Day with his soon-to-be-ex-wife, Erin, at her parents' large and elegant house in Beverly Hills. But already there were hints that the never-less-than-volatile couple had rowed again and Axl had, in fact, spent Christmas hanging out with his cronies at his small West Hollywood apartment. I never really found out, for sure. When I finally caught up with him, a couple of days after my failed attempt at putting Slash and Duff on the radio, Axl dismissed my enquiry as to whether he'd had a good Christmas with a curt, 'Christmas is for amateurs'. But then, he was in a bad mood. As usual, his goat had been too easily got by some trifling bit of shit in the rock press a more mature Axl would probably have dismissed with the contempt it deserved.

Probably. Anyway, once he'd calmed down and I'd made enough sympathetic noises, said the right words, he started to relax and eventually he did tell me about his Christmas, in a round-about sort of a way. Yes, he'd been planning on spending the actual day with Erin and her parents. Yes, they'd had a fight. Yes, he'd been spending most of what was left of the holidays with his rag-tail posse of road buddies and acolytes. And yes, he'd been doing some other things that he wasn't going to tell me about.

'I had the worst New Year's and Christmas in my fuckin' life, man, as far as I was concerned. I'm in a good mood tonight 'cos it's fuckin' over and I fuckin' lived through it,' he scowled at my shoes, myopically. 'I, like, hibernated, didn't see anybody. People say that's wrong. But it wasn't wrong ... Then last night I had, like, eight people here and I was, like, in shock ... You know, I was into it but it's eight people that are really close friends ... Immediately it was, like, OK, we haven't seen each other and it's all heavy talk – this happened with my family, this happened with my girlfriend, dah dah dah. It was just heavy. Heaviness all round.'

We were sitting in the lounge of his small, two-bedroom apartment. Axl sat with his back to the balcony window, an undraped glass wall, the lights of LA twinkling noxiously in the darkness behind his head. 'Want some coke?' he asked me at one point. I hesitated. 'Look at your face!' he sneered. 'Look at you! I don't mean that. I mean this,' he said, holding up a can of Diet Coke. He got up to get me one. 'People always think the worst,' he was saying to himself.

I asked Axl what presents he'd got for Christmas and he sighed elaborately and declared that he'd been given, as he put it, 'some cool things that I'll probably never get 'round to using. Nothing I was particularly looking for, I don't think.'

Why, what had he particularly been looking for then? There were a number of things, he said, although not easy to specify. Still suffering from the Christmas/New Year hangover, peace on Earth and goodwill to all men was somewhere on the list, I'm sure – although, with the proviso, as Axl put it, of 'peace and love, man, but if you fuck with my garden I'm gonna kick your ass!'

The word Axl used most often in connection with his hopes and dreams for the future – oddly, I thought at the time, although now, looking back, I don't think so at all – was 'security'. 'It's like . . . I'd like to walk away knowing that, like, I can support my kids for whatever they want for the rest of their lives. I've never known any security in my whole life, you know? Not financial; not emotional. I'd like to have that security now.'

I can't be absolutely positive – it's been some time since we last spoke, of course – but judging by the reports we've all read since, I would guess Santa's still looking for a stocking big enough for that one.

As for that unbroadcastable Capital Radio interview, the full unedited transcript, is as follows:

Duff [singing]: Doe, a deer, a female deer . . .

Me [explaining]: It's a live show, so you can say or do whatever you like, but . . .

Slash: Can we say 'fuck' in it?

M: If you must, but try and keep it to a minimum, OK?

S: Oh, cool. OK.

M: So, imagine it's a Saturday night in London.

S: Is it raining? Most likely . . .

M: Just follow me, OK? I'm gonna start. Right. Slash. Duff. Thank you both for coming on my show . . .

S: Well, thank you for letting us watch you come.

[Much sniggering.]

M [starting again]: OK, here on Capital FM I'm talking to Slash and Duff from Guns N' Roses. It's the day after New Year's Day. Did you both have a good time over Christmas and New Year?

D: Oh, yes! Oh, yes!

S: Fucking wonderful . . .

D: Oh, yes! We're gonna go and do our record pretty, uh . . . like in two weeks.

S: Yeah, so anybody who's been wondering, it will happen.

M: That's good, because you know what people have been saying in England – that you're never gonna make another record because you're such bad boys you'll never get it together . . .

D [blowing a huge raspberry]: AAHHH! PUUHHHSSSSTTTTT!! They're WRONG!

M: Do you have anything to add to that, Slash?

S: Yeah! Fuck YOU . . . Ha, ha! No. We're gonna make another record. We've just been through a lot of shit, you know. It'll be fine. Just relax. It's gonna be a really good one, too. It's gonna be very . . .

D [interrupting]: Imagine, like, riding on the tube. Getting, like, one of those tube tickets and riding on the tube and then, like, getting lost on the Piccadilly tube, and then you go to the Thames tube and then it's like you get on another tube and you get lost and lost and lost . . . That's what happened to our band, kind of like in the fuckin' . . . broad scale of things. And we ended up on the Thames river in the rain. That's, basically, what happened . . .

M: The band were on the River Thames in the rain and that's why the new album didn't get made last year?

S [nodding enthusiastically]: We were drunk, we were lost and we had nowhere to go . . . And my top hat got fuckin' ruined . . .

D: And now we're back dry in the, er . . . somewhere dry.

S: No, no, the thing is, it's not like we're . . . um . . . I won't mention any names. But we're not like some bands who make records like jerking off . . .

D: POISON?

S: No, no . . . It just means a lot to us, so we're just taking our time with it and . . .

D: WARRANT!?

S: Sshhh . . .

D: BRITNEY FOX!?

S [giggling]: It'll come back to haunt you, I promise you.

D: No, I'm just kidding. No, what happened was . . . the album went wuuhhh!, and then we went wuuhhh! . . .

S: No one expected . . . I thought – no offence to Lemmy or any of those guys – but I thought it would be like a Motörhead album, it would just come out and, you know, no big deal . . . Yeah, right.

D: We went through a lot of stuff and then, after that, it took us a while to recoup and deal with our own lives.

S: You get places to live . . .

D: And deal with our own lives.

S: And girlfriends . . .

D: And deal with our own lives.

S: Oh! That's true! We all broke up with our old ladies today.

D: Divorce!

M: This is an official announcement, is it?

D: OK, this is in England – that's many area codes away, right? Well, I got divorced, girls . . .

M: OK, before we get any further . . .

D: No, let's get much further!

S: No, this is deep! This is deep!

M: We're gonna go much further, but first we're gonna play a Guns N' Roses track. Which track shall we hear?

D: 'Nightrain'!

S: No! No, no, no, no, no, no, no . . . 'You're Crazy'.

D: You're crazy . . .

S: I'm nuts, but no, play 'You're Crazy' . . .

D: OK, 'You're Crazy'.

S: No, no, no, no, no, no, no, no! Fuck, I can't remember the name of it . . .

D: 'NIGHTRAIN'!

S: No! Everybody plays 'Nightrain' . . . Um . . . [starts snapping fingers] . . . um . . .

D: Are you going down?

S: No, no, no, no, no! Um . . .

D: We don't even remember our own record . . . 'It's So Easy'?

S: No, the one – ' . . . pulls up her skirt'. The song we never play anymore?

[Both start humming two completely different riffs loudly. The interview has already descended into full-blown Spinal Tap absurdity.]

D [looking at me]: You know the song we're talking about . . . [starts humming again]

S: No, wait, wait! We have to figure this one out. [Both start singing and humming and clicking fingers.]

S: God, this is horrible ... Um ... 'My way, your way ...'

D: 'ANYTHING GOES'!

S: 'Anything Goes'!

M: OK, this is 'Anything Goes' ...

D: By us, yes!

[I back-announce the record and we get back into interview mode. Sort of.]

M: What were we talking about?

S: Nothing in particular ... We got rid of our girlfriends, that was major.

D: That was major! And both on the same day!

S: On the same day! It was serious ...

M: OK, let's talk about the girlfriends ...

D: No. Let's talk about music.

S: Yeah, sure. It'd be more ...

D: I don't, uh ... naw.

S: We already got good new ones!

D [whispering]: I can't talk about this, I got lawsuits and shit ...

S: Yeah, OK, OK, OK, OK. All right, never mind. Yeah. No. I have a new girlfriend. He's ... he doesn't really have a new girlfriend, because he's still married ...

D: No, I'm not! I just can't talk about it ... Mick, let's talk about you for a second.

S: That's a cool shirt.

D: What's going on with you, back home? Do you have a girlfriend back there?

S [nudging him]: She's here! Her name's ...

D: That's right! Oh, she's beautiful! You did good! You guys over in England, Mick is fuckin' happening. He's got a fuckin' happening girlfriend ...

M [fumbling]: That's very nice of you to say so, but getting back to the interview ...

D: Me and Slash both have Corvettes now, can you believe that shit?

M: The question everybody wants answered is, what have you been doing this year, why hasn't your album come out, and when will it come out?

S [shaking his head]: We've been adjusting ...

D: But we have thirty-five songs!

S: We have thirty-five new songs. But we've had to . . . Let me put it this way . . .

D: Put it some fuckin' way, please. I tried to earlier.

S: The first fuckin' time we . . . Can I say that?

D: Yeah, do.

S: The first fuckin' time we came to England, we like, we were just like . . . like . . . just . . . here's the plane ticket, everybody go, and we're all wuh-ooh-uh! And we get drunk and fucked up and sick in the street and stuff. Things changed . . .

[Both start talking at once.]

D: We just sat in the street across from the Marquee and just drank. We didn't know. We thought we'd just be like some opening band and stuff, and we got there and the place was sold out!

S: We thought it was the greatest thing ever. Now we have homes . . .

D: But fuck that, England was like our homecoming ground . . .

S: No, no, no, but the changing thing, that's what's important.

D: That's what's been happening this year, yeah. But the transformation from England to like now is . . .

S: But we haven't changed.

D: No, we haven't changed.

M: Well, you're still drunk, anyway.

S: It's the day after New Year's. YOU'RE drunk, too!

D [laughing]: Mick, are you going to be able to use this interview?

M: I'm gonna give it a shot.

S: We're not built for rock star shit.

D: We aren't! We aren't! [Goes into long, incoherent rant about a fight he got into at a club on New Year's Eve] And the guy was bigger than I was, but I just went CAH-BOOOM! And . . . his eyes crossed, like you see in the cartoons, like that? And he went down. And then everybody dragged him back and dragged me back, but they were dragging him past me and I fuckin' biffed him three more times in the head! They said I broke his jaw . . .

S: Nasty [Suicide – former Hanoi Rocks guitarist] stuck his arm in through the crowd and got one in there, too!

D: So we go through this shit all the time, people trying to fuck with us. I was telling you earlier, if anybody fucks with my homeboy here, Slash – and it's happened before, like if a big guy was gonna hit him – I've stepped right in front of him.

S: Sure, and I can hide in the crook of his knee . . .

D: I beat up a guy for him once. And he'd do that for me.

S: But not to sound stupid, because we're starting to sound stupid . . .

D: Because we're drunk! We're drunk! Of course we're gonna sound stupid.

S: No, but we're a fuckin' band . . .

D: Yeah . . . that's what it comes down to.

M: All right, let's play some more music. What this time? It doesn't have to be Guns N' Roses.

[Both simultaneously.]

D: 'SCARRED FOR LIFE'! ROSE TATTOO!

S: 'Scarred for Life'. Rose Tattoo . . .

[Duff goes into invisible-guitar routine, singing at the top of his voice. We come back from the record.]

D: Oh, I fucked up . . .

S: We are intelligent, though.

D: We're not right now, though. Mick, you got me drunk!

S: We just like to have fun. Go out there and jam. It's like this, to put it bluntly, we go out there and we play, and we're very conscientious about our music, and we're sick of fucking talking about it.

D: Yeah, that's a good point.

S: It's true.

D: That's a good point.

S: It's like, it's old . . .

D: We don't mind talking to you because you know what it's all about. But most people go, 'So what's it like being a ROCK STAR?' Like, what? What is a rock star?

S: It's a hard stone that shines. Ha ha ha!

M [deciding enough is enough]: So let's clear it up for everybody . . .

S: In England? We love you guys.

D: We really do love you guys.

S: We fucking kicked ass in London, that first time.

D: I love the Marquee. I love London.

S: We did suck in a couple of places, though . . .

D: When we go back we're gonna do the Marquee . . .

S: No, man, it's gone.

D: Oh yeah, it's that new place.

S: I think we're gonna do Wembley.

D: No, let's do that biker club! Let's do that biker club! I don't wanna do Donington again.

S: Not Donington, Wembley . . .

[Much discussion ensues over the pros and cons of Wembley Stadium versus Donington Park, with everybody talking at once.]

S: Do two bands, that's cool. Five bands on the bill, all day long . . . it's just . . .

D: No way. No Donington.

M: Well, wherever it is, I know you're both looking forward to playing live again as much as your fans are.

S [pulling face]: Man, we have to get out. When we get this record done, we'll go.

D: Hear this? Hear this? Hear this? [Duff grabs the sides of the table and bangs his head with an audible thump against it.]

S [disdainfully]: What was that?

D: Oh, you do it, too? OK, together . . . one, two, three, four!

[Both lean over and, as one, head-butt the table together, making an even more audible THUMP on the tape.]

M [desperately trying to wrap it up now]: You heard it live and exclusive on Capital Radio . . . I'd like to thank Duff and Slash for joining me this evening . . .

[Much braying of laughter in the background.]

S: Anybody who stayed tuned, thank you for listening . . . Ha ha ha!

D: Yeah! I thank you! Because, uh . . . hah . . .

M: What are we going out on?

[Long pause.]

S: 'We are the Road Crew' by Motörhead?

D: YES! [singing] We are the ROAD CREW . . . da-nah-nah-nah-nah-naaaawww . . .

S [above the noise]: We had a band called Road Crew once. 'Rocket Queen' came from that track . . .

D: Right! Lemmy, hi from Duff and Slash! And the rest of you boys, 'Filthy' and all you guys . . .

S: Hallo!

D: Lemmy, you rock!

[We say our 'radio' goodbyes.]

D: SEE YA! We'll see ya soon!

S: Mick, thank you for holding the mike for so long. I couldn't even hold my dick that long . . .

D: I've seen you do it! Remember, when we were on the road, and I pretended I was, like, asleep and you talked to your girlfriend on the fuckin' phone and you'd have your little rag and you'd go, 'Get the Coke bottle, baby.' I was pretending to go to sleep and he's there beating off, and shit.

M: And on that happy note . . .

D: I'd be trying to get to sleep and he'd be like, 'Oh, baby. I'm saving a load of come in my rag for you . . .'

[Tape ends abruptly.]

CODA

It would take another book of its own to fully describe what happened next. But the essentials go like this: Guns N' Roses did eventually make their next album – two double albums released simultaneously called *Use Your Illusion* I and II – the latter featuring a song called 'Get in the Ring', which contained my name and some unflattering, and wholly untrue, lines in it about me. Then they toured the world for nearly three years, recorded a so-so covers album and effectively broke up. That is, there was still a 'group' called Guns N' Roses but only Axl survived from the original line-up and it was another thirteen years before they released their next album, *Chinese Democracy*. By this time, Slash and Duff – and drummer Matt Sorum – had formed their own hugely successful breakaway group called Velvet Revolver. By then, Duff had long since gone straight, taken a business degree and grown into one of the more genuinely interesting figures in rock music. Slash, meanwhile, has become a bigger star in the twenty-first century than all of them put together through his involvement in the Guitar Hero computer game series. Oh, and the original line-up of Guns N' Roses is definitely getting back together in 2010. Or maybe 2011 . . .